NCO Guide

0 11557 03273 4

NCO Guide

8th Edition

Revised by
CSM Robert S. Rush, USA (Ret.)

STACKPOLE
BOOKS

Published by
STACKPOLE BOOKS
5067 Ritter Road
Mechanicsburg, PA 17055
www.stackpolebooks.com

NCO Guide and its predecessor, *The Noncom's Guide,* have been published by Stackpole Books since 1948.

Printed in the United States of America

10 9 8 7 6 5 4 3 2 1

Cover design by Wendy A. Reynolds

All photographs courtesy of the U.S. Army

Library of Congress Cataloging-in-Publication Data

Rush, Robert S.
NCO guide / by CSM Robert S. Rush, USA (Ret.). — 8th ed. rev.
p. cm.
Includes bibliographical references and index.
ISBN 0-8117-3273-8 (alk. paper)
1. United States. Army—Non-commissioned officers' handbooks. I. Title: Non-commissioned officer guide. II. Title.

U123.R87 2006
355.00973—dc22

2006002779

ISBN 978-0-8117-3273-4

In honor of noncommissioned officers
past, present, and future

Deeds, not words

The NCO Creed

No one is more professional than I. I am a Noncommissioned Officer, a leader of soldiers. As a Noncommissioned Officer, I realize that I am a member of a time-honored corps, which is known as "The Backbone of the Army."

I am proud of the Corps of Noncommissioned Officers and will at all times conduct myself so as to bring credit upon the Corps, the Military Service, and my country, regardless of the situation in which I find myself. I will not use my grade or position to attain pleasure, profit, or personal safety.

Competence is my watchword. My two basic responsibilities will always be uppermost in my mind—accomplishments of my mission and the welfare of my soldiers. I will strive to remain tactically and technically proficient. I am aware of my role as a Noncommissioned Officer. I will fulfill my responsibilities inherent in that role. All soldiers are entitled to outstanding leadership; I will provide that leadership. I know my soldiers, and I will always place their needs above my own. I will communicate consistently with my soldiers and never leave them uninformed. I will be fair and impartial when recommending both rewards and punishment.

Officers of my unit will have maximum time to accomplish their duties; they will not have to accomplish mine. I will earn their respect and confidence as well as that of my soldiers.

I will be loyal to those with whom I serve, seniors, peers, and subordinates alike. I will exercise initiative by taking appropriate action in the absence of orders. I will not compromise my integrity, nor my moral courage. I will not forget, nor will I allow my comrades to forget, that we are professionals, Noncommissioned Officers, leaders!

Contents

Foreword

Stackpole Books has published the *NCO Guide* and its predecessor titles for over fifty years. We revise this book frequently so that it reflects the latest information needed by our Army's noncommissioned officers in the performance of their duties and for their own professional development. We seek the best-qualified senior NCO authors for this work, such as Command Sergeant Major Robert Rush, who revised this edition.

We believe the information in the *NCO Guide* represents virtually all the duties a noncommissioned officer is expected to perform, and we welcome comments and input from serving noncommissioned officers in all components.

One thing that impresses us each time we revise the *Guide* is the amount of knowledge, the numbers of skills, and quantity of information an NCO needs to effectively lead the soldiers in America's modern Army.

Given the very high reputation our Army has with the American public, a clear vote of thanks is due to our noncommissioned officers for the fine job they are doing leading and teaching America's young men and women who enter this ancient and honorable service.

Preface

When I was going through training as an infantryman during the 1960s, the drill sergeant's familiar refrain was, "If you don't learn this, you'll die in Vietnam!" Studying the *NCO Guide* will not guarantee your survival or even ensure your success or failure; however, it will assist you in keeping yourself and your soldiers up to date on NCO career development and promotions, finance and personnel policies, awards and decorations, customs and courtesies, and other important areas. The training portions speak not so much of a book of *do*'s and *don't*'s as one to lead you through a series of decision points to arrive at a solution best for your current situation. Tuck it in your DCU trouser pocket before you deploy and you will have one more tool to assist you in your duties of leading soldiers.

NCOs become good NCOs by using their time productively to study their profession and themselves. They read Army regulations, field manuals, military journals, and other official literature to hone their professional edge. They research military topics in sources ranging from on-post libraries to Army listings on the World Wide Web. They spend many off-duty hours studying college texts or using alternative educational resources to pursue degrees to further develop their usefulness as leaders.

The *NCO Guide* is aimed at the corporals, sergeants, first sergeants, and sergeants major who will turn to it when they need self-help guidance or information that will benefit fellow soldiers. The *Guide* is an educational resource and ready reference to key Army subjects. It draws from education, experience, training, and hundreds of sources. The *Guide* begins with a discussion of how and why the Army continues to change and ends with how to make the most of a transition from service to civilian life. Readers will also find information on the developmental aspects of soldiering, fitness, education, promotion, and dozens of other necessary topics relating to a noncommissioned officer's duties. It serves as a desktop reference when the reader or a fellow soldier has questions about pay, benefits, entitlements, personal appearance, uniforms, insignia, assignments, and personal and professional problems. The *NCO Guide* also contains aids that quickly lead soldiers to official or other publications that may contain updates.

The eighth edition has been fully revised and expanded to include topics all NCOs must understand. It contains new or updated information about our responsibilities as NCO leaders: leadership counseling, battle-focused training, the Army values, personnel and property accountability, master fitness principles, weight control, the Army Physical Fitness Test, the NCO Education System and civilian education, professional reading and writing and multimedia, life insurance, the new thrift savings plan, and medical and dental insurance. It also addresses sensitive contemporary leadership issues such as professional ethics, fraternization, AIDS, discrimination, sexual harassment, and homosexuality.

Readers will also find sections about the military justice system, including military discipline, the law of land warfare, command authority and soldier rights, nonjudicial punishment, the Manual for Courts-Martial, and its Uniform Code of Military Justice. Also provided is information about awards and decorations, with several pages of full-color photographs portraying those medals.

This edition of the *NCO Guide* has reformed content and improved relevancy. All new material was tightly composed and edited to contain less mundane detail, flow more logically, and be more readable and useful. It is also more practical and less vulnerable to problems associated with information that changes prior to publication or while in print. Field manual numbers are being changed to reflect the DOD number system; within the text, the new number is provided parenthetically after the old. Because of the large number of MOS-specific schools, discussion of schools is restricted to those that apply most—such as the NCO Education System, drill sergeant, airborne, recruiter, etc.

Even though retired, I continue to use my copy of the *NCO Guide* to both remind myself of benefits I may have, as well as to explain to others how the Army operates.

Robert S. Rush, Ph.D.
CSM, USA (Ret.)

Acknowledgments

The Internet is a wondrous thing! By using the many sites available to all soldiers, I was able to ensure that the latest information is included in this update. Many sites contributed to this revision, including the following: USAPA, the Army's Publishing Agency, which lists every current regulation; Army Knowledge Online, Department of Veterans Affairs; Defense Activity for Nontraditional Education Support; Army Family Advocacy Program; Army Community Services; Civilian Health and Medical Program of the Uniformed Services; American Forces Information Service; Total Army Personnel Command; Enlisted Records and Evaluation Center; Army Career and Alumni Program; Training and Doctrine Command; Army and Air Force Exchange Service; Army Training Support Center; Association of the United States Army; Office of the Chief of Public Affairs; Defense Finance and Accounting Service; Department of Education; and Reimer Digital Library.

The following organizations also contributed: the Office of the Sergeant Major of the Army; Army News Service; *SOLDIERS* magazine; Army Continuing Education Services; Army Safety Center; Army Family Liaison Office; Judge Advocate General's Corps; DOD Still Media Records Center; the U.S. Army Center of Military History; and the Army Community and Family Support Center.

I am indebted to my Stackpole editors for their professional support and guidance during production of the *NCO Guide,* 8th edition. I also want to thank all those who over the years have led me to a better understanding of our Army. Lastly, I thank my wife, Edith, not only for everything she has done and the support she has shown toward this project, but also for the many years she put up with a ragged old ranger who was seldom home. Without her support and understanding, I would have failed before I had even started.

PART I

Leading Soldiers

1

America's Army at War

> We remain an Army at War. It is a war unlike any other in our Nation's history, prosecuted not by states, but by extremists employing irregular means to erode our power and resolve. Our adversaries threaten the ideas that form the bedrock of our society, endangering our freedoms and way of life. Fueled by an ideology that promotes intractable hatred, this war will endure in some form for the foreseeable future. The Army, in service to the Nation, must therefore be prepared to sustain operations during a period of persistent conflict—a blurring of familiar distinctions between war and peace. This is the most significant aspect of the 21st century security environment.
>
> —Army Posture Statement 2006

Our Army of the future incorporates intellectual ingenuity, technological innovation, and the values that have always shaped America's Army throughout its more than 200-year history. To be successful in the new millennium, our Army needs skilled, versatile, and highly motivated NCOs who are capable of accomplishing their mission in changed environments; NCOs, confident in their ability to train soldiers in individual through small-unit tasks relevant to their units' mission, who use creative approaches to maximize their subordinates' full potential; and lastly, NCOs who can ably lead their soldiers in battle. These are the deeds NCOs do.

America's Army is the best land combat force in the world, serving the nation every day at home and abroad. It is often the commitment of our Army into trouble spots that makes the difference between the success and failure of America's defense policy. Land forces remain decisive and provide the most visible and sustained form of U.S. commitment, and when ground troops deploy, the world knows the United States means business. We are no longer forward based as we were during the Cold War with divisions in Germany and Korea. In the near future, only three brigade-sized units will be permanently stationed overseas: one in Germany, one in Italy, and one in Korea; the remainder based here in the United States will be able to quickly deploy to crises spots overseas.

Soldiers and the units they serve in are expected to accomplish whatever mission they are assigned, regardless of circumstances, location, funding, or priority. Although appropriations are now climbing, and attitudes have changed, there are always challenges—and rewards. A reporter asked a noncommissioned officer assigned to the 1st Battalion 87th Infantry if he was worried about being killed during Operation Anaconda. The sergeant replied, "I didn't worry about me getting out of there alive. I was worried about some of the casualties that we initially took earlier on in the day. I was concerned for them. It didn't really cross my mind. I knew we had a job to finish."

DUTY, INTEGRITY, HONESTY, COMPASSION: THE ARMY'S NCO CORPS

> My plans would have amounted to little had there not been trained NCOs available to build my decision. . . . Throughout my career, at every level of command to the position I now hold, I have relied on my NCOs. Whatever I entrusted them with, they accomplished to standard when given the full set of resources, including authority and responsibility to do so.
>
> —Lt. Gen. John P. Otjen, USA (Ret.),
> former commander, First U.S. Army

Deeds, Not Words

We have the finest noncommissioned officers corps in the world and much of the Army's success is directly attributable to NCO leadership. Noncommissioned officers are famous for their abilities in getting things done, whatever that might be. However, here I must caution that a leader must be concerned not only with the *quality* of unit achievements, but also with the *process* by which the achievements are attained. Many ethical conflicts occur when not in combat because some members of our profession forget that the real test occurs on the battlefield. Our Army's future has to be based on a solid foundation of moral-ethical values, for any lessening of this standard compromises and corrupts our ability to lead soldiers and, in the long run, diminishes the support of the American public.

Army leaders speak of three fundamental truths: The Army is people; our nation's citizens trust their Army to do the right thing; and we are a values-based organization. No matter how intellectually or technologically advanced we get, we can never forget these fundamental truths. The Army way of life

Soldier securing perimeter in Samarra, Iraq.

should inspire us to a sense of purpose that will sustain us in the brutal realities of combat and the ambiguities of operations other than war. Our values of fairness and of concern for the individual are supported by our national values, but they also contribute to unit loyalty and cohesiveness. These values are also useful. They create standards of behavior that we as members of a professional Army need to hold to in order to be successful. These values then become the standards of the unit.

Standards are those principles or rules by which behavior is measured as acceptable and tasks are measured as successfully accomplished. Once the standard becomes a criterion for acceptance into a section, company, or battalion and all share the values and understand the standards that flow from them, soldiers will measure other soldiers and the result will be a more cohesive organization, a real team.

Field Manual (FM) 100-1 (FM 1), *The Army,* capstones its guiding beliefs, standards, and ideals succinctly in one word—duty. *Duty* means to fulfill your obligations. It is behavior required by moral obligation, demanded by custom, or enjoined by feelings of rightness. It requires the impartial administration of standards without regard to friendship, personality, rank, or other bias.

Integrity is your personal set of values. It is the thread that weaves throughout the fabric of the professional Army ethic. Integrity means *honesty,* uprightness, the avoidance of deception, and steadfast adherence to standards of behavior. Integrity means that personal standards are consistent with professional values and demands a commitment to act according to the other Army values. Integrity is the most important character trait of any leader, and we all make decisions based on the integrity of those reporting to us. Integrity can be ordered, but it can only be achieved by encouragement and example. As NCO leaders we must not only be technically and tactically competent, but also commit ourselves to the highest standards of ethical conduct and foster soldier commitment to the values of the profession.

How many times have commanders and senior NCOs "blinked" at how an objective was accomplished? At how, for the division run, where no one falls out, the less fit are culled from the ranks during the first formation? Soldiers see and understand these shenanigans for what they are: ethical lapses by their leaders. We must eliminate the mind-set that produces such directives as "I don't care how you do it, just do it."

If a leader puts a positive spin on a report in peacetime, what will happen in war? There is no time in combat to verify reports, question the accuracy of information, or wonder about the reliability of equipment or someone's word. When leaders initial a safe as being checked without actually checking it and then punish a soldier for not having checked the motor pool, all credibility is lost. Soldiers know the difference between right and wrong and no matter how much is said to justify something wrong, they hold the leader in less regard. However, leaders who make it clear that they will not tolerate ethical ambivalence and who demonstrate by their actions that they hold themselves to the same standard promote mutual confidence and understanding among their soldiers. There is no senior-subordinate difference when it comes to doing what is right.

NCOs play a key role in setting "command climate." Every organization, no matter whether a squad, company, brigade, or higher echelon, has only so much energy to expend to accomplish a given mission. That energy can be wasted or it can be used wisely. In a unit with a positive healthy climate, that energy is, or can be, even more than the sum total of the energy of its members. The energy of an organization can be wasted as well. If you are forced to expend energy looking over your shoulder, preparing to cover yourself for some inspection, building a wall of numbers and statistics to look good, you will have little energy left to teach your soldiers, be innovative, or accomplish your mission. It is only through steadfast, ethical leadership that soldiers and units can reach their full capabilities and be most effective. Soldiers in units with a good moral climate understand right from wrong.

All soldiers make mistakes. Errors of omission (such as not knowing how to do something and doing it wrong) should receive little notice outside of additional training. However, errors of commission, such as submitting a doctored report or lying to protect oneself, should result in immediate punishment. If we make a decision that is contrary to that expected of us, then we must also take responsibility for our actions.

FM 100-1 (FM-1) also adds *compassion* to the core qualities of *courage, competence, commitment,* and *candor.* Compassion is much more than a cursory interest in others. It means sincere involvement in helping to find solutions to problems and improving welfare; talking with and listening to subordinates, not simply talking at them; doing something about hardships or problems, not paying lip service to them; teaching individuals by counseling, not by abusing them.

Caring means fostering a command climate that challenges people, convinces them that their contributions make a difference, and allows them to feel good about themselves and the Army they serve. We have to take the time to see, hear, and resolve problems before they affect our units and our soldiers.

What Is Expected of NCO Leaders?

Up to now, NCO duties have centered around maintaining good order and discipline within units; serving as small-unit and/or technical skill leaders; training soldiers in individual skills; and ably leading teams, squads, and sections in combat and in support of combat. All leaders are responsible for accomplishing the unit's mission, ensuring subordinates' welfare to include physical, moral, personal, and professional well-being, setting and exemplifying the highest professional and ethical standards, and treating subordinates with dignity, respect, fairness, and consistency.

Good senior NCOs, along with officers, will foster a moral-ethical climate in which leaders teach, individual character has the opportunity to mature, and recognition of achievement and tolerance of honest mistakes foster personal and professional growth. They show them what right looks like. Leaders must nurture a human relations environment that treats all soldiers, regardless of race, creed, color, gender, religion, or national origin, as soldiers. NCO leaders who deal daily with soldiers affect values and behavior by establishing day-to-day procedures, practices, and working norms; by their personal example; and by building discipline, cohesion, motivation, consistency, and fair play.

NCOs ensure that a soldier behaves as a soldier, both on and off duty. "We don't do that in this organization." The NCO takes immediate action when a soldier's conduct affects good order and discipline. Soldiers who infringe on other soldiers' rights need to be told to modify their behavior or go elsewhere. There is no substitute for observing for oneself what is going on at the muddy boots level. No PowerPoint presentation listing everything, including boot sizes and numbers of shoelaces, will ever come close to "eyes on the target." We expect all noncommissioned officers, regardless of rank, to form the habit of getting down in the trenches with the soldiers, of seeing what is taking place, of measuring it against one's own scale of values, and ordering changes as necessary.

We expect our small-unit leaders to lead by example and to practice the professional Army ethic; to enforce Army standards on appearance and conduct; to supervise maintenance of equipment, living areas, and work places; to instill discipline; and to take care of subordinates. Those NCOs serving in staff positions must never forget their responsibilities to train, mentor, and look out for the well-being of other soldiers in their sections.

Current trends suggest that independent leadership is increasingly exercised by junior officers and noncommissioned officers who lead our soldiers. As our Army becomes more involved in operations other than war (OOTW) and the "battlefield" becomes defined in new ways, many decisions will be made by soldiers operating in environments away from their superiors. We must develop in our soldiers the ability to take the appropriate action on their own initiative in support of the commander's intent.

In such an environment, *self-discipline* is vitally important. If we can trust a corporal with a color guard to render proper respect to the flag when no one is watching, then we can also trust that corporal to do what he or she believes is right when faced with an ethical dilemma. Trained properly and understanding what is right and what is wrong, our soldiers will invariably do what is ethically right. But if they observe their senior leaders bending the rules for one reason or another, they will find it more difficult to justify the harder right. Moral character develops out of repeating good actions; it cannot be ordered, but it can be imitated. The best discipline is self-discipline; the individual does what he knows is right because he wants to do the right thing. It is especially important for young soldiers to learn this immediately. As former Chief of Staff of the Army (CSA) General John Wickham once said:

> During the initial tour the young soldier's life is lived mainly at the squad level with his primary chain of command ranging up through platoon and company/battery/troop level. Therefore the brand of leadership that is exercised by the soldier's squad leader, platoon sergeant, platoon leader, first sergeant and company commander is absolutely critical.

NCOs must *motivate* soldiers, help them grow, develop them personally and professionally, and inspire them to achieve their maximum potential. We have to allow our subordinates to learn from honest errors, while ensuring that they correct their mistakes. Not correcting mistakes breeds mediocrity. If you walk by a deficiency and say nothing, it becomes the standard.

When told of a soldier not performing to standard, many senior leaders question how effective the immediate leader is in counseling, mentoring, or teaching the soldier his or her job. We must make soldiers want to excel, and those soldiers who do not strive for the highest rungs and who are content to reside at the lowest level of performance can do so elsewhere.

Everyone tells us we have the best soldiers in the world. Let us treat them as the professionals they are. They are beyond the stage of needing baby-sitters. We must foster their faith in us by ensuring that we give them the respect and confidence they deserve. Anything else will result in compromise and will impair our ability to lead soldiers into the next century. If we and our subordinate leaders foster strong *esprit* in our soldiers by being personal and professional examples of excellence and by treating them as professionals, there is no doubt they will act professionally.

You do not have to stop soldiers who have pride in themselves and their unit. You just need to steer them. Former U.S. Army Forces Command (FORSCOM) Command Sergeant Major Richard Cayton once said, "Your soldiers will walk a path and they will come to a crossroads; if you are standing at the crossroads, where you belong, you can guide your soldiers to the right path and make them successful."

I have found no soldier, active, guard, or reserve, who wants to fail. But many do, not for lack of effort (we expend a lot of that), but for lack of knowing how. Some NCOs are unfamiliar with their training responsibilities, and some officers are reluctant to let their NCOs have their piece of the training pie. We should all consider the following:

- No soldier should ever have to do his duty ill-trained or ill-prepared to do it.
- NCOs are responsible for the proper conduct of individual, crew, squad, and section level training.
- No NCO should ever stand before his soldiers unconfident or incompetent to lead or train them.
- All soldiers should hold their NCOs in high regard and want to follow their lead and example.
- Each NCO must accept full responsibility for his or her soldiers' success and failure.

Leading in the Twenty-First Century

When we entered the mechanized age at the turn of the twentieth century, our Army found an increasing need for a different type of noncommissioned officer—one who was familiar with the technical aspects of his field as well as basic soldiering skills. Today, the NCO Corps again sits at the crossroads. Army Transformation and the Global War on Terrorism are leading to an increased reliance on the small-unit leader. A smaller force will require senior NCOs to move away from some of the more traditional roles and become skilled artisans in developing and training NCO leaders who have direct responsibility for training our soldiers in these new technologies.

A senior NCO's primary duty is much like that of the master guildsman of old. It is to ensure that subordinate leaders are trained as skilled professionals and future leaders. If a sergeant stands in front of his soldiers unconfident and unfamiliar with the task he is to train, several things happen. First, the sergeant loses credibility with his soldiers, and the training is not learned or accomplished. Second, training resources and time are wasted and the task is either rescheduled or, more commonly, listed as unsatisfactory and collective training is begun.

Let us now look at the relationship between the commander and his senior NCOs concerning training. FMs 25-100 (FM 7-0) and 25-101 (FM 7-10) specify that senior noncommissioned officers—sergeants first class through sergeants major—are an integral part in the planning and execution of soldier, team, and squad training, and that they should be made responsible for how well their soldiers are trained.

Some compare commanders to architects, who design the Mission Essential Task List (METL) for their organizations. Subordinate officers take the METL and extract those collective tasks necessary for successful completion at their level. Senior NCOs at each echelon take the collective tasks and determine which individual soldier tasks are necessary to be completed in order for the unit to complete its mission. Just as the architect relies on the contractor to transform his design into a building, the officer must rely on the NCO to put his intent into effective individual and leader training programs that make up the building blocks for the collective tasks that support the unit METL.

In a 1994 *Military Review* article Gen. Gordon Sullivan wrote, "Concentration on basics will mean that we reduce the number of tasks on a unit's mission essential task list, not increase them. Football has six basics—run, pass, catch, block, tackle, and think. We must look to the same type of basics. Without excellence in the basics, versatility is impossible." This holds true today.

Some leaders believe that making important collective, leader, and individual tasks nondiscretionary robs the leader of creativity and initiative. The fact is that senior leaders have to provide sufficient structure to ensure superior performance from leaders newly introduced into their position. It is only when the boundaries are clear that creativity and initiative become free from timidity rooted in uncertainty. NCOs who know they have to build a mousetrap will look for better ways to build it.

The NCO Creed states that officers will be given time to accomplish their duties and that they will not have to do ours. We give officers that time by ensuring that soldiers are trained to standard in individual tasks before we attempt training them in collective tasks. This development of training occurs not only at the beginning and end, but is ongoing throughout. Since both the commander and his senior NCO are involved with the development of the training plan at different levels, collective and individual, each must sequence and talk through the different stages. Too much reliance on either collective or individual tasks will result in failure to meet the overall objective. Tankers will never get to Tank Table XII if everyone concentrates only on Tank Table VIII. Without this corporate "buy-in" by both officers and NCOs, training in units becomes little more than a list of discrete, nonrelated, often poorly resourced events. However, when everyone buys into the plan, training will be successful.

The following chapters cover many areas, from the uses of military history to the history of the role of the NCO to the "master trainer" concept for identifying individual training needs and conducting After Action Reviews (AARs). How-to's for conducting NCO induction ceremonies, marksmanship ranges, and physical fitness programs are also addressed. The unifying factor in all revolves around the noncommissioned officer and his or her responsibilities to the soldiers. Much of the book consists of quick reference guides regarding promotion, assignments, the Uniform Code of Military Justice, and other topics that will assist in your role as a noncommissioned officer. Officers expect you to provide your soldiers with the best training possible, so that when the time comes, they will know that they are competently trained and well led, and will have confidence that they can fight and win in combat. A soldier dying for lack of training is nothing less than criminal. Your job and responsibility is to ensure that this does not happen.

So, where do you go from here? If you are serious about leading in the twenty-first century with all its technology, and are still expecting your soldiers to fight and—if necessary—die, you must focus your efforts on training, leading, and mentoring your soldiers and supporting your fellow noncommissioned officers so they can perform the same duties for the men and women in their charge. I am certain that noncommissioned officers will continue to produce a quality force that will serve the Army and this nation as well in the new century as it had in the last century.

Today, as the Army wrestles with fundamental changes in the way it operates and is organized, an array of disconcerting issues face soldiers and the NCOs who lead and train them. With the nation at war, members of the Army have had to deal with seemingly ever-increasing deployments and assaults on their character because the bad behavior of a few of their fellow soldiers sullied the Army's reputation.

Perhaps. But selfless service calls for personal sacrifice and dedication to duty, regardless of the circumstances. No one gets rich on Army pay. If elements of the nation seem less than caring, well, that's just how it is—so don't sweat it. According to the annual national polls, the military is still the highest-rated institution in the nation. And in the Army family, plenty of good people do care and go about their business because it must be done. The Army's Sgt. Maj. Kenneth O. Preston has commented:

> Today's global environment challenges us to be a Culture of Innovation. Our operational Army is adapting to its threats on the battlefield daily. So too must our Institutional Army adapt to ensure our training and processes move at the speed of an Army at war,

> supporting a nation at war. I always encourage Soldiers to collaborate, think out of the box, and find innovative solutions to today's toughest problems. Phrases like "that's the way we've always done it" or "if it ain't broke, don't fix it" are unacceptable excuses today.

This is excellent advice for anyone. Sergeants and their soldiers have enough to concern themselves with on a daily basis. Mission tasks, seemingly endless deployments, leading soldiers in combat, maintaining good order and discipline, keeping fit, appearance, meeting the standards of service, upholding their sworn or affirmed oath to defend the Constitution and obey the orders of superior officers—these are some of the unchanging principal requirements of soldiering in a changing Army, in a dangerous world.

Remember that "the Army is people" and "your soldiers are your credentials." Nothing could be truer.

ARMY ROLES, MISSIONS, AND FUNCTIONS

The Army exists to serve the American people, to protect enduring national interests, and to fulfill national military responsibilities. The Army is charged to provide forces able to conduct prompt, sustained combat on land as well as stability and reconstruction operations, when required. The Army provides the Joint Force with capabilities required to prevail in the protracted Global War on Terrorism and sustain the full range of its global commitments. The bulk of the active-duty army is either in Iraq, returning from Iraq, or preparing to go to Iraq. Brigades of the National Guard now account for about 40 percent of the combat brigades deployed to Iraq and Afghanistan. Simultaneously, the Army is undertaking one of its most profound transformations since the Pentomic era of the 1950s.

When it comes to fighting and winning a major regional conflict, no one is in our league. The Army has demonstrated both in operations in Afghanistan and Iraq that we own the battlefield, day and night. But ownership can be slippery. To win the next battle, the Army will have to quickly get to trouble spots with a sustainable fighting force. It will have to dominate the information war, acting promptly on incoming data to strike targets deep in enemy territory with a new generation of indirect fire weapons. And commanders at all levels will have to maneuver quickly and decisively, leaving an enemy with no options except withdrawal or surrender.

The roles, missions, and functions of the military are defined as follows: Roles are the broad and enduring purposes for the services that are established by Congress in law; missions are the tasks assigned by the president or secretary of defense to combatant commanders in chief (CinC); and functions are specific responsibilities assigned by the president or secretary of defense to enable the services to fulfill their legally established roles. Simply stated, the primary function of the services is to provide forces that are organized, trained, and equipped to perform a role—to be employed by a CinC in the accomplishment of a mission.

Hundreds of thousands of soldiers are involved in vital roles, missions, and functions on a daily basis. In 2005, approximately 640,000 soldiers are serving on active duty, while 315,000 from all components—Active (155,000), Army National Guard (113,000) and Army Reserve (47,000)—are deployed or forward-stationed in more than 120 countries to support operations in Iraq, Afghanistan, and other theaters of war and also deter aggression, while securing the homeland. Soldiers from the Army National Guard and the Army Reserve are making a vital contribution, with 150,000 soldiers mobilized and performing a diverse range of missions worldwide. In addition to their duties overseas, soldiers from all components including the Guard and the Reserve are supporting civil authorities during disaster relief operations, such as those which occurred in Louisiana and Mississippi.

Assigned Army missions affect how the military is structured, trained, and employed. The Army's new regional focus, combined with major troop reductions overseas, puts enormous emphasis on strategic mobility. Airlift and sealift mobility improvements being made today will enable deployment of an Army light division and a heavy brigade to any crisis area in about two weeks, and two heavy divisions in about a month.

Regardless of how roles, missions, functions, and force structures change with the new post-Cold War era, NCOs play a vital role in the effort. The effort is worth making because the objective, as always, is safeguarding our country while maintaining and improving combat readiness for twenty-first-century Army missions.

CURRENT TRENDS IN THE ARMY

- Today war is the norm; peace is the exception.
- There is an enormous pool of potential combatants armed with irreconcilable ideas.
- Our adversaries seek adaptive advantage through asymmetry.
- We have near peer competitors in niche areas of military science.
- Conventional force-on-force conflicts are still possible.
- Our homeland is part of the battlespace.
- The Army is adapting to these challenges now; it's called "Army Transformation."

Army Transformation

Transformation is a process that recognizes the changing nature of military competition and cooperation, which our Army is addressing through new combinations of operational doctrine, military capabilities, people, and organizations.

Among other initiatives, the Army is currently transforming from a division-based to a brigade-based force. These are the new modular, self-sufficient, and standardized Brigade Combat Teams (BCTs), that can be more readily deployed and combined with other Army and joint forces to meet the precise needs of the combatant commanders for today's new type of warfare.

Combat and Support BCTs

The modular BCT is a stand-alone, self-sufficient, and standardized tactical force of between 3,500 and 4,000 soldiers. These units are more capable of independent action than current division-based organization, with strategic responsiveness greatly improved.

There are three common organizational designs for ground BCTs and five for support brigades. The three designs include a heavy BCT with two armor-mechanized infantry battalions and an armed reconnaissance battalion; an infantry BCT with two infantry battalions and an armed reconnaissance and surveillance battalion; and a Stryker BCT with three Stryker battalions and a reconnaissance and surveillance battalion.

Four of the five types of support brigades perform a single function each: aviation, fires, sustain, and battlefield surveillance. The fifth type is the maneuver enhancement brigade, which is organized to provide engineer, military police, air defense, chemical, and signal capabilities. Modularity increases each unit's capability by building in the communications, liaison, and logistics capabilities needed to permit greater operational autonomy and support the ability to conduct joint, multinational operations—capabilities that previously were at much higher organizational echelons.

Army transformation is well underway. The 3rd Infantry Division and the 101st Airborne Division have both reorganized and now have four maneuver brigades each, with the 10th Mountain Division and the 4th Infantry Division in the process of reorganization. By the end of 2006, the Army will have added 10 new brigades, with a potential for five more in 2007. The Army National Guard is converting 34 divisional or separate brigades to modular designs. By the end of transformation, the Army will have 77 and potentially 82 total BCTs. The Army Reserve is developing Army Reserve Expeditionary Packages to better generate and distribute critical force capabilities in support of the BCTs. And with the conversions, many military occupational specialties (MOSs), active and reserve, once necessary for a Cold War adversary, are now being reduced, with the positions going to increase infantry, military police, civil affairs, intelligence, and other critical skills for the war we now fight.

The goal for this larger pool of available forces is to enable the Army to generate forces in a rotational manner, while enhancing soldier stability. At the current operational tempo, this modular force structure will allow active component soldiers to spend at least two years at home following each deployed year; the reservist at least four years at home following each deployed year; and the National Guardsman five years at home following each deployed year.

Divisions, Corps, and Armies

The Army toyed with the idea of creating new command and control units for the transformed Army. It called them Units of Employment—X (UEx) and—Y (UEy), but in the end decided to retain current division and corps names, with the current two-star and three-star ranks. Both the transformed division and corps, with about 800 and 1,000 soldiers respectively, are capable of functioning as a joint task force and a joint force land component command. When the Army's restationing plan is complete, the ten active division headquarters will all be based in the United States.

Field army headquarters will also continue to exist, albeit modified for Army transformation needs, primarily as joint forces land component commands. Third, Fifth, Sixth, and Seventh U.S. Army have been designated to date. The number of the field army in the Pacific is yet to be determined.

Transformation Stationing Plan

The active division headquarters and BCT designations were influenced by a desire to preserve the lineage and honors of the units and divisions to which they are assigned, so that soldiers assigned to a modular BCT will have a shoulder patch. Lineage and honors for the support and maneuver support brigades will be determined in due course. The following table shows the currently planned stationing of the BCT units.

ANTICIPATED ACTIVE DIVISION AND BRIGADE COMBAT TEAM LOCATIONS:

Fort Benning, Ga.	1 BCT affiliated with the lineage of the 3rd Infantry Division
Fort Bliss, Tex.	1st Armored Division headquarters: 4 BCTs
Fort Bragg, N.C.	82nd Airborne Division headquarters: 4 BCTs
Fort Campbell, Ky.	101st Airborne Division headquarters: 4 BCTs
Fort Carson, Colo.	4th Infantry Division headquarters: 4 BCTs
Fort Drum, N.Y.	10th Mountain Division headquarters: 3 BCTs
Fort Hood, Tex.	1st Cavalry Division headquarters: 4 BCTs
Fort Hood, Tex.	3rd Armored Cavalry Regiment: 1 BCT
Fort Knox, Ky.	1 BCT affiliated with the lineage of the 1st Infantry Division
Fort Lewis, Wash.	2nd Infantry Division headquarters: 3 Stryker BCTs (SBCT)

Fort Polk, La.	1 BCT affiliated with the lineage of the 10th Mountain Division
Fort Richardson, Alaska	1 BCT affiliated with the lineage of the 25th Infantry Division
Fort Riley, Kan.	1st Infantry Division headquarters: 3 BCTs
Fort Wainwright, Alaska	1 SBCT affiliated with the lineage of the 25th Infantry Division
Fort Stewart, Ga.	3rd Infantry Division headquarters: 3 BCTs
Schofield Barracks, Hawaii	25th Infantry Division headquarters: 1 BCT / 1 SBCT
Fort Irwin, Cal.	11th Armored Cavalry Regiment: 1 BCT (-)
Korea	1 BCT affiliated with the lineage of the 2nd Infantry Division
Germany	2nd Armored Cavalry Regiment: 1 SBCT
Italy	173rd Airborne Brigade: 1 BCT

Transformation Training and Readiness Cycle

To maximize force availability, the Army will phase unit readiness, deployment, and soldier stability through the following stages:

Reset. In this phase, a unit is organized, stabilized and regenerated, to include modular conversion if necessary, for the upcoming ready and/or deployment cycle.

Training. The unit reaches readiness standards in individual and collective training. The training phase concludes with a validation or certification exercise that transitions the unit to the ready phase.

Ready Phase. For the remaining period of the operational cycle, the unit continues to improve its collective readiness, and deploys when required.

Along with restructuring, the Army is transitioning from an individual replacement manning system to a unit focused system, with soldiers over the long term being stabilized at the same post for extended periods to increase combat readiness and cohesion, reduce turnover, and eliminate many repetitive training requirements.

NEW THREATS

The end of the Cold War had three key strategic events: the collapse of international communism, the demise of the USSR, and an end to bipolar competition. These events, in turn, are affecting power and security relationships throughout the world. One result is the relative dispersal of power away from the states of the former Soviet Union toward regional power centers. Another is the potential struggle within regions as the dominant states vie for position within the emerging power hierarchy. A third is that in many regions the "lid has come off" long-simmering ethnic, religious, territorial, and economic disputes.

Terrorism

The United States continues to face a variety of threats from terrorist organizations such as al Qaeda and Sunni Muslim extremist groups. The primary threat for the foreseeable future is a network of Islamic extremists hostile to the United States. The network is transnational and has a broad range of capabilities, which include mass-casualty attacks. The most dangerous and immediate threat is Sunni Islamic terrorists that form the al Qaeda associated movement.

Osama bin Ladin and his senior leadership no longer exercise centralized control and direction. We now face an al Qaeda associated movement of like-minded groups who interact, share resources, and work to achieve shared goals.

Islamic terrorists hit the Pentagon.

Some of the groups in the movement provide safe haven and logistical support to al Qaeda members, others operate directly with al Qaeda, and still others fight with al Qaeda in the Afghanistan/Pakistan region.

Remnants of the senior leadership still present a threat. As is clear in their public statements, Bin Ladin and al-Zawahiri remain focused on their strategic objectives, including another major casualty-producing attack against the U.S. homeland.

The Global Jihadist Movement

The global jihadist movement predates al Qaeda's founding and was reinforced and developed by successive conflicts in Afghanistan, Bosnia, Chechnya, and elsewhere during the 1990s. As a result, it spawned several groups and operating nodes and developed a resiliency that ensured that destruction of any one group or node did not destroy the larger movement. Since 2001, extremists, including members of al Qaeda and affiliated groups, have sought to exploit perceptions of the U.S.-led global war on terrorism and, in particular, the war in Iraq to attract converts to their movement. Many of these recruits come from a large and growing pool of disaffected youth who are sympathetic to radical, anti-Western militant ideology. At the same time, these extremists have branched out to establish jihadist cells in other parts of the Middle East, South Asia, and Europe, from which they seek to prepare operations and facilitate funding and communications. Foreign fighters appear to be working to make of the insurgency in Iraq what Afghanistan was to the earlier generation of jihadists—a melting pot for jihadists from around the world, a training ground, and an indoctrination center. In the months and years ahead, a significant number of fighters who have traveled to Iraq could return to their home countries, where they might strengthen existing extremist networks with their new skills and experience in the communities to which they return.

Another goal is the overthrow of "apostate" Muslim governments, defined as governments which do not promote Islamic values or support or are friendly to the United States and other Western countries. The goals also call for withdrawal of the United States and other Coalition forces from Muslim countries, the destruction of Israel, and restoration of a Palestinian state, and recreation of the caliphate, a transnational state based on Islamic fundamental tenets.

Underlying the rise of extremism are political and socioeconomic conditions that leave many, mostly young male adults, alienated. There is a demographic explosion or youth bubble in many Muslim countries. The portion of the population under age 15 is 40 percent in Iraq, 49 percent in the Gaza Strip, and 38 percent in Saudi Arabia. Unemployment rates in these countries are as high as 30 percent in Saudi Arabia and about 50 percent in the Gaza Strip.

Educational systems in many nations contribute to the appeal of Islamic extremism. Some schools, particularly the private "madrasas," actively promote Islamic extremism. School textbooks in several Middle East states reflect a narrow interpretation of the Koran and contain anti-Western and anti-Israeli views. Many schools concentrate on Islamic studies focused on memorization and recitation of the Koran and fail to prepare students for jobs in the global economy.

Groups like al Qaeda capitalize on the economic and political disenfranchisement to attract new recruits. Even historically local conflicts involving Muslim minorities or fundamentalist groups such as those in Indonesia, the Philippines, and Thailand are generating new support for al Qaeda and present new al Qaeda-like threats.[1]

---

[1] From the State Department's *Country Reports on Terrorism, 2004* (April 2005).

Although terrorism is our most important challenge today, President George W. Bush has named Iran and North Korea as states that are threats to the United States. There also remains uncertainty about the future of Russia and China—two major powers undergoing great change—plus other issues, such as the dynamics on the Korean peninsula; the prospects for lasting peace or continuing conflict in the Middle East; genocidal, ethnic, religious, and tribal conflict in Africa; the global impact of the proliferation of military technology; and an array of upcoming leadership changes.

COUNTRY AND REGION REPORTS

Afghanistan

Afghanistan, once the safe haven for Osama bin Ladin, has started on the road to recovery after decades of instability and civil war. Hamid Karzai's election to the presidency was a major milestone. Elections for a new National Assembly and local district councils—held in late 2005—completed the process of electing representatives. President Karzai still faces a low-level insurgency aimed at destabilizing the country, raising the cost of reconstruction and ultimately forcing Coalition forces to leave. The development of the Afghan National Army and a national police force is going well, although neither can yet stand on its own. There is also a broad coalition of military forces from NATO that provides stability operations and force training in Afghanistan.

Iraq

Iraq's December 2005 national parliamentary elections have brought to Iraq its first permanent democratic government in several decades. However, domestic tranquility for the Iraqi people will largely depend on the ability of Iraqi forces to provide security. Iraq's most capable security units have become more effective in recent months, contributing to several major operations and helping to put an Iraqi face on security operations. Insurgents have targeted new recruits in order to undermine the effectiveness of existing Iraqi security forces.

The lack of security is hurting Iraq's reconstruction efforts and economic development, causing overall economic growth to proceed at a much slower pace than many analysts expected a year ago. Alternatively, the larger uncommitted moderate Sunni population and the Sunni political elite may seize the postelectoral moment to take part in creating Iraq's new political institutions if victorious Shiite and Kurdish parties include Sunnis in the new government.

Iran

Iran is important to the United States because of its size, location, energy resources, military strength, and its hostility to U.S. and Western interests. It actively supports terrorist groups in the region, such as Hezballah, and could encourage increased attacks in Israel and the Palestinian Territories to derail progress toward peace. Iran also aids insurgents in Iraq in their drive to oust the United States from that country and ultimately the Middle East. In the near term, Iran's goal is a weakened, decentralized, and Shiite-dominated Iraq that is incapable of posing a threat to Iran. The country's mullah-dominated government will also continue its weapons of mass destruction and ballistic missile programs. Its drive to acquire nuclear weapons is a key test of international resolve and the nuclear nonproliferation treaty.

The government in Tehran has the only military in the region that can threaten its neighbors and Gulf stability. Its expanding ballistic missile inventory presents a potential threat to states in the region. As it fields new longer range medium-range ballistic missiles (MRBMs), Iran will have missiles with ranges to reach many of our European allies. Although the country maintains a sizable conventional force, it has made limited progress in modernizing its conventional capabilities. Air and air defense forces rely on out-of-date U.S., Russian, and Chinese equipment. Ground forces suffer from personnel and equipment shortages. In addition, the equipment is also poorly maintained. Intelligence services estimate that Iran can briefly close the Strait of Hormuz, relying on a layered strategy using predominately naval, air, and some ground forces. Last year it purchased North Korean torpedo and missile-armed fast attack craft and midget submarines, making marginal improvements to this capability.

Iran is and will remain a threat to the national security interests of the United States for the foreseeable future.

Syria

The Syrian government likely weighs opportunities and risks with an unstable Iraq. It sees the problems we face in Iraq as beneficial because our commitments in Iraq reduce the prospects for action against Syria. However, it is probably concerned about potential spillover of Iraqi problems, especially Sunni extremism, into Syria. We have little evidence of active regime support for the insurgency, but Syria offers a safe haven to Iraqi Baathists, some of whom have ties to insurgents. Syria continues to support Lebanese Hizballah and several rejectionist Palestinian groups, which its government argues are legitimate resistance groups. While the country is making minor improvements to its conventional forces through purchases of modern antitank guided missiles and overhauling of some aircraft, it cannot afford major weapon systems acquisitions.

North Korea

After more than a decade of declining or stagnant economic growth, Kim Jong Il's military capability has significantly degraded. The North's declining capabilities are even more pronounced when viewed in light of the significant improvements over the same period of the Republic of Korea (ROK) military and the US-ROK Combined Forces Command. Nevertheless, the North maintains a large conventional force of over one million soldiers, the majority of which may be deployed south of Pyongyang.

North Korea has sought to develop nuclear weapons, and its regional neighbors and the U.S. are seeking to forestall this development diplomatically.

The North Korean People's Army remains capable of attacking South Korea with artillery and missile forces with limited warning. Such a provocative act, absent an immediate threat, is highly unlikely, counter to Pyongyang's political and economic objectives and would prompt a South Korean—Combined Forces Command (CFC) response it could not effectively oppose.

China

Beijing's military modernization and military buildup is tilting the balance of power in the Taiwan Strait. Improved Chinese capabilities could threaten U.S. forces in the region should a major reason for hostilities emerge.

China remains keenly interested in Coalition military operations in Afghanistan and Iraq and is using lessons from those operations to guide the People's Liberation Army (PLA) modernization and strategy; however, it will take several years before these lessons are incorporated into the armed forces. China continues to develop or import modern weapons. Priorities include submarines, surface combatants, air defense, ballistic and anti-ship cruise missiles, and modern fighters. The government, however, also faces technical and operational difficulties in many areas. The PLA continues with its plan to cut approximately 200,000 soldiers from the Army to free resources for further modernization, an initiative that began in 2004.

China is increasingly confident and active on the international stage, trying to ensure it has a voice on major international issues, secures access to natural resources, and counters what it sees as U.S. efforts to contain or encircle China.

Russia

Despite an improving economy, Russia continues to face endemic challenges related to its post-Soviet military decline. Seeking to be a great power, the Russian government has made some improvements to its armed forces, but has not addressed difficult domestic problems that will limit the scale and scope of military recovery. Defense should continue to receive modest real increases in funding, unless Russia suffers an economic setback. Budget increases will help Russia create a professional military by replacing conscripts with volunteer servicemen and focus on maintaining, modernizing, and extending the operational life of its strategic weapons systems, including its nuclear missile force.

Balkans

International peacekeeping forces in Bosnia and Kosovo continue to operate in a complex environment that poses significant challenges to the establishment of a stable and enduring peace. The Bosnian factions should continue to generally comply with the military aspects of the Dayton Accords and Stabilization Force (SFOR) directives. Montenegro's potential drive for independence from Serbia presents the next potential crisis. Ethnic Albanians from across the political spectrum in Kosovo continue to insist on independence from Serbia. U.S. and allied forces expect to be involved in stability operations for the mid-term.

South Asia

The tense rivalry between India and Pakistan over Kashmir is our most important security concern on the subcontinent. While neither side wants war, both see their security relationship in zero-sum terms. India's larger economy and more robust military is balanced by Pakistan's threat to retaliate with nuclear weapons if the two nations go to war. With frequent low-level clashes, the potential for miscalculation and rapid escalation is constant.

The South Asian drug trade presents another serious regional concern, with many production and trafficking areas outside effective government control. Afghanistan and Pakistan will remain significant opium producers, with Pakistan and Iran also serving as key drug transit nodes. Destabilized governments as well as other economic and political imperatives will continue to limit the effectiveness of regional counterdrug efforts.

Latin America

The scourge of narcotics trafficking, related money laundering, weapons and contraband smuggling, and insurgency all combine to provide threatening conditions for some countries and governments of the region and for U.S. interests. The potential for more serious insurgency and more widespread terrorism and crime in several areas of Central and South America and the Caribbean continues to demand our vigilance.

In summary, the threats facing the United States remain high although we will not likely see a global "peer competitor" within ten years. On the other hand, the world remains a very dangerous and complex place and there is every reason to expect U.S. military requirements to be at about the same level of the past several years, and that use of U.S. military forces will be required along the full spectrum of operations.

2

The Role of the NCO

BRIEF HISTORY OF THE NCO CORPS[1]

Throughout our Army's 225-year history, NCOs have performed vital functions as small-unit leaders, technical experts, trainers, and, perhaps most important, guardians of the Army's standards. The history of the U.S. Army and of the noncommissioned officer began in 1775 with the Continental Army. The men who faced the opening rounds of the American Revolution exemplified the ideal of citizen-soldiers. However, patriotism alone was not sufficient to ensure victory in an age where linear tactics dominated the battlefield. There was little systematic about NCO duties until Inspector General Friedrich von Steuben standardized them at Valley Forge. With the publication of his now famous "Blue Book," he established the ranks of sergeant major, quartermaster sergeant, first sergeant, sergeant, and corporal, and their corresponding responsibilities. A truly American NCO emerged with the blending of traditions of the British, French, and Prussian armies.

The lessons of the Revolutionary War battlefields, especially the value of sergeants and corporals, had to be relearned the hard way during the War of 1812. In 1825, the first attempt was made to establish a systematic method for noncommissioned officer selection. The appointment of regimental and company NCOs remained the duty of the regimental commander. In 1829, instructions were published to train NCOs so that they had "an accurate knowledge of the exercise and use of their firelocks, of the manual exercise of the soldier, and of the firings and marchings." In 1840, an effort was made to give the NCO corps greater prestige by adopting a distinctive sword. The model 1840 NCO sword remains the sword of the NCO corps and is still used on special ceremonial occasions. During Mexican War battles, an outnumbered American force gained victory by applying the concept of combined arms operations. These tactics succeeded in part because career NCOs within the ranks of infantry,

[1] Much of this overview has been extracted from the Center of Military History's *The Story of the Noncommissioned Officer Corps,* which was written in 1989 for the Year of the NCO, and reissued updated and with additional chapters in 2003.

artillery, engineers, and dragoon regiments mastered the necessary skills of working together.

The Civil War was the last major use of linear tactics. Much deadlier weapons, and horrible casualties, added emphasis to the sergeant's role in holding units together. As both sides shifted to more open formations, NCOs took on added leadership responsibilities. This experience, and new tactics, served the Army well in operations against the Indians after the war. Although short in duration, the Spanish-American War tested the ability of both regular and National Guard NCOs to make a swift transition from peace to combat. Overcoming disease and tropical heat, these troops captured Santiago, Cuba.

The United States entered the twentieth century as a new world power. NCOs soon faced duty on foreign shores including the Philippine Insurrection and China's Boxer Rebellion. On the eve of World War I sergeants and corporals from the active and reserve components experienced excellent training when troubles along the border with Mexico prompted a temporary mobilization. Sergeants and corporals deployed to France as part of the American Expeditionary Forces (AEF). Massing a huge army and deploying it overseas taxed the abilities of the nation—but the NCOs came through. Many were real heroes, and their roles in the trenches of the first modern war spanned the widest array of technical and tactical specialties to that date. After WWI, in a cost-cutting move, Congress reorganized the NCO ranks into five grades: master sergeant, technical sergeant, staff sergeant, sergeant, and corporal. Until the 1930s, NCOs usually stayed with their regiment; to leave meant giving up their stripes, which belonged to the regiment.

World War II made more demands upon the noncommissioned officer corps and had a greater impact upon the NCO's role and status than any previous conflict in American history. By the end of the war, there were 23,328 infantry squads in 288 active infantry regiments. More than seventy separate battalions, including armored infantry and rangers, raised the total number of such squads to over 25,000, all needing noncommissioned leaders. Drafted, trained, and promoted during the hectic months of the early war years, these citizen-soldiers carried out their duties as noncommissioned officers superbly in countless engagements on every front during World War II, but especially those areas where small-unit leadership was at a premium.

The 1950–53 "police action" in Korea sent NCOs into combat as part of a United Nations (UN) force when the Cold War heated up. Despite the onrush of technology, some fundamental NCO functions had to be performed in time-honored fashion. The United States and the Soviet Union, each armed with nuclear weapons, spent the decades after World War II engaged in a new kind of rivalry. The Cold War placed different demands on the NCO corps than did conventional combat. Education became essential to the creation of a professionally competent soldier. Although formal instruction for officers began with the establishment of West Point, peace time leadership programs for NCOs began only after World War II. The precedent set when the garrison forces in Germany established a school at Sonthofen soon spread across the Army. Two senior grades, E-8 and E-9, were created in 1958, and the rank of sergeant major reappeared.

Eight years of fighting in Southeast Asia provided a challenge to the corps. Beginning with small-scale deployments of advisers to help the Army of the Republic of Vietnam, the American presence grew to over a half-million men. The Vietnam era's heavy requirement for small-unit tactical leaders, technical specialists, and trainers strained the available pool of NCOs. At the same time, the 365-day tour of duty disrupted the traditional ability of the NCO Corps to provide the Army with continuity and experience in the field. In 1966, the chief of staff created the position of sergeant major of the Army.

In the last half of 1971, the Army implemented the Noncommissioned Officer Education System (NCOES). This progressive system was designed to educate NCOs in subjects and skills needed to enhance their performance and abilities. The products of the NCOES were prominent during the liberation of Grenada in 1982 and during operations in Panama and Kuwait in 1989 and 1992, respectively, and, presently, in places such as Bosnia, Macedonia, the Middle East, and Africa. Today, their presence is felt across the battlegrounds of Afghanistan, Iraq, and countless other countries, as well as in units training in the United States. It is to these small-unit leaders and soldiers who had trained so hard and well during the late 1980s through the early 1990s that the laurels of victory fell. Brig. Gen. John S. Brown, USA (Ret.), Chief of Military History, wrote: "The characteristic that most distinguished Americans from their late-twentieth-century adversaries was the caliber of their NCOs. No army exceeded and few approximated the combination of experience, leadership, and technical knowledge represented by sergeants through command sergeant major. This does not diminish the roles that officers and other ranks played; it just highlights what has made the US Army what it is today."

Except for short periods of national emergency, the Army has normally had to operate with limited funds. Training continued during lean periods because NCOs knew how to improvise. Looking back over the more than two centuries that have passed since the creation of the U.S. Army, it is clear that the evolution of the NCO's role and status to a modern, professional identity was not always smooth, as the Army leadership and Army doctrine tried to keep pace with these developments. Today's NCO retains the duties and responsibilities established by Von Steuben in 1778, and has added to this rich heritage the roles of small-unit leader, trainer, technician, and guardian of Army standards.

MILITARY HISTORY AND NCO LEADERSHIP

What NCOs do today is not new. Despite profound changes in the outward appearance of noncommissioned officers during the last century, the mission "to protect and defend" remains. From the stand-up battles of the Civil War and enforcement of peace in the American West to the war of maneuver in the Gulf, peacekeeping in Bosnia and Kosova, and now the war on terrorism in Afghanistan, Iraq, and other regions of the world, the essentials of small-unit leadership and, therefore, the duties of the NCO have remained the same. Although many NCOs have an active interest in the "big picture" of military history, the true applicability of military history for the NCO lies in relating the big picture to the basic NCO duties of soldier accountability, reconstituting small units, and the unit cohesiveness built by NCOs through small-unit training.

Senior noncommissioned officers traditionally have been the keepers of their organization's lineage and traditions. Serving as role models and mentors, they pass on and inculcate the traditions and organizational ethos into newly arrived soldiers.

The staff ride is an important leader development technique that analyzes battles on the actual terrain where historic events took place. Illustrating the complexity of human conditions during combat, military history can help NCOs bridge the gap between peacetime training and war. Although most unit staff rides study decision making at the higher levels, including maneuver, logistics, and politics, some units integrate the different perspectives of officers and NCOs. When staff rides incorporate the human conditions under stress of battle, such as why and how they fought, and the combat duties and responsibilities of the different ranks, as well as the equally important and necessary lessons learned regarding casualty evacuation and reporting, resupply, and training and integration of replacements, NCOs learn more about their present-day duties. When NCOs can make comparisons between past and present—when they realize, for example, that instead of moving as a member of a fire team, soldiers were moving as a member of a company in line—they better understand the greater role that NCOs of all branches and occupational specialties play in achieving victory on the decentralized battlefield. Further information on staff rides and Army history in general can be found on the World Wide Web at *www.army.mil/cmh-pg,* the Center of Military History web site.

The U.S. Army Center of Military History book *The Story of the Noncommissioned Officer Corps* also includes portraits of NCOs in action. It views NCO leadership responsibilities and addresses them through extracted documents, including Baron von Steuben's historic *Regulations for the Order and Discipline of the Troops of the United States,* published in 1789. The book also presents an evolution of NCO rank insignia and a gallery of noncommissioned heroes.

Here is an extract of one such noncommissioned officer fighting in Afghanistan:

> The platoon sergeant surveyed his soldiers as they debarked the CH-47 helicopter after their days of trudging up and down the

ridges of Shah-I-Kot fighting the Taliban and al Qaeda. His soldiers were finally relaxed after days of pumping adrenaline.

They were light infantrymen who took pride in their craft, their buddies, and their organization. There was nothing flashy or fancy about them. They were like every other doughboy, dogface, grunt, or crunchy who fought with his boots on the ground and today they were bearded, dirty, and tired, but their weapons gleamed. As infantrymen, they lived under the stars and got wet when it rained; shivered when it was cold; were excited when moving to contact; exhausted when moving to daylight; and felt the adrenaline rush when shot at.

The platoon sergeant submitted the daily status, ensured that his soldiers were fed and kept their equipment serviceable. When the packing list for the upcoming operation arrived, he had all of the soldiers repack their rucks and then he and his squad leaders inspected each. The rucksacks were loaded with ammunition, batteries, night vision and communications gear for the operation itself and "hawk" gear consisting of gortex, fleece liners, and polypropylene underwear to keep warm when the big heat tab in the sky went down, water and food.

When they boarded the CH-47 for the flight into combat the platoon sergeant checked each man's name against the manifest as they quietly filed by, each lost in his own thoughts and mortality. During the long flight soldiers dozed to the drone of the engines,

First Combat.

heads bouncing against their chests, back against the cabin wall, or leaning on another soldier's shoulders. The signal came to get ready five minutes out and soldiers shuffled and arranged their equipment. The platoon sergeant made his final check and received the thumbs[-]up from his squad leaders. He could see the stress on the faces around him and hoped that his own did not reveal his last thoughts before landing. The nose of the CH-47 rose abruptly and the crew chief yelled one minute. A load whine and shock on landing, the ramp drop, and soldiers spilled into the whirlwind of gravel and dust kicked up by the rotors.

They landed in what appeared an onion patch high up on one of the ridgelines so they would now have to fight 2,000 meters straight up. The rough terrain was more an obstacle than the elevation, although breathing was a task. They were above 9,000 feet and it was a real effort to hump the rucksack or even just to move around at that altitude. Although warned to expect altitude sickness, there was none in his company and no cold weather injuries, due to the watchful eyes of the junior NCOs.

Throughout the combat operation the platoon sergeant kept daily accountability, arranged for Medivac of those soldiers wounded, and kept them resupplied with ammunition, water, and rations, and then ensured that everyone ate. On the tenth day, he and the other members of his platoon boarded helicopters for the return flight to their initial staging area. As the platoon sergeant watched his soldiers move toward their tents at Bagram Air Base, he knew they had accomplished the mission assigned them.

History has been recorded in many ways during the U.S. military's existence. Official museums operate throughout the Army and benefit thousands of interested soldiers. At Fort Bliss, Texas, soldiers can visit the NCO Museum. At Fort Knox, Kentucky, they can visit the Patton Museum of Cavalry and Armor, and at Fort Benning, the Infantry Museum. At Fort Bragg, North Carolina, the 82nd Airborne Division Museum is chock-full of paratrooper and glider infantry history. The largest collections of military equipment are maintained at the Ordnance Museum at Aberdeen, Maryland, and the Transportation Corps Museum at Fort Eustis, Virginia. Soldiers interested in the history of women in the Army can visit the Women's Army Corps Museum at Fort Jackson, South Carolina. The Finance Museum is also located there. Visitors to the Pentagon should visit a small alcove called the Hall of Heroes to read the names of the nation's Medal of Honor recipients. Virtually all major installations and many minor ones have some kind of history facility, and all are worth visiting. Locations and hours of operation for Army museums can be found on the web at *www.army.mil/cmh-pg/museums/museums.htm*.

A more detailed history of the NCO can be found in Ernest F. Fisher's *Guardians of the Republic: A History of the Noncommissioned Officer Corps of the U.S. Army* (Stackpole Books, 2000).

NCO INDUCTION CEREMONY—PRESERVING THE TRADITION

From their first day as an NCO, new corporals and sergeants must realize that they are part of a fellowship which puts the mission and subordinates before self, and though battered at times, the professionalism of the soldiers within the NCO Corps will never falter. One way to preserve the NCO tradition is to honor newly promoted noncommissioned officers when they join the NCO Corps, a tradition that can be traced to the Army of Frederick the Great.

As FM 7-22.7, *The Army Noncommissioned Officer Guide,* makes clear, induction ceremonies are a rite of passage and not an opportunity for hazing. The importance of recognizing the transition from "just one of the guys or gals" to a noncommissioned officer should be shared among the superiors, peers, and soldiers of the newly promoted. The induction ceremony should be held separate and to serve as an extension of the promotion ceremony. Typical Army promotion effective dates occur on the first day of a month and when possible, so should the induction ceremony.

As the senior NCO of the command, the battalion command sergeant major (CSM) serves as the host of the NCO induction ceremony. The first sergeants are the CSM's assistants and they compose the "Official Party." If desired, a guest speaker for the ceremony may be included and also is a part of the official party. A narrator will serve as the Master of Ceremonies.

The ceremony is to be conducted with pride in a dignified and solemn manner. All of the unit's NCOs should be in attendance. It should be conducted by the command sergeant major (CSM). This ceremony should be held at least quarterly. Unit colors, guidons, and historic artifacts should be displayed. Family and guests may be present.

The sponsor should be the NCO who recommended the candidate for promotion.

The NCO Creed will be personalized with the candidate's name at the heading and the CSM's and candidate's signature blocks at the bottom. Additionally, distinctive unit insignia or shoulder sleeve insignia can be added to link the candidate with the organization.

What follows is a sample sequence of events for a battalion-level NCO Induction Ceremony that can be modified to fit other size units:

The CSM makes appropriate opening remarks. Recommend inclusion of the deeds of a past or present NCO who exemplifies the intent behind the NCO Creed.

CSM directs the Personnel NCO: "Read the Creed of the Noncommissioned Officer."

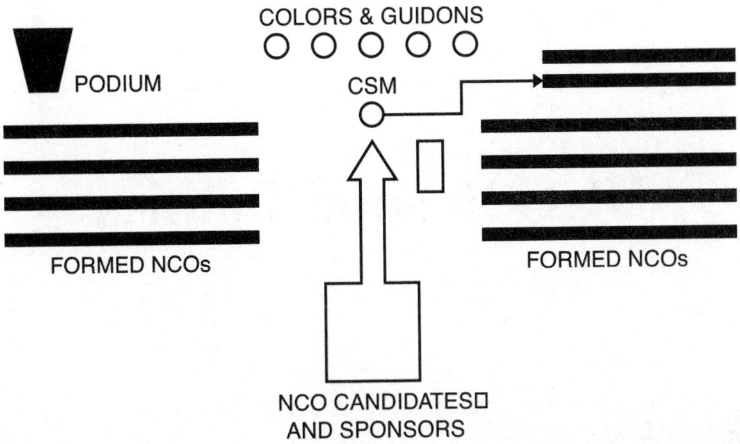

NCO Induction Ceremony

On completion the CSM asks, "How many candidates are there for induction?"

Personnel NCO responds, "Sergeant Major, we have _____ candidates."

CSM addresses the sponsors and candidates: "Who is the first candidate and sponsor?"

Sponsor responds, "Sergeant Major, the first candidate is Sergeant/ Corporal _______________

I, Sergeant _______________ am his sponsor."

CSM directs, "Bring your candidate forward."

The sponsor and the candidate move forward and halt in front of CSM.

Signing of the Creed

Both CSM and candidate sign the creed. Both CSM and candidate symbolically "wet down" the stripes (optional).

After the signing and wetting down of stripes, the candidate and sponsor move to a predesignated position.

When all candidates have been inducted, the CSM proposes a toast or appropriate salute to the newly inducted NCOs.

All assembled NCOs then pass down the line of newly promoted NCOs, shake their hands, and say, "Congratulations! Welcome into our corps." (This is a very important part of the ceremony.)

3

NCO Responsibilities

PRINCIPAL NCO DUTIES

An NCO leads by example, trains and enforces standards, maintains discipline, takes care of soldiers, and adapts to a changing world. NCO responsibilities are divided into twelve broad categories:

1. **Individual training of soldiers in military occupational specialties (MOSs) and in basic soldiering skills.**
   - Train soldiers to fight, win, and live.
   - Teach soldiers the history and traditions of the Army, military courtesy, personal hygiene, appearance standards, and drill and ceremonies.
2. **Personal and professional development of soldiers.**
   - Fix responsibility. Give soldiers tasks they can do based on their abilities, experience, and know-how. Train soldiers to take on increasingly difficult or complex tasks.
   - Train soldiers to replace you, just as you trained to replace your superiors.
   - Hold soldiers responsible for their actions.
   - Ensure that required publications are available and convenient.
   - Help soldiers cope with personal and professional problems. Until the problem is resolved, you have a soldier with a problem in your unit, so it is your problem, too.
   - Counsel soldiers on their strengths and weaknesses; build on strengths and help them strive to overcome weaknesses.
   - Recommend promotions and awards through the NCO support channel, but do not promise them.
   - Recommend that good soldiers attend service school specialist or career development courses as needed and as appropriate.
3. **Accountability for the squad, the section, or the team.**
   - Know what each soldier in the unit that you lead is doing during duty hours (and off-duty hours as well when a problem spreads from off duty to on duty).

- Know where your soldiers live and how to contact them.
- Know why a soldier is going on sick call or other appointments, how he or she is treated, and what is wrong.
- Use the unit to accomplish as many missions as possible, but never volunteer troops for missions to make yourself look good in the eyes of superiors. Know your team's limitations.
- Know the readiness status or operating condition of unit weapons, vehicles, and other equipment.

4. **Military appearance, physical fitness, and training.**
   - Make corrections when you see something wrong wherever you may be and to whomever is concerned. Be polite and diplomatic.
   - Supervise the physical fitness training and development of your soldiers, in accordance with FM 21-20 (FM 3-22-20), *Physical Fitness Training,* and AR 350-15, *The Army Physical Fitness Program.*
   - Ensure that you and your soldiers meet the Army's weight and body fat standards in accordance with Army Regulation (AR) 600-9, *The Army Weight Control Program.*
5. **Physical and mental well-being of the soldier and his or her family.**
   - Know your soldiers' family situations and help them if they have problems.
   - Make sure your soldiers know what services and benefits they and their families are entitled to. Your personnel service NCO can provide this information.
6. **Supervision, control, motivation, and discipline of subordinates.**
   - Counsel soldiers and maintain counseling records.
   - Support subordinate NCOs. Similarly, when they are wrong, tell them so, but do it privately.
   - Teach your soldiers about the Uniform Code of Military Justice.
   - Recommend commendations and passes.
   - Recommend bars to reenlistment, or elimination actions, if appropriate. Weeding out the bad soldiers will encourage good soldiers to stay.
   - Conduct corrective training when required.
   - Keep soldiers informed—do not let them be surprised by details, field training exercises, inspections, or other events.
   - Enforce the Army Equal Opportunity Program.
7. **Communication between the individual soldier and the organization.**
   - Use, and insist that soldiers use, the chain of command and support channels.
   - Listen and act on soldiers' suggestions and complaints, but be able to distinguish between bellyaching and real concerns.
   - Support and explain reasons for current policies.
   - Try to develop a feeling of loyalty and pride in your team and unit.
   - Do not complain to, or in the presence of, your soldiers.

8. **Plan and conduct day-to-day unit operations.**
   - Provide input to the training NCO for individual skill training.
   - Conduct team training.
   - Supervise events as required by training schedules.
9. **Maintain established standards of performance.**
   - Treat all soldiers with the respect they deserve, and ensure that your soldiers do the same.
   - Explain clearly what you expect from soldiers.
   - Conduct special training to correct weaknesses.
   - Train soldiers to standards set by soldiers' manuals and other literature.
   - Provide up-to-date information for appropriate levels of self-development tests.
   - Be professional.
10. **Maintenance, serviceability, accountability, and readiness.**
    - Inspect soldiers' equipment often. Use the manual or approved checklist. Hold soldiers responsible for repairs and losses.
    - Learn how to use and maintain the equipment that soldiers use. Be among the first to operate new equipment, whether tanks or word processors.
    - Enforce maintenance and supply system procedures.
    - Encourage economy, and deal with soldiers who abuse equipment.
    - Keep up-to-date component lists and conduct inventories. Know what is on hand and turn in excess or unserviceable equipment.
11. **Appearance and condition of unit billets, facilities, and work areas.**
    - Ensure that decorations in soldiers' rooms and common areas do not impact on good order and discipline of the organization.
    - Conduct fire and safety inspections and drills.
    - Set and enforce cleanliness standards.
    - Eat in the mess hall and observe mess operations.
12. **Advise on, support, and implement policy established by the chain of command.**

THE CHAIN OF COMMAND

The importance of the chain of command to success is nothing new in military affairs. How well any institution works depends upon how effectively orders and information are passed from top to bottom and back. The role of the NCO in making the chain work is vital.

The chain is defined as the succession of commanders from a superior to a subordinate through which command is exercised. There is only one chain of command in the Army, but it is paralleled and complemented by the NCO support channel. Both are communication channels used to pass information up and down. Neither is a one-way street, nor are the two entirely separate. In order for the chain of command to work, the NCO support channel must be operating.

THE NCO SUPPORT CHANNEL

The NCO Support Channel begins with the command sergeant major and ends with the lowest-ranking NCO. This channel functions orally through the command sergeant major or first sergeant and normally does not involve written instructions; however, either method may be used, and both are considered directive in nature. In addition to passing information, this channel is used for issuing orders and getting jobs done. The channel leaves the commander free to plan, make decisions, and program future training and operations.

Some of the tasks with which the NCO support channel assists the chain of command are the planning and conducting day-to-day unit operations, training soldiers in individual and small-unit collective tasks, caring for soldiers and their families on and off duty, accounting for and maintaining individual and unit equipment under their control, and ensuring that soldiers meet the standards for physical training (PT) and height and weight.

Sergeant Major of the Army

The sergeant major of the Army is the senior sergeant major grade of rank and designates the senior enlisted position of the Army. The individual who occupies this office serves as the senior enlisted advisor and consultant to the chief of staff of the Army in the following areas: problems affecting enlisted personnel and solutions to these problems; professional education, growth, and advancement of NCOs; and morale training, pay, promotions, and other matters concerning enlisted personnel.

Command Sergeant Major

The command sergeant major (CSM) is the senior NCO of the command at battalion level or higher. He or she executes policies and standards, and advises the commander on training, appearance, and conduct of enlisted soldiers. Activities of the local NCO channel emanate from the CSM. The CSM administers the unit Noncommissioned Officer Development Program (NCODP).

First Sergeant

The position of the first sergeant is similar to that of the command sergeant major in importance, responsibility, and prestige. The first sergeant is in direct and daily contact with sizable numbers of enlisted personnel, requiring of him or her outstanding leadership and professional competence. The first sergeant is the senior NCO in companies, batteries, and troops. Although heavily involved in company administration, the first sergeant's principal duty is the individual training of enlisted members of the unit.

Platoon Sergeant

The platoon sergeant is the principal assistant and advisor to the platoon leader and, as such, is second in command. It is normal for platoon sergeants to become the platoon leader during the absence or disability of commissioned officers of the platoon.

Section, Squad, and Team Leaders

Section, squad, and team leaders are responsible for the personal appearance and cleanliness of their soldiers, for property accountability and maintenance, for the whereabouts of their soldiers at all times, and for the ability to perform the primary mission at all times.

THE NCO AND THE OFFICER

There is no such thing as NCO business or officer's business. It is all Army business. Officers and NCOs in units determine the exact division of responsibilities by considering the mission, the situation, and the abilities and personalities of the leaders. Officers and their principal NCO should complement one another, i.e., if one walks around with a dark cloud overhead, the other should be a ray of sunshine, or one may focus on training and the other on maintenance. The following are general types of tasks for officers and NCOs.

- Officers command, plan, establish policy, and manage the Army; NCOs conduct the daily business of the Army within established policy.
- Officers focus on collective training leading to mission accomplishment; NCOs focus on individual training, which leads to mission capability.
- Officers are primarily involved in units and unit operations; NCOs place their major focus on individual soldiers and team leading.
- Officers concentrate on unit effectiveness and readiness; NCOs ensure that all subordinate NCOs and soldiers are individually ready and functioning as effective unit members—and that equipment in their possession is also ready and functioning.

PRECEDENCE AND RELATIVE RANK

The determination of rank and precedence among enlisted personnel is used when determining, among two or more individuals of equal rank, which one will be responsible for functions within the enlisted support channel. Date of rank is also used as the first determinant in computing standing on DA promotion boards.

Among enlisted personnel of the same grade of rank in active military service, including retired personnel on active duty, precedence or relative rank is determined as follows:

1. By date or rank.
2. When dates of rank are the same, by length of active service in the Army.
3. When 1 and 2 above are the same, by length of total active service.
4. When the foregoing tests are not sufficient, by age.

ENLISTED INSIGNIA OF GRADE

AIR FORCE	ARMY	MARINES	NAVY
Chief Master Sergeant of the Air Force (CMSAF)	Sergeant Major of the Army (SMA)	Sergeant Major of the Marine Corps (SgtMajMC)	Master Chief Petty Officer of the Navy (MCPON)
Chief Master Sergeant (CMSgt) Command Chief Master Sergeant	Command Sergeant Major (CSM) Sergeant Major (SGM)	Sergeant Major (SgtMaj) Master Gunnery Sergeant (MGySgt)	Fleet/Command Master Chief Petty Officer Master Chief Petty Officer (MCPO)
Senior Master Sergeant (SMSgt) First Sergeant (E-8)	First Sergeant (1SG) Master Sergeant (MSG)	First Sergeant (1stSgt) Master Sergeant (MSgt)	Senior Chief Petty Officer (SCPO)
Master Sergeant (MSgt) First Sergeant (E-7)	Platoon Sergeant (PSG) or Sergeant First Class (SFC)	Gunnery Sergeant (GySgt)	Chief Petty Officer (CPO)
Technical Sergeant (TSgt)	Staff Sergeant (SSG)	Staff Sergeant (SSgt)	Petty Officer First Class (PO1)
Staff Sergeant (SSgt)	Sergeant (SGT)	Sergeant (Sgt)	Petty Officer Second Class (PO2)
Senior Airman (SrA)	Corporal (CPL) Specialist (SPC)	Corporal (Cpl)	Petty Officer Third Class (PO3)
Airman First Class (A1C)	Private First Class (PFC)	Lance Corporal (LCpl)	Seaman (Seaman)
Airman (Amn)	Private E-2 (PV2)	Private First Class (PFC)	Seaman Apprentice (SA)
Airman Basic (AB) (no insignia)	Private E-1 (PV1) (no insignia)	Private (Pvt) (no insignia)	Seaman Recruit (SR)

OFFICER INSIGNIA OF GRADE

AIR FORCE	ARMY	MARINES	NAVY
General of the Air Force	General of the Army	(None)	Fleet Admiral
General	General	General	Admiral
Lieutenant General	Lieutenant General	Lieutenant General	Vice Admiral
Major General	Major General	Major General	Rear Admiral (Upper Half)
Brigadier General	Brigadier General	Brigadier General	Rear Admiral (Lower Half)
Colonel	Colonel	Colonel	Captain
Lieutenant Colonel	Lieutenant Colonel	Lieutenant Colonel	Commander
Major	Major	Major	Lieutenant Commander

OFFICER INSIGNIA OF GRADE

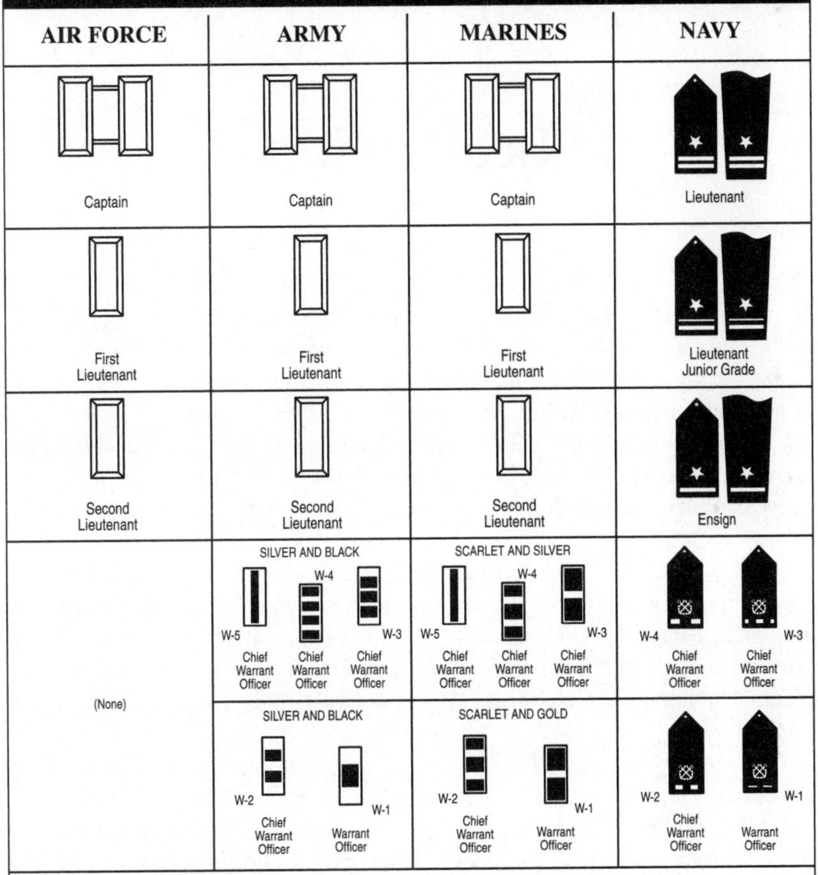
AIR FORCE
ARMY
MARINES
NAVY
Captain
Captain
Captain
Lieutenant
First Lieutenant
First Lieutenant
First Lieutenant
Lieutenant Junior Grade
Second Lieutenant
Second Lieutenant
Second Lieutenant
Ensign
(None)
SILVER AND BLACK
W-5 Chief Warrant Officer
W-4 Chief Warrant Officer
W-3 Chief Warrant Officer
SCARLET AND SILVER
W-5 Chief Warrant Officer
W-4 Chief Warrant Officer
W-3 Chief Warrant Officer
W-4 Chief Warrant Officer
W-3 Chief Warrant Officer
SILVER AND BLACK
W-2 Chief Warrant Officer
W-1 Warrant Officer
SCARLET AND GOLD
W-2 Chief Warrant Officer
W-1 Warrant Officer
W-2 Chief Warrant Officer
W-1 Warrant Officer

COAST GUARD

Coast Guard officers use the same rank insignia as Navy officers. Coast Guard enlisted rating badges are the same as the Navy's for grades E-1 through E-9, but they have silver specialty marks, eagles and stars, and gold chevrons. The badge of the Master Chief Petty Officer of the Coast Guard has a gold chevron and specialty mark, a silver eagle, and gold stars. For all ranks, the gold Coast Guard shield on the uniform sleeve replaces the Navy star.

4

Leadership

The terms *noncommissioned officer* and *leader* are synonymous. To be one is to be the other. In order to be an NCO, you must continually *develop* and *exhibit* certain *performance* behaviors, skills, and knowledge. Above all, NCO performance must be in accordance with Army values.

Regardless of where, when, under what circumstances, or by whom it is exercised, leadership boils down to getting soldiers to willingly carry out orders and accomplish the mission. The more expert the leader, the more likely that soldiers will follow.

NCOs must be able to motivate and inspire soldiers to carry out missions for the greater good of the Army. Good leaders acquire leadership attributes through a never-ending process of individual study, education, training, and experience. Although many principles of leadership exist, the ability to lead by example has stood the test of time, rigors of battle, and correct performance of duty.

Discipline

Military discipline relies for the most part upon self-discipline, respect for properly constructed authority, and the embracing of the Professional Army Ethic with its supporting individual values. Maintenance of discipline is a function of command and the first responsibility of the NCO leaders. Leaders must ensure that all soldiers present a neat and soldierly appearance, and must take action in cases where conduct is prejudicial to good order and military discipline.

NCOs must take action to quell any quarrel, fray, or disorder among persons subject to military law and apprehend the participants. In order to fulfill your duty, you may have to risk physical injury, so proceed with judgment and tact, but *take action.* In public, you may request the civilian police to take an offender into custody when no military police are available. Make on-the-spot corrections of uniform or courtesy violations wherever possible, and handle minor infractions as much as possible through the NCO support chain.

You must exercise your military authority with promptness, firmness, courtesy, and justice. One of your most effective nonpunitive disciplinary measures is extra training or instruction.

Training or instruction given to an individual to correct deficiencies must be not only directly related to the deficiency observed but also oriented to improving performance. For example, soldiers having dirty weapons can be required to clean their own weapons, as well as other soldiers' weapons. This requirement reinforces the standard that weapons must be clean, and it gives soldiers additional practice at cleaning weapons, so that in the future the soldiers will understand the standard.

NEW DIRECTIONS IN LEADERSHIP DOCTRINE

The Army defines leadership as "the process of influencing people by providing purpose, direction, and motivation, while operating to accomplish the mission and improve the organization." Leadership, despite the great strides in technology, remains the same—influencing and motivating people to get a job done. The new FM 22-100 (FM 6-22) consolidates five current manuals and one Department of the Army FM on all aspects and levels of leadership. The new manual discusses character-based leadership, clarifies values, establishes attributes as part of character, and, most importantly, focuses on improving people and organizations for the long term. Rather than provide a one-size-fits-all leadership model, Army leadership doctrine now outlines three levels of leadership—*direct, organizational,* and *strategic*—and identifies four skill domains that apply at all levels: *interpersonal, conceptual, technical,* and *tactical.* The discussion on actions outlines for each level what leaders do—what turns character into leadership.

Direct leadership is the work of first-line supervisors, whether they be in line or staff positions. It is face-to-face communication between soldiers, so it clearly applies at the tactical level in teams, squads, sections, platoons, and companies, even on battalion and brigade staffs. Besides communicating, team building, supervising, and counseling, NCOs need to think analytically and creatively, considering multiple perspectives and their decisions' intended and unintended consequences. Just as we train technically and tactically, we must now develop this ability to handle ideas, thoughts, and concepts.

Organizational leadership occurs at levels from battalion through corps. Here, because of increased unit size and complexity, organizational leaders influence, operate, and improve their outfits through programs, policies, and systems. At this level, it is more often that failure or success derives from one of these procedures than from an individual's success or failure. Senior NCOs must concern themselves with the higher organization's needs—as well as those of their subordinate units and leaders—learn to filter information, and decide how best to gather, analyze, and evaluate it.

Strategic leadership occurs at the highest military levels, whether in institutional settings stateside or operational contexts around the world. Here, the strategic leader provides the vision that focuses the force, from which flow the goals, plans, and benchmarks that shape the Army of the future. To support their vision, strategic leaders continually emphasize the Army's core messages to soldiers, their families, and their elected leaders.

Although the familiar concept "be, know, do" remains the centerpiece of the 1999 edition of *Military Leadership* by providing a specific framework with 23 dimensions that describes a leader of character and competence, leadership doctrine now flows from the axiom "Leaders of character and competence act to achieve excellence." Above all, the new doctrine anchors leaders of character and competence in moral bedrock—our Army values.

Be—Values and Attributes

Character describes who a person is inside, and at the core of Army leaders are Army values. Those values—*loyalty, duty, respect, selfless service, honor, integrity,* and *personal courage* (LDRSHIP)—capture the professional military ethos and describe the nature of our soldiers. Our common values help us to understand the purpose of our missions and devise appropriate methods to accomplish them. Values are the foundation of all that we are and do.

In addition to values, practice of leadership involves exercising *will, initiative, discipline, intelligent judgment, obedience,* and *cultural awareness.* These personal attributes, combined with the *military and professional bearing, physical and mental fitness,* and *self-control,* create a soldier's overall temperament to be a leader.

Know—Skills

Leaders develop skills in a variety of areas, grouped under four headings. Leaders must utilize their *interpersonal skills;* know their people and how to work with them as individuals and teams. Knowing, understanding, and applying job-related ideas constitute *conceptual skills.* Knowing how to use equipment and being proficient with it are *technical skills.* Those who combine the skills with people, concepts, and equipment to fulfill military missions have the *tactical skills* necessary for Army leadership. Although the Army provides some leadership training in NCO schools, no one knows the relevant areas of study and practice like the NCOs themselves, and it remains an individual's responsibility to develop new skills, whether for new jobs, equipment, tactics, or different people.

Do—Leadership Actions

The new definition of leadership focuses on *behavior,* something that can be seen and evaluated.*Influencing, operating,* and *improving* are basic leadership actions. Leaders demonstrate influence through communicating, decision-making, and motivating. At the direct level, NCOs influence face-to-face with instructions, encouragement, and recognition. A leader's influence obviously applies in the day-to-day business of operating—accomplishing missions. As part of operating, a leader is responsible for detailed, suitable planning; careful, proficient executing; and continual assessing and adjusting. Assessing change is essential to improving an organization. This new doctrinal emphasis means that a leader's influence today involves preparing for tomorrow. Improving the organization is not itself a new concept, for good leaders get their people ready for contingencies and strive to leave the unit better than they found it. Just pushing troops to meet immediate demands has never been enough. Leaders must also provide for their future. They are responsible for developing individual subordinates, building teams, and fostering learning in the organization. The best test of a leader's effectiveness is to observe how the unit operates when he or she is absent. If soldiers do what is right when the leader is absent, then the NCO has trained and led them well.

The traditional measure of leadership is whether an organization performed its tasks, fulfilled its obligations, and accomplished its missions—all short-term goals. Long-range leadership success is more difficult to assess, especially with turnover in commanders every eighteen months or less, and with the changes, differences in leader intent to subordinate officers, and NCOs who are normally in the unit for two or three commanders. Nevertheless, rather than be preoccupied with perfection and short-term gains that look good but do little to better the organization, some leaders work to build a climate that encourages prudent risk taking and creativity, exercises command that tolerates honest mistakes, promotes learning, and develops leaders who know how to help individual soldiers become the best they can be, so that in the long run units are capable of even more in the future. Effective leaders understand the stresses of training, combat, and inevitable change, and care for soldiers as they accomplish their missions under pressure. In a supportive, ethical climate, leaders demand the best from their soldiers and teach and mentor them so that they constantly improve.

Soldiers learn leadership every day. Simply by watching other leaders and performing their duties, they will learn leadership. Those who deliberately apply the process—study examples of leadership, reflect on their own experiences, apply lessons learned, and seek feedback—become better leaders now and for the future.

The following principles of leadership are not used as a laundry list in the new doctrine; however, they are still applicable as mind jogs to keep leaders focused. A good leader continues to seek self-improvement, strengthens personal attributes, and knows his or her soldiers and the unit.

Technical and tactical knowledge are essential to leadership. Be proficient with your weapon and all other items of unit equipment. Develop technical and tactical skills and knowledge through practice and study.

Seek responsibility and take responsibility for your actions. Pay attention to what is going on, figure out what needs to be done, and take responsibility for doing it.

Make sound and timely decisions. Problem solving, decision making, and planning are all part of a leader's responsibilities. Identify the problem, analyze and develop courses of action, make a plan, decide on a course of action, implement your plan, and assess it. Implementing your plan will utilize your abilities to communicate, coordinate, supervise, and evaluate your plan. This seven-step problem-solving process is described in FM 22-100 (FM 6-22), *Military Leadership.*

Know your soldiers and look out for their well-being. Show you care. Make the needs of the people in your unit coincide with unit tasks and missions. Reward individual and team behavior that is supportive. Develop morale by alleviating causes of personal concern so that your soldiers can concentrate on their jobs. Ensure that your soldiers are properly cared for and have proper equipment and tools to do their work.

Keep your soldiers informed. Your ability to communicate can make the difference between success and failure. Be available. Discuss upcoming training and other missions with soldiers. Get feedback from your soldiers. Make sure that short-range and long-range training plans are available to your soldiers to help them plan for personal situations.

Develop a sense of responsibility in your subordinates. Challenge them—especially those who exhibit potential to handle more responsibilities. Delegate. Do not be afraid of losing some power or authority. By delegating, you actually increase the power of your unit because you give subordinates a chance to think and carry out their plans and thus increase their motivation and your means of accomplishing your mission.

Ensure that subordinates understand tasks and have good supervision. Eliminate psychological and physical barriers that sometimes inhibit good communication.

Train your soldiers as a team. Army success depends on team cohesiveness. Cohesion demands mutual respect, trust, confidence, and understanding among soldiers. Cohesion and discipline go hand in hand.

Employ soldiers and your unit according to capabilities. Develop capabilities through individual and unit training under your leadership and guidance. Be aware of fatigue and the draining effects of fear. Train soldiers to meet unit standards. If you have the desire, you can become increasingly efficient as a leader.

LEADING SOLDIERS IN THE TWENTY-FIRST CENTURY

Most of the qualities and skills that are required to lead soldiers today will also be required in the future. Look to Field Manual (FM) 7-27.7, *Army Noncommissioned Officer Guide,* and FM 22-100 (FM 6-22), *Military Leadership,* to determine what it takes to lead soldiers in the new century. Determine what your organization expects of you; learn who your immediate leader is and what he or she expects of you; and assess the level of competence and the strengths and weaknesses of your subordinates. Identify the key people outside of your unit whose willing support you need to accomplish the mission.

Demonstrate tactical and technical competence; that is, know your business. Teach your subordinates. Be a good listener. Treat your soldiers with dignity and respect. Stress the basics, including courage, candor, confidence, commitment, and compassion. Set the example through selfless service, and abide by Army values. Set and enforce the standards. Lead by Example.

AR 600-100, *Army Leadership,* states why leadership is extremely important today, and will be tomorrow:

> In an era when technological advantages have narrowed, and access to information of all kinds is relatively limitless, the most effective and efficient way for the Army to maintain its competitive edge is by enhancing the effectiveness of people and organizations. Good leadership can facilitate this goal. Whether preparing for war, fighting a war, or supporting a war, leadership skills, knowledge, and behavior must be consistent with the war-fighting doctrine of the U.S. Army.

Teaching Army Values

Soldiers learn and draw strength from leaders who encourage the development of values as inalienable professional attributes. Leaders, in turn, are expected to live by and exemplify those values. Internalizing these values—living by them—is what builds professional soldiers in America's Army. Values and traditions are the soul of the Army. As an institution, we must be unwavering in upholding them.

As noted earlier, the Army has seven bedrock values to which all soldiers must adhere:

Loyalty is to bear true faith and allegiance to the U.S. Constitution, the Army, your unit, and other soldiers.

Duty means to fulfill your obligations.

Respect is to treat people as they should be treated.

Selfless service means to put the welfare of the nation, the Army, and your subordinates before your own.

Honor is to live up to all Army values.

Integrity is doing what's right, legally and morally.

Personal courage is to face fear, danger, or adversity (physical or moral).

In addition, two characteristics go hand in hand with values: *teamwork* and *discipline.*

You must teach and stress to your soldiers the values of the professional. Your role is not to change their long-held personal values; we all have individual differences. But impress upon them the importance of professional values. Development of the seven basic soldierly values is vital as well. Also develop their *candor,* which is honesty and faithfulness to the truth. Teach them to be *competent;* their working knowledge and ability contribute directly to mission success. Develop in them a sense of the mental and moral strength—courage—that they will need to enable them to retain control and continue the mission when they are in harm's way. And make them understand that commitment to unit accomplishment takes priority over personal wishes, wants, pleasures, and, perhaps, needs.

Although these attributes are not new, there is a renewed interest in them. The *Soldier's Code* and the new *Soldier's Creed* best encapsulize the compact between the soldier, the leader, and the Army.

Soldier's Code

I. I am an American soldier, a protector of the greatest nation on earth—sworn to uphold the Constitution of the United States. I will always perform my duties to the utmost of my abilities and will strive to exhibit the moral and physical courage expected of a soldier. Throughout my years as a soldier and after, I will put my obligations before self. My word is my bond.

II. I will treat others with dignity and respect, and expect others to do the same. I will not tolerate soldiers being treated differently because of race, color, sex, religion, or national origin. I will notify my chain of command if I observe instances which affect the good order and discipline of the organization.

III. I will honor my country, the Army, my unit, and my fellow soldiers by living the Army values. I will obey the lawful orders of my superiors and will uphold the standards established by the leadership.

IV. No matter what situation I am in, I will never do anything for pleasure, profit, or personal safety which will disgrace my uniform, my unit, or my country.

V. I expect my leadership to discipline me when I do wrong and commend me when I exceed expectations. I rely on my leadership to establish an organizational climate where I can learn and grow as an individual. Lastly, I am proud of my country and its flag. I want to look back on my time in the Army and say that I am proud to have served my country as a soldier.

The Soldier's Creed

I am an American soldier.
I am a warrior and a member of a team. I serve the people of the United States and live the Army Values.
I will always place the mission first.
I will never accept defeat.
I will never quit.
I will never leave a fallen comrade.
I am disciplined, physically and mentally tough, trained and proficient in my warrior tasks and drills. I always maintain my arms, my equipment[,] and myself.
I am an expert and I am a professional.
I stand ready to deploy, engage, and destroy the enemies of the United States of America in close combat.
I am a guardian of freedom and the American way of life.
I am an American Soldier.

SOLDIER TEAM DEVELOPMENT

When you talk to soldiers in good units, you will usually hear the words "us" and "we," rather than "I" and "me." Unit members look out for and take care of one another. The unit has developed its own workable ways of accomplishing missions to standard, rather than relying heavily on being guided by outsiders and regulatory material. The excellent unit has a steady high-performance rhythm, and members have effective skills for coping with stress and pressure. The unit has high standards, ethical values, and its own way of expressing how well it is performing. Members will voluntarily work however hard and long is necessary based on unit operational needs.

Building strong soldier teams is critical in the Army. Readiness is the goal.

An outnumbered and overpowered team can achieve its mission goal when it has a strong desire—the spirit—to do so. Spirited soldiers believe in their cause. Your leadership should produce a winning spirit; it is critical to building a cohesive team. You should build cohesion in numerous other ways as well. Respect your soldiers and help them develop physically, socially, emotionally, and spiritually. Doing so will give them the stamina necessary for sustained performance under stress, and will teach them to mature, work together, and face danger with hope and purpose. Signs of self-discipline, initiative, effective judgment, and confidence will be positive indicators of your effort.

Do a mental assessment of your soldiers' willingness and ability to work as a cohesive unit. Listen, observe, and monitor. In each new situation, you must reassess and correct to retain and build teamwork. Practice verbal and nonverbal communication. Encourage development of your unit's "vocabulary"—short-cut words and terms—to communicate complex messages. *Ensure that those words and terms always comply with the commander's intent.*

Teach your soldiers to use the chain of command so that decisions are made at the right level. Give them their own planning and decision-making responsibilities as well so that they know the mission and operate within the commander's guidance. Combat teamwork requires training so that soldiers think on their feet and communicate effectively.

Every new soldier in your unit will go through a formation stage, the process of checking out other soldiers and his or her leaders. As trust develops, the soldier will participate more actively in unit missions. You must help by answering a new soldier's questions about your team, its work, and the soldier's personal concerns. Develop the soldier's strengths into unit strengths.

Put the new soldier to work as soon as possible. Afterward, watch for signs that he or she is trying to exert independence. The soldier will be trying to find his or her range and limits as a unit member. You will know this is happening when you begin to feel resistance to your leadership. Share with the soldier your thoughts and feelings about the unit and ask him or her to do likewise, to teach the soldier to pass information back and forth. This will help dissolve a communication barrier before it can form. You want the soldier to depend on you and others on the team, and vice versa, to build cohesion.

Deployment: when having trained soldiers counts.

Constantly guide your developing team. Retain control. Listen. Establish lines of authority and develop individual and team (squad, section, platoon, battery, company, troop) goals.

Training is paramount. Train your soldiers as a unit during peacetime. Focus your team on training to standard. Treat each job, task, or detail as a training opportunity. Use mission opportunities to motivate and challenge soldiers while you train them in their wartime missions. With the world as it is today, one day your company might be in garrison, the next week in a distant country.

Training in combat is different. Time will be critical. Soldiers' lives will be at stake. The field manual and experienced combat veterans emphasize that the NCO leader must use every available opportunity to sharpen survival skills. In combat, you must teach your soldiers to know the enemy, what the threat is, and how to respond to hostile activity. Training is conducted during real operations, which causes extreme stress, so you must help your soldiers use coping skills. (Turn to FM 22-51 [(FM 4-02.22)], *Leader's Manual for Combat Stress Control,* for more information.) Realistic training during peacetime and the ways you demonstrate your ability on the battlefield will contribute to your soldiers' self-confidence.

LEADING SOLDIERS IN COMBAT

In a combat zone, noncommissioned officers continually train their soldiers for what lies ahead, ensure they are rehearsed, inspected before operations commence, and when under fire led by example. It is training and discipline (instilled by pride and training, maintained by good leadership) that keeps soldiers alive.

A squad of military police from the 617th MP Co., Kentucky National Guard, defeated more than three times their number, killing and capturing most of the insurgents in a battle that occurred at a time and place of the enemy's choosing. The squad's soldiers believed even before this fight that their NCOs were the best in the Army, and that they have the best squad in the Army.

On this Sunday afternoon, on the southeastern outskirts of Baghdad, 40 to 50 heavily armed Iraqi insurgents attacked a convoy of 30 civilian tractor trailer trucks that were moving supplies for the coalition forces. The MP squad had been following the convoy from a distance behind the last vehicle, and when the convoy halted in the kill zone, the squad sped up, paralleled the convoy up the shoulder of the road, and moved to the sound of gunfire.

Leadership under fire. The squad was committed to the fight when the three noncommissioned officers stepped out of their vehicles. Several of the squad fell wounded during the first moments of contact. The squad leader dismounted and grabbed the team leader out of the first vehicle after she had radioed the contact report to higher. The squad leader staff sergeant and team leader sergeant rushed the nearest ditch about 20 meters away and began clearing it of enemy. The fire of the two NCOs plus that from the high mobility multipurpose wheeled vehicles (HUMMVs) turned the ambush into a killing ground for the ambushers.

Combat loading. The sergeant runs low on ammo and runs back to a vehicle to reload. She moves to her squad leader's vehicle and blindly reaches her arm into it to find ammo, because each vehicle is packed the same. The day before the squad had taken the recently issued new type bandoliers and experimented with mounting them in their vehicles. Once they determined how, they preloaded a second basic load of ammo into magazines, put them into the bandoliers, and mounted them in their vehicles—the same exact way in every vehicle—with load plans enforced and checked by leaders!

Training for the unexpected. With an AT-4 antitank rocket, the medic destroyed insurgents firing out of a building at the wounded. The past week his squad leader forced him to train on it, though he did not think as a medic he would ever use one.

Discipline and training. That's what makes the difference, and it is up to NCOs to ensure standards are maintained. On a battlefield, you must ensure that your soldiers remain informed. The soldier wants to know all he can about his situation. Keep the news flowing as regularly as the situation permits. Do not speculate or allow rumors to grow. The unit's supporting Army Public Affairs team or detachment, American Forces Radio and Television Service, and the chain of command will all be able to provide pieces of accurate information. As you are informed, and especially when the bits and pieces form a complete picture of some sort, pass along the news as quickly and as objectively as possible. Avoid distractions, however; keep your soldiers focused on their mission.

Suppress fearful behavior because it can spread.

Teamwork provides results on and off the battlefield. You will be the key to sustaining cohesion among your soldiers. Focus on teamwork, training, and weapons and gear maintenance. Do everything within your power to ensure timely supply of needed items, and learn the supply system.

PROFESSIONAL ETHICS

Of the fourteen general principles of ethical government conduct, the one listed first is so placed for a reason—"Public service is a public trust, requiring [soldiers] to place loyalty to the Constitution, the laws, and ethical principles above private gain"—because it goes to the heart of selfless and ethical service. Developing, achieving, maintaining, and teaching high ethical standards is NCO business.

Noncommissioned leaders and supervisors frequently face ethical problems that, if not handled properly, can damage—or destroy—unit cohesion, discipline, and effectiveness. You must do what is right, and enforce correct conduct and behavior standards. And you must always set the example.

No Middle Ground

Nothing says more and *nothing* says less about an NCO than the way he or she acts or behaves on and off duty. The honorable corporal, for example, is not the one whose conduct is exemplary on duty but despicable off duty, when he or she mentally or physically abuses family members. An honest sergeant is not the one who accomplishes a key task, then later falsely reports sick-in-quarters because of a hangover. A loyal staff sergeant is not the one whose NCO tells his soldiers how good they are and then turns around and bad-mouths them for incompetence in front of others.

The Professional Army Ethic

Fortunately, most NCOs do not fit into the portraits illustrated above; instead, they try to live the Professional Army Ethic.

Most NCOs are aware of the Department of Defense (DOD) Standards of Conduct. All NCOs have attended periodic common military training based on the Department of Defense Joint Ethics Regulation. Basically, the law and regulations address proper and improper ways to accept gifts, handle financial matters, seek part-time employment, use position or rank, raise funds, teach, speak in public, and write for compensation. The law also impels soldiers to always act with integrity, to use Army property and soldiers for government business only, to never use official position for personal gain, and to never coerce a soldier to help pay for a gift for a superior. These are easy requirements to meet, really, when you look at larger ethical issues.

When faced with an ethical matter, tackle it with the following reasoning process: Identify the problem; know the relevant rules; develop and evaluate courses of action; and choose the course that best represents Army values. FM 22-100 (FM 6-22), *Military Leadership,* explains the process. The manual also states, "The ethical development of self and subordinates is a key component of leader development. . . . Leaders must make a personal commitment to the Professional Army Ethic and strive to develop this commitment throughout the force."

NCOs may also turn to FM 7-27.7, *The Army Noncommissioned Officer Guide,* which makes this point: "If the NCO is the 'backbone' of the Army, then the Professional Army Ethic is the 'heart' of the NCO Corps, and from that heart springs our pride."

NCOs, if they must, may lead with the full legal force of general military or delegated command authority under the provisions of AR 600-20, *Army Command Policy.* NCOs rarely need to lean on regulations, however. Instead, they instinctively do what is right, for the right reasons, when necessary, no matter how hard doing so may be. NCOs earn their stripes every day. An NCO who is reported and placed under the scrutiny of command or the public embarrasses and discredits the Army, whether the problem involves personal conduct or a more serious breach of ethics, as described in the following section. And more important, a soldier who has or causes ethical problems distracts his or her leaders from mission accomplishment.

The Cost of Unethical Conduct

The abuses at Abu Ghraib and other instances of unethical and unsoldierly conduct committed by a few soldiers have done much to embarrass and severely damage the credibility and morale of the majority of U.S. soldiers who serve with honor and distinction. These acts of unethical, criminal conduct have accelerated the loss of public support for the war effort.

NCOs must uphold and enforce ethical behavior and conduct standards to retain the trust and confidence of superior officers, including commissioned troop leaders who may face extremely hard ethical decisions on a future battlefield. The effort on your part, at your level, will help enable the Army to maintain the unwavering support of the nation.

PERSONAL CONDUCT

NCOs should be above reproach at all times. This does not mean that a slip automatically spells disaster. Keep this in mind when your subordinates err.

Never lend money to other soldiers for interest. Be careful about lending money to anyone based only on a verbal agreement, no matter how much is involved. Of course, if a friend or coworker asks for a small sum occasionally, to tide him over on a heavy date or to buy lunch, give it to him if you can afford to. But never telegraph through the outfit that you are an "easy touch." If you do, every freeloader in the unit will hit you up for small loans, which they will seldom repay. Young soldiers are particularly vulnerable to this sort of thing. Guard against it yourself and advise your subordinates to do the same. Be alert for soldiers who are habitual borrowers. They're heading for trouble, and if they are your subordinates, soon their trouble will be yours.

If a friend is really in trouble and you can help with a loan, then do so—what are friends for? But have him back it up by signing a promissory note. This note is merely insurance against the unexpected, not an indication of distrust; his note will enable you to claim any unpaid debt against his estate, should he die. If your friend cannot pay you back all at once, be sure to give him receipts for each payment he does make. This will help you both later on if there is any disagreement.

Gambling

NCOs should never gamble with subordinates, no matter what the circumstances. Gambling can be as addictive and as ruinous to some people as alcohol and drugs are to others. When you acquire financial responsibility for other people—your family—they must always come first. Don't allow what can be an innocent and pleasant pastime to develop into a compulsion that will wreck your family. Never allow sharks—card, pool, loan, or otherwise—to operate in your unit.

Adultery

Adultery is punishable under the Uniform Code of Military Justice (UCMJ). The best advice you can receive in regard to this subject, and the best you can give someone else about it, is this: Don't do it. If you do, and are found out, take responsibility for your actions.

At some point in your career, though, the temptation to err will be strong, especially where alcohol and sex are readily available, the idle hours are long, and diversions are few. Remember, what you do in the heat of passion may come back to haunt you in years to come. Precisely how a person deals with this problem depends on the individual. Keep up an active correspondence with your spouse. Go easy on the intoxicants. Concentrate on your military duty, and cultivate your hobbies.

Should you succumb, you will have to live with your indiscretion. Repeated unfaithfulness becomes general knowledge in a small, tightly knit military community. Your soldiers will lose respect for you; and if continued, someone in the chain of command will tell you to straighten up, or else. Adultery hurts everyone—you, your spouse, family, friends. A single person who enters into an adulterous relationship with a married man or woman is not much better off than the married person who is unfaithful. The single person's career (and life) can be as easily ruined by adultery as that of a married person.

Lying

Society would crumble if it were not for the accepted social lie. We all know that nobody wants to listen to someone else's personal problems. And nobody in his right mind tells everyone just exactly what he thinks of them. Military life is no different from civilian life in this regard.

Never lie to cover up mistakes, however, whether yours or those of your subordinates. Lying to anyone in the line of duty is wrong. Once those in your unit lose faith in you because of a lie discovered, no matter how small that lie may be, you may never be able to recover that confidence. And once you get away with a lie, it sometimes becomes necessary to tell more and more of them to cover up the initial one, until you create a tissue of lies that sooner or later will tear and expose the truth.

Indebtedness

Ensure that you pay off your debts. Keep tight control of your budget. Do not allow yourself to fall behind on credit payments. This will require restraint and self-denial at times. A letter of indebtedness from a creditor will harm your career as well as damage your reputation in the business world and make it harder for you to get credit when you really need it.

Our whole economy operates on indebtedness, and most of us are in debt for something: homes, cars, credit card services, and so on. You will, from time to time, counsel your soldiers on their indebtedness. Help them to learn to budget and overcome a vicious cycle.

Self-Perception

NCOs have always been important. In units in which the NCOs are enthusiastic, mission oriented, and supportive of one another, things click. In units where NCOs put themselves before their men and their organization, things go clunk. May you always serve in units that click, but should you have the misfortune to be assigned to one that clunks, turn things around. Don't wait for the officers to catch on; clue them in. As for your fellow NCOs, by your example demonstrate my old regiment's motto, one that I believe fits the NCO Corps: "Deeds, not words." Rise to the occasion and do what has to be done. Do not try to find ways to get out of doing things. Do not look back. Get the job done. Never let there be any mistake that you represent the NCO Corps at its finest.

5

Contemporary Leadership Issues

The War on Terrorism is a different kind of war, a world war, where deployments take soldiers from the United States to the mountains of Afghanistan, the desert of Iraq, the streets of Baghdad, the jungles of the Philippines; to Bosnia, Kosovo, and any other location where terrorism is located and must be rooted out. Battles may range from the 10,000-foot peak, where infantry is king and no terrain is impassible to foot soldiers in search of a hard-to-pin-down terrorist foe; to the sands of the desert, where Abrams tanks and Bradley fighting vehicles reign supreme.

THE LAW OF WAR

The Army has been tarred by a few soldiers operating outside the bounds of military discipline and law. Although their misdeeds have been exposed by fellow soldiers and investigated by the chain of command, their actions have brought great discredit to not only themselves, but the Army and our nation.

The United States and its armed forces abide by the laws of war. Soldiers are expected to comply with both the spirit and intent of these laws in all of their actions. Officers and noncommissioned officers of the Army are the main safeguard to ensure that its soldiers abide by these laws in both peace and war. It is only this respect for, and obedience to, the rule of law that differentiates our Army from savages. Nevertheless, the very nature of war can lead some of the fighting forces to fall prey to violence and disorder and to participate in unlawful actions. Such actions, at whatever level and for whatever reason, cannot be permitted. Only when all members understand that every member of the Army must be absolutely opposed to any unlawful conduct—and that any such conduct will be met with immediate action—will the United States be living up to its national goals. If leaders accept an unlawful order or permit unlawful actions by any member of their organization, it is no different than if they themselves committed the act. If something feels wrong, question it. If you walk by, you may be acquiescing to establishing a standard for patterns of abuse: "But sir, Sergeant Jones saw us doing this and said nothing, so we assumed it was OK."

"Is this correct, Sergeant Jones?"

The September 11, 2001, al Qaeda attacks against the United States were more than crimes—they were acts of war. However, al Qaeda, without regular armed forces, territory, or citizens to defend, also presents unprecedented military challenges. The Geneva Conventions legally do not apply to acts of terrorism because al Qaeda is not a nation-state and has not signed the treaties. Al Qaeda members also do not qualify as legal combatants because they hide among peaceful populations and launch surprise attacks on civilians—violating the fundamental principle that war is waged only against combatants. As such, the U.S. administration has concluded that al Qaeda and the Taliban are not legally entitled to the protections of the Law of War, such as treatment afforded those who have POW status.

That said, U.S. forces comply with the law of war during the conduct of military operations and related activities in armed conflict. During peacekeeping and peace enforcement and all other Military Operation Other Than War (MOOTW), U.S. forces apply Law of War principles. Because of the broad applicability of these legal principles, commanders are responsible both for their own conduct as well as the actions of troops under their command. The rules of engagement generally embody the command guidance governing the use of force to accomplish a given mission. Commanders will develop rules of engagement that are trained to soldiers and followed during operations. Noncommissioned officers enforce the rules of engagement.

Attacking noncombatants and protected property is illegal. You must be able to distinguish "noncombatants" from "combatants" and distinguish "protected property" from "military objectives." Combatants are defined as follows: Anyone engaging in hostilities in an armed conflict on behalf of a party to the conflict. Combatants are lawful targets unless "out of combat." Military objectives are lawful targets. Commanders must ensure that any use of force, even that directed against what would be a lawful military objective under the Law of War, complies with the mission statement. Military objectives are defined as combatants, defended places, and those objects that by their nature, location, purpose, or use make an effective contribution to military action (FM 27-10, *The Law of Land Warfare,* para. 40; Geneva Protocol (GP) I, art. 52(2)).

RULES OF ENGAGEMENT

The DOD *Dictionary of Military Terms* defines Rules of Engagement (ROE) as "Directives issued by competent military authority that delineate the circumstances and limitations under which United States forces will initiate and/or continue combat engagement with other forces encountered."

Army training about ROE envisions two general circumstances for using weapons: in self-defense and to accomplish the mission. Whether ROE are "permissive" (allowing more use of force) or "restrictive" (limited use of force) depends on the anticipated conditions extant in the mission—e.g., the presence or absence of quantities of small arms and light weapons; existing, organized opposition groups, armed and unarmed; competency of local security forces, etc.

Some ROE are included in unit "standing operational procedures" (SOP) and form the basic structure from which changes are made to develop operational-specific ROE issued to forces just prior to the start of an operation.

REMEMBER THAT IN ALL CASES AND REGARDLESS OF ROE, A SOLDIER ALWAYS HAS THE INHERENT RIGHT OF SELF-DEFENSE.

SECURITY

The U.S. Army in its past has been uncommonly careless about security when in the combat theaters. Analysts believe that in past wars this resulted in almost a quarter of our casualties. And it is not very much different today. Use alternate routes if possible; never react exactly the same for similar situations, even though you achieve success the first few times. The enemy will soon discern your techniques and design work-arounds. Heed the advice of the U.S. ground commander in Iraq:

GEN. GEORGE W. CASEY'S "FLAT-ASSED COMMONSENSE RULES"

- Make security and safety your first priorities.
- Help the Iraqis win—don't win it for them.
- Treat the Iraqi people with dignity and respect. Learn and respect Iraqi customs and cultures.
- Maintain strict standards and iron discipline everyday. Risk assess every mission—no complacency!!
- Information saves lives—share it and protect it.
- Maintain your situational awareness at all times—this can be an unforgiving environment.
- Take care of your equipment and it will take care of you.
- Innovate and adapt—situations here don't lend themselves to cookie-cutter solutions.
- Focus on the enemy and be opportunistic.
- Be patient. Don't rush to failure.
- Take care of yourself and take care of each other.

FRATERNIZATION

The Army has always had policies concerning senior-subordinate relationships. This is nothing new, and it is not just a problem relating to gender.

Army policy states that relationships between soldiers of different rank that involve, or give the appearance of partiality, preferential treatment, or the improper use of rank or position for personal gain, and that are prejudicial to good order, discipline, and high unit morale, will be avoided. Leaders must counsel those involved or take other action, as appropriate, if relationships between soldiers of different rank:

- Cause actual or perceived partiality or unfairness.
- Involve the improper use of rank or position for personal gain.
- Create an actual or clearly predictable adverse impact on discipline, authority, or morale.

Unprofessional relationships include relationships between persons of different ranks in the same chain of command, the same unit, or a closely related unit and include (a) dating and close male-female friendships and (b) frequently spending off-duty time together, regardless of gender. Because of the possible repercussions of dating, courtship, and marriage between persons of different ranks, whether or not in the same unit, guidance should be sought from the first sergeant, the commanding officer, or the staff judge advocate.

This policy is based on the principle of good judgment and common sense. An association between an officer and an enlisted soldier, or relationships between enlisted soldiers, might not be considered fraternization yet may still be inappropriate. Just because a certain relationship does not break the law does not mean it is acceptable or appropriate, and leaders have the responsibility to articulate what is improper. When a relationship between soldiers violates this policy, the Army is firmly committed to corrective action.

The above does not negate a leader's responsibility in the professional development of their soldiers. Leaders cannot stop mentoring, coaching, and teaching soldiers because they fear being accused of fraternization or worse. They must continue to encourage individual study and professional development, and mentor the continued growth of their subordinates' military careers. If they are professional and treat each soldier as a soldier instead of as a male, a female, or a member of a minority, then many of the problems will disappear.

EQUAL OPPORTUNITY

The policy of the Army is to provide equal opportunity and treatment for soldiers without regard to race, color, religion, gender, or national origin, and to provide an environment free of sexual harassment both on and off post. To execute this, commanders often turn to their senior noncommissioned officers to provide advice and assistance on equal opportunity (EO) matters. To achieve the Army EO goal of ensuring fair treatment of all soldiers, NCO leaders must develop, establish, and maintain a climate of discipline that corrects those who exhibit inappropriate social behavior that could affect the unit's work environment.

When commanders and their subordinate leaders remain too focused on the next mission and not enough on the behavior of their soldiers, and NCOs fail to keep the problem away from an already overworked leadership, then the threats to the Army posed by sexual harassment, extremism, racial separatism, and gender discrimination can become major issues that detract from readiness and our ability to accomplish the mission.

There is a direct correlation between behavior in an organization and its human relations environment. A poor climate can foster stereotyping and hate, and a unit with poor human relations can become a breeding ground for inappropriate behavior and unhealthy attitudes. Likewise, a strong human relations climate fosters open communications, promotes tolerance of diversity, encourages dialogue, and is reflective of Army values.

For more than twenty years, Headquarters, Department of the Army (HQDA), has placed responsibility for equal opportunity in the hands of unit commanders and has articulated the connection between equal opportunity and unit readiness by enforcing the policy through the traditional chain of command. AR 600-20, *Army Command Policy,* is the starting point to learn about the Army Equal Opportunity Program. Chapter 6 establishes the program and is explicit in affixing responsibility for equal opportunity to the chain of command; it states:

> The chain of command, whether military or civilian, has the primary responsibility for developing and sustaining a healthy climate. This responsibility entails, but is not limited to, promoting positive programs that enhance unit cohesion, esprit, and morale; communicating matters with EO significance to unit personnel and higher headquarters; correcting discriminatory practices by conducting rapid, objective, and impartial inquiries to resolve complaints of discrimination; encouraging the surfacing of problems and preventing reprisal for those who complain; and taking appropriate action against those who violate Army policy.

Under current regulations, commanders have the legal authority to deal with cases of unlawful discrimination or sexual harassment. AR 600-20, paragraph 4-4, "Soldier Conduct," provides that ensuring proper conduct of soldiers is a function of command. Commanders rely on all leaders in the Army to "Take action against military personnel in any case where the soldier's conduct violates good order and discipline." Although chapter 6 is not punitive, the commander's inherent authority to impose administrative sanctions and the specific offenses under the Uniform Code of Military Justice (UCMJ) provide commanders with the authority sufficient to enforce Army policy on discrimination and harassment. Figures 4-7 and 6-1 in Department of Army Pamphlet (DA Pam)

350-20, *Unit Equal Opportunity Training Guide,* list sexual harassment behavior and equal opportunity violations subject to UCMJ violations.

Sexual Harassment and Gender Discrimination

The Department of Defense defines sexual harassment as a form of sex discrimination that involves unwelcome sexual advances, requests for sexual favors, and other verbal or physical conduct of a sexual nature when:

- Submission to such conduct is made either explicitly or implicitly a term or condition of a person's job, pay, or career, or
- Submission to or rejection of such conduct by a person is used as a basis for career or employment decisions affecting that person, or
- Such conduct has the purpose or effect of unreasonably interfering with an individual's work performance or creates an intimidating, hostile, or offensive working environment.

This definition emphasizes that workplace conduct, to be actionable as "abusive work environment" harassment, need not result in concrete psychological harm to the victim, but rather need only be so severe or pervasive that a reasonable person would perceive, and the victim does perceive, the work environment as hostile or offensive. Any person in a supervisory or command position who uses or condones any form of sexual behavior to control, influence, or affect the career, pay, or job of a military member or civilian employee is engaging in sexual harassment. Similarly, any military member or civilian employee who makes deliberate or repeated unwelcome verbal comments, gestures, or physical contact of a sexual nature in the workplace is also engaging in sexual harassment.

Sexual harassment can include verbal abuse, profanity, off-color jokes, sexual comments, threats, barking, growling, oinking, or whistling at passersby to indicate a perception of their physical appearance. It also includes nonverbal abuse such as leering, ogling (giving a person the "once-over"), blowing kisses, licking lips, winking, leaving sexually suggestive notes, and displaying sexist cartoons and pictures. Unwanted physical contact such as touching, patting, hugging, pinching, grabbing, cornering, kissing, blocking a passageway, and back and neck rubs may also constitute sexual harassment.

Gender discrimination is defined as discrimination based solely on an individual's gender in a subgroup "female" or "male." It is distinguished from sexual harassment because it does not have a sexual component. Discrimination based on gender is often linked to a set of assumptions based on sex role stereotypes concerning the abilities, competence, status, and roles of the particular subgroup resulting in a disparate treatment or impact on those groups. Operations in Afghanistan, Iraq, and other parts of the world have changed many of the peacetime perceptions of women in combat, and taboos about the "other" sex have gone by the wayside. One of your duties as a noncommissioned officer is to ensure that your soldiers are treated fairly. If it affects your soldiers, it affects you. It all hurts unit cohesion.

EXTREMISM

Although the Constitution guarantees freedom of speech and association, soldiers do not have the right to use these freedoms to infringe upon the rights of others.

Policy

Chapter 4-12 of AR 600-20, *Army Command Policy,* makes it clear that participation in extremist organizations or activities is inconsistent with the responsibilities of military service. It defines extremist organizations and activities as those "that advocate racial, gender, or ethnic hatred or intolerance; advocate, create, or engage in illegal discrimination based on race, color, sex, religion, or national origin; advocate the use of or use force or violence or unlawful means to deprive individuals of their rights under the United States Constitution or the Laws of the United States, or any state, by unlawful means."

By regulation, soldiers are prohibited from the following actions in support of extremist organizations or activities:

- Participating in a public demonstration or rally.
- Attending a meeting or activity with knowledge that the meeting or activity involves an extremist cause when on duty, when in uniform, when in a foreign country (whether on or off duty or in uniform), when it constitutes a breach of law and order, when violence is likely to result, or when in violation of off-limits sanctions or a commander's order.
- Fund-raising.
- Recruiting or training members (including encouraging others to join).
- Creating, organizing, or taking a visible leadership role in such an organization or activity.
- Distributing literature on or off a military installation of which the primary purpose and content concern advocacy or support of extremist causes, organizations, or activities, and it appears that the literature presents a clear danger to the loyalty, discipline, or morale of military personnel, or if the distribution would materially interfere with the accomplishment of a military mission. Penalties for violations of these prohibitions include the full range of statutory and regulatory sanctions, both criminal (UCMJ) and administrative.

Command Authority

Commanders have the authority to prohibit military personnel from engaging in or participating in any other activities that the commander determines will adversely affect good order and discipline or morale within the command.

This includes, but is not limited to, the authority to order the removal of symbols, flags, posters, or other displays from barracks; to place areas or activities off-limits (see AR 190-24); or to order soldiers not to participate in those activities that are contrary to good order and discipline or morale of the unit or pose a threat to health, safety, and security of military personnel or a military installation.

Command Responsibility

Any soldier involvement with or in an extremist organization or activity, such as membership, receipt of literature, or presence at an event, could threaten the good order and discipline of a unit. In any case of apparent soldier involvement with or in extremist organizations or activities, whether or not violative of the prohibitions above, commanders must take positive actions to educate soldiers, putting them on notice of the potential adverse effects that participation in violation of Army policy may have upon good order and discipline in the unit and upon their military service. These positive actions include educating soldiers regarding the Army Equal Opportunity Program. Commanders will advise soldiers that the goals of extremist organizations are inconsistent with Army goals, beliefs, and values concerning equal opportunity, and that any participation in extremist organizations or activities will be taken into consideration when evaluating soldiers' overall duty performance, including appropriate remarks on evaluation reports, and making selections for positions of leadership and responsibility.

HOMOSEXUALITY

The armed forces must maintain personnel policies that exclude persons whose presence would create an unacceptable risk to the armed forces' high standards of morale, good order, discipline, and unit cohesion, which are the essence of military capability. That exclusion must apply to persons who demonstrate a propensity or intent to engage in homosexual acts. The Department of Defense has stated that the suitability of persons to serve in the Army is based on their conduct and their ability to meet required standards of duty performance and discipline.

Homosexuality is incompatible with military service.

A "homosexual act" means any bodily contact, actively undertaken or passively permitted, between members of the same sex for the purpose of satisfying sexual desires, and any bodily contact (for example, hand-holding, slow dancing, or kissing) that a reasonable person would understand to demonstrate a propensity or intent to engage in such an act.

A "statement by a person that he or she is a homosexual or bisexual or words to that effect" means language or behavior that a reasonable person would believe was intended to convey the statement that a person engages in, attempts to engage in, has a propensity to engage in, or intends to engage in homosexual acts. This may include statements such as "I am a homosexual," "I am gay," "I am a lesbian," "I have a homosexual orientation," and the like.

A "homosexual marriage or attempted marriage" means that a person has married or attempted to marry a person known to be of the same biological sex (as evidenced by the external anatomy of the person involved).

Separation Policy

Homosexual conduct is grounds for separation from the Army.

Only a soldier's commander is authorized to initiate fact-finding inquiries involving homosexual conduct. A commander may initiate a fact-finding inquiry only when he or she has received credible information that there is a basis for discharge. Commanders are responsible for ensuring that inquiries are conducted properly and that no abuse of authority occurs.

A fact-finding inquiry may be conducted by the commander personally or by a person he or she appoints. It may consist of an examination of the information reported or a more extensive investigation as necessary. The inquiry should gather all credible information that directly relates to the grounds for possible separation. Inquiries shall be limited to the actual circumstances directly relevant to the specific allegations.

If a commander has credible evidence of possible criminal conduct, he or she shall follow the procedures in the *Manual for Courts-Martial,* ARs 27-10 and 195-2. A commander will initiate an inquiry only if he or she has credible information that there is a basis for discharge. Credible information exists when the information, considering its source and the surrounding circumstances, supports a reasonable belief that a soldier engaged in homosexual conduct. It requires a determination based on known facts, not just a belief or suspicion.

A basis for discharge exists if the soldier has engaged in a homosexual act, the soldier has said that he or she is a homosexual or bisexual, the soldier has made some other statement that indicates a propensity or intent to engage in homosexual acts, or the soldier has married or attempted to marry a person of the same sex. Credible information exists, for example, when a reliable person states that he or she observed or heard a soldier engaging in homosexual acts or saying that he or she is a homosexual or bisexual or is married to a member of the same sex. Credible information also exists when a reliable person states that he or she heard, observed, or discovered a soldier making a spoken or written statement that a reasonable person would believe was intended to convey the fact that the soldier engages in, attempts to engage in, or has the propensity or intent to engage in homosexual acts.

Additionally, credible information exists when a reliable person states that he or she observed behavior that amounts to a nonverbal statement by a soldier that he or she is homosexual or bisexual—that is, behavior that a reasonable person would believe intended to convey the statement that the soldier engages in, attempts to engage in, or has the propensity or intent to engage in homosexual acts. Commanders or appointed inquiry officers shall not ask, and soldiers shall not be required to reveal, whether a soldier is heterosexual, homosexual, or bisexual. However, upon receipt of credible information of homosexual conduct, commanders or appointed inquiry officials may ask soldiers if they engaged in such conduct. The soldier should first be advised of the DOD policy on homosexual conduct and rights under the UCMJ. The prohibition against homosexual conduct is a long-standing element of military law that continues to be necessary in the unique circumstances of military service.

AIDS

Military readiness, medical, and personnel policies associated with HIV-AIDS look to protect the Army's ability both to fulfill its Constitutional role and to confidentially identify, evaluate, and provide an appropriate level of care for infected members.

Active duty soldiers are tested biennially for the AIDS virus, reserve component soldiers every five years. Soldiers who are HIV-positive will not be deployed outside the continental United States (CONUS) (Alaska, Hawaii, and Puerto Rico are considered CONUS in this definition). The fact that HIV-positive soldiers are nondeployable does not preclude their assignment to table of organization and equipment (TOE) or modified TOE (MTOE) units, except for Ranger and Special Forces units, which are totally closed. Soldiers who are HIV-infected are eligible for all military professional development schools and may also attend formal military training to qualify them for reclassification, provided the schooling does not exceed twenty weeks.

Mandatory testing and HIV prevention awareness are being emphasized Armywide. You must teach your soldiers—and implore them to teach their families—to understand how to avoid and prevent the spread of the dreadful disease. For more information, request from the Association of the U.S. Army a copy of its Institute of Land Warfare Paper No. 6, titled "AIDS and Its Impact on Medical Readiness."

ENVIRONMENT

FM 25-101 (FM 7-10), *Battle-Focused Training,* states that leaders must protect resources, including land used for training. Soldiers must understand that they are stewards of our environmental resources. At a minimum, abide by the following rules, which will do much to assist in keeping you and your organization out of trouble:

- Avoid maneuver damage and report observed damage as soon as possible.
- Do not dig, cut down, or "dismember" trees, or otherwise alter the environment unless you have approval from proper military authority (usually your commanding officer).

- Do not contaminate the soil or water with petroleum, oil, or lubricants (POL). Report POL leaks or spills immediately to your chain of command.
- Do not burn or bury garbage, refuse, or rubbish.
- Do not use tracers during training, do not set off pyrotechnics, and do not allow open flames in areas that are likely to catch fire.
- Obey posted environmental signs.
- Include environmental preservation in training plans.

MEDIA

NCOs have a role to play in teaching soldiers about the media. If your soldiers see unescorted members of the press—newspaper, magazine, radio, or television reporters and crew members—they should inform their chain of command.

Bona fide members of the press provide a service to the nation. Still, commanders often shun coverage because mission security and soldiers' lives come before the media's "right to know." The military-media relationship continues to be marked by a contest of wills regarding the right to know versus operational security.

Animosity between the military and the media does a disservice to both and to the nation. For years, annual national polls have shown that citizens rate the military at the top of lists of the most credible of all vital national institutions. The press nevertheless is entitled under the First Amendment to investigate military activities and report news to the nation.

When approval is granted, soldiers must guard against making comments about troop strength, position, direction, condition, tactics, strategy, or other factors an enemy may use to gain an advantage. Giving operational information will result in operations security (OPSEC) leaks—the kind that compromise the mission and destroy units.

Sergeants should train their soldiers so they know how to respond to questions without detracting from the mission or violating OPSEC. The "Five Knows" to train soldiers are as follows:

- Know the role and purpose of the American press, who do a job vital to democracy by keeping the public, your loved ones, and other soldiers informed.
- Know whom you are talking to by verifying that media members in your area are escorted by an Army Public Affairs officer or NCO, or are registered by the corps or division public affairs office. Verify registration through command or staff channels.
- Know who will hear you, that whatever you say could be in the hands of the enemy within minutes because of modern press technology, which is not secure.

- Know your rights. It is your choice whether to speak to reporters—unless your leaders have decided that doing so would interfere with or jeopardize the mission.
- Know your limits; that is, do not talk about anything above your level, and do not speculate or repeat rumors. Remember that your comments represent your personal opinions and knowledge, not necessarily the views of your unit or the Army.

For more information about media training, contact your servicing Army public affairs office.

6

Problem Solving and Counseling

HELPING YOUR SOLDIERS SOLVE THEIR PROBLEMS

Extended overseas deployments, marital strife, substance abuse, failure to comprehend or to comply, inability, a medical condition, weight control, failing or a low score on the Army Physical Fitness Test, no pay due, nonpayment of just debts, spouse or child abuse, poor self-management skills—the kinds of problems that soldiers can encounter go on and on. Small problems often are easily resolved without assistance. Some problems, though, are bigger than the individual, who may require our assistance with them before they spiral out of control.

Recognizing Soldiers with Problems

Some soldiers will come to you, explain their problem, and seek your guidance or assistance. Others will not. Those who do not may be hard to spot, unless you know what to look for during daily contact. Watch for signs when you speak with or observe your soldiers.

If a soldier who is normally on time to work begins to show up late, he or she might be losing sleep for any number of innocent reasons. Sleep loss can also be caused by partying late into the night, or because of substance abuse. Observe the soldier's appearance. Is it neat? Does he or she look disheveled? Do you smell alcohol on the soldier's breath? If married, is the soldier getting along well with his or her spouse? Does the soldier have teenage children who stay out late, and does the soldier wait up?

Something is wrong when a soldier who usually has a good attitude and behaves properly suddenly develops an improper attitude or exhibits irrational behavior. If deployed overseas, did he or she receive unpleasant news from home; or does the soldier feel unfairly treated, or is there some other cause of the problem? Is the soldier lashing out or venting because emotional release is needed?

The only effective way to identify and deal with the myriad problems that crop up in Army units is to stay tuned in to your soldiers. Try to:

- anticipates stressful events;
- stress the value of problem-solving and conflict-resolution skills, respect, self-accountability, walking away when emotions are at a peak, and being in control of a situation;
- encourage soldiers to be open about their concerns and problems at the first signs of stress;
- be supportive and nonjudgmental;
- listen to what and how something is being said;
- balance a leadership approach with a supportive response to a soldier's or family's explanation of their problems;
- teach soldiers that it is their personal obligation to take responsibility for their actions and to seek help before a problem becomes a crisis;
- be aware of the unit grapevine and alert to concerns and rumors.

Obtaining Information and Assistance

The table on page 67 shows some of the staff office and support agencies that can help soldiers with advice and assistance in their personal affairs. In all cases, personnel should first contact the right person in their chain of command for guidance: immediate supervisors, squad leaders, first sergeants, or unit commanders. Number one (1) in the table indicates primary or key contacts; number two (2) indicates other contacts, as applicable.

LEADERSHIP COUNSELING

Effective counseling helps subordinates develop personally and professionally. In the past, many soldiers perceived counseling as bad—because the only time their leaders spoke to them was to correct deficiencies or to check the block for the mandatory monthly counseling. Now there is a different reason to counsel. The Army values of loyalty, duty, and selfless service require that we counsel subordinates, while the values of honor, integrity, and personal courage require us to be honest and straightforward with our feedback. Lastly, the value of respect requires that we find the best method in which to convey that feedback so that our subordinates understand it. The new doctrine mandates two-way communication and encourages the development of a plan of action (if required).

This is pretty clear guidance—and for good reason. Effective leadership is the Army's key to success not only in training and combat, but also in developing soldiers. Soldiers watch leaders very carefully, and your competence, candor, and evenhandedness will help establish and maintain their faith in you. As a leader you can suggest alternatives, persuade, urge, advise, direct, punish, and reward using directive, nondirective, or combined approaches to counseling. Counseling can range from a few words of praise or guidance with a hand on a shoulder to long, structured sections.

Guide for Obtaining Information and Assistance

	YOUR CHAIN OF COMMAND	PERSONNEL NCO OR OFFICER	REENLISTMENT NCO	JUDGE ADVOCATE	INSPECTOR GENERAL	FINANCE OFFICER	CHAPLAIN	HOUSING OFFICER	TRANSPORTATION OFFICER	AMERICAN RED CROSS	ARMY COMMUNITY SERVICES	ARMY EMERGENCY RELIEF	EDUCATION OFFICER/ADVISOR
Appeals	1	2		2	2		2						
Assignment, reassignment, MOS, and proficiency pay	1	1				2							
Reenlistment	1		1										
Personnel matters: promotion, reduction, discharge, retirement Veterans' benefits	1	1	2	2									
Complaints (requests for assistance)	1	2	2	2	2	2	2	2	2	2	2	2	
Debts and civilian creditors	1	1		2		2	2				2		
Dependents' schools	1	1									2		
Family and religious affairs	1	2					1			2	2		
Travel of dependents, shipment of POV and household goods	1	2				2			1		2		
Medical service (individual and dependents)	1	1											
Pay, allowances, and incentive pay	1	2				1							
Leaves and passes	1	2											
Insurance, all types (SGLI and commercial)	1	1				2							
Legal assistance, including U.S. and foreign law, wills, and powers of attorney	1			1									
Military education	1	2	2										
Nonmilitary education	1	2											2
PX, commissary, QM sales store	1				2								
Government quarters, off-post housing	1	2						1					
Registration/operation of privately owned vehicle (POV), registration of firearms	1												
Entry into U.S., passport, visa, naturalization, immigration, birth certificate (children born in foreign country)	1	2		1							2		
Home conditions and emergency leave	1	2					2			2	2	2	
Emergency financial assistance	1	2				1				2	2	2	
Postal service	1												
Drug and alcohol rehabilitation program	1						2				1		

1. Primary source
2. Other sources as appropriate

What was once described as formal counseling has been updated and is now known as developmental counseling, which in essence means that counseling should progress toward some type of conclusion. The two major categories are event-oriented and performance-oriented (professional) growth. Event-oriented counseling focuses on a specific event or situation, such as instances of superior or substandard performance, reception and integration counseling, crisis counseling, referral counseling, promotion counseling, or separation counseling. Department of the Army (DA) Form 4856-E, JUN 99, *Developmental Counseling Form,* is now used in place of the JUN 85 edition. *Performance-oriented counseling* is required under the NCO Evaluation Report (NCOER) system and consists of a review of *past* performance over a given period as well as the joint establishment of performance objectives and standards for the next period. *Professional growth counseling* focuses on the *future,* where you assist subordinates in establishing short- and long-term goals and objectives to achieve organizational and personal goals.

The counseling approach you use will depend on the circumstances and how well you know the soldier and his or her duties. The directive approach is good for immature or insecure soldiers, while the combined and nondirective methods encourage open communication. The directive and combined approaches give the counselor an opportunity to use his or her experience, while the nondirective approach develops the soldier's personal responsibility. All three methods require you to listen, observe, and respond appropriately. Appendix C of FM 22-100 (FM 6-22) goes into more detail about developmental counseling, as well as the different counseling approaches, effective communication, how to be an active listener and keep the dialogue moving, what to interpret from silence at various points during counseling, and how to respond under friendly and hostile circumstances.

The Directive Approach

The directive approach is the quickest method but does not encourage maturity and is often suited to "I talk, you listen" situations in which the counselor must correct a soldier who is the problem. The directive approach is commonly used when making on-the-spot corrections. You give advice, offer solutions, and tell the soldier what must be done. This approach may also be used to praise on the spot.

The directive approach is simple, quick, and provides immediate solutions, but it has shortcomings. Your dominant influence may cause resentment because the soldier may feel that you are taking the ability to solve the problem away from him or her. The approach may address only symptoms of the real problem. And decisions are made by the leader, not the soldier, so the soldier may later blame the leader if the solution did not fix the problem. Sometimes, regardless of its shortcomings, you must use the directive approach to counsel an unresponsive soldier who will not connect bad behavior or conduct with the consequences.

The Nondirective Approach

The nondirective approach encourages maturity but takes considerable time and requires the greatest counseling skill. NCOs using the nondirective approach to counseling will find that it is more relaxed and focused on the soldier's self-discovery toward finding a solution. The soldier can verbalize and work out solutions through personal insight, judgment, and realization of the facts. The counseled soldier must understand, however, that he or she must be willing to openly discuss the subject and must take responsibility for the solution.

Often, a soldier will come to you with a problem, a concern, or perhaps a good idea. This is the time, if it is convenient, to use the nondirective approach. If it is not a convenient time, you should set a better time and appropriate place. During counseling, avoid offering solutions; let the soldier work it out, if possible. Certainly, you must guide the conversation to keep it focused on the subject, but make the soldier realize that the session is on his or her time. This way, the soldier may be less inclined to become defensive or to feel guilty.

Counseling is leading.

Try to establish rapport. Display sincere interest. Give the soldier an opportunity to state the problem. Don't interrupt. Ask leading, open-ended questions to clarify the nature and scope of the problem. Let the soldier respond. Listen for responses that indicate the soldier is approaching a resolution. Approve the soldier's solution if it is honest and may work.

If you are unable to help the soldier, refer him or her to someone who can, such as the local chaplain, finance officer, legal officer, or whoever else is appropriate. If time permits, go with the soldier. Briefly tell the official about the problem, then depart. After the soldier returns to your control, follow up to ensure the problem has been or will be resolved. As far as possible, keep superiors informed about the situation, your actions, the soldier's actions, and the resolution.

The Combined Approach

The combined approach is moderately quick but may take too much time in some situations. Using the combined approach, you apply parts of the directive and nondirective approaches to adjust your counseling style as the tone of the conversation and the requirements of your role as counselor change. You can adapt to emphasize what is best for the soldier.

This approach assumes that the soldier will eventually take charge of solving the problem but needs some help along the way. Use the ethical decision-making process and related problem-solving process in FM 22-100 (FM 6-22) to help guide the soldier. If you work from directive to nondirective, listen for information that defines the problem and allow the soldier an opportunity to suggest his or her own solutions. You may add your own suggestions as well. But remember, the counseling goal is to get the soldier to "own" or resolve the problem.

Lastly, when you counsel a member of the opposite sex, ask the person whether he or she would mind if another person of his or her gender were present during counseling. You must show that you care—avoid violating the soldier's confidence—but maintain a professional distance. To avoid an allegation of harassment or other wrongdoing, you may decide that it is in your and the soldier's best interest to have a third party present. Use your judgment, but err on the side of caution.

ALCOHOL AND DRUG ABUSE

Abuse of alcohol or the use of illicit drugs is inconsistent with Army values and the standards of performance, discipline, and readiness necessary to accomplish the Army's mission. As an NCO, you will at some time in your service encounter soldiers who depend on or abuse alcohol and other drugs. A drug is defined as "any substance which by its chemical nature alters structure or function in the living organism." This definition includes alcohol, glue, and aerosols, among many other potential sources. The harm and misery done to soldiers by substance abuse are incalculable.

Soldiers who use or sell drugs do not belong in the U.S. Army. Any soldier who relies on alcohol to make it through the day or who feels he or she must turn to some drug to get by or get high should have the personal courage to quit or to seek help from the local Army Substance Abuse Program. Command referral is an almost sure ticket out of the Army.

Alcohol Abuse

It is Army policy to maintain a workplace free from alcohol. At all levels alcohol will not be glamorized or made the center of attention at any military function. It should not become the purpose for, or the focus of, any military social activity. Impairment due to alcohol use while on duty is no longer tolerated, and AR 600-85 now stipulates that soldiers on duty will not have a blood alcohol level equal to or greater than 0.05 grams of alcohol per 100 milliliters of blood. So watch the benders from the night before!

Drug Abuse

AR 600-85 is clear that drug abuse in today's Army is unacceptable: Abusers "have violated the special trust and confidence that the Army has placed in them." Several years ago, the Army introduced a stricter policy about substance abuse that basically says "zero tolerance," and in 2001 the separations policies in effect for drug-using officers and NCOs were expanded to include all soldiers.

Treatment issues in the Army Substance Abuse Program do not affect command administrative or disciplinary decisions made in the best interest of the Army, meaning that command referral of a soldier into a treatment plan in no way prevents disciplinary action or separation processing.

Urinalysis testing is commonplace and random. Soldiers prescreening positive for substance abuse, will have their samples verified by a supporting forensic laboratory. Discharge for misconduct under AR 635-200, chapter 14 (for enlisted), will be initiated and processed to the separation authority for all soldiers involved in illegal trafficking, distribution, possession, use, or sale of illegal drugs, with the exception of self-referrals, and soldiers may face the consequence of a court-martial and the punishment it may direct, including confinement, loss of all pay and allowances, and a less than honorable (e.g., bad conduct or dishonorable) discharge. Note that the separation authority is not required to approve the discharge.

Prevention and Control (AR 600-85, *Army Substance Abuse Program*)

The Army Substance Abuse Program (ASAP) is a command program that emphasizes readiness and personal responsibility—one in which alcohol, other drug abuse, and all related activities are addressed as a single program. The programs are generally short-term and conducted in a manner that supports the military organization. Even though a soldier is enrolled in the program, unit commanders retain their authority to make personnel decisions such as initiation of separation from service, bar to reenlistment, and extension on active duty to permit reenlistment; they may also require soldiers to attend field training or deployments, even when such actions may interfere with the treatment plan. The ultimate decision regarding separation or retention of abusers rests with the NCO's chain of command.

You can help, too, by educating your soldiers. Motivate any abuser to recognize the advantages of self-referral. Otherwise, it is your responsibility to ensure that identified abusers receive command referral to the program. Abusers who do not cooperate and who are not rehabilitated will be separated.

ASAP and Efficiency Reports

A soldier's voluntary participation in the ASAP is not normally mentioned in an NCO Evaluation Report, but raters may make note of incidents of alcohol or drug abuse not derived from ASAP records. Once a soldier has been identified in a report as having a substance abuse problem, his or her voluntary entry into the ASAP or successful rehabilitation may be mentioned in subsequent reports.

FAMILY ABUSE

Frequent moves and deployments guarantee that military families will spend a lot of time in transition. This perpetual change can lead to individual and family strain, financial pressure, and the removal of valuable support networks. Transitions also lead to shifts of control as spouses endure frequent or long separations and learn to survive independently. Soldiers also face greater work demands and longer workdays, which inevitably add pressure to family relationships.

A soldier's spouse and children should be the most important people in his or her life. Nothing about service, no family issue at home or in quarters, and no external pressure or stress can justify abusive treatment of loved ones. This, not only applies to ourselves and our home life, but that of our soldiers. Every leader is responsible for acting upon known or suspected cases of family violence. As leaders, we must learn to detect such cases. We must create an environment of support and caring that encourages victims to come to us for assistance. As leaders, we must be familiar with the Family Advocacy Program and other resources locally available. If our families are in trouble, so too is soldier and unit readiness. We must be advocates of family well-being by linking soldiers with services that can help their families work together through stress and change. It is crucial that we connect soldiers with these services at the first signs of stress—before a problem evolves into a violent crisis.

When soldiers and families get involved in violent incidents, their behaviors often suggest that they are trapped in a "cycle of violence": *Tension building* (i.e., demands increase, stress builds up, "walking on eggshells," put-downs) leads to *explosion* (i.e., hitting, threatening, pushing, humiliating, controlling) followed by *honeymoon* (i.e., denial of the problem). The honeymoon period gives the spouse hope for change—"It's over now"; "It won't happen again"; "It only happened because . . ."; "Everything is OK now"—when the abuser makes promises, cries, declares love, and gives presents. But with the onset of stress, the cycle begins again.

It is wrong to verbally abuse (curse, defame, intimidate, belittle, embarrass, malign) or inflict physical pain (slap, hit, punch, kick, or otherwise harm) or neglect (omit necessary care for) the people who rely on you for their support, welfare, and safety—and who probably love you very much. Deal with the problems leading to the abuse. Do not vent frustration on family members. Cool off. Regroup your emotions. Refocus your attitude. Ask for forgiveness, and show loved ones that they come first. If you cannot, or if you have tried to avoid an abusive nature but failed, then call the local Army family advocacy office to get help. If you supervise an abusive soldier or know someone else who is an abuser, follow the guidance in this section.

Prevention and intervention in family violence is a community responsibility: No single individual, agency, or organization can implement an effective and comprehensive program. Teamwork is the key. NCOs are major team members for the success of this mission because they are frequently on the "front line" when it comes to assisting soldiers and families.

If a dependent of a soldier reports abuse to you, it is your duty to immediately report the matter to your chain of command. Your superiors, acting within command channels, may take it upon themselves to investigate the allegation. If you know that the abuse victims need protection, you should also inform the military police or local civilian authorities. Take care of the soldier and the family.

Child and spouse abuse are extremely sensitive matters. Senior leaders throughout the Army take a grim view of abusive soldiers. It is important to stress to an abusive soldier that most reported incidents of abuse or neglect lead to treatment and assistance, not to prosecution. Family advocacy officials will work to preserve and protect the family unit. Program officials can verify whether a soldier is an abuser, and then treat and rehabilitate both the abuser and the victims. A soldier's participation in the program is not intended to harm a military career; it is designed to be supportive and offer needed assistance. If abuse continues, however, officials may make recommendations regarding criminal or administrative actions. In cases where violence continues and when persons refuse to cooperate, command involvement must be initiated.

The Lautenberg Amendment addresses domestic violence and firearms. As such, this amendment may or may not apply. For further information, check the *Army Family Advocacy Program Guide for Noncommissioned Officers* at *www.child.cornell.edu/army/ncoguide/ncoguide.html* and AR 608-18, *The Army Family Advocacy Program* (2004).

ABSENCE WITHOUT LEAVE (AWOL) AND DESERTION

AWOL is not the serious problem that it once was; however, it is still a problem, especially with younger soldiers. Factors influencing a soldier to go AWOL are numerous: job dissatisfaction, personality clashes, deployment stress, and family and financial problems, to name just a few. First-line NCOs are usually first to notice changes in attitudes and performance and can do much to alleviate a soldier's urge to go AWOL by using the same preventive measures that work well in other situations: Stay attuned to your soldiers' needs and problems, conduct regular professional and personal counseling. "An ounce of prevention is worth a pound of cure."

After a soldier goes AWOL, unit leaders must store the soldier's personal belongings and turn in organizational issue items. Leaders change the soldier's status on unit manning documents and the duty roster, report the matter to higher authority, conduct an immediate inquiry to determine the soldier's location, notify the provost marshal (within forty-eight hours), and mail a notification letter to next of kin (on the tenth day). All of these steps are described in DA Pam 600-8, *Management and Administrative Procedures* with the official next-of-kin letter in AR 630-10.

On the thirty-first day of a soldier's absence the unit commander drops the member from the unit rolls (dropped from rolls [DFR]). If considered a "special category" absentee, the soldier may be dropped sooner. A special category soldier is one with access to top secret information during the last twelve months or a current assignment to a special mission unit, according to AR 630-10, which also covers defection to another country. When placed into a DFR status, the former member is declared a deserter or defector.

When the soldier is dropped, the unit commander prepares a charge sheet, *Department of Defense* (DD) Form 458, for desertion (or defection) and any other military infractions under the Uniform Code of Military Justice (UCMJ). Next, the commander prepares DD Form 553, *Warrant for Apprehension*. These two documents, along with DA Form 4187, *Personnel Action Request* (entering the soldier into DFR status), constitute a deserter packet. The packet is necessary for a warrant to be entered into the FBI National Crime Information Center for apprehension.

If the soldier returns to military control prior to submission of the DFR packet, the soldier will be carried only as AWOL and remain assigned to the unit. DFR packets submitted after a soldier has returned to the unit could put the commander and the Army at risk of erroneous arrest and lawsuits. So follow proper reporting procedures to the letter.

If your commander is unsure about what to do in a particular case, the Army Deserter Information Point (ADIP) operates a twenty-four-hour information line that can be reached at Defense Switched Network (DSN) 536-3711 or commercial (502) 626-3711. The ADIP is located at Fort Knox, Kentucky.

PART II

Training Soldiers and Self

7

Training in Operational Assignments

> In no other profession are the penalties for employing untrained personnel so appalling or so irrevocable as in the military.
>
> —Gen Douglas MacArthur (1933)

Since the late 1880s noncommissioned officers have been referred to as the "backbone of the Army" not just because of their ability to train soldiers, but because they maintained good order and discipline within the unit. It has only been within the past hundred years that sergeants and corporals assumed the individual training role from officers, and it has only been in the last ten years that senior noncommissioned officers have been given the responsibility by regulation to plan and conduct training of soldiers, sections, squads, teams, and crews. Today we have the world's best NCO Corps, and the Army leadership now entrusts us with what was once considered "officers' business." It is up to the Noncommissioned Officer Corps to uphold that trust and execute the responsibility. Our soldiers' lives, the success of Army missions, and our nation depend on it.

Training is a primary leadership mission of *all* noncommissioned officers. Every enlisted soldier has an NCO. It is that NCO's responsibility to ensure not only that the soldiers get that training, but that the training is presented in a professional manner, by expert, qualified trainers, and that the soldiers' proficiency at duty performance is increased and sustained as a demonstrated result of that training. Soldiers in transportation units, supply operations, signal units, and higher staff sections need training in combat, technical, and professional duty skills just as much as soldiers in frontline combat units.

What follows is a detailed look at today's noncommissioned officers and their role in training soldiers. Along with describing Army training doctrine, this section provides thoughts on senior NCOs and their training responsibilities, as well as techniques on how to determine collective, leader, and individual tasks for the small-unit leader; what an After Action Review should "feel like"; and some thoughts on running marksmanship ranges.

BATTLE-FOCUSED TRAINING

Training for war is the Army's number one priority during peacetime. Training management is the process used by Army leaders to identify training requirements and then plan, resource, execute, and evaluate training. Battle focusing is the process of deriving peacetime training requirements from wartime missions. Battle-focused training allows commanders to purposefully narrow the focus of the unit's training efforts to that number of vital tasks that are essential to wartime mission accomplishment.

The training management cycle begins with an understanding of the wartime mission and the establishment of a mission essential task list (METL). Once the METL is developed, it becomes the training focus for the unit. The unit is assessed in terms of unit training proficiency. These two basic elements, the METL and the training assessment, define the framework of the training plan. Knowing where you are (training assessment) and knowing where you are headed (METL) are half the battle to conducting effective training.

To be effective trainers, NCOs must know their unit's mission and the individual, leader, and collective tasks that support the wartime mission, as well as understand the roles that other units—combat, combat support, and combat service support—play in the overall scheme.

NCO Responsibilities

These regulations are important to NCOs in their roles as trainers.

AR 600-20, *Army Command Policy,* prescribes policy on basic responsibilities of command, military discipline and conduct, and enlisted aspects of command. Paragraph 3-2 of the *Noncommissioned Officer Support Channel* says: "NCO support channel will assist the chain of command in accomplishing the following:

- Training of enlisted soldiers in their MOS as well as in the basic skills and attributes of a soldier.
- Teaching soldiers the mission of the unit and developing individual training programs to support the mission.
- Administering and monitoring the NCO professional development program, and other unit training programs."

FM 25-100 (FM 7-0), *Training the Force,* is the Army's standardized training document and provides the necessary guidelines on how to plan, execute, and assess training at all levels.

In paragraph 1-9, it states: "The CSM and NCO leaders must select the specific individual tasks, which support each collective task, to be trained during the same period. NCOs have the primary role in training and developing individual soldier skills. . . . Officers at every level remain responsible for training to established standards during both individual and collective training."

In paragraphs 4-3 and 4-4 the FM mandates that all NCOs are responsible "for conducting individual training to standard and must be able to explain how individual task training relates to collective mission essential tasks."

FM 25-101 (FM 7-10), *Battle-Focused Training,* assists leaders in planning, executing, and assessing battle-focused training programs. Paragraphs 3-5 and 3-6 note: "The key is to train the trainer so he can train his soldiers. This requires the NCO to identify essential soldier and small-unit and team tasks (drills) that support the unit METL and then

- To assess strengths and weaknesses,
- To formulate a plan to correct deficiencies and sustain strengths, and
- To execute the training to standard."

Paragraph 4-2 defines roles in executing training: "Senior NCOs ensure:

- Prerequisite training is completed so that soldiers' time is not wasted.
- Leaders are trained and prepared to train their sections, squads, teams[,] or crews. They train the trainers.
- Training is conducted to standard and meets the training objectives.

"Unit leaders are the primary trainers. They are responsible to

- Know their units' and soldiers' training needs and, based on that assessment, plan appropriate time to train tasks to standard.
- Ensure training is conducted to standard.
- Before presenting training to the soldier, trainers must prepare for the training."

AR 350-17, *Noncommissioned Officer Development Program,* provides doctrine and guidelines for the synchronization of the Noncommissioned Officer Development Program (NCODP) into the Army's leader development program. Paragraph 4.g says that "Commanders of battalions, separate companies, and equivalent organizations will:

- Be responsible to develop and implement an effective NCODP.
- Ensure the program supports the unit mission and enhances development of noncommissioned officers."

Paragraph 4.h says that "Command sergeants major (CSM), first sergeants, or senior NCOs of battalions, separate companies, or equivalent organizations will:

- Implement the commander's directives and guidance on the unit's NCODP.
- Be responsible for content, pertinence, and implementation of the unit's NCODP."

As with all leader training, the NCODP is a command responsibility. The program reflects command priorities and expectations for leader development, jointly determined by commanders and their senior NCOs.

AR 350-41, *Training in Units,* outlines essential training functions accomplished in units and complements FM 25-100 (FM 7-0) and FM 25-101 (FM 7-10). The regulation explains training requirements and strategy that relate directly to battle-focused training and the METL development process. Chapter 6 addresses leader development. It also covers Army policy about the following: soldier training courses; physical fitness; weapons qualifications; nuclear, biological, chemical (NBC) training; the combat lifesaver program; code of conduct; survival, evasion, escape, and resistance (SEER) training; law of war training; and modernization training. Appendix B of AR 350-41 lists required common military tasks (CMT) subjects to be taught in all Army units and schools.

Paragraph 2-32 reiterates existing guidance that "Battalion-level and company-level commanders will assign primary responsibility for collective training to officers, and primary responsibility for soldier training to NCOs. NCOs will also train most sections, squads, teams[,] and crews."

The Senior NCO as Master Trainer

Emerging prominently from current Army training doctrine is the relatively new role of senior NCOs as "master trainers." Having fifteen to twenty-five years' service and the benefits of the Army's advanced NCO schools, our senior NCOs are the equivalent of the guild masters of the olden days.

Masters trained midlevel journeymen in the more advanced skills of the craft. They taught the journeymen how to train apprentices. Above all, the masters set the standard and enforced it within the trade. Those who did not meet the masters' standards were dismissed from the trade.

The commander can be viewed as the architect who designs the master blueprint for the organization. The subordinate officers take the blueprint and extract those parts necessary for successful completion of their parts of the operation. The senior noncommissioned officers at each echelon take the blueprints and determine which individual tasks are necessary to successfully complete the project and then, while they are at it, look to see whether there is an easier, more cost-effective way to achieve the same goals. Sometimes the best plans in the world are never accomplished because someone doesn't know how to lay the foundation.

The NCO master trainer must know exactly what is needed to meet the officer's "architect" specifications. Just as a master of masonry did not care whether he was building a cathedral or a post office—his only concern was to ensure that the blocks of stone were cut exactly to the architect's standards—the NCO ensures that standards are met on the individual tasks that contribute to mission accomplishment. Just as the architect relies on the contractor to transform his design into a building with doors, walls, and windows, the officer must rely on the noncommissioned officer to put his intent into tangible individual and leader training that will build the collective tasks and ultimately the unit METL.

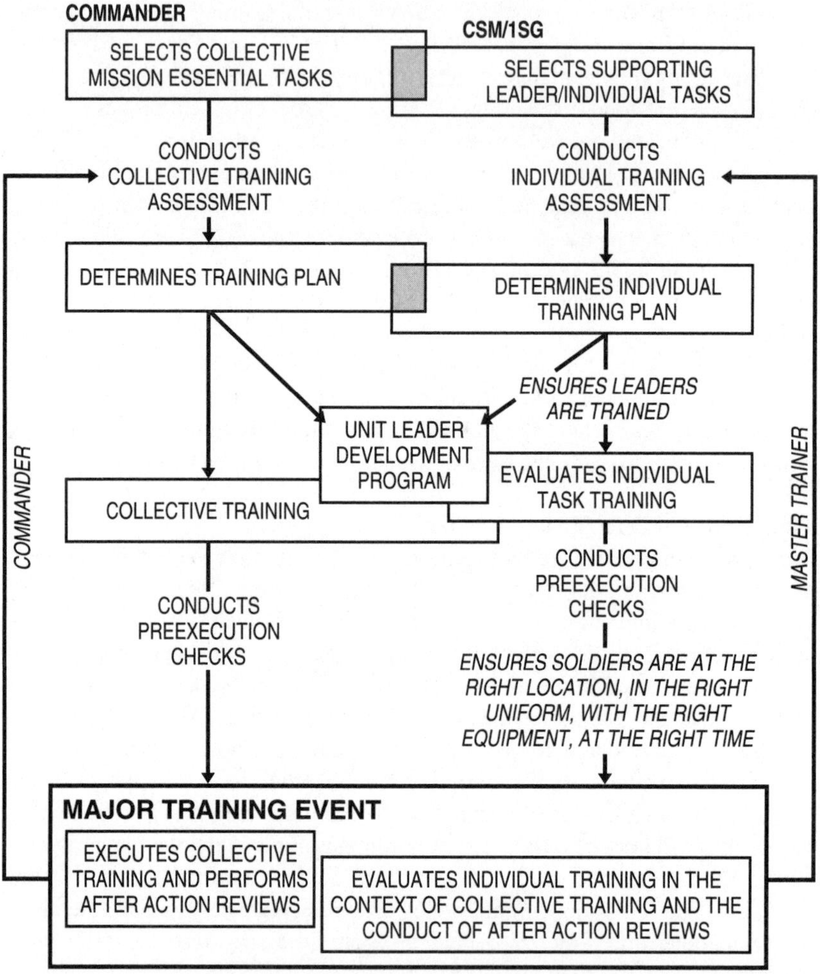

Commander/Senior NCO Roles

As the Army's master trainers, senior NCOs at the battalion and company level hold primary responsibility for planning and executing to standard all individual and most small-unit training in a manner that is supportive of, and synchronized with, collective and leader tasks. This is why it is important for the commander and his master trainer to sequence their work and talk through each stage of their unit's training plan.

Basic NCO roles and responsibilities for each echelon must be well understood within the NCO support channel.

Brigade and Higher Command Sergeants Major

Brigade and higher command sergeants major implement the commander's training guidance by establishing essential elements of individual and small-unit training that apply organization-wide and ensure that training standards are not compromised. They design collective training programs that apply to individual and small-unit training and assist subordinate command sergeants major in developing critical individual tasks that support the unit METL.

Battalion Command Sergeant Major

The battalion command sergeant major is the battalion master trainer. As such, he or she implements the commander's guidance and instructions by establishing essential elements of individual training that apply battalion-wide and inspecting training to verify that it is conducted to standard and meets the training objectives. This includes developing the individual and NCO leader task list that supports the battalion METL; conducting pre-execution checks to ensure that leaders are trained before they train the soldiers; ensuring that preliminary training for section, squad, team, and crew has the right focus, and soldiers' time is not wasted; and ensuring that soldiers in low-density MOSs are trained. The command sergeant major also assists and trains the first sergeants in developing their critical individual and NCO leader task lists that support their company's METL.

Company First Sergeants

The first sergeant (1SG) is the company master trainer and must be fully involved in all aspects of NCO and individual training. Similar to the battalion sergeant major, the first sergeant, with the assistance of the company commander, develops the individual and NCO leader task list that supports the company METL. As master trainer, the first sergeant ensures that preliminary training for section, squad, team, and crew has the right focus (i.e., training individual soldiers to drive a truck before teaching convoy procedures); that leaders are trained and prepared to train their sections, squads, teams, or crews (to include personally conducting some NCO training); that detailed inspections and checks are performed before the execution of training and that soldiers are at the right location, in the right uniform, with the right equipment, at the right time; that training is conducted to standard and meets the training objectives; and that adequate time is scheduled to repeat tasks not performed to standard the first time. In conjunction with platoon sergeants, first sergeants develop basic skills programs for incoming NCOs that focus on those tasks necessary for successful accomplishment of each NCO's duty position.

Platoon, Section, and Squad Sergeants

Platoon, section, squad, team, and crew leaders are the primary trainers of soldiers. Platoon sergeants, with the assistance of platoon and squad leaders, must prepare a list of essential common tasks and MOS specific tasks for each soldier's duty position. All platoon NCOs must know their units' and soldiers' training needs and, based on that assessment, plan appropriate time to train tasks to standard. Before training their soldiers, they must ensure that they are themselves trained. Platoon-level NCOs ensure that detailed inspections and checks are performed before training commences, that training is executed to standard, and that soldiers are retrained when standards are not met. Squad, team, and crew leaders should be prepared to conduct opportunity training whenever time is available.

EXAMPLES OF TRAINING GUIDANCE

Examples to assist NCOs in developing their training programs include the following.

Quarterly/Yearly Individual Training Guidance (ITG)

In conjunction with the commander's training guidance, the ITG focuses the leaders at all levels on those collective, leader, and individual tasks to be emphasized during the year. This development and assessment of individual training does not occur solely at the beginning and at the end of the training, but is ongoing. The ITG allows leaders and soldiers to train to the individual standards before being evaluated during collective tasks. The following is a sample of an Individual Training Guidance put forth by a battalion sergeant major:

1. *Actively mentor and train all soldiers.* Train up-and-coming specialists on junior leader tasks. Give each of your soldiers/subordinate leaders clearly defined goals for each month/quarter. Focus on team aspects of individual training. It is every soldier's responsibility to assist those who are weaker in getting to the objective. Foster an attitude of mind that produces individuality, self-reliance, resourcefulness, and adaptability. Our ultimate goal is to have soldiers with a dogged wiry endurance who will push on regardless of their circumstances.
2. *New leader training.* NCOs recently assigned or promoted need to be validated on the tasks critical to both the NCO's and the unit's mission accomplishment. Identify those tasks needing training to bring each new NCO up to a minimum level of proficiency in the critical tasks necessary to perform the unit's mission. This should include the most critical common leader tasks, leading physical training (PT), land navigation, and how to train marksmanship.
3. *Evaluation of individual tasks.* Every collective task we do, whether at battalion, company, or platoon, will have a minimum of three individual tasks identified and evaluated within the collective task. Individual tasks are to be taught to soldiers by their first-line leaders in both field

and garrison. The individual task will then be evaluated under field conditions during unit training of collective tasks/missions. During platoon/squad After Action Reviews (AARs), dissect collective tasks into their supporting individual tasks to determine which tasks most affected unit performance. Once identified, these individual tasks are recorded as T (trained), P (practice), or U (untrained) in the leader book. You must primarily test individual tasks within the framework of collective training. Individual testing by itself does not give an accurate picture of how successfully the task would be accomplished when soldiers are tired and under stress.

4. *Identify weaknesses.* There is very little time on the schedule for companies/platoons to do collective tasks not already mentioned, but there is time to train leaders and soldiers on individual tasks where they are weak. It is up to us to identify those weaknesses and ensure that the training occurs.
5. *Common task training (CTT).* Look at the tasks identified for the CTT test. Using your unit METL and supporting collective tasks, identify those tasks most important to your mission accomplishment. Don't wait until the last minute to test your soldiers; do a paper drill, or test your soldiers at company level. Testing should be at platoon and lower, with spot checks by company/battalion to see if the standards are being maintained. The best way to skin this cat is to do one or two of the tasks on the CTT monthly so you don't have to crunch at the last minute. Be smart; if one of the tasks is to maintain your M-16 series rifle, schedule the task when you are going to clean the rifles anyway; evaluate while you are on mission.

NONCOMMISSIONED OFFICER DEVELOPMENT PROGRAM (NCODP)

The NCODP is a component part of the Army leader development program and equally applicable to TDA (table of distribution and allowances, which are nonfighting units) and TOE (table of organization and equipment, which are units expected to deploy and either fight or support the war-fighting effort). NCO professional development training is structured to the needs of the unit NCOs as assessed by their unit officer and NCO leadership.

Program Objectives

The NCODP has the following objectives:

- Strengthen the leadership skills and professional attributes within the NCO Corps.
- Assist and provide guidance in the continuing development of NCOs.
- Increase the confidence of the NCO as a leader.

- Realize the full potential of the NCO support channel.
- Improve unit effectiveness and combat readiness.

Although the Enlisted Personnel Management System (EPMS) and the Noncommissioned Officer Education System (NCOES) provide a valuable foundation for NCO development, the NCODP builds upon those contributions. It is only through the application of skills, knowledge, and behavior in the unit that soldiers become quality NCOs.

NCODP Responsibilities

The ultimate responsibility for noncommissioned officer professional development belongs with the unit commander, but the perpetuation of high ideals and professional standards for NCOs, and ultimately for those enlisted under their charge, must be accomplished by NCOs themselves through a continued and sustained process. The NCODP is an organized way in which to accomplish this. There are no fill-in-the-block time limitations. NCO and unit needs will vary from unit to unit and each NCODP should be structured and adjusted to fit the battle focus of each particular unit's NCO needs.

Command sergeants major at all levels above battalion have hands-on responsibility for NCODP definition, implementation, management, and inspection in subordinate units. Commensurate with the master trainer discussion above, the battalion command sergeant major is the battalion master trainer for the unit's NCODP, with the first sergeant being the master NCODP trainer in each company. It is, however, platoon sergeants and sometimes section and squad leaders who are the primary trainers. They are responsible, as mentioned earlier, for implementing the basic skills program for each incoming subordinate.

Program Fundamentals

There are certain "fundamentals" that belong in any NCODP. First, the NCODP should be implemented at the lowest level feasible and should include tasks applicable to all affected NCOs regardless of career field at that level. Battalion NCODP should concentrate on those areas where formal training is appropriate for all units in a command, attuned to the geography, mission, and shortfalls of a unit (examples: convoy operations, cold-weather training, etc.). Company-level NCODP focuses on those subjects that apply to those NCOs in the company. Platoon NCODP should include subjects focusing on the MOS of the NCOs within the platoon. NCODP at the company and platoon levels will be battle-focused on those tasks that directly apply to the supporting collective tasks of a company METL.

The training task and method to train must be identified well enough in advance to identify instructors, obtain resources, plan and rehearse lessons, and allow NCOs to arrange schedules and workloads to attend the training. First sergeants should ensure that company training schedules reflect the NCODP training.

Total NCO development occurs when training covers the entire spectrum of NCO duties; however, remember that the primary purpose of unit-battalion-level NCODP remains to prepare corporals, sergeants, staff sergeants, and platoon sergeants to conduct battle-focused training at the squad/team/crew and individual levels so that no NCO leader is unprepared to teach his or her soldiers. If we train our platoon NCOs only to be good administrators, but don't teach them how to lead soldiers, then we have failed both the NCO and the soldiers they lead.

The skills that NCOs need to ensure that their soldiers can fight, win, and survive on the battlefield vary from unit to unit, but certain proficiencies, known as Common Leader Combat Skills (CLCS), are applicable to every unit, from the most forward infantry squad to a maintenance section in the corps's rear area. Although they are taught to NCO leaders in the Army service schools, they should be made an integral part of any NCO development program. The following tasks constitute the CLCS: occupy assembly area, break contact, conduct fire and movement, react to indirect fire, react to air attack, consolidate and reorganize, conduct continuous operations, move (traveling,

Operational training at a MOUT site.

traveling overwatch, bounding overwatch), apply troop-leading procedures, operate in an NBC environment, defend, react to ambush, and disengage. All of these skills are addressed in FM 7-8 (FM 3-21.8), *The Infantry Rifle Platoon and Squad (Infantry, Airborne, Air Assault, Ranger).*

NCOs are responsible for their duty performance. Having the appropriate mission training plans and soldier's manuals on hand, as well as unit NCODP, and mentoring by the chain of command will assist the NCO in building proficiency on new tasks and in sustaining proficiency on tasks already known. With skill builds will.

Techniques and Tips for Training NCOs at Unit Level

Force Leaders at All Echelons to Make Decisions. Push the decision-making process down to the lowest level that has the knowledge to make the decision. Set down objectives, but don't dictate how to perform the task. Let the NCO make the hard choices. There will be errors in judgment, but in peace those can be readily corrected. Give NCOs the freedom to make mistakes, but NOT the freedom to fail. "It" is done until the task is done to standard, whether once or twenty times. The chain of command should identify any errors to the NCO to preclude him or her making the same mistake twice, but control of the problem should not be taken away.

Mentoring Development of Aspiring NCOs. Mentoring usually occurs two levels down and usually outside the mentored NCO's chain of command, i.e., the CSM mentors PSGs, 1SGs mentor squad leaders. This helps both the mentor and mentored; one gets the advice and counsel of one who is senior and reasonably distant, and the other gets the view from the trenches. This day-to-day training and mentoring allows a solid senior/subordinate relationship and enables the senior NCO to take charge of the development of those NCOs who are junior in grade and experience. The senior NCO can begin the molding process that establishes a foundation for further development.

Leading Subordinates in Execution of the Activities of the Day. Such leadership is exemplified in understanding the instruction or task before beginning; in giving clear, concise instruction; and in being a demanding, willing teacher and an aggressive role model. No school can duplicate the example that a good unit NCO leader makes on a young soldier.

Conducting Unit Instruction. An often neglected area, unit instruction is possibly the most important tool used in developing NCOs. To be effective, the instruction has to be meaningful, well planned, and professionally presented. Design the classes so they are progressive and fill the needs of both the NCO and the unit. Match the training to the echelon that is getting the training (i.e., platoon sergeants receive training from the 1SG on how to maintain duty rosters, or platoon sergeants teach their squad/team leaders how to supervise construction of a fighting position).

Unscheduled Time. An NCO may be given a requirement to read a book, view a lesson, or write a report when things get quiet, when he or she has staff duty, charge of quarters (CQ), or when the NCO is without troops.

NCO Self-Development

Encourage your NCOs to enroll in the Army Correspondence Course Program. MOS-related courses and the Army precommission correspondence course all build on those battle competencies desired in NCOs. Taking the courses will broaden the NCO professionally and increase the knowledge of the unit as a whole. It will also assist the NCO in progressing through the ranks, for it shows board members that this NCO has the initiative to better his or her military education without being sent to a resident school.

The NCO Development Program must also address the long-term education of the NCO. An individual reading program will build on the NCO's analytical abilities, knowledge of leadership, and Army values. This not only extends the NCO's knowledge, but fosters an interest in reading. It encourages the NCO to analyze what he or she reads, to learn from the past, and to plan for the future.

Increasing an NCO's Civilian Education. This in no way, shape, or form advocates making college graduates of the NCO Corps, but helps the sergeant accomplish the day-to-day tasks. If all NCOs can comprehend what is being written, then there will be less confusion in determining which tasks are to be accomplished, their priority, the implied tasks, and the intent of the commander.

There are thousands of years of NCO experience in each brigade or group, and hundreds in each company. Tap that experience and make your program the best there is.

DEVELOPING INDIVIDUAL TRAINING TASKS

One of the hardest, yet most important, tasks for an NCO to accomplish is determining what is important to train. There is not enough time in a training year to train all the tasks in a skill level 1 book and common task manual, as well as to know all the collective tasks for the MOS, whether active, guard, or reserve.

Training Plan Overview

As discussed in FM 25-101, collective, leader, and individual training requirements come together in a training plan. The following charts and discussion explain the planning process.

Figure 1 illustrates the training management cycle, from identification of training tasks through the After Action Review (AAR) assessment; the planning, execution, and assessment cycles are in FM 25-101.

The chart illustrates how collective and individual training are interrelated. We can see that the unit leader development program is an integral part of the

Overview, Development, and Execution of Training Plan□

Identification of Collective Tasks to AARs

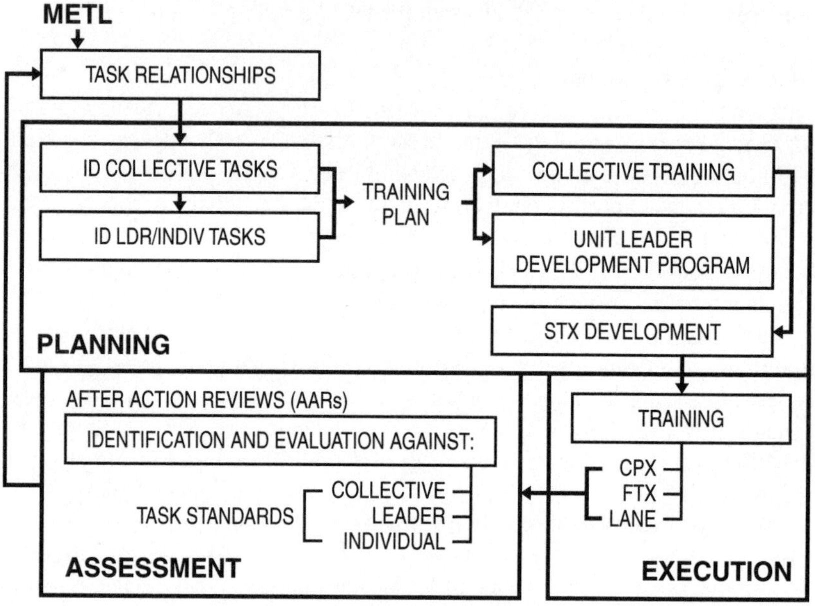

Figure 1.

training program. We use it to train the leader tasks necessary to perform the collective tasks. That is why it is so necessary to battle-focus the leader development program. That way, when we begin to train the collective tasks with our soldiers, we are able to devote the time to the collective task rather than trying to train ourselves at the same time.

Figure 2 is an extension of Figure 1 and shows where the commander gets the information to develop the training plan. Note the cyclical nature of the planning from one year to the next, where prior AARs become input to the next training plan.

Mutually Supporting Training Tasks

Figure 3 shows a sample of how a unit's collective, leader, and individual soldier tasks are sequentially derived from a brigade METL. This chart is an amplification of the figures on pages 2-10 and 2-15 of FM 25-101. Note that the lower unit's METL and supporting individual and leader tasks support the higher unit's METL. Each level has its own supporting leader tasks and individual tasks that are applicable to all soldiers within that command. Although not shown on

Where the Training Plan Comes From

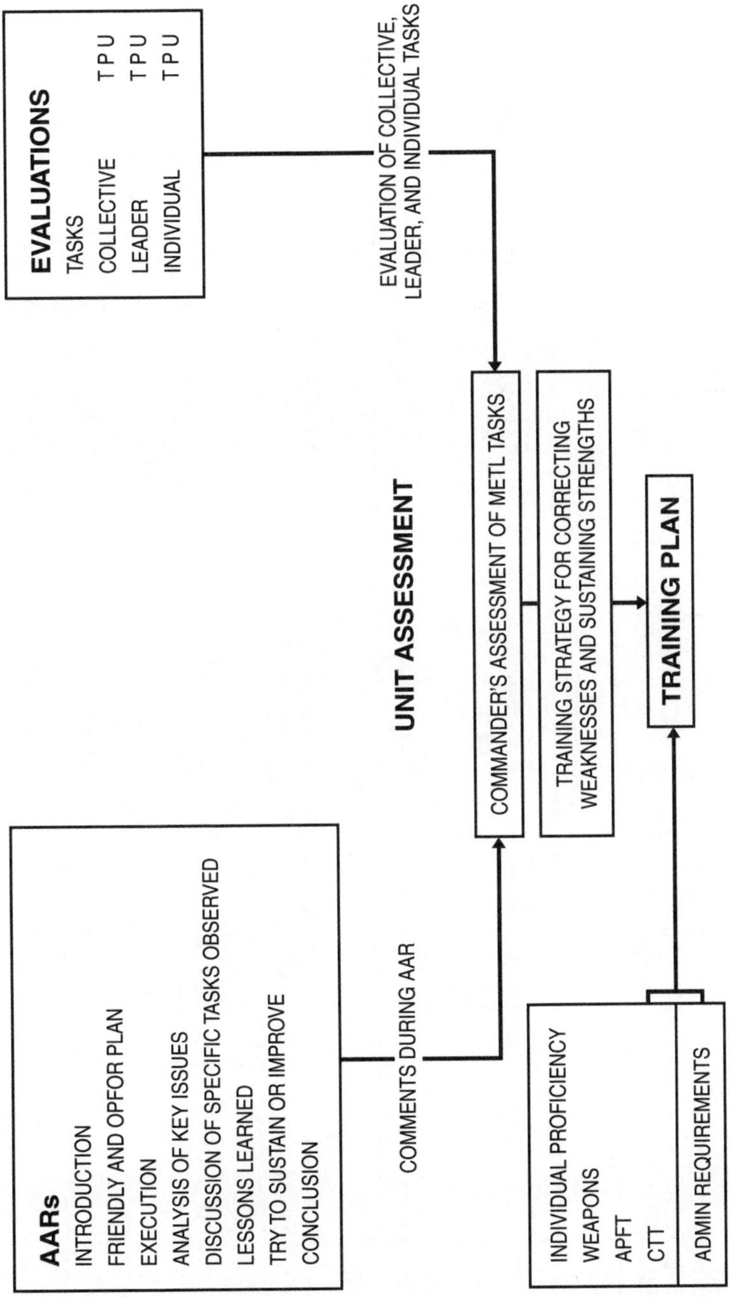

Figure 2.

Example Brigade to Individual Soldier Task Relationship

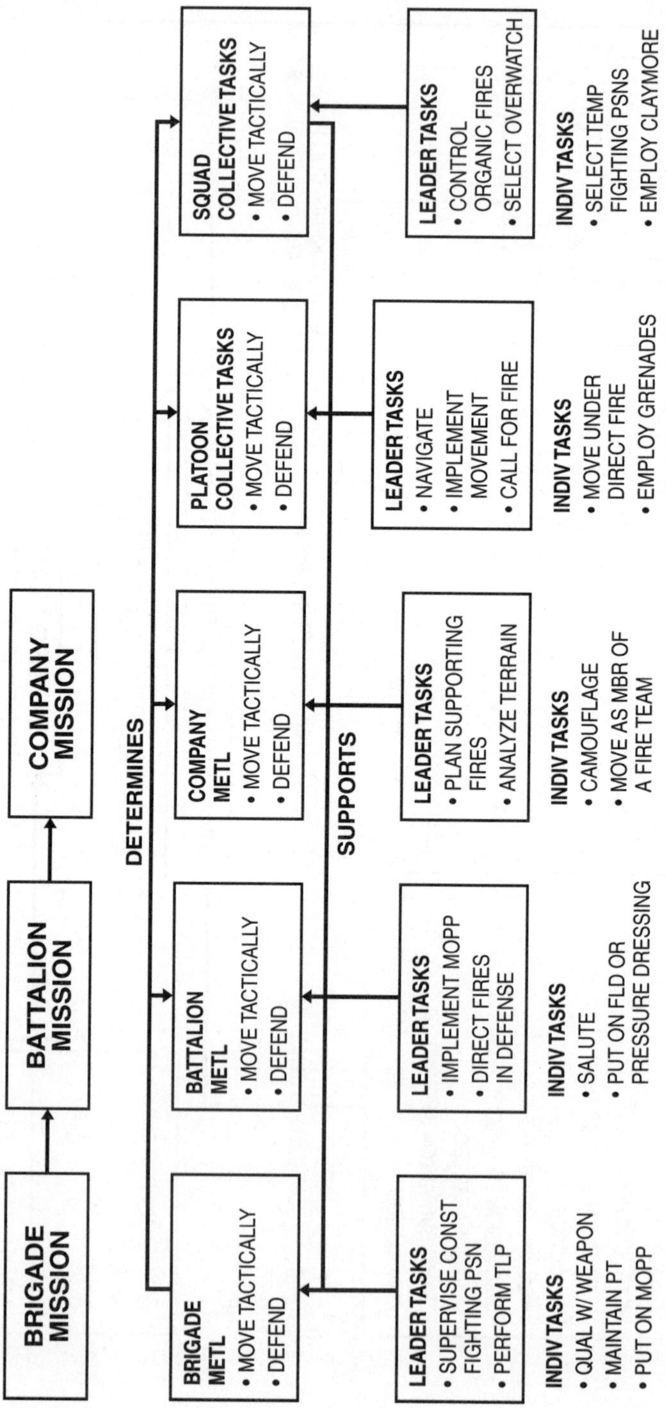

Figure 3.

the chart, there are also staff tasks for each tier of command. With all the different MOSs in the brigade, few critical individual and leader tasks apply to all soldiers. The larger the organization, the more generic the tasks.

Lanes Integrate Collective, Leader, and Individual Tasks

Once training tasks have been defined, use lanes to certify the individual, collective, and leader tasks as shown in figure 4. Lanes are drills designed to teach each unit task and to test collective, leader, and individual proficiency. Note the input to the design of the lanes.

Lane Development and Relationship□ Between Collective and Individual Tasks

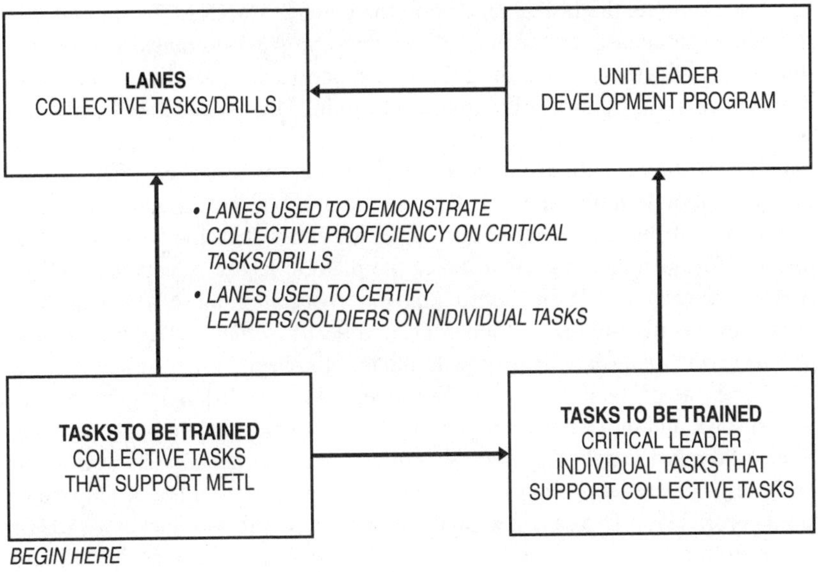

Figure 4.

We use lanes to train our subordinates and ourselves before we go to the field. We want to certify individual and leader skills prior to field exercises because soldiers react differently under stress. For example, a squad leader may demonstrate proficiency in determining which movement techniques to use with his squad on a sand table, but on a lane, when he is tired and thinking about the next hill, he may not be as proficient.

Identifying and Prioritizing Collective Tasks

There is nothing more important than a solid foundation in the leader and individual tasks. Collective tasks and missions fail because leader and individual tasks were not accomplished to standard. Fortunately, many of these tasks apply to more than one collective task, such as preparing a fragmentary order or navigating from one point to another. If a leader can control organic fires in a defense, then chances are he or she can do the same in an ambush.

The lowest echelon to have an METL is a company. Platoons have supporting tasks that support the company METL. Look at figure 5. Leaders can use this flow chart to determine platoon supporting tasks. Using the company METL and commander's guidance as well as the mission training plan (MTP), a collective task list can be developed that supports the company METL. Squad leaders, acting together, and using the platoon tasks and the platoon leader's guidance, then develop their own supporting tasks.

For example, the task *defend* is on the company METL. To support this mission essential task, one of the platoon supporting tasks is *ambush*. There are thirty-one collective tasks in the MTP that support this task. Given competing requirements, this is probably too many to train. This means that the platoon leader, using the commander's intent and input from the other leaders in the platoon, must reduce the list to critical tasks to be accomplished when preparing the platoon training plan. It is far easier to evaluate a small number of critical tasks during an exercise than a laundry list that looks good but is impossible to execute. In this instance the platoon leader selects *prepare for combat, move tactically,* and *consolidate and reorganize,* all of which apply to almost every mission the platoon does, and *occupy objective rally point* and *perform point ambush,* which apply to the mission itself.

Once one of the tasks is rated T (trained), we establish a program to sustain the task and move on to another that is either untrained or needs practice. Some of the tasks such as *prepare for combat* or *move tactically* as well as the battle drills have such an impact on other tasks that they must not be allowed to slip in proficiency. Dependent upon the training we want to achieve, we add or delete from the list as necessary. Some of the other tasks, such as the Military Operations in Urban Terrain (MOUT) tasks, are dependent upon the situation and might wait until all of the primary tasks are trained, unless they apply to the company METL.

Selecting Complementary Leader and Individual Tasks

The process of selecting leader and individual tasks to complement the collective tasks is shown in figure 6.

It is similar in structure to the collective task process. After the collective tasks to be trained have been identified, NCOs use the MTPs, soldiers' manuals of common tasks (SMCTs), and soldiers' manuals for specific MOSs to find those individual and leader tasks that apply. As mentioned earlier, many of

Identification of Tasks for the Collective Task List

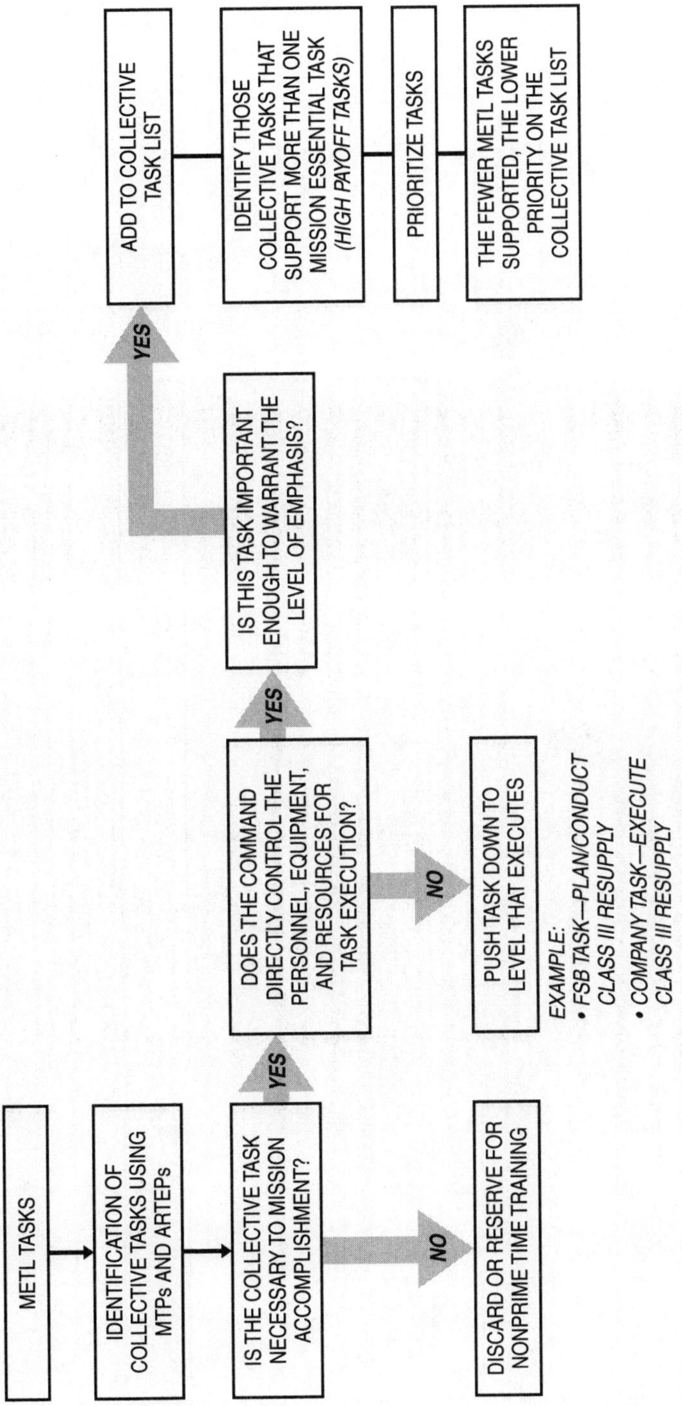

Figure 5.

Identification of Tasks for the Leader/Individual Task List

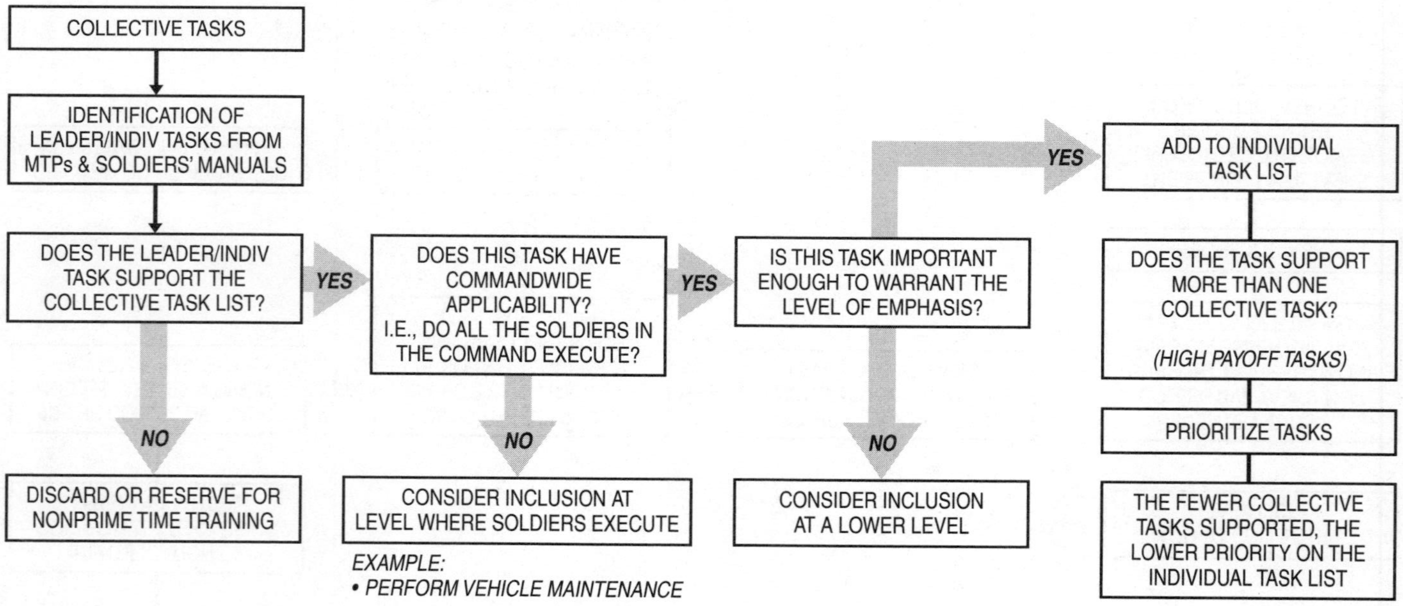

Figure 6.

the individual tasks are applicable to more than one collective task. The lower the level, the more tasks apply and the more the effort must be made to prioritize the tasks.

To prioritize tasks, you look at whether the task applies to everyone at each level. Ask yourself if all soldiers perform the task. Next look at how critical the task is to your unit. Ask yourself if the task is critical to mission accomplishment. All soldiers need to know how to *camouflage self and equipment,* but I would venture to say that the task is more critical to soldiers in an infantry company than to soldiers in support organizations not in direct contact with the enemy. Indeed, the required training of yearly CTT subjects should not be on the individual task list if they are not critical to the unit's collective tasks, even though they have to be trained.

Once we have our list of individual and leader tasks, we check to see how many collective tasks each supports. We then prioritize the task list from most important to least, and train the most critical first. Some of the tasks may have already been accomplished in an earlier exercise, so we also want to look at the training rating of those tasks when we establish our training program. Once we achieve the standard, we establish a program to sustain the task and move to other tasks. Remember, similar to the collective tasks, some of the individual and leader tasks have such an impact that they can't be allowed to slip in proficiency and must be continuously evaluated.

After determining which collective tasks the unit will accomplish in the field, we take the individual task list and match it against the tasks to be trained. Moreover, as with collective tasks, you add or delete tasks to achieve the training objective that needs to be accomplished. The collective tasks aren't the only ones evaluated in the field; so are the supporting leader and individual tasks.

CONDUCTING THE AFTER ACTION REVIEW

After Action Reviews (AARs) help to provide soldiers and units with feedback on mission and task performances in training and in combat. AARs identify how to correct deficiencies, sustain strengths, and focus on performance of specific METL training objectives. Key to the AAR is the spirit in which it is given. The environment and climate surrounding an AAR must be one in which the soldiers and leaders openly and honestly discuss what actually transpired, in sufficient detail and clarity that everyone not only will understand what did and did not occur and why but, most important, will have the strong desire to seek the opportunity to practice the task again.

The Squad After Action Review A One-Act Play[1]

The rifle squad filed quietly into the AAR tent—soldiers' eyes squint as they adjust to the change in light. Everyone shuffles

[1] Published by Sgt. Maj. Robert S. Rush in *Army Trainer,* January 1994.

around as they find chairs and drink water. Yellow keys are in all but three soldiers' multiple integrated laser engagement simulation (MILES) harnesses. The squad had just completed a tactical exercise in which it sustained heavy losses in an ambush.

Moments later the observer/controller enters the tent and walks to the front of the squad between the terrain table and charts.

Observer/Controller (OC): "Welcome to the After Action Review for the Squad React to Ambush Lane. I am Sergeant First Class Hall and I walked with you on the lane as your observer/controller. Before we begin the AAR, let me orient you to the sand table. The top of the table is north, the blue string on the left is the Snake River, and the white powder is the primary trail through the area. The vegetation represents the wooded area, and the red string represents your start point and your direction of travel. Any questions on the sand table? No questions? Then let's begin. If you look at the butcher paper, you will see the sequence for the AAR.

AAR Briefing Sequence

Introduction
- Training objectives: Evaluate squad on drill *react to ambush* and supporting collective, leader, and individual tasks
- Map orientation

Planning
- Squad mission
- Higher intent
- Squad leader's plan
- OPFOR plan

Execution
- What happened?
- How it happened?
- Why it happened?
- Specific leader and individual tasks that affected mission accomplishment

Summarization

"Although your mission did not specify React to Ambush, the lane was set up for you to be ambushed while you were performing your mission. OK! Squad leader, what was your mission?"

Squad leader (SL): "Sergeant Hall, my mission was to conduct an area recon along the river to detect OPFOR [opposing forces]

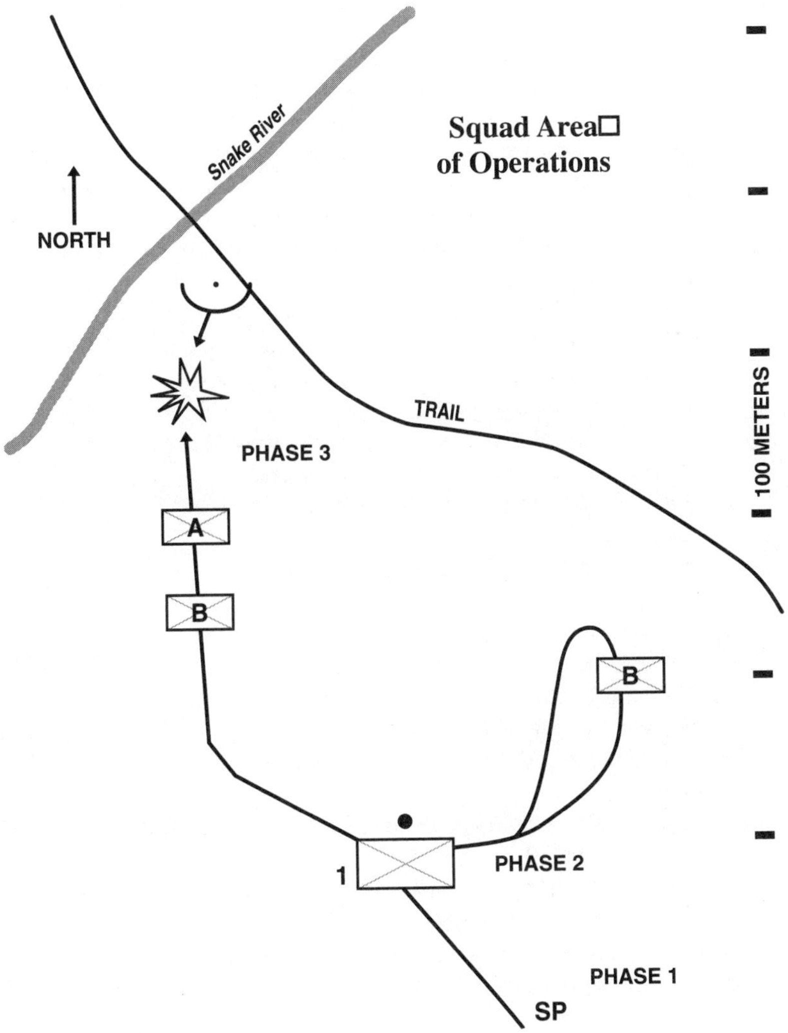

infiltration routes in the area and destroy any enemy units of fewer than four men."

OC: "What was your commander's intent?"

SL: "The commander wanted us to recon our zone's crossing sites and report all enemy in the area and destroy those elements that contained fewer than four men."

OC: "What was your plan?"

SL: "I planned to move my squad using traveling overwatch along the river. If I found a crossing site that was recently used, I'd set up an ambush along the trail the OPFOR was using."

OC: "OK, OPFOR commander, your plan."

OPFOR: "I had two four-man teams in the area—one walking along this trail and one in an ambush position by our previous crossing site. That team had an M60 machine gun. I hoped that the BLUFOR [blue-forces, friendly forces] squads would find the trail used by the roving patrol and follow it back to the crossing site, where they would be ambushed. Since our maneuver area was small, each of the teams had the additional task of moving to the other's assistance if contact was made."

OC: "All right, squad leader, what happened?"

SL: "Well, we crossed the friendly forward lines about 0900."

OC: "What formation were you in?"

SL: "Traveling overwatch."

OC: "Really! B-Team leader, how close were you to A-Team?"

B-Team Leader (BTL): "About 20 meters."

OC: "Squad leader, what formation were you in?"

SL: "Traveling."

OC: "Continue with execution."

SL: "We had moved about 100 meters when the lead fire team saw movement to its 11 o'clock."

OC: "A-Team leader, what did you see?"

A-Team Leader (ATL): "I didn't really see soldiers, but the bushes were moving and there was no wind."

OC: "Good observation. Squad leader, what were your actions?"

SL: "I had the A-Team leader select a good overwatch position and then I had B-Team move right."

OC: "B-Team leader, what did the squad leader tell you?"

BTL: "He didn't really tell me. He pointed out where the enemy was and signaled that he wanted me to take my team into the trees on the right."

OC: "What did you do?"

BTL: "I brought my team into the trees and tried to turn to the left to get behind the enemy."

OC: "A-Team leader, could you follow the B-Team's movement?"

ATL: "No, I lost them as soon as they went into the woods."

OC: "Squad leader, did the B-Team do what you wanted them to do?"

SL: "Not really. I wanted SGT Charles to go to the woods and set up an overwatch so that I could move A-Team."

OC: "Everyone, what is the arm and hand signal for bounding overwatch or cover me?"

The squad members begin patting the top of their heads with their right hands.

OC: "What happened when the team disappeared into the woods?"

SL: "Well, I changed my plan and tried to follow their movement through the woods by the noise they made, but after about five minutes everything was quiet."

OC: "B-Team 203 Gunner, talk to me."

B-Team Gunner: "The woods were really thick, I had a hard time watching the team leader. I couldn't see Smith, the rifleman, on my left. I tried to signal the team leader that Smith was missing, but he wouldn't turn around. The team leader finally stopped and signaled that he heard noises to the front. We all froze. The noise got louder as whatever it was moved toward us, and then Smith broke out of the woods. He was lucky we didn't shoot him."

OC: "Smith, what happened?"

Smith: "I was having a hard time following Maxwell. Then I came to a small trail and followed it. It was a lot easier than breaking brush. After a couple of minutes I couldn't hear anyone, so I decided to double back through the woods. It was really quiet and I started to get nervous. Finally, I broke through the thicket and saw everyone pointing their weapons at me."

OC: "OK, OPFOR commander, what was happening on your side?"

OPFOR: "My team on the trail did not know they had been detected until we heard noises on our left flank. It sounded like they were coming close so my trail team moved back to the ambush site."

OC: "Squad leader, you now have your A-Team in an overwatch position, and your B-Team somewhere in the trees. What were your actions?"

SL: "I hoped that the B-Team would pop out of the woods where we could see them."

OC: "What would have happened if they had popped out in front of A-Team? How were you planning to control your organic fires?"

The A-Team rifleman speaks up. "We would have waited to identify them positively as the enemy."

OC: "Sounds good. Now, what would have happened if B-Team had engaged enemy in the woods? Could you have supported them?"

A-Team Rifleman: "Not from where we were."

OC: "B-Team leader, what happened then?"

BTL: "I went back to where we had entered the woodline, then SSG Thomas signaled me to bring my team back."

OC: "All right, squad leader, your squad is together again, what were your actions?"

SL: "I didn't want to go down the trail or through the thick woods on the right. On our left, where the river was, there looked like an area that was reasonably open but still offered some concealment."

OC: "Let's back up a bit. Were you in radio contact with your platoon leader?"

SL: "Yes, I had called him when we crossed the LD [line of departure]."

OC: "Not after?"

SL: "No, I didn't think it was necessary."

OC: "Don't you think that the platoon leader would want to know that you modified your route? He might find it difficult to support you if he doesn't know where you are."

SL: "I should have called the platoon leader with the change."

OC: "OK, let's continue. What movement formation were you in?"

SL: "Traveling overwatch."

OC: "Again, B-Team leader, what was the distance between you and A-Team?"

BTL: "About 20 meters."

OC: "Same mistake as before. Continue, SSG Thomas."

SL: "We moved ahead another 200 meters toward the river. I could see the river through the trees to our front and a big trail on our right."

OC: "What was the terrain like?"

SL: "It was pretty much flat with thick trees and brambles along the river itself. On the right across the trail was a gentle rise into thicker trees."

OC: "What happened then?"

SL: "When the A-Team was about 50 meters from the edge of the woodline, we were ambushed. The enemy had a machine gun."

OC: "A-Team SAW [squad automatic weapon] gunner, what were your actions?"

A-Team SAW Gunner: "As soon as they started firing, I fired a couple of rounds and got down."

OC: "I see a yellow key in your harness. What happened?"

A-Team SAW Gunner: "I didn't get down fast enough."

OC: "A-Team leader, were you in grenade range."

ATL: "No."

OC: "Squad leader, what were your actions?"

SL: "I wanted to break contact because they had a machine gun. I tried to maneuver B-Team to the flank so that they could support A-Team's withdrawal."

OC: "B-Team leader, what happened?"

BTL: "We were also in the kill zone. Two others and I were hit when we tried to move to the right."

OC: "OPFOR commander, tell me about your ambush."

OPFOR: "The squad basically paralleled the trail into our ambush site. We could see them for about 250 meters. I was able to reposition the ambush to where they were walking right into us. We held fire until they were just out of grenade range."

OC: "What did the friendly squad look like?"

OPFOR: "There was good dispersion among the team members but it seemed like the teams were right up on one another. I had the machine gun shoot from the left, where there was cover, to the right. I directed my rifleman to shoot at the leaders."

OC: "Good plan. Squad leader, how effective was the OPFOR plan?"

SL: "Well, just after I had told the B-Team to maneuver, I was hit."

OC: "Where were you located?"

SL: "Up by A-Team."

OC: "A-Team leader, looks like you were in charge. What did you do?"

ATL: "I knew that my SAW gunner was down. I called to Jones and Murphy to cover me. I crawled over, checked the gunner, and got his SAW. I then yelled out for everyone to bound back by buddy teams, A-Team first, while I covered them. I don't know how many were left in B-Team.

"My two guys went back about 20 meters and set up another position. I was hit when I got up to pull back."

OC: "Sergeant Adams, you did a good job! A-Team 203 grenadier, what happened then?"

A-Team Grenadier: "Brown in B-Team pulled back past us and began supporting us from a small depression in the ground. Jones and I pulled back to that location also. Then you stopped the exercise."

OC: "Let's look at the next chart and talk about some of the collective/leader and individual tasks that applied to this mission. Some of the leader and individual tasks identified on the chart were not accomplished because of the way the lane went. Squad leader, how do you think you did analyzing the terrain?"

TASK: React to Ambush

	Trained	Practice	Untrained
COLLECTIVE TASKS			
React to ambush	T	P	U
Move tactically	T	P	U
Overwatch, support by fire	T	P	U
LEADER TASKS			
Analyze terrain	T	P	U
Implement movement techniques	T	P	U
Control organic fires	T	P	U
Direct fire movement against an enemy position	T	P	U
Control fire team movement	T	P	U
Reorganize following contact	T	P	U
INDIVIDUAL TASKS			
Move as a member of a fire team	T	P	U
Move under direct fire	T	P	U
Select temporary fighting position	T	P	U
Engage targets	T	P	U
Employ hand grenades	T	P	U
Report enemy information	T	P	U

SL: "I thought it was OK at the beginning, but I sort of lost it when I had the problems with controlling B-Team."

OC: "We'll address that later. You told me earlier that you did not go through the woods for control reasons. But tell me, why didn't you use that slight high ground on the right to overwatch with?"

SL: "I didn't think that we would make contact when we did. I wasn't expecting an ambush."

OC: "OK, your mission is now to set up an ambush. Given that area, where would you put it?"

SL: "Probably where the OPFOR put it."

OC: "Squad leader, when do you use traveling, traveling overwatch, bounding overwatch?"

SL: "Not expected, possible, expected."

OC: "How long prior to the ambush had you seen the enemy?"

SL: "About ten minutes."

OC: "So contact was . . ."

SL: "Expected."

OC: "But you kept in traveling overwatch. Where were you in the formation?"

SL: "Just behind the A-Team, so I could control movement."

OC: "OK, B-Team leader, how far behind the squad leader were you?"

BTL: "Pretty close, I guess about 20 meters."

OC: "What formation have we just described?"

BTL: "Traveling."

OC: "Squad leader, when contact was made, how easy was it to control B-Team?"

SL: "Control was pretty easy. I could yell at him and he could hear. My only problem was that I was getting near misses from the ambush."

OC: "So you were suppressed along with A-Team?"

SL: "Yes."

OC: "Had you been back with B-Team and the interval about 50 meters, what do you think could have been different?"

SL: "It would have been a lot easier to maneuver my B-Team where they could support A-Team's pullback."

OC: "B-Team leader, how hard was it to control your fire team's movement?"

BTL: "It wasn't hard. My men followed where I went."

OC: "Grenadier, how about it?"

B-Team Grenadier: "The team leader needs to turn around more, some of the brush was really thick."

OC: "Valid point. Team leader, how far apart are you supposed to be from A-Team in traveling overwatch?"

BTL: "50 meters."

OC: "Why were you so close?"

BTL: "So I could hear the squad leader."

OC: "Squad leader, why where you so close to A-Team?"

SL: "So that I could control them better."

OC: "What kind of guidance did you give the A-Team leader?"

SL: "I would use my hand to point the direction that I wanted him to go."

OC: "No specific instruction?"

SL: "I guess not. I wanted to be up front in case something happened."

OC: "Do you trust the A-Team leader?"

SL: "Absolutely."

OC: "Then let him do what he's paid to do—lead a team. You lead a squad."

SL: "Roger."

OC: "B-Team leader, why did you go off into the woods with your team?"

BTL: "I believed that was what the squad leader wanted."

OC: "Are you sure?"

BTL: "Well, SSG Thomas is new and I was trying to help him out."

OC: "Where did your expanding on his intent get the squad?"

BTL: "We lost contact with the enemy and forced the squad leader to change his plan."

OC: "The moral of the story is . . ."

BTL: "Let the squad leader plan for the squad."

OC: "OK, good. Now let's carry the discussion one step farther. What were your thoughts when the squad leader directed you to move to the right flank when contact was made?"

BTL: "I knew that we wouldn't make it, but decided since I hadn't really done what he wanted me to do earlier, that I would execute no matter what."

OC: "What should you have done?"

BTL: "What the squad leader wanted me to do was right. He didn't dictate *how,* but *what.* I should have bounded by buddy team in rushes to the flank. It probably would have taken a little longer, but we might have gotten out with fewer casualties."

OC: "The moral to this story is, work within the leader's intent, don't read into it more than there is. Leaders, what leader tasks do you need to relook before you go back out on the lane?"

SL: "I need to put myself in the enemy's place when I analyze terrain to determine better what movement techniques and formation to put my squad in. I also have to watch both teams to ensure that they are in the movement technique I want them in. I will also let the team leaders do their job."

OC: "Good critique. A-Team leader?"

ATL: "I should have thought to throw smoke before we began breaking contact. That probably would have stopped some of the casualties."

OC: "Good comment and good job. You really played heads-up out there today. B-Team leader?"

BTL: "Try not to second-guess the squad leader, and maneuver my team within his intent. I have also got to look back more often at my team to see if there are any problems."

OC: "Good. Now from left to right, how do you think you did on individual tasks?"

B-Team Rifleman: "Move as a member of a Fire Team—I need to stay in my lane and watch the team member on my right."

B-Team Grenadier: "Engage Targets—The M203 is just extra weight when using MILES. We would have had a better chance of breaking the ambush if I could use TP [training practice] rounds or there was a laser device for the grenade launcher."

OC: "You're right, the problem with duplicating MILES kills with the grenade launcher makes it hard for the squad leader to use all of his systems properly. The squad leader has the same combat systems as the company commander; where the company has mortars, the squad leader has 203s; for direct fire the company has M60s and the squad SAWs; for maneuver the company has platoons, and the squad fire teams. While there are fire markers for mortar fire, there is no system for 203s, and though using 203 TP is one solution to the problem, I don't consider it the approved one. As accurate as you gunners are, someone would get hurt fast. Enough said. Next man."

B-Team SAW: "I don't know what task this falls under, but we need to keep the team leader informed."

OC: "Bad news does not get better with age." *Points to next soldier.*

A-Team Rifleman: "Move as a member of a Fire Team—I thought our distance between members and control was good in A-Team."

A-Team Grenadier: "Engage targets—I agree with Maxwell, the B-Team grenadier. From my last position, I could have pasted the ambush site with 203 rounds without getting return fire."

A-Team SAW: "Move under direct fire—I need to get down quicker."

OC: "Those are all good comments. You all did a good job in identifying the critical tasks. Now, let's see how the leader and individual tasks affected the collective tasks.

"React to ambush—untrained; both fire teams were in the kill zone and the squad was unable to react. The squad suffered more than 30 percent casualties. Move tactically—untrained; the squad did not employ the movement technique ordered by the squad leader. The squad leader did not select the proper movement technique based on the likelihood of enemy contact. Initial contact with the enemy was made with the entire squad rather than with a team.

"SSG Thomas, although I rated your squad untrained for the two collective tasks observed, there were sparks of brilliance. Your plan was well thought out, and your squad showed enthusiasm and determination even when everything began to go wrong. I did not observe any systemic problems and those problems that were identified should be easily correctable. Are there any further comments from anyone? *(Pause)*

"If not, this concludes the AAR. I enjoyed walking with you and wish you good luck on the next mission. May the force be with you."

MARKSMANSHIP[2]

Every noncommissioned officer, regardless of MOS, must know how to train soldiers in basic rifle marksmanship skills. Marksmanship proficiency is critical and basic to soldiering and is required for any unit deployed to a wartime theater. There is nothing else as important to a soldier, or as important for teaching NCOs how to train soldiers, than conducting marksmanship training.

The unit's combat mission must be considered when establishing training priorities. This not only applies to the tasks selected for the unit's METL but also the conditions under which the tasks are to be performed. If a unit may be employed in an urban environment, the effects of range, gravity, and wind may not be too important, but automatic or burst fire, quick fire, and assault fire would be. The reverse may be true of a unit that expects to engage the enemy at long ranges with rifle fire.

Marksmanship training is an individual task, and as such should be NCO led to the greatest extent possible. Each echelon of NCO leadership has a different piece of the planning and training pie. The command sergeant major is primarily responsible for the collective individual weapons training of his or her unit. At the company level, the first sergeant is responsible for the collec-

[2] Based on article published by Sgt. Maj. Robert S. Rush in *NCO Journal,* fall 1994.

tive individual weapons training of his or her company. Platoon sergeants train the trainer in the fundamentals of rifle marksmanship and ensure that the training is executed to standard, and the section/squad/team leaders, knowing their soldiers better than anyone else, are the primary trainers of their units.

Sergeant Major	**First Sergeant**	**Platoon Sergeant**	**Section /Squad Leaders**
Plan/resource	Resource/evaluate	Evaluate/train	Train

"First Sergeant, we are having problems zeroing some of our soldiers. We may have to change the rotation times for the firing orders, so that we can train the soldiers on how to achieve tight shot groups."

Dry firing is becoming a lost art within the U.S. Army. The term "dry fire" means to simulate the firing of live rounds with an empty weapon. Soldiers given proper dry-fire training move to the firing line and assume good, comfortable firing positions. They fully understand the aiming process, and breath control and correct trigger squeeze are second nature. Dry fire is an excellent training technique to use as concurrent training, opportunity training, or as a primary technique to maintain marksmanship proficiency.

While initial dry-fire training should focus on establishing a steady position, each phase should involve the full simulation of firing a shot—establishing a steady position, aim, breathing, and trigger squeeze.

If the firer, who is the best judge of position, can hold the front sight post "rock" steady through the fall of the hammer, this indicates a good position. Once the supported position has been mastered, the firer should work on the various unsupported positions.

Some of the other exercises that can be used during dry fire are the shadow box method (used to verify proper aiming), the dime/washer exercise (used to practice trigger squeeze), and the use of the Riddle sighting device (used to determine proper sight picture), all of which are explained in FM 3-22.9, *Rifle Marksmanship, M16A1, M16A2/3, M16A4, and M4 Carbine.*

"Sir, we don't have enough time to run all the soldiers through the qualification course on the Weaponeer. We need more Weaponeers."

The Weaponeer is a computerized training device that very closely approximates the live firing of an M16A1 rifle. It's an excellent marksmanship training device that can be used for skill development, problem diagnosis, remedial training, and evaluation. However, it's not a cure. Overreliance on Weaponeer use or other simulators, while avoiding more conventional means of preparatory marksmanship training, wastes good marksmanship training time. Use the Weaponeer or other computerized systems as diagnostic devices, letting each soldier spend a few minutes on them to determine what shooting problems there are and then relying on more conventional methods to help correct those problems.

"Specialist Jones is missing the farthest target. He's the best shot. There must be something wrong with the target mechanisms."

For many years, the Army's primary marksmanship program meant zeroing at twenty-five meters and practicing and qualifying on pop-up targets that provided only hit-or-miss data. This, coupled with the simplified approach to training that taught that the M16 bullet had a flat trajectory that was not influenced by wind and gravity, made it difficult for leaders to learn about bullet trajectory. Without knowledge of where bullets were hitting, target misses were blamed on bad rifles, bad shooting, or bad target mechanisms.

"Sergeant Jones, look at my shot group. What am I doing wrong?"

Training is more effective when leaders are directly involved in training their soldiers. First-line leaders, assisted by—if not one themselves—marksmanship trainers (in FM 23-31 known as instructor trainers), must teach and coach their own soldiers during basic rifle marksmanship and on the firing line. A good instructor-trainer must understand the training phases and techniques for developing marksmanship skills, and he must possess the following qualifications:

(1) ***Knowledge.*** Have a thorough knowledge of the rifle, proficiency in firing, and a thorough understanding of this manual and supporting manuals.
(2) ***Patience.*** Relate to the soldier calmly, persistently, and patiently.
(3) ***Understanding.*** Enhance success and understanding by emphasizing close observance of rules and instructions.
(4) ***Consideration.*** Enhance soldier enthusiasm for firing by encouraging firing abilities.
(5) ***Respect.*** Soldiers respect technical expertise, especially those alert for mistakes and patiently makes needed corrections.
(6) ***Encouragement.*** Encourage soldiers by convincing them to achieve good firing performance through practice.

An added benefit to marksmanship training is that it is one of the best methods in which to train subordinate leaders in how to train soldiers.

"The Commanding General is going to visit us at the qualification range Friday."

"Oh no, another dog-and-pony show!"

Many believe that "dog-and-pony" shows are a waste of time, and they are when it comes to pretty charts, designated parking areas, and briefing NCOs whose primary mission is to brief the VIPs. However, there are good points to such shows.

NCOs are prepared to teach classes, and teach them well, because they have done their homework. Soldiers get more out of training because sound training was conducted. We should consider soldiers the VIPs.

Other methods could be used to get better training out of the meager time and resources we have available for marksmanship training. What we have to remember is that an effective marksmanship program will reflect the interest that we place on it. We should provide the necessary refresher training to maintain standards, while conducting new and more advanced training to continue the improvement of individual shooting skills. A good program will focus on the tasks most important for mission accomplishment and will advance the soldier from more basic skills to those more complex. This will result in all soldiers being able to perform all shooting skills required in combat, the ultimate live-fire range.

8

Training at Service Schools

> America's Army is the envy of the world. Other nations look to model our tanks, our helicopters, our equipment, but the one area they wish they could model most is our NCO corps. Those nations recognize the depth and maturity of our corps and the value of our education system. We look at our past heritage for inspiration, to today's heroes for motivation, and then look to the future warrior and ask "what if." Sergeants continue to pass the torch of training, education, values, and ethos from our Greatest Generation to today's Next Greatest Generation.
>
> —Sgt. Maj. of the Army Kenneth O. Preston

NONCOMMISSIONED OFFICER EDUCATION SYSTEM (NCOES)
NCOES is an integral part of the Enlisted Personnel Management System (EPMS) and sustains the Army with trained leaders and technicians. The NCOES applies to all enlisted personnel of all components of the Army and is an integrated system of resident training—service school and NCO academy—that, combined with supervised on-the-job training, individual study, and on-the-job experience, provides job-related training for NCOs throughout their careers. The NCOES is designed to provide progressive, continuous training from the primary through the senior level.

Five skill levels representing progressively higher levels of performance capability, experience, and grade characterize the EPMS, and five levels of training have been established in support of these skill levels. Completion of initial entry training provides the soldier with the foundation of professional and technical knowledge needed to perform at the first duty station; combined with subsequent individual training in the unit, the soldier qualifies at skill level 1. The next four levels of training (primary, basic, advanced, and senior) are taught through the NCOES.

As an NCO you, as well as your soldiers, must realize the importance of NCOES to professional development and career progression. Do not look at

Enlisted Training System

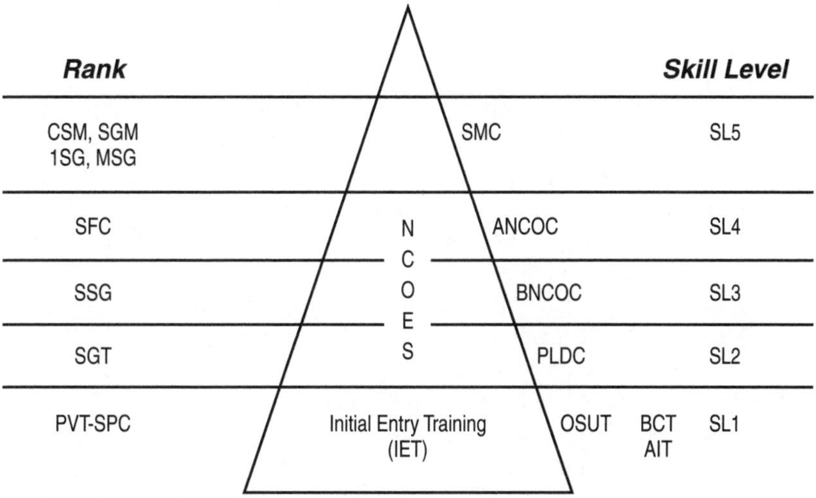

attendance as "a break" from routine duties. Most soldiers can easily pass any phase of NCOES, but to score in the top 20 percent is an achievement. Not only is graduation from the school a discriminator, but having board members see that you were among the best is also a discriminator. While in school, help those around you who need it, as you are all working together toward a common goal: graduation.

Graduation from the appropriate level NCOES school is a prerequisite for promotion. Full linkage of NCOES to promotions ensures that NCOs acquire the appropriate skills, knowledge, and duty performance needed to assume the duties and responsibilities of the next higher grade. The linkage aligns NCO professional and leader development with the Army philosophy of "select, train, promote, utilize."

Commanders and their senior NCOs at every level understand that NCOES training must receive high priority and that soldiers must attend school when scheduled. A strong, competent, and highly motivated NCO corps is every leader's responsibility, and promotion linkage ensures training the right soldier at the right time for the next level of leadership. Keeping a soldier away from school because he is needed hurts both the unit and the soldier—one because the unit never learns to do without its hard chargers, and the other because the sergeant stagnates in rank.

Command sergeants major, in concert with Army selection boards, ensure that soldiers who need NCOES training receive it. Soldiers who are not otherwise qualified will not be sent for training merely to fill a quota. In the past, the

Army's NCO academies were plagued by soldiers who did not want or deserve to be there.

Human Resources Command (HRC) schedules soldiers for resident training at Basic Noncommissioned Officers' Course (BNCOC), Advanced Noncommissioned Officers' Course (ANCOC), and the U.S. Army Sergeants Major Course (USASMC), while local selection authority governs attendance at Primary Leadership Development Course (PLDC). Soldiers are selected for PLDC based on a battalion-level (or equivalent) order of merit list. To be eligible, a soldier must accomplish the following:

- Have trained on 70 percent of all MOS tasks in his or her individual soldier's job book within the past six months.
- Have passed the Army Physical Fitness Test within the past six months.
- Meet the weight standards.
- Be eligible for reenlistment.
- Be recommended by his unit commander.

Time Remaining in Service

Regulatory guidance on the time remaining in service (TRS) obligation incurred after attending military schools is found in AR 614-200, chapter 4 ("Enlisted Assignments and Utilization Management"). Soldiers who are selected for and attend service schools incur a TRS obligation based on the length of the course, which begins upon completion of the course. Soldiers selected for special training programs must meet the TRS obligation prescribed for the program selected; the maximum TRS obligation is thirty-six months. NCOES courses require an obligation of six months, except the Sergeants Major Course, which incurs a twenty-four-month obligation. For example, to attend the Basic Noncommissioned Officers' Course (BNCOC), you must have six months remaining on your enlistment from the time you graduate. Soldiers with insufficient TRS to meet the prescribed TRS obligation must reenlist or extend before attending training. Voluntary retirements will not be approved for soldiers until after they have completed all TRS obligations, including those resulting from school attendance.

Profile Policy (Noncommissioned Officer Course Attendance)

Soldiers may not attend NCOES courses with a temporary profile. If you are scheduled for an NCOES course and you are on a temporary profile, or if the recovery period of the profile overlaps with your course report date, you should immediately notify your unit school's NCO and your installation training office. They will in turn notify the HRC NCOES section to cancel your reservation. Soldiers may attend NCOES courses with a permanent designator 2 (P2) physical profile with a copy of DA Form 3349 as long as they can meet the minimum course graduation requirements. Soldiers may attend NCOES courses with a permanent designator 3 (P3) or permanent designator 4 (P4) physical profile with a copy of DA Form 3349 that has been reviewed by a medical screening board. Soldiers who have not been medically screened and classified with appropriate limitations may not attend NCOES courses. Soldiers who have been before a medical screening board, awarded medical limitations, and allowed to retain their MOS or reclassified will be eligible to attend NCOES and will be required to meet course prerequisites up to the limits of their profile.

Pre-Execution Checklist

Effective February 1, 2000, all soldiers reporting to ANCOC/BNCOC must have in their possession a completed Pre-Execution Checklist, signed by the soldier and the unit commander. This checklist is found in Appendix H, U.S. Army Training and Doctrine Command (TRADOC) Regulation 350-18, *The Army School System* (TASS).

References: DA Message 152117Z Dec 99, DA Message 021858Z Dec 99, and DA Message 091600Z Apr 99.

Authorized NCOES Codes

The following letters and digits must be entered on a soldier's Personnel Qualification Record (PQR) so that HRC career managers may make accurate decisions. Soldiers are individually responsible for periodically reviewing their PQR to ensure that the codes are current and correct. If a soldier's NCOES code is incorrect, he or she must act immediately through the local personnel service center to correct the error. The soldier or the Personnel Service Center (PSC) can send a copy of the academic report (DA Form 1059) to Commander, U.S. Total Army Personnel Command, ATTN: TAPC-EPT-FN, 2461 Eisenhower Avenue, Alexandria, VA 22331-0457. The computer that screens for promotion and school selection eligibility will delete you from the eligibles before the board convenes if your code shows that you have not successfully completed the prerequisite NCOES for the school or grade. The eligibility/status codes are:

A — Sergeants Major Academy graduate (resident or nonresident program).
F — Sergeants Major Academy selectee (resident or nonresident program).
C — Sergeants Major Academy nongraduate (resident or nonresident program).
D — Sergeants Major Academy declinee (resident or nonresident program).
S — Advanced NCO Course graduate.
T — Advanced NCO Course selectee.
M — Advanced NCO Course nongraduate.
W — Basic NCO Course graduate.
2 — Primary NCO Course graduate.
0 — Has not completed any NCOES course.

NONCOMMISSIONED OFFICER ACADEMIES (NCOAS)

The mission of NCO academies is to provide NCOES training to qualified soldiers, to train them in the fundamentals of leadership, to prepare them to train subordinates, to offer them increased educational opportunities, to prepare them to work in all kinds of environments, to instill them with increased self-confidence and a sense of responsibility, and to provide selected personnel with specific critical MOS training. To ensure that soldiers are provided equal opportunity to attend NCOES courses, the NCOA network has been divided into geographic training regions. If certain NCOES training is not available within a region, that region's student population may receive its training at the nearest NCOA that offers the training. Appendix D, AR 351-1, lists the NCOA regions.

NCOA courses do not award an MOS, an additional skill identifier (ASI), or a higher skill level. Leadership courses offered in academies emphasize training management and leadership skills that focus on senior and subordinate relationships, needs of the soldier, discipline, counseling, and techniques of soldier motivation. While NCOAs ensure that students maintain high standards of military courtesy, conduct, and fitness, the level of discipline should not detract from the learning environment.

Overweight soldiers who report at any of the four NCOES courses are tape-tested by instructors to determine body fat content. If they are over the limit for their age, gender, and height, they are denied enrollment and sent home. Overweight soldiers returning to the unit are barred from reenlistment for failing an Army school, removed from any promotion list, and might ultimately be separated if they fail to make satisfactory progress in the weight-control program. And almost as important, the funds wasted on the round-trip ticket and airfare could have been used for another soldier.

Listed below are the Army's NCO academies (listed by location) with their courses and web sites, which contain welcome letters and provide packing lists, directions, phone numbers, and mailing addresses:

Aberdeen Proving Grounds, MD; BNCOC/ANCOC
www.goordnance.apg.army.mil/

Camp Jackson, Korea; PLDC
www.ncoa.korea.army.mil/

Fort Benning, GA; PLDC/BNCOC/ANCOC
www.infantry.army.mil/ncoa/

Fort Bliss, TX; PLDC/BNCOC/ANCOC/USASMC
www.airdefense.bliss.army.mil/secure/ncoa/

Fort Bragg, NC; PLDC
www.bragg.army.mil/ncoa/default.htm

Fort Campbell, KY; PLDC
www.campbell.army.mil/ncoa/ncoa.htm

Fort Drum, NY; PLDC
www.drum.army.mil/garrison/ncoacad/index.htm

Fort Eustis, VA; BNCOC/ANCOC
www.eustis.army.mil/ncoa/
Fort Gordon, GA; BNCOC/ANCOC
www.gordon.army.mil/rncoa/
Fort Hood, TX; PLDC
www.hood.army.mil/NCOA/
Fort Huachuca, AZ; BNCOC/ANCOC
www.huachuca-usaic.army.mil/SCHOOL/NCOA/index.htm
Fort Jackson, SC; BNCOC/ANCOC
www.jackson.army.mil/ncoa/index.htm
Fort Knox, KY; PLDC/BNCOC/ANCOC
www.knox.army.mil/school/ncoa/ncoa.htm
Fort Lee, VA; BNCOC/ANCOC
www.quartermaster.army.mil/NCO/
Fort Leonardwood, MO; BNCOC/ANCOC
www.wood.army.mil/mncoa/default.htm
Fort Lewis, WA; PLDC
www.lewis.army.mil/ncoa/index.htm
Fort Polk, LA; PLDC
www.jrtc-polk.army.mil/ncoa/
Fort Richardson, AK; PLDC
www.usarak.army.mil/ncoa/index.htm
Fort Rucker, AL; BNCOC/ANCOC
www-rucker.army.mil/NCOA/test%20web%20page.htm
Fort Sam Houston, TX; BNCOC/ANCOC
www.ncoa.amedd.army.mil/
Fort Sill, OK; PLDC/BNCOC/ANCOC
www.sill.army.mil/usancoa/
Fort Stewart, GA; PLDC
www.stewart.army.mil/Display.asp?Page=55A55D2D-9BC5-48C6-9FFD-8E45D30C5A04
Grafenwoehr, Germany; PLDC
www.grafenwoehr.army.mil/7ATC/default.htm
NCOA Hawaii; PLDC
(not available)
Updates can be found at
www.hrc.army.mil/site/active/epncoes/ncoalink.htm

Primary Leadership Development Course

The four-week, non-MOS-specific Primary Leadership Development Course (PLDC) is conducted at sixteen noncommissioned officer academies (NCOAs) worldwide. The course provides basic leadership training for soldiers selected for promotion to sergeant. The Primary Leadership Development Course provides an opportunity to acquire the skills, knowledge, and behaviors needed to lead a team-size unit and serves as the foundation for further training and development. PLDC is a branch-immaterial course conducted in an NCO academy live-in environment using the small-group instruction method with practical application, followed by hands-on, performance-oriented training conducted in a field environment, culminating with an extensive field training exercise (FTX). Training focuses on self-discipline; professional skills; leading, disciplining, and developing soldiers; and caring for soldiers and their families. Other areas include the planning, executing, and evaluating of individual or team training and the planning and executing of missions/tasks assigned to a team-size unit. Successful completion of PLDC establishes the foundation for further training and leader development. Small-group leaders assess the students' leadership potential and evaluate their ability to apply lessons learned and effectively lead their classmates in a tactical environment.

Attendance at PLDC is mandatory for promotion to sergeant. Priority of attendance goes to the sergeants who have not previously attended, E-4 promotable (P), and E-4 serving in leadership positions. Soldiers may appear before promotion boards; however, they cannot be promoted until they complete PLDC. Conditional promotions may occur when a soldier meets the cutoff score while operationally deployed.

Noncommissioned Officer Education System Equivalency for PLDC
Personnel support battalion (PSB) commanders may grant active component (AC) Primary Leadership Development Course (PLDC) equivalency to soldiers that successfully complete any of the following training:

Reserve Component Primary Leadership Course (RC-PLC)

Reserve Component Primary Noncommissioned Officer Course (RC-PNCOC)

Reserve Component Primary Leadership Development Course (RC-PLDC), BNCOC (must have completed phases I and II), or ANCOC (phase I)

Any of the several Marine Corps NCO Courses above the Corporal's Course

Any branch of service Officer Candidate School (OCS)

Reserve Officer's Training Course (ROTC) (from any service) advanced camp

U.S. Army or USMC Warrant Officer Candidate School

The following courses, among many others, are not equivalent to AC PLDC: any nonresident corresponding study programs, courses taught at the USMC institute in Washington, D.C., or any U.S. Air Force or U.S. Navy NCO training.

Soldiers must provide valid documentation before the personnel support battalions can process actions to select soldiers for promotions, schools, and other EPMS matters.

Basic NCO Course

Combat Arms (CA) /Combat Support (CS) /Combat Service Support (CSS) BNCOC is conducted at proponent service schools. Successful completion of BNCOC is a prerequisite to be considered for promotion to sergeant first class. Training lengths vary from two to nineteen weeks; with an observer/controller, (OC) attendance is currently aligned with Unit Focus Stabilization, Units of Action, and Brigade Combat Teams. A two-week common core supplements leadership training received at PLDC. Phase 2 (technical track) is hands-on, performance-oriented training normally conducted at the proponent service school with instruction in the MOS-specific areas, as well as in troop-leading procedures, physical fitness, and safety training. There may be gaps in time between phase 1 and phase 2 for those soldiers attending schools in two separate locations. Soldiers may also attend NCOES in an out-of-sequence order: technical track prior to common core. The common core VTT (video teletraining) concept is becoming the responsibility of the MACOM (Major Army command)/Installations. The technical track scheduling remains a DA (Department of the Army) responsibility.

The priority for BNCOC goes to a SSG (staff sergeant) by date of rank and then to a SGT (P) by promotion points as soldiers compete against their peers for a seat in a BNCOC. All soldiers attending BNCOC are scheduled via an automated system called the BNCOC Automated Reservation System (BARS). The system provides HRC with an order of merit listing of soldiers eligible to attend BNCOC. The order of merit listing emanates from criteria established

You get what you put into it.

by Headquarters, Department of the Army. The report enables HRC to identify the best qualified soldiers for training and nominate them to their commander for verification that the soldier is qualified to attend BNCOC. Commanders have the option of canceling the Human Resource Command nomination if the soldier is unqualified. If the commander cancels the nomination, HRC will then select a replacement.

The Army Training Requirements and Resources System (ATRRS) has a history file showing every soldier scheduled, whether the soldier arrived for training or was a no-show, and if the soldier was released, failed, or graduated. It is better to be a cancellation than a no-show; if there is a cogent reason you cannot attend, make sure your chain of command notifies the NCOES section.

Conditional Promotions to Staff Sergeant

The Office of the Deputy Chief of Staff for Personnel (ODCSPER) approves conditional promotions to staff sergeant for those soldiers who have met a cut-off score, but have not completed the Basic Noncommissioned Officer Course (BNCOC) through no fault of their own. Sergeants promoted to staff sergeant without BNCOC may be promoted conditionally. Conditional promotions are contingent upon the successful completion of the required level of NCOES. Those soldiers who receive a conditional promotion revert to their former rank and have their names removed from the local promotion standing list if they fail to meet the BNCOC requirement within one year of promotion or as scheduled by HRC. Soldiers not scheduled within one year will not lose their rank for nonattendance. Conditional promotions and NCOES were delinked effective January 1, 2004. Soldiers who fail to attend due to overweight, APFT failure, or any other reason will become the responsibility of the local commander to take action.

ADVANCED NCO COURSE

Soldiers who attend the Advanced Noncommissioned Officer Course (ANCOC) are selected by the Department of the Army SFC (sergeant first class) Advanced Noncommissioned Officer Course Selection Board. The zone of consideration is announced by HRC before each board convenes. Scheduling is done by the soldier's career branch who can answer any questions. The priority for ANCOC attendance is the SFC and the SSG(P) who has not attended.

The Advanced NCO Course (ANCOC) stresses common core and MOS-related tasks, with emphasis on technical and advanced leadership skills and knowledge of military subjects required to train and lead other soldiers at the platoon or comparable level.

ANCOC is a two-phased course, with phase 1 a twelve-day non-MOS-specific course taught in a resident service school (a noncommissioned officer academy live-in environment using classroom instruction with practical application). This course uses training support packages and the small-group process to teach the theory and principles of battle-focused common leader training and the war-fighting skills required to lead a platoon-size element in combat. This phase is a prerequisite to attending the MOS-specific training in phase 2. The phase 2 course lengths vary with MOS requirements.

An NCO must be an ANCOC graduate to be considered for promotion to MSG. All soldiers selected for promotion to SFC who have not previously attended ANCOC are automatic selectees. All SFCs with a date of rank of April 1, 1981 or later, must successfully complete ANCOC in order to be considered for promotion to MSG.

HRC announces the zone of consideration before each board convenes. An NCO must be an ANCOC graduate to compete for promotion to MSG (master sergeant). All soldiers selected for promotion to SFC who have not previously attended ANCOC are automatic selectees. Scheduling is done by the soldier's career branch. Priority for ANCOC attendance are SFC and SSG (P) who have not attended. HRC centrally manages ANCOC selection through a DA selection board. Soldiers attend ANCOC either in a temporary duty (TDY) en route status or TDY and return. Additionally, there may be an alternate ANCOC selection list based on the number of NCOs selected for promotion to SFC.

In keeping with "select-train-promote," the Army now sends NCOs to ANCOC only after selection for promotion to SFC, and soldiers normally attend ANCOC within a year after the release of the appropriate SFC selection list. Commanders may defer NCOs scheduled to attend ANCOC only once for operational reasons; other than this one operational deferment, the only deferment requests considered are for medical or compassionate reasons. No-shows at ANCOC for any reason other than those mentioned above result in the NCOs losing their promotion status.

Soldiers who report to ANCOC and fail to meet the enrollment requirement or fail to meet the course's academic requirements also will forfeit their promotion list status and their conditional promotion to SFC. Soldiers who fail to complete ANCOC will have to recompete for promotion during a subsequent SFC promotion board to regain ANCOC eligibility and/or SFC.

U.S. Army Sergeants Major Course (USASMC)

This nine-month course is the capstone of the NCOES. USASMC prepares master sergeants and first sergeants for senior troop and staff assignments throughout the defense establishment. Only the best qualified attend the sergeants major course, and being selected to attend is a large step forward in an NCO's career because course completion is mandatory for promotion to sergeant major and command sergeant major. The curriculum design broadens the senior NCOs already acquired knowledge and is quite different from the MOS-related training accomplished at the basic and advanced levels of the NCOES. The course provides an intellectually stimulating educational experience as well as a detailed study of contemporary subjects. The curriculum focuses on leadership, resource management, training management, and military operations at the highest levels throughout the Army.

Attendance at the USASMC is a permanent change of station to Fort Bliss, Texas. Spouses and families are an essential and vital part of the academy experience, and they are included in many educational, social, and recreational activities, many of which will assist students and their spouses in their new assignments.

Nonresident Sergeants Major Course

The U.S. Army Sergeants Major Academy Nonresident Course (NRC) is a two-year program that parallels the resident course curriculum. Graduates of both the resident and nonresident courses receive identical consideration for all personnel management decisions. Participation in this program is highly selective and consists of senior noncommissioned officers in the ranks of master sergeant, first sergeant, sergeant major, command sergeant major, and the equivalent ranks from sister services and allied nations.

Much like the resident course, the NRC provides an intellectually broadening educational experience as well as a detailed study of contemporary leadership subjects. Phase 1, the correspondence phase, consists of six modules with six to twelve lessons each, for a total of fifty-three lessons. There is a comprehensive exam at the end of each module to validate the student's knowledge of the material learned for each lesson. Phase 2 is conducted in residence at the U.S. Army Sergeants Major Academy, Fort Bliss, Texas. Those students satisfactorily completing phase 1 requirements are eligible to attend the seventeen-day resident phase during which period students complete the final graduation requirements and become graduates of the Sergeants Major Course.

Dismissal from Courses

Camp commandants may remove students from NCOES courses before course completion for disciplinary reasons, lack of motivation, academic deficiencies, or other valid reasons, such as illness or injury. Failure of a student to maintain established academic, physical fitness, conduct, and weight-control standards at any time during a course is cause for elimination. Failure to maintain standards may constitute an infraction of the Uniform Code of Military Justice (UCMJ) or may indicate a lack of motivation or aptitude.

Students whose actions during training constitute a probable violation of the UCMJ may be suspended, dismissed, or reported to a commander exercising court-martial jurisdiction. Students who show a probable lack of motivation will be counseled.

If disenrollment is determined to be appropriate and adequately documented, the commandant notifies the student in writing of the proposed action, the basis for the action, and the consequences of disenrollment. The student has the right to appeal but must submit any appeal within two days after receipt of written notification. A disinterested command sergeant major reviews the appeal.

Soldiers eliminated from the 1SG Course and the USASMC are not eligible for reentry. Those eliminated academically from other NCOES courses will not be eligible for further NCOES training for a period of six months.

NCOs dismissed for cause from an NCOES course face a mandatory bar to reenlistment or separation proceedings. "For cause" can mean for lack of discipline or motivation or for other problems, such as insubordination or alcohol abuse.

FUNCTIONAL COURSES FOR NCOS

Unlike NCO academy courses, functional courses are not generally mandatory—but they are quite important to day-to-day activities and mission-critical operations. Specifically identified senior NCOs, such as command sergeant major, first sergeant, battle staff, operations, and intelligence position selectees, either must or should attend the associated functional course. Additionally, NCOs who currently serve in one of these positions should voluntarily seek enrollment in the associated functional course. Functional courses are both career enhancing and beneficial from a professional viewpoint. The better armed you are with the skills, knowledge, and behaviors you may derive from such courses, the better prepared you will be on the job.

Command Sergeants Major Course (CSMC)

The CSMC is a five-day course designed to prepare promotable master sergeants (P) and sergeants major to perform the duties of a battalion command sergeant major. Subject areas include transition of the new command sergeant major as the senior enlisted advisor to the commander, interpersonal relationships with the command and staff, assigning and utilizing soldiers, boards, caring for soldiers and their families, and contemporary issues. It is highly recommended that your spouse attend the Command Sergeants Major Spouse Course, which runs concurrently with the CSMC.

First Sergeant's Course

All first-time first sergeants must attend with the goal of attending within six months of appointment, although soldiers on short tours of thirteen months or less will not be required to attend FSC while in the short tour area.

The course consists of two phases. Phase I contains thirty-one self-study lessons, with an examination upon completion. Phase II includes three weeks of interactive small-group instruction and is conducted here at Fort Bliss, at certain Army Reserve and National Guard Centers in the United States, or by Video Teletraining (VTT) at locations worldwide. Major subjects of study include training management, unit administration, communicative skills, discipline and morale, logistics and maintenance, tactical operations, and physical fitness training. No priority is given to MOS or unit status in the selection of students. The major commands select about 90 percent of each class, and HRC selects the other 10 percent. HRC's selectees attend the course in a TDY en route status, generally to an overseas duty position. Candidates for this five-week course must meet the physical fitness and weight standards. The course is conducted at the U.S. Army Sergeants Major Academy.

Battle Staff Noncommissioned Officer Course (BSNCOC)

The Battle Staff NCO Course trains battalion and brigade staff noncommissioned officers in the grades staff sergeant through sergeant major to serve as integral members of the battle staff and to manage the day-to-day operations of battalion or brigade command posts. Major subjects of study include plans, orders, and annexes; graphics and overlays; military intelligence, and combat service support operations.

This course consists of two phases. Phase 1 contains twenty-three self-study lessons with an examination upon completion. Phase 2 consists of academic instruction followed by a command post exercise that includes interactive small-group instruction. It is conducted at the USASMA, Fort McCoy, Wisconsin, or at one of the video teletraining (VTT) locations certified to instruct the BSNCOC. The length of phase 2 depends on where the student attends the course.

Drill Sergeant Course

The Drill Sergeant Course is a functional course providing qualified NCOs with specialized training, resulting in the awarding of the "X" skill qualification identifier. The nine-week (forty-five days) resident course is conducted at three Drill Sergeant Schools (DSSs) and consists of twelve major subject areas. The course objective is to refine noncommissioned officers' skills of leadership, instructional techniques, and counseling, which, combined with occupational specialty skills, will ultimately enable them to train civilians to be soldiers.

Recruiting Course

The purpose of this course is to provide selected enlisted personnel with the skills, knowledge, and techniques required to perform as U.S. Army and Army Reserve recruiters. The curriculum is divided into five major segments: introduction to recruiting, management, eligibility, prospecting, and sales techniques/communication skills. The largest segment is devoted to the study of sales techniques and communications skills and is designed to equip the Army recruiter with the abilities that will effectively enable the recruiter to persuade qualified men and women to enlist in the U.S. Army. This course is held at Fort Jackson, South Carolina.

Equal Opportunity (EO)

The Defense Equal Opportunity Management Institute (DEOMI) curriculum consists of two resident courses: a fifteen-week EO Advisor Course and a six-week EO Program Manager Course. A three-phase Reserve Component EO Advisor Course, consisting of two two-week resident phases and one nonresident phase, is conducted for Army National Guard (ARNG) and U.S. Army Reserve (USAR) personnel.

SPECIALIZED COURSES FOR NCOS

Soldiers may apply for a number of additional qualification training courses. (Soldiers are sometimes directed to take certain language training in connection with special assignments.)

Air Assault Course

Obstacle courses, physical training, aircraft safety, Pathfinder operations, combat assaults, sling-loading operations, rappelling from UH-60 Black Hawk helicopters, twelve-mile road marches with rucksack and rifle—this ten-day course is packed with challenge. To attend, soldiers must receive permission from their commander and pass the APFT (in the seventeen- to twenty-one-year-old age group).

Airborne Course

Airborne training is available on a voluntary basis for enlisted personnel, without regard to current assignment, who will be assigned to an airborne unit after training. This functional training is conducted by the U.S. Army Infantry School and is designed to qualify volunteers in the use of the parachute as a means of deployment, and through mental and physical training, to develop leadership, self-confidence, and an aggressive spirit. Graduates receive an additional skill identifier (P). Eligible personnel volunteering for airborne training should submit applications according to the instructions contained in AR 614-200 and should be physically qualified for parachute duty in accordance with AR 40-501.

Language Training

The Defense Language Program is designed to provide personnel the minimum essential professional linguistic skills needed to meet specific Army requirements. Basic language training is provided through the Defense Language Institute, Presidio of Monterey, California. Training requires full-time attendance. Nonresident training is conducted in education centers, units, or established language training facilities using approved materials. Details of the management of the program are set forth in AR 350-20, AT 611-6, and AR 621-5. An additional skill identifier (L) is usually awarded to graduates of the program.

Ranger Training

This voluntary training conducted by the U.S. Army Infantry School, Fort Benning, Georgia, is designed to develop leadership skills and provide a knowledge of Ranger operations involving direct combat with the enemy. Nonairborne enlisted graduates receive a special qualification identifier (G) for their MOS code, while those who are airborne qualified receive a V. Ranger training is available on a voluntary basis principally for enlisted soldiers who are in the following MOSs: any Infantry or Special Forces MOS, 12B—Combat Engineer, 13F—Fire Support Sergeant, 14S—Avenger Crewman, 19D—Cavalry Scout, and 19K—Armor Crewman. Ranger School is now also available to combat support and combat service (MCS/CSS) support soldiers within the combat arms exclusion policy. Because many of the the tasks evaluated at Ranger School are outside the CS/CSS arena, successful completion of a Pre-Ranger program is essential for CS/CSS student success. Submit applications according to the instructions contained in AR 614-200. In my opinion, this is the best small-unit leadership training in the Army, if not the world, bar none!

Special Forces Training

Special Forces training is available for all male soldiers with any MOS, however, combat arms branches are preferred. Applicants must be in the rank of SPC specialist (P) through SSG and meet the course criteria as outlined in AR 614-200, chapter 5, section I, Special Forces Assignments (policy and selection criteria). Soldiers who meet the prerequisites and who volunteer for Special Forces training must be airborne qualified and must attend and successfully complete the three-week Special Forces Selection and Assessment Course, which assesses tactical skills, leadership, physical fitness, motivation, and a student's ability to cope with stress. Students are in a TDY (temporary duty) and return status during the course. Those who pass are scheduled to attend the Special Forces Qualification Course. Soldiers who attend the qualification course must complete a common phase, an MOS-specific phase, and a final phase that combines and tests what was learned in the first two phases. Depending on the MOS (weapons, engineering, communications, medical, intelligence), the qualification course can vary from twenty-six to fifty-seven weeks, depending on the MOS. Language training may also be required. The primary training site for Special Forces training is Fort Bragg, North Carolina.

DISTANCE LEARNING

The Army has entered the digital age with soldiers attending classes at their post; where through digital and video teleconferencing (VTC) links they attend courses presented by schools and instructors located at far-off institutions. Soldiers attending courses, whether through a resident school, a Total Army Schools System (TASS) Training Battalion, or a digital learning facility, receive the same credit for successfully completing training, with documentation in the soldier's Military Personnel Records Jacket (MPRJ) reflecting identical codes for any of the training types. All diplomas, certificates, or DA Form 1059 will be the same and not reflect nonresident, distant learning, reserve component, or other similar remarks. Promotion and evaluation boards will not discriminate against soldiers who completed their professional military training through distant learning.

First priority for all components is mission immediate training required for mobilization, activation, deployment, or other critical, time-sensitive requirements. Second priority is to HQDA directed/quota-managed training, such as MOS reclassification and NCOES courses with the reserve components, and NCOES, Additional Skill Identifier (ASI) and Special Qualification Identifier (SQI) courses, and MOS reclassification for active duty. Third priority is to reserve component ASI/SQI courses and civilian training. The remaining priorities are for functional training courses, self-development courses, and training courses provided to the civilian community.

Soldiers may split their training phases, with some at the resident school or at a TASS Battalion and the remainder conducted through distant learning while at their home station. One of the considerations for determining training location is whether the costs of TASS or distant learning exceed the costs of sending a soldier to the proponent school for the full resident course.

9

Self-Development

SETTING PROFESSIONAL GOALS

Weapon systems superiority is not the only bedrock of American Army success; leadership development also is, and everything you do should focus in that direction.

Self-development means both development of the self as a leader and development of oneself. Unlike thirty years ago, no one remains at one rank forever. The retention control points force you to move up or get out. Promotion in any MOS has certain elements applicable to all. With promotions being competitive, you must do the best you can at whatever you do. Identify yourself to the chain of command (and the board) through your good actions and as a soldier who is above his peers, whether holding a table of organization and equipment (TOE) or a table of distribution and allowance (TDA) position.

Secondly, seek leadership positions as early as possible within your career management field (CMF). You should be performing duties in your primary MOS at the authorized or next higher grade. Take advantage of any opportunity to serve in a leadership position at the next higher grade, as you might not get the opportunity again. Next is physical fitness. For a soldier, physical fitness is essential; nothing more need be said. Additionally, it is important to round out your career with duty in both TOE and TDA units. A number of high-priority assignments—drill sergeant, recruiting, ROTC, and active and reserve components—provide unique professional development opportunities for NCOs and a chance to catch your breath and reflect.

Finally, you should take advantage of every opportunity to attend military and civilian schools. Begin taking Army correspondence courses early in your career. Take college courses if you are in a position to do so. The additional military and civilian education that you achieve on your own shows the chain of command that you are a self-starter seeking to improve yourself. Additionally, it will improve your chances for promotion by converting educational credit into promotion points. Remember, however, that your leaders recommend you for promotion because of your duty performance.

THE NCO ROAD MAP TO SUCCESS

Rank	Assignments	Positions	Military Schools	NCOES	Promotion
Sergeant	The focus during this stage of your career should be on developing your leadership skills, technical expertise, and tactical knowledge.	Almost all positions held while a SGT should be in TOE organizations so that you can develop your skills in leading soldiers and improve your MOS knowledge. Leadership positions you can hold are team leader (TL) and squad leader (SL).[1]	There are many MOS-specific schools available to you at this grade.[2] Non-MOS-specific schools available to you are air assault, and airborne.	The Basic NCO Course (BNCOC) is a requirement for promotion to the rank of staff sergeant. BNCOC is an MOS-specific course that provides SGTs (P) with the technical, tactical, and leadership training necessary to prepare them to lead and train soldiers.	

[1] A very small number of exceptionally qualified SGTs may be DA selected for recruiting duty. Recruiting duty is vital and necessary to ensure an accession of highly motivated men and women into our Army. Recruiting duty is a stabilized three-year tour. Twelve months before completing your tour you must contact your career advisor and request to return to a TOE unit.

[2] For more information regarding prerequisites and availability of these schools, see your battalion school's NCO and the *Army Formal Schools Catalog*, DA Pam 351-4.

THE NCO ROAD MAP TO SUCCESS

Rank	Assignments	Positions	Military Schools	NCOES	Promotion
Staff Sergeant	The critical assignment at this stage of your career is squad leader. In order for you to be considered "branch qualified" at this grade level you should have at least 18 to 36 rated months of squad leader time.	It is during this stage of your career that you may start serving in other TOE assignments. However, before requesting a TDA position you should ensure that you have built a solid base of troop time. There are many different positions you can hold as a SSG, including squad leader, platoon sergeant, drill sergeant, reserve component duty, observer/controller, recruiter, TRADOC instructor.	Non-MOS-specific schools available to you are Recruiting School, Drill Sergeant School, Battle Staff Course.	The Advanced NCO Course is a requirement for promotion to SFC. ANCOC prepares SSGs (P) to become technically and tactically proficient at skill level 4 and 5 tasks. Currently SSGs selected for promotion to SFC will automatically attend ANCOC.	A DA centralized board selects SSGs for promotion to SFC. The board relies entirely on your Official Military Personnel File (OMPF), your Personnel Qualification Record (DA Forms 2-1 and 2-A), and your military photograph. The condition of your OMPF and the quality of your photo are the basis for promotion.

THE NCO ROAD MAP TO SUCCESS

Rank	Assignments	Positions	Military Schools	NCOES	Promotion
Sergeant First Class	The critical assignment at this stage of your career is platoon sergeant. More than any leadership assignment, platoon sergeant is the assignment you must have and excel in if you want to advance to MSG and SGM/CSM. You should attempt to hold this assignment for 18 to 30 months.	The primary positions you can hold as a SFC are platoon sergeant and first sergeant. TDA positions include reserve component duty, recruiter, drill sergeant, ROTC instructor, TRADOC instructor.	Schools available to you at this level are Ranger, Pathfinder, Battle Staff, Recruiter, First Sergeant, Drill Sergeant, and EO.	Upon completion of ANCOC you have completed all necessary levels of NCOES until selected for promotion to SGM; then you must attend the Sergeants Major Academy (SMA).	As with the DA centralized board for promotion to SFC, there is a DA centralized promotion board for selection to MSG.
Master Sergeant	The critical assignment for a master sergeant is first sergeant. Demonstrated superior performance while serving in a first sergeant position (strive for 24 months) is the best message to the SGM/CSM selection board.	The primary positions you can hold are first sergeant, detachment sergeant, and operations sergeant. TDA positions at this level are reserve component duty, ROTC instructor, TRADOC instructor.	Schools at this level are limited to the following: Battle Staff, First Sergeant, Ranger, and EO.	The final level in this NCOES is the Sergeants Major Academy, which is a requirement for promotion to SGM/CSM.	A DA centralized board selects soldiers for attendance at the SMA. A DA centralized board selects MSGs for promotion to SGM/CSM.

NCO Road Map for Success

The following career development guide uses a standard format for each grade covered. It includes rank, key leadership assignments, duty positions, military schools, and the Noncommissioned Officer Education System (NCOES). Much is extracted from enlisted newsletters at the G1 web site at *www.hrc.army.mil/site/Active/enlist/ENLIST.htm.*

You should actively seek information and guidance from your chain of command, mentors, and career advisor. You must play an integral part in the decision and assignment process in order to achieve the goals you have set for yourself. The bottom line is, if you do not help make the decisions, someone else will make them for you.

Your career branch is there to assist you in determining what is right for you, both professionally and personally. You should maintain communication with your branch to inquire about your next move, school, or promotion. For further information or assistance, contact the Soldier Assistance Center at (703) 325-7792/3 or toll free at (800) ALL ARMY, or check the web site listed in the paragraph above.

DA Pam 600-25, *Noncommissioned Officer Professional Development Guide,* was revised in 2002 to better provide noncommissioned officers with more robust career development guidance. The new pamphlet specifically identifies the duties, prerequisites, required institutional training, and recommended self-development for NCOs in each MOS by career management field and skill level. The pamphlet is available in a portable data file (PDF) through the Soldier Support Institute's web site at *www.usassi.army.mil/references.html.*

Individual Study: Enhancing Your Leadership Abilities

The learning process is an individual endeavor and is not just about more schooling. Develop yourself by *observing* both good and bad leaders in action; listen to your subordinates' comments, aspirations, and frustrations to gain their perspective; and read about wartime leaders to obtain a perspective that few experience, but all should study. Analyze your experiences and think about how you can be better. Soldiers who do not think about their experiences will stagnate, continue to live with their existing mental models, and never fully develop their potential.

Remember, however, that you cannot evaluate your own effectiveness with total objectivity; consider others' perceptions and attempt to reconcile the differences between their perceptions and your own. Seldom formal, these talks might take place over the hood of a Humvee, sitting against a tree in the field, in the motor pool, through e-mails with someone you seldom meet, or even over a cold drink at a social event.

The Self-Development Process

Every NCO has the professional responsibility to continually seek self-improvement and self-development wherever the soldier is and no matter what the soldier is doing. Self-development focuses on maximizing leader strengths, minimizing weaknesses, and achieving individual goals.

Just as having an accurate understanding of friendly and enemy unit strengths and weaknesses is paramount to successful military operations, having an accurate understanding of individual strengths and weaknesses is paramount to the development of an effective self-development action plan. Follow your assessment with frank discussions with those you trust to identify what makes you strong in some areas and weak in others. Develop your action plan to highlight and prioritize the specific actions that you should take to achieve your self-developmental goals.

Your action plans should focus on the following activities that categorize your goals over time:

- Immediate goals focus on accomplishing tasks related to the current job and are therefore very specific.

Job training is continuous . . . Here, soldiers in Afghanistan conduct battle drills to maintain proficiency.

- Near-term goals are somewhat broader in scope and develop leaders for their responsibilities at the next operational assignment.
- Long-term goals are the activities that have the broadest scope, focusing on tasks that prepare leaders for their duties and responsibilities beyond their next operational assignment.

Noncommissioned officer self-development activities are the broadest in nature and are limited only by your imagination. These activities include attending military and civilian education courses, participating in professional organizations, reading professional materials, seeking challenging assignments, practicing critical leader technical and tactical tasks, and participating in leadership activities in both the military and civilian communities.

ARMY CONTINUING EDUCATION SYSTEM (ACES)

The Army Continuing Education System (ACES) through its many programs promotes lifelong learning opportunities and sharpens the competitive edge of the Army, 2010 and beyond. ACES is committed to excellence in service, innovation, and deployability. Today's soldier can take advantage of numerous educational programs. The comprehensive web site for Army education is at *www.armyeducation.army.mil/*.

Your *Army Continuing Education System Record,* DA Form 669, can serve a very important purpose during your military career or it can collect dust. Maintained at your local Army Education Center, it contains information used by education counselors to document your pursuit of higher education. Semester after semester throughout your career, you should (whenever the mission allows) contribute course completion slips to your record. Consider it as making regular deposits to an intellectual savings account that grows enormous interest—the kind that Army promotion boards and civilian employers will have for you as your educational value increases.

You should invest in yourself. The Army does and benefits in the process. The Army Continuing Education System's mission is, in part, to improve the combat readiness of the Army by planning, researching, and implementing educational programs and services to support the professional and personal development of quality soldiers and their adult family members, according to AR 621-5. In support of the mission, ACES supports five goals, three of which apply to soldiers:

- Develop confident, competent leaders.
- Support the enlistment, retention, and transition of soldiers.
- Provide personal development opportunities for soldiers.

The ACES meets its mission goals by providing quality educational programs and services throughout the Army. Education and training mutually support and enhance the combat readiness of the Army and are essential elements in the NCO Development Program. ACES programs and services are designed to expand soldiers' skills, knowledge, and behavior. Programs and services discussed later in this chapter contribute to the three pillars of leader development: institutional training, operational assignments, and self-development.

Individual development, supported by ACES, is a planned, progressive, sequential program that leaders use to enhance and sustain the leadership plan discussed earlier.

Under the guidelines of AR 621-5, NCOs and the soldiers they lead should meet the following educational objectives:

- Master academic skills needed to perform duties of their primary MOS and meet prerequisites for the NCO Education System.
- In cases of exception to the enlistment rule regarding having a high school diploma, earn a high school diploma or equivalent before completing a first enlistment.
- Earn a college degree, license, or professional certificate in an MOS-related discipline, as recommended in DA Pam 600-25,*U.S. Army Noncommissioned Officer Professional Development Guide.*

Army Education Center Counselors

Counselors are wonderful people who are critical to the success of the ACES mission. They help soldiers establish realistic education goals and continue to provide counseling through attainment of the goals. They also help soldiers get the maximum benefit from limited tuition assistance and other resources. AR 621-5 requires that soldiers new to an installation receive education counseling within the first thirty days of their arrival, and then receive follow-up counseling as needed.

Soldiers should not need a regulatory push to receive counseling; they should virtually run to get the valuable advice and assistance that counselors provide. Counselors help with school selection; application procedures, which can be lengthy and complex; prerequisite assessments; and financial aid. When they cannot help locate financial aid for formal courses of instruction, counselors can recommend free alternative methods of obtaining educational credit. (See Defense Activity for Nontraditional Education Support) (DANTES), College Level Examination Program (CLEP), and Graduate Record Examinations (GRE) below.) Nevertheless, soldiers must take the first step and call the local Army Education Center, make an appointment, and speak with a counselor. There, a soldier can increase MOS proficiency, prepare for the GED or CLEP, and pursue personal enrichment.

Army Learning Center (ALC)

Army Learning Centers (ALCs) are the military education elements of the Army Education Center. The on-post ALC is the primary source for self-development materials. All services at the ALC are free of charge.

Military Publications and Training Aids. The ALC has thousands of military references, including Army regulations, field manuals, technical manuals, Department of the Army circulars, and pamphlets, which can be checked out. Additionally, the ALC has a wide selection of training aids (computers with CD ROM- and DVD-based training courses), video and audio training programs, microfiche readers, as well as the older training education center (TEC) machines, etc., to meet the training needs of the population served.

Self-Development Materials. The ALC has numerous materials focused on the self-development pillar of leader development. Some of these materials include videotapes on military training; the Annenberg Project Center for Public Broadcasting (AP/CPB) Program; the Dick Cavett Speed Reading Program; the NCO Read-to-Lead Program; study guides for most DANTES tests; ACT, SAT, CLEP, and GED video programs; Guidance Information Systems III (a college database program); and college catalogs on microfiche. Each ALC is equipped with state-of-the-art computer systems. All computers have Internet access and are loaded with a minimum of Microsoft (MS) Office 97 and Guidance Information Systems III software. ALC customers can use these computers for research, preparing college papers, registering for an Army correspondence course, job searches, or any other self-developmental activity.

Army Correspondence Course Program

Army correspondence courses are available through the Army Institute for Professional Development. Courses are designed for your professional development and include individual subcourses on specific topics developed by respective proponent schools. You may enroll in this program as an individual student or via the group enrollment program. Group enrollment allows an NCO to use these courses to supplement individual training. It provides professionally designed training for the NCO supervisor and awards promotion points for those who successfully complete each subcourse. The ALC provides assistance in determining applicable courses and aids in resolving administrative problems individuals may have with courses or schools.

Of special interest are the Green Book *(www.atsc.army.mil/accp/grnbook.asp)* courses, which combine two series of correspondence courses. The Primary Leadership Subjects cover math skills, reading comprehension, study methods, management, and writing mechanics/composition. The second course, Basic Leadership Subjects, is for those students ready to attend the Basic Noncommissioned Officer Course (BNCOC). It contains lessons on communications, behavioral sciences, and briefings/visual presentations.

High School Completion Program (HSCP)

The HSCP is an off-duty program that provides soldiers and adult family members the opportunity to earn a high school diploma or equivalency certificate. Tuition assistance is authorized for soldiers up to 100 percent of the costs of courses, subject to the following: ACES will pay tuition assistance only to accredited institutions and will not pay fees covering such items as books, matriculation, graduation, and parking.

Montgomery GI Bill enrollees must finish a high school completion program or earn an equivalent certification during their first enlistment. The HSCP is open to all non-high school graduates.

Functional Academic Skills Training (FAST)

The FAST Program, formerly called Basic Skills Education Program, provides instruction in academic competencies necessary for job proficiency and preparation for advanced training. FAST, available at Army Learning Centers, helps improve soldiers' job performance and helps them meet reenlistment eligibility and MOS classification requirements.

Because this program is self-paced, using instructional material (software at those ALCs that are computer equipped), FAST is available during duty and off-duty hours. FAST covers reading, writing, arithmetic, and other subjects that soldiers must comprehend to excel in service.

COLLEGE DEGREE PROGRAMS

Thousands of degree programs are available to soldiers—too many to list here. But you may use dedicated resources to find out more information about obtaining an Associate in Arts or Associate in Science degree, a Bachelor of Arts or Bachelor of Science degree, or a Master of Arts or Master of Science degree. A recent edition of the *Army Veterans Education Guide* contained brief articles with the following information:

- What to look for in a college.
- How to use your educational benefits.
- How to select a college major.
- What to understand about Servicemembers Opportunity Colleges (SOC).

You may obtain the guide through your local Army Education Center.

If you want to take college courses but are concerned about your ability to comprehend course material, use DA Pam 351-20, the *Army Correspondence Course Program Catalog*. It contains numerous courses covering practically every MOS in the Army, as well as courses in basic math, English, and science. For example, suppose you want to earn an electrical engineering degree. You could contact your local education center to request the basic electricity course listed in the pamphlet. The course is open to "any student who meets the basic qualifications for correspondence study." After successfully completing seventeen sequential electricity subcourses, you should be fully prepared to enroll in a college course that deals with the subject of electricity. Apply this method to other subjects and you will see the value of "boning up" through correspondence studies.

Servicemembers Opportunity Colleges (SOC)

The SOC is a network of schools across the country and overseas that have recognized and responded to soldiers' expectations for postsecondary education. They must have liberal entrance requirements, allow soldiers to complete courses through nontraditional modes, provide academic advisement, offer maximum credit for experiences obtained in service, have residence requirements that are adaptable to the special needs of soldiers, have a transfer policy that recognizes traditional and nontraditional learning obtained at other schools, promote the SOC, and provide educational support to servicemembers.

Under the Servicemembers Opportunity Colleges Army Degree (SOCAD) Program, a part of SOC, there are degree and certification programs wherein a soldier is normally awarded a degree or certificate for an academic or technical course of study, with the programs developed to provide common curricula in disciplines related to Army MOSs. Course work taken from colleges and universities to complete an Army Career Degree, however, does not substitute for military training core courses of the Noncommissioned Officer Education System (NCOES). This course work, however, should be complementary and supportive of the soldier's career development.

Army Career Degrees provide soldiers credible options for completing college while making the Army their career. NCOs receive a briefing on the SOC Army Career Degree as well as other degree options when they attend their Basic Noncommissioned Officer Course (BNCOC). This new program allows soldiers to maximize the learning achieved through their Army career development while permitting them to complete degree programs through distance learning anywhere in the world.

The SOCAD student agreement gives the soldier a one-time evaluation of everything the soldier has done that can be credited toward the college degree and lists what the soldier must take to graduate. The SOCAD colleges require soldiers to take no more than 25 percent of their course work with that college to receive their degree—not necessarily on campus, but from their offerings and elsewhere. Once a soldier completes residency, future courses taken at other colleges will be accepted and applied toward the soldier's original degree plan.

eArmyU

Another new initiative toward assisting soldiers in achieving their educational goals is eArmyU. This program is entirely on-line, offering soldiers a streamlined "portal" approach to a variety of postsecondary degrees and technical certificates. All courses allow soldiers to study on their own schedule. Highly motivated soldiers can complete degree and certification requirements regardless of work schedules, family responsibilities, and deployments.

eArmyU Benefits. All eligible soldiers receive 100 percent tuition up to $250 per semester hour, whichever is less, with a ceiling of $4,500. Tuition Assistance (TA) covers tuition, fees, books, academic advisement, library resources, and administrative and technical support. Tuition Assistance for eCourse enrollees is on a course-by-course basis, subject to the availability of funds. Effective February 1, 2005, eligible E4, E5, and E6 soldiers, with less than ten years service, who reenlist may participate in the Technology Package (laptop) option, if they meet eligibility requirements. Added to the existing education programs and services available, this on-line program helps to ensure that all soldiers have the opportunity to fulfill their personal and professional educational goals while simultaneously building the technology, critical thinking, and decision-making skills required to fully transform the Army.

Soldier Eligibility. To be eligible for participation in this program, soldiers must be regular active-duty or active guard reserve enlisted soldiers with at least three years remaining on their enlistment. Soldiers may extend or reenlist to meet this requirement. More information on eArmyU can be found at *www.earmyu.com/default.asp*.

College Credit for Military Experience

Army Education Center counselors can help you complete DD Form 295, *Application for the Evaluation of Learning Experiences during Military Service*. The completed form is used to inform institutions, agencies, and employers about in-service educational achievements. Schools use the form to determine how many and what kinds of college credits to award to soldiers based on military education, training, and experience. Your pursuit of a degree should include completing and forwarding DD Form 295 to the college or university of your choice.

The American Council on Education evaluates Army service school courses and recommends the number of semester hours of credit that civilian schools may award based on a soldier's military training and experience. Examples include vocational, lower-level baccalaureate and associate's degrees, upper-level baccalaureate, and graduate-level credits. These recommendations are published in the *Guide to the Evaluation of Educational Experiences in the Armed Services* (ACE Guide).

Independent Study and Examination Programs for College Credit

If you are working on an undergraduate (associate's or bachelor's) degree, you should know about independent ways to earn credit through the following programs: Defense Activity for Nontraditional Education Support (DANTES), including the College Level Examination Program (CLEP) and Defense Subject Standardized Tests (DSST); American College Testing Proficiency Examination Program (ACTPEP); Graduate Record Examinations (GRE); and Annenberg Project and Center for Public Broadcasting (AP/CPB).

The DANTES, CLEP, DSST, ACTPEP, GRE, and AP/CPB offerings all require independent study. Many subject packets include texts, workbooks, and audio or videotapes that are used in conjunction with the paper materials. Most of the for-credit tests offered by these programs and agencies are worth three or four semester hours of credit each. The GRE, which includes a general exam and subject exams, is worth much more. The GRE sociology examination, for example, is worth thirty semester hours of undergraduate credit, fifteen lower division (100 and 200 level) and fifteen upper division (300 and 400 level).

DANTES independent study and examination program services are available to all eligible active-duty soldiers. One important aspect of DANTES is the College Level Examination Program (CLEP), which also enables students to earn credit by examination. The examinations measure knowledge of the basic concepts and applications involved in courses that have the same or similar titles. They are divided into two types: general examinations and subject examinations.

The general examination measures college-level achievement in five basic areas of the liberal arts: English composition, social sciences and history, natural sciences, humanities, and mathematics. The test material covers the first year of college, often referred to as the general or liberal education requirement.

Subject examinations measure achievement in specific college courses and are worth course credit. Examples of test titles include Introduction to Business Management, General Psychology, Western Civilization, and American Literature.

Each civilian educational institution has its own evaluating criteria for using CLEP test scores to determine credit. You should have official transcripts forwarded to the registrar of the college or university at which you desire to receive credit (some institutions require that a minimum number of semester hours of classwork be completed before CLEP credit will be accepted). Another type of subject test that, like CLEP, substitutes for college classroom work is the DANTES Subject Standardized Tests.

THE SKILL RECOGNITION PROGRAM

The Skill Recognition Program provides ways to get recognition within the civilian sector for skills learned in service. This recognition can come in the following forms.

Army Apprenticeship

This program provides participants with documentation of apprentice skills acquired while in the Army that is understood by civilian industry. It improves the performance and motivation of soldiers, provides a recruiting incentive for MOSs that are related to skills with apprenticeships, and improves the supervisor-soldier relationship.

Occupations with apprenticeships are those that are learned through experience and on-the-job training and are supplemented by related technical instruction. They involve manual, mechanical, or technological skills and knowledge requiring a minimum of 2,000 hours of work experience plus related instruction. They do not fall into the categories of selling, management, clerical, or professional skills requiring advanced knowledge and academic degrees. These apprenticeship occupations are identified in Department of Labor pamphlets; Appendix I, AR 621-5; and DA Pam 621-200, *Army Apprenticeship Program Procedural Guidance.*

Enrollment is open to soldiers who perform satisfactorily on the job and possess an MOS (primary or secondary) that relates to the program and that has been registered with the Bureau of Apprenticeship Training. Also eligible are soldiers who possess a qualifying MOS in which they were initially registered but are no longer serving because of priorities and mission requirements.

Army training programs will not be altered to meet civilian standards for skill recognition programs. As a prerequisite to registration, certification, or formal recognition, however, some civilian agencies might require additional nonmission-related training or experience before recognizing a soldier as fully qualified. When this is necessary, the soldier must acquire the additional training and experience through local trade or vocational schools, or by other means. Programs stress individual initiative. An individual cannot be enrolled in more than one occupational skill area within an apprenticeship program at any one time. The soldier may, however, change to another occupational area or program as many times as desired, provided prerequisites are met.

THE GI BILL

Valuable education benefits offered under the GI Bill are available today for would-be college graduates and for those soldiers who wish to pursue certain kinds of training. Originally named the Servicemen's Readjustment Act of 1944, which was signed into law by Pres. Franklin D. Roosevelt on June 22 of that year, the GI Bill—now called the Montgomery GI Bill after its latest champion, Congressman G. V. "Sonny" Montgomery—takes the following forms: the Montgomery Active Duty GI Bill and the Montgomery Selected Reserve GI Bill. The post-Vietnam Veterans Educational Assistance Program (VEAP) is also covered by the Montgomery GI Bill. Valued at hundreds of dollars a month for up to thirty-six months, a wide range of benefits at various levels are available. I cannot stress strongly enough that you should take full advantage of the benefits to which you are entitled.

The Montgomery Active Duty GI Bill (MGIB)

The Montgomery Active-Duty GI Bill (chapter 30, U.S. Code [USC]) provides up to thirty-six months of benefits. Soldiers covered by category I of this program are entered active duty after June 30, 1985, and contributed a nonrefundable $100 a month for the first twelve months of service. Active-duty members may begin using their benefits after completing two years of service. Members of the National Guard who are in the Active Guard and Reserve Program also are covered by this contributory program, but they must have entered service after November 29, 1989, and must not have previously served on active duty. (See category IV.)

Soldiers with remaining benefits under the Vietnam Era GI Bill (chapter 34, USC) are entitled to benefits through an automatic conversion to category I of the Montgomery Active Duty GI Bill. A Vietnam-era soldier who never used his or her benefits is today entitled to thirty-six months of entitlements under the Montgomery program. Vietnam-era soldiers do not have to contribute to the program to receive benefits, including an additional allowance paid for dependents. Soldiers in category II—thousands of whom are senior NCOs today—can verify their benefits by contacting the local or regional Department of Veterans Affairs (DVA) office.

NCOs who are supervising soldiers who declined to take part in the contributory GI Bill active-duty program or who may be affected by the drawdown should inform their soldiers that they may be covered under category III of the Active-Duty GI Bill. Effective February 3, 1991, the law was amended to allow members who originally declined to participate, or who were not eligible to participate, the opportunity to contribute and participate before involuntary separation from the Army. On October 23, 1992, the law was further expanded to allow the same opportunity to those soldiers who voluntarily separated from service under the Special Separation Benefit and Voluntary Separation Incentive programs. Members in category III earn one month's benefit for each month of active-duty service, up to thirty-six months.

Category IV covers those soldiers on active duty on October 9, 1996, with money remaining in a Veterans Educational Assistance Program (VEAP) account on that date who elected MGIB by October 9, 1997. It also applies to those full-time National Guard who entered active duty under title 32, USC, between July 1, 1985, and November 28, 1989, and elected MGIB during the period October 9, 1996, through July 8, 1997. In any instance all have to have had their military pay reduced by $100 a month for twelve months or made a $1,200 lump-sum contribution.

The Montgomery Selected Reserve GI Bill

The Montgomery Selected Reserve GI Bill (chapter 106, USC) is available to members of the Army Reserve and the Army National Guard. It applies to members who entered Selected Reserve status after June 30, 1985. To receive up to thirty-six months of entitlements under this program, members must have a six-year commitment that began after September 30, 1990. Members must also have completed initial active duty for training, be high school graduates or have equivalent certificates, and serve in an active reserve or National Guard unit and remain in good standing. Soldiers entering the National Guard or Army Reserve on or after October 1, 1992, have their eligibility end fourteen years from their beginning date of eligibility, or on the day they leave the

Selected Reserve. Soldiers entering service prior to October 1, 1992, have either ten years from beginning date of eligibility—their period of eligibility ends ten years from their beginning date of eligibility—or on the day they leave the Selected Reserve.

The Veterans Educational Assistance Program (VEAP)

The VEAP (chapter 32, USC) is a program in which a soldier makes contributions from his or her military pay, which are matched on a $2 for $1 basis by the U.S. government. This program is for soldiers who entered service between January 1, 1977, and June 30, 1985; who opened a VEAP account before April 1, 1987; who contributed from $25 to $2,700 (refundable); and who completed their first period of obligated service. Benefit entitlement is one to thirty-six months, depending on the number of monthly contributions. Changes in the law in 1997 allow soldiers who have at least $1 remaining in their VEAP account to transition to the Montgomery Active-Duty GI Bill. See your education counselor for details.

Monetary Value of the GI Bill

As indicated above, the monetary value of the benefit program you qualify for will depend on various factors, including the date you entered the military, your status in the military, how long you have been or were in service, and the character of a previous discharge or separation. Also, if you are in a contributory program, the amount of money the government will contribute depends on how much you contribute, up to a maximum matching contributory amount.

In-service benefits are worth less, monetarily, than postservice benefits and normally cover only tuition and fees. But here is the kicker: Under current federal law, if you receive a college or university assistantship, fellowship, or grant that pays or offsets part or all of your tuition and fees or research expenses, you may still be entitled to receipt of education benefits—meaning that monthly entitlements received from the DVA are yours to keep.

Entitlement retention applies to serving, separated, and retired soldiers who compete for and receive school assistantships and the like, and who can work at the school a specified number of hours—normally at least twenty—per week.

TUITION ASSISTANCE PROGRAM

The Tuition Assistance (TA) Program provides financial assistance for voluntary off-duty education programs in support of a soldier's professional and personal self-development goals. All soldiers (officers, warrant officers, enlisted) on active duty, and Army National Guard and Army Reserve on active duty, pursuant to U.S. Code Title 10 or Title 32, are authorized to participate in the TA program. Soldiers receive a maximum total yearly amount of up to $4,500 at a rate of 75 percent of tuition costs, or up to $250 per semester hour (SH), whichever is less. Before obtaining TA, soldiers must visit an education counselor to declare an educational goal and create an educational plan.

Various rules and certain service- or usage-oriented restrictions cover the programs and situations described above. Visit your Army Education Center or local DVA office, obtain counseling, and get the most recently published copies of the following pamphlets:

- DVA Pam 27-82-2, *A Summary of DVA Benefits.*
- DVA Pam 22-90-2, *Summary of Educational Benefits.*
- DVA Pam 22-90-1, *Avoiding VA Education Overpayments.*

When you decide to apply for benefits, first make sure the education or training program you choose is approved by the DVA, then complete and submit DVA Form 22-1990 at least two months prior to the beginning of the program. If you choose to use some of your benefits while in service, your commander and local education assistance officer must sign the form. Depending on your personal situation, you also may need to provide a copy of your marriage license, divorce decrees from any previous marriages, and children's birth certificates. Provide these documents, if they apply, because the level of your education benefits may be increased according to the number of legal dependents.

Except for the Selected Reserve program, education benefits expire ten years from the date of your last discharge or release from active duty. The DVA can extend the ten-year period by the amount of time you were prevented from training during the period because of a certified disability or being held by a foreign government power. Certain other extensions apply as well and are covered in DVA Pam 22-90-2.

You may use GI Bill benefits for the following purposes:

- To seek an associate's, bachelor's, master's, professional, or doctoral degree at a college or university.
- To participate in a cooperative training program.
- To participate in an accredited independent study program leading to a college degree.
- To take courses leading to a certificate or diploma from a business, technical, or vocational school.
- To work and train in an apprenticeship or job training program offered by a company or union.
- To take a correspondence course.
- To participate in a program abroad that leads to a college degree.
- To take remedial, deficiency, and refresher courses, under certain circumstances.
- To receive tutorial assistance for a deficiency (such as in math), if you attend school at least half-time.
- To participate in the DVA work-study program, provided you attend school or train three-quarters or full-time.

Soldiers with private pilot licenses are entitled to benefits leading to more advanced flying certification. This program has been extended indefinitely.

You may be entitled to benefits under more than one education program, or you may be eligible for vocational rehabilitation if you have a service-connected disability. In either case, you are strongly encouraged to discuss your education plans with a local DVA counselor. If local counselors are unavailable, contact DVA regional offices. DVA toll-free telephone service is available in all fifty states, Puerto Rico, and the U.S. Virgin Islands. Call (800) 827-1000.

Other Financial Aid

The U.S. Department of Education (DOE), in *The Student Guide,* will inform you and your family members about federal student aid programs and how to apply for them. Its advice is to contact the financial aid administrator at the school that you, your spouse, or your children are interested in and ask about the total cost of education. Ask the state higher education agencies about state aid. Check the local library for state and private financial aid information. Check with companies, foundations, religious organizations, fraternities or sororities, and civic organizations such as the American Legion. Also ask about aid through professional associations. *The Student Guide* is free and may be available at the local Army Education Office.

A FINAL THOUGHT ON EDUCATION

Buy bonds. Series EE savings bonds may be entirely tax-free when used for education. If you have children, and are considering the rising cost of education, purchasing bonds on a regular basis is a smart way to invest in their future and protect your financial security. For example, assuming an annual interest rate of 6 percent, putting just $50 a month into bonds for a one-year-old child who will begin college at age eighteen will yield $17,356. Investing $100 a month will yield $34,712. If you are an NCO with an older child, one who is twelve and who will begin college in six years, putting $50 a month into bonds will provide $4,227; $100 a month will yield $8,454—minimum!

If you are a young NCO, say a sergeant with five or six years in service, you may purchase bonds for yourself, hold them five years or so, then use them to augment other financial aid you will apply toward a bachelor's or master's degree.

Beginning with Series EE bonds purchased in 1990, the interest earned can be excluded from federal income tax if you pay tuition and fees at colleges, universities, and qualified technical schools during the same year the bonds are cashed. The exclusion applies not only to your own educational expenses, but also to those of your spouse and any other dependent according to the Savings Bonds Public Affairs Office in Washington, D.C. Some restrictions apply. Contact your unit savings bond coordinator for more information.

PROFESSIONAL READING AND WRITING

NCOs must read to remain abreast of changing events and policies, and soldiers rely on their leaders to keep them informed. Writing ability is critical for similar reasons. To keep up, NCOs need to be able to comprehend what they read, to be clear in their writing, and to know how to use the software products on their computer. The ability to read, rapidly understand, and respond in writing to memorandums, letters, reports, and other documents hinges on a command of comprehension, grammar, vocabulary, and related skills. To write clearly and efficiently, you must organize your thoughts, put them in order of precedence, and tell up front what you want the reader to get from your paper.

NCOES Contribution to Literacy

The Army considers reading comprehension so important that soldiers attending primary, basic, and advanced NCOES courses must read at the tenth-grade level and Sergeants Major Course (SMC) students must read at the twelfth-grade level. Were this policy not in effect, soldiers unable to read at a high level would be at a disadvantage against those who could and would fare poorly during the course.

This requirement carries over to duty performance. Senior leaders, officer and NCO, routinely read inches-high piles of official documents that flow through local mail distribution systems, and junior leaders pore through field manuals or memorandums of instruction preparing classes for their soldiers.

Writing is as important as reading. NCOs who have a hard time putting thoughts on paper, even if otherwise excellent leaders, limit their influence to those they directly supervise. Some intended meanings get through to the busy readers, but too many remain buried because of poor writing skills. Largely due to formal training provided by the NCO Education System (NCOES), thousands of NCOES graduates understand that the Army writing standard puts the bottom line up front, meaning putting the intended meaning of their writing in the first sentences and paragraph. For further information on how to write in the Army style, read TRADOC Pam 350-5, *Effective Staff Writing,* and DA Pam 600-67, *Effective Writing for Army Leaders.*

Write and Read to Succeed

Write directly and to your audience. If you can convey an idea with a single understood word instead of a series of words or one that no one understands, do so, rather than flashing how erudite you might be. If you are writing to sell a program or an idea, put it into as few words as possible; senior leaders look at hundreds of documents every day, and those not concise or clear fall by the wayside—even if they represent the day's best idea—because they were too long to read, confusing, or had the main point buried somewhere in the text. Any person able to read and summarize a ten-page paper in two or three paragraphs that convey the meaning of the longer paper is a cherished asset in any organization.

When writing, watch your sentence structure, grammar, punctuation, mechanics, usage, tense, relational agreement, and jargon that can contribute to reader confusion. The easier your writing is to understand, the better chance you have of making your point. Remember that those who have a difficult time comprehending what they read will have even more difficulty if what they read is poorly written.

PERSONAL REFERENCE LIBRARY AND RECOMMENDED READING

Whatever your literary pursuits, you need basic reference books to be an adept communicator. Make sure you have *Webster's Eleventh New Collegiate Dictionary* in your personal reference library, as well as the *Army Dictionary and Desk Reference,* by Maj. Tim Zurick (Stackpole Books), and *Guide to Effective Military Writing,* by William A. McIntosh (Stackpole Books.)

Also read *The Story of the Noncommissioned Officer,* which is available through the Government Printing Office (GPO). Write to Superintendent of Documents, U.S. Government Printing Office, Washington, DC 20402. Additionally, you should have *Guardians of the Republic: A History of the Noncommissioned Officer Corps of the U.S. Army,* by Ernest F. Fisher (Stackpole Books).

The U.S. Army Chief of Staff's Professional Reading List

Historically, one of the most important, distinguishing characteristics of outstanding soldiers has been a challenging personal professional development program based largely on reading. On June 14, 2000, in coordination with the Army's 225th birthday, the chief of staff established a professional reading list to represent his personal commitment to self-study as a critical aspect of professional development. This is not a mandatory reading list, but it is recommended, and the chief of staff's intent will be met if every year each leader reads and thoughtfully reflects on a few good books. The list is supportive of leader professional development, and as such is broken into four subordinate lists: sublist 1, appropriate for cadets, soldiers, and junior NCOs; sublist 2, appropriate for company-grade officers and company cadre NCOs; sublist 3, appropriate for field-grade officers and senior NCOs; and sublist 4, appropriate for senior leaders at levels of responsibility above brigade. The chief of staff's list is at *www.army.mil/cmh-pg/reference/CSAList/CSAList.htm.*

What follows are the books and poetry that most affected my attitudes toward service as an NCO and that I have recommended for my NCOs to read. Many are on the chief of staff's professional reading list. Most lend a historical perspective and deal with issues we have all faced or will face in the future:

soldier motivation and morale, ethics, training, and leadership, most especially that of the small unit in extreme circumstances. Lastly, many look at leaders who are looking at themselves.

Nonfiction Books

American Military History, Maurice Matloff
Brave Men, Ernie Pyle
Co. Aytch, Sam Watkins
Common Sense Training, John Collins
Embattled Courage, Gerald Linderman
The Face of Battle, John Keegan
GI: The US Infantryman in World War II, Robert S. Rush
Hell in Hürtgen Forest, Robert S. Rush
A Message to Garcia, Elbert Hubbard
The Military in America, Peter Karsten
Morale, John Baynes
Rise and Fall of the Great Powers, Paul Kennedy
Small Unit Leadership, Dandridge (Mike) Malone
Thinking in Time, Richard E. Neustadt and Ernest R. May
This Kind of War, T. R. Fehrenbach
We Were Soldiers Once and Young, Harold Moore and Joe Galloway

Fiction Books

The Centurions, Jean Larteguy
Forgotten Soldier, Guy Sager
Once an Eagle, Anton Myrer
Starship Troopers, R. A. Heinlein

Poetry

"If," Rudyard Kipling
"The 'Eathen," Rudyard Kipling
"The Quitter," Robert W. Service

I would also recommend the following books: *From Dawn to Decadence,* by Charles Barzun, for a synopsis of the past 500 years; *Battlecry of Freedom,* by James M. McPherson, for perhaps the best overview of the American Civil War; and *There's a War to Be Won,* by Geoffrey Perret, for World War II. The U.S. Army Center of Military History has hundreds of books available at no cost to units with publication accounts through the Government Printing Office. Stackpole Books, the *NCO Guide's* publisher, offers more than a hundred other titles of interest to the military reader. If you study strategy or individual soldiers and soldiering, for example, you will enjoy the Osprey Campaign series books, which include three on the infantryman in WWII by the author of the *NCO Guide. Army Times* is also a useful source of military news, features, and other information, although not as vital now that the Army has most information on its web sites. The print editions of the *NCO Journal* and *SOLDIERS* are now published on-line and are recommended sources of current information on units and people in the Army.

Professional associations, including the Noncommissioned Officers Association (NCOA) and the Association of the U.S. Army (AUSA), publish *NCOA Journal* and *AUSA News,* respectively. The AUSA also mails its monthly Army magazine to members. More on these associations will follow in respective sections below.

Trade magazines and Army professional journals that apply to your MOS should be read to keep up with trends, changes, and other matters related to your specialty. Combat arms soldiers may read *Infantry, Armor, and Field Artillery Professional Bulletin.* Other combat arms, combat support, and combat service support publications are available as well, including *Army Logistician* magazine and *Combat Service Support Guide,* a Stackpole Books publication by Maj. John E. Edwards. Check with your first sergeant or command sergeant major for other recommendations.

If you are stationed overseas, read the *Stars and Stripes,* which is published in several editions to provide daily news, sports, features, columns, and other information to soldiers and their families. Daily offerings from *USA Today,* the *Wall Street Journal,* the *Herald Tribune,* and certain other major newspapers serve soldier-readers who are stationed at major installations abroad. There are also Internet sites for most major newspapers, which you can access to remain abreast of world developments.

WRITING FOR PROFESSIONAL DEVELOPMENT

Your professional development should be shared. Writing will develop your professional skills and your writing abilities through the discipline of writing for publication. Other factors being equal, an NCO who writes well is more valuable and is promoted faster than one who doesn't. As you learn, share your knowledge by writing about it. Submit material to the following:

- *NCO Journal.* The editor is always on the hunt for good material. Here are the guidelines: Keep the reader in mind; address the subject to a wide audience; write conversationally; keep it simple and short (four double-spaced pages fill a magazine page); and include photos or other illustrations. The editor also wants letters from NCOs who agree or disagree with what they read in the journal, or who have a better idea about aspects of NCO business. Book reviews are also welcomed. Include the title, author, publisher, date published, price, whether it is hardbound or softbound, and number of pages. For more information, contact the editor and ask for a reprint of "Wanted: Writers." The address is *NCO Journal,* ATTN: Editor, USASMA, Fort Bliss, TX 79918.

- *The AUSA Institute of Land Warfare (ILW).* The ILW wants to hear from you. Request a copy of "Manuscripts Wanted" from the institute at 2425 Wilson Boulevard, Arlington, VA 22201, or call (800) 336-4570. The AUSA needs land warfare papers, essays, and books. You may also submit material to Army magazine at the same address. Write and ask for a copy of the magazine's style requirements.
- *Center for Army Lessons Learned (CALL).* If you have learned a valuable professional lesson, relate it in writing to the CALL. Send material to Commander, Combined Arms Command, ATTN: ATZL-CTL, Fort Leavenworth, KS 66027-7000. Lessons shared help drive doctrinal and force structure improvements.
- The different branch journals.

Regulations about For-Profit Writing

Before you try to make money selling what you write, consult the *Department of Defense Ethics Guidelines.* Visit your local ethics counselor at the Judge Advocate General's Office to discuss your topic, research methods, data resources, commercial intention, and proposed business relationship with your publisher. Let the counselor be your guide. If you get the nod to proceed, then go for it. If the counselor recommends that you not publish, then discuss alternatives—switching, for example, from nonfiction to autobiographical fiction—but do not twist sound guidance into an illegal framework, based on a profit motive. Put the Professional Army Ethic first.

If you are on active duty, do not allow a publisher to print your official rank before your name on a cover or to use your rank to solicit for sales, because doing so is a conflict of interest in most for-profit cases; it could make potential customers believe that, contrary to federal law, the government endorses your work.

The Department of Defense (DOD) ethics guidelines give potential enlisted soldier-authors a lot of leeway. Officers in procurement and acquisition positions have much more restrictive guidance to follow. Just remember, however, that certain restrictions apply, some of which will depend on your subject matter and your own position. Further, and it should go without saying, do not disclose classified information. Again, you are strongly encouraged to visit your local ethics counselor before selling a manuscript.

THE ARMY ON-LINE AND THE WORLD WIDE WEB

The Army has entered the Information Superhighway in a big way, with thousands of sites currently on-line and more being published daily. Increasingly, computer literacy is becoming important for NCOs because it enables them to receive and transmit text and supporting communications across vast electronic networks. No longer do you have to thumb through old copies of the *Army Times* or look for the latest Human Resources Command (HRC) message to find information vital to your career. Just enter the HRC home page and view the most up-to-date information concerning your MOS. Entire books are online at the Center of Military History's home page. Need to prepare a class on the most current techniques to breach a minefield? Try the Center for Army Lessons Learned. It's all there—you just have to look.

The Internet, intranets, electronic mail, and remote access are all high-technology methods to transmit and receive information to and from the computers we use every day. These forms of communication were practically unheard of fifteen years ago; now they are essential for doing business. Nearly all companies and organizations throughout the world have their own graphical web pages that are used both to advertise and to make available vast quantities of information. With a modem and a personal computer (PC), NCOs can reach out and communicate with—or retrieve information from—anyone, anywhere in the world.

The Internet

The Internet is the worldwide free enterprise network of computers that links distant sites together. It is a combination of tens of thousands of computer servers linked to computer users via telephone lines or direct circuits. Each server is a separate "site" with a unique name. Although the U.S. Department of Defense originally developed the Internet as a means of transmitting research data, it uses the "net" to communicate routine electronic mail (e-mail) as well as to post great quantities of current information.

Intranets

Intranets are simply proprietary internal versions of the Internet within a large organization. Intranets are primarily used as graphical bulletin boards where current information and commonly used text reference materials are posted. This greatly enhances document access and information flow between workers.

Web Pages

A web page is the graphical presentation of a document on the Web. Usually each page contains one type or grouping of information with links to other sub-pages or to other web pages at different sites. Web pages can be as simple as text pages or as complex as pages with pictures, animated images, video clips, and attached sound files.

Electronic Mail (E-mail)

E-mail is the electronic transmission of messages and documents across one or more networks, computer to computer. This form of communication has literally exploded in the past few years. E-mail is generally a stand-alone system or a separate module within a software package that uses any one or more of the following to transmit data: local area networks (LANs), wide-area networks

(WANs), telephone connections, or the Internet. If you or your soldiers have not registered for an Army Knowledge Online (AKO) account, go to *www.us.army.mil*. The Army's intent is to have every soldier (active, guard, and reserve) and DA civilian with a transportable e-mail account that they can use in any organization to which they belong.

Remote Access

Remote access actually refers to three separate capabilities to electronically connect to an organization via a dial-in modem: (1) a remote connection to the e-mail system; (2) a remote connection to an organizational LAN, with subsequent enabled connections directly to other PC workstations; and (3) a remote connection to the organization's private intranet or, if allowed, to the Internet. All remote access connections would be from a distant location carried over commercial telephone lines. The three types of connections may be kept exclusive of the other types or they may be interconnected. A computer with a modem (and usually a log-on name and password) is all that is needed.

U.S. Army On-line

Listed below are some of the more popular web sites that deal with military issues. At the time of writing, all of the listed links worked.

ACES GI to Jobs website	*www.armyeducation.army.mil/COOL*
Adjutant General Directorate	*www.hrc.army.mil/site/active/tagd/-index.htm*
APFT Score Converter	*www.everettsoftware.com/APFT16.htm*
Army and Air Force Exchange Service	*www.aafes.com/*
Army Career and Alumni Program (ACAP)	*www.acap.army.mil/*
Army Continuing Education System	*www.armyeducation.army.mil/*
Army Correspondence Course Program	*www.atsc.army.mil/accp/aipdnew.asp*
Army Distance Learning	*www.tadlp.monroe.army.mil/*
Army Electronic Product Support (AEPS)	*www.aeps.ria.army.mil/*
Army Enterprise Architecture	*www.army.mil/ciog6/offices/SAISIO/-SAISIOE/ent_arch_home.html*
Army home page	*www.army.mil/*
Army Housing	*www.housing.army.mil/*
Army Knowledge Online access page	*www.us.army.mil*
Army National Guard	*www.arng.army.mil/*
Army Publishing Agency (USAPA)	*www.usapa.army.mil/*
Army Reserve	*www.goarmy.com/reserve/nps/*
Human Resources Command Army Reserve	*www.hrc.army.mil/site/reserve/*

Army Retirement Services	*www.armyg1.army.mil/rso/mission.asp*
Army Sergeants Major Academy	*www.bliss.army.mil/usasma/default.htm*
Army Training Information Management Program (ATIMP)	*www.atsc.army.mil/atimp/*
Army Training Requirements and Resources System (ATRRS)	*www.atrrs.army.mil/*
Army Vision 2010	*www.army.mil/2010/*
Army Public Affairs	*www4.army.mil/ocpa/*
Assignment Satisfaction Key (ASK) (active duty enlisted only)	*www.isdrad06.hoffman.army.mil/ask/-index.html*
Association of the United States Army	*www.ausa.org/*
Available electronic forms	*www.army.mil/usapa/eforms/*
CALL (Center for Army Lessons Learned)	www.*call.army.mil/*
Career Branch Newsletters	*www.hrc.army.mil/site/active/enlist/-cb-let.htm*
Center of Military History (CMH)	*www.army.mil/cmh-pg/default.htm*
Combat Developments Directorate for Combat Service Support	*www.cascom.army.mil/DCD_CSS/-Multi/index.htm*
Command and General Staff College	*www.cgsc.army.mil/*
Common Task Testing	*www.atsc.army.mil/itsd/ctt.asp*
Corps and Division Doctrine	*www-.cgsc.army.mil/cdd*
Defense Finance and Accounting Service	*www.dod.mil/dfas/*
Defense News	*www.defensenews.com/*
DefenseLink	*www.defenselink.mil/*
Department of Veteran's Affairs	*www.va.gov/*
DOD Dictionary	*www.dtic.mil/doctrine/jel/doddict/-acronym_index.html*
Enlisted National Guard Association	*www.ngaus.org/*
GulfLink	*www.gulflink.osd.mil/*
Headquarters, Department of the Army	*www.hqda.army.mil/hqda/*
Installations & Facilities	*www.army.mil/organization/*
Instant Map "Mapquest"	*www.mapquest.com/*
Leadership Resources	*www.wyattresources.net/leadership.html*
Medals and Ribbons	*www.hrc.army.mil/site/active/tagd/-awards/index.htm*
Military Family Research Institute	*www.mfri.purdue.edu/*
Military Network	*www.military-network.com/*
My Pay Military and Civilian	*www.dod.mil/dfas/*
Military Review Magazine	*www.leavenworth.army.mil/milrev/-index.htm*

NCO Education System Newsletter	*www.hrc.army.mil/site/active/EPncoes/-newsletter.htm*
NCOES Information Paper	*www.hrc.army.mil/site/active/enlist/-guide/ncoes.htm*
Office of the Chief, Army Reserve (OCAR)	*www.armyreserve.army.mil/usar/home/*
Pentagon Library	*www.hqda.army.mil/library/*
Per Diem	*www.secureapp2.hqda.pentagon.mil/-perdiem/*
Human Resources Command, Enlisted Promotions	*www.hrc.army.mil/site/active/select/-enlisted.htm*
Human Resources Command	*www.hrc.army.mil/indexflash.asp*
PS Magazine	*www.logsa.army.mil/psmag/psonline.cfm*
Retention and Reenlistment	*www.armyreenlistment.com/*
Soldiers Magazine Online	*www4.army.mil/soldiers/*
Thrift Savings Plan	*www.tsp.gov/*
Training and Doctrine Digital Library	*www.train.army.mil/*
Training Support Center (ATSC)	*www.atsc.army.mil/*
TRICARE home page	*www.tricare.osd.mil/*
TRICARE OCHAMPUS	*www.defenselink.mil/dodgc/doha/-tricare.html*
U.S. Army Reserve	*www.armyreserve.army.mil/usar/home/*
U.S. OPM Retirement Programs	*www.opm.gov/retire*
USAJOBS (OPM)	*www.usajobs.opm.gov*
Veteran's Affairs OEF/IF web site	*www.seamlesstransition.va.gov/*

PROFESSIONAL ASSOCIATIONS

The Noncommissioned Officers Association (NCOA)

The NCOA is a federally chartered, nonprofit, fraternal association founded in 1960. Its purpose is to accomplish the following:

- Uphold and defend the Constitution and support a strong national defense with a focus on military personnel issues.
- Promote health, prosperity, and scholarship among its members and their families through legislative and benevolent programs.
- Improve benefits for soldiers, veterans, and their families and survivors.
- Help soldiers, veterans, and their families and survivors in filing benefit claims.

Through its office near the Pentagon, NCOA actively lobbies Congress, the White House, the Department of Veterans Affairs, the military services, and other federal agencies to fulfill its goals. The association also supervises the following: major nonpartisan voter registration drives in the United States and abroad, a nationwide network of coordinators who monitor state and local administrative and legislative activities affecting NCOA members, a nationwide outreach program for hospitalized veterans, and fellowship and intern programs for undergraduate college students.

The NCOA is a leader in advocating improvements in benefits for enlisted soldiers. The association's director of marketing said, "The NCOA has been instrumental in the development of the Montgomery GI Bill, creating severance pay for enlisted soldiers, providing equity in hazardous duty pay, and fair unemployment compensation for former soldiers." The NCOA's registered lobbyists submit testimony to Congress and maintain liaison with other federal agencies to ensure that laws are implemented and policies developed with equity for enlisted military personnel and veterans.

Annual membership for NCOs is $30. The association offers many member benefits, including the Certified Merchants Program and the Buying Network, which provide substantial discounts on commercial products and services. Members may also receive *NCOA Journal* and may qualify for the competitive NCOA *VISA* card. Members with families may purchase CHAMPUS Aid, a health insurance supplement offered through Academy Insurance Group, Inc. The association also offers a motor club that provides roadside assistance and towing. Additionally, property and casualty insurance is offered, and each member receives free accidental death and dismemberment insurance.

For more information, write to Noncommissioned Officers Association, ATTN: Membership Processing, P.O. Box 105636, Atlanta, GA 30348-5636; call (800) 662-2620; or check their website at *www.ncoausa.org*.

The Association of the U.S. Army (AUSA)

The AUSA is a private, nonprofit organization established in 1950. It supports active and reserve component members, Army civilians, retirees, and Army families. Its goals are as follows:

- Being the voice for all components of America's Army.
- Fostering public support of the Army's role in national security.
- Providing professional education and information programs.

AUSA focuses on issues that affect soldiers during and after service. The association pushes for pay equity, adequate military housing, cost-of-living allowances, and standard subsistence allowances for all personnel.

Regular membership costs are stepped according to grade, $25 for E-5 through E-7 and $30 for E-8 through E-9. Among its membership benefits are opportunities to participate in chapter activities and discount product and service programs. Members in the rank of sergeant and above receive *AUSA News* and *Army* magazine. Corporals who elect to pay a discounted $20 per year for membership will receive both the newspaper and the magazine. Corporals and other soldiers whose pay grades are E-4 and below may opt to join for $12 per year, but the reduced fee does not include *Army* magazine.

For more information, check the AUSA web site at *www.ausa.org;* call (800) 336-4570; write to Association of the U.S. Army, 2425 Wilson Boulevard, Arlington, VA 22201; or e-mail *ausa.info@ausa.org.*

National Guard Enlisted Association (EANGUS)

EANGUS exists to "promote the status, welfare, and professionalism of the enlisted members of the National Guard of the United States" and "promote adequate National Security." It handles and maintains active communications with the Department of Defense, the National Guard Bureau, the National Guard Association, and other military support organizations in Washington, D.C.

EANGUS has a home page on the Internet at the following address: *www.eangus.org*. Users can access Thomas (the congressional database system), Senate, House, EANGUS *New Patriot* magazine and newsletter, *Congressional Quarterly,* legislative updates, and more. E-mail capability will put you in touch with the various departments at the national office that can answer your questions regarding membership, events, and legislative issues.

For more information, call toll-free (800) 234-EANG; write to Enlisted Association of the National Guard of the United States, 3133 Mt. Vernon Avenue, Alexandria, VA 22305; check their web site at *www.eangus.org* or e-mail to *eangus@eangus.org.*

10

Personal Fitness Improvement

Noncommissioned officers are expected to take part in and lead physical training sessions. Nothing improves credibility in front of troops more than setting the example during rigorous fitness training. And more importantly, the many battles in which American troops have fought and continue to fight underscore the important role physical fitness plays on the battlefield. If we fail to prepare our soldiers for their physically demanding wartime tasks, we are guilty of paying lip service to the principle of "Train as you fight." It is difficult to survive in 130-degree heat while wearing body armor when you or your soldiers aren't in shape.

FM 21-20 (FM 3-22-20) *Physical Fitness Training* (Oct 98), is directed at leaders who plan and conduct physical fitness training. It provides guidelines for developing programs that will improve and maintain physical fitness levels for all Army personnel. These programs will help leaders prepare their soldiers to meet the physical demands of combat. Our physical training programs must do more for our soldiers than just get them ready for the semiannual Army Physical Fitness Test (APFT).

THE ARMY PHYSICAL FITNESS PROGRAM

The Army's Physical Fitness Program objective is to enhance combat readiness by developing and sustaining a high level of physical fitness in soldiers as measured by the following criteria:

- Cardiorespiratory endurance.
- Muscular strength and endurance.
- Flexibility.
- Anaerobic conditioning.
- Competitive spirit, the will to win, and unit cohesion.
- Self-discipline.
- Body fat composition as prescribed by AR 600-9.

- A healthy lifestyle that includes good nutrition, avoidance of smoking, and avoidance of drug use.
- Ability to cope with psychological stress.

A good fitness program can also reduce the number of soldiers on profile and sick call, invigorate training, and enhance productivity and mental alertness.

Physical Fitness and Deployment

If time permits, you should train your soldiers on the most physically demanding mission essential task list (METL) tasks; such as foot marches under combat loads, lifting and loading equipment, obstacle courses, and individual movement techniques in battle gear. Exercise your soldiers five days per week regardless of unit type, alternating aerobic activities with muscular strength and endurance exercises in accordance with (IAW) FM 21-20.

Consider conducting physical training (PT) during hot periods of the day to facilitate acclimatization. It takes eight to fourteen days to acclimate to a hot, humid climate. Ensure that you adjust the exercise intensity to meet the heat index with undue risk to your soldiers. Have your soldiers drink sufficient water and maintain appropriate mineral levels in the body.

If the mission and conditions permit, conduct physical training and testing while deployed. Do anything that you can to keep your soldiers ready for any contingency.

On redeployment resume physical training as soon as practicable. You can be assured that a long deployment will lower your unit's physical fitness level from what it was before you deployed. MOS specific tasks such as those listed above will be easy, but returning to runs, push-ups, and sit-ups will be less so. Begin with lower numbers of repetitions and shorter, slower runs and over a period of sixty to ninety days increase the intensity to predeployment levels.

At Home Station

AR 350-31, *Unit Training*, mandates that soldiers be afforded the opportunity to exercise during duty hours at least three times per week. While many units exercise five times per week, many soldiers in headquarters and administrative units have to exercise on their own time.

Soldiers in many Army units are required to take part in daily PT. Students attending NCO Education System (NCOES) courses are required to do PT five times per week, except when in the field overnight, in compliance with Training and Doctrine Command (TRADOC) Regulation 351-17, *NCO Training in TRADOC NCO Academies*. Students are required to lead fitness training on a rotational basis and are evaluated by NCO academy small-group leaders on their ability to plan and conduct the training. All NCOES courses require that students take and pass the Army Physical Fitness Test (APFT). For those soldiers returning from combat operations Global War on Terrorism (GWOT) deployment and reporting directly to a NCOES course with thirty or fewer training days, the requirement for taking the APFT is waived. Those attending NCOES for more than thirty training days must meet APFT standards prior to graduation.

THE FOUR FITT PRINCIPLES—FREQUENCY, INTENSITY, TIME, AND TYPE

- Frequency means doing PT at least three—preferably five—times a week. Intensity of cardiorespiratory (CR) workouts must be at the proper training heart rate (THR), depending on current fitness level. The THR is most accurately calculated as follows: (1) Subtract your age from the number 220 to determine your maximum heart rate (MHR); (2) take your resting pulse (while completely relaxed) for thirty seconds and multiply the number of pulses by two to determine your resting heart rate (RHR); (3) determine your heart rate reserve (HRR) by subtracting the RHR from the MHR; (4) calculate your THR based on 60 to 90 percent of your HRR by multiplying the percentage (that is, 0.6, 0.7, 0.8, or 0.9) by the HRR, then adding the result to your RHR to determine your

The perfect push-up.

THR—that is, the number of heartbeats per minute that you must maintain during aerobic exercise to achieve a training effect (and burn fat).

- Intensity, for muscular strength and muscular endurance workouts, refers to the percentage of maximum resistance used for a given exercise and is expressed as "repetition maximum." Basically, for strength training you would exercise close to your one-repetition maximum but with fewer repetitions per set (heavy weight, few repetitions, several sets); for endurance training you would exercise well below your one-repetition maximum with many repetitions per set (light weight, many repetitions, several sets).
- The time component of the FITT principles means that at least twenty to thirty continuous minutes of intense exercise are necessary to improve CR endurance. For muscular strength and endurance, exercise time equates to the number of repetitions done. FM 21-20 (FM 3-22-20) states that, for moderately fit soldiers, eight to twelve repetitions with enough resistance to cause muscle failure improves both endurance and strength.
- The last FITT principle, type, refers to the kind of exercise performed. The basic rule is that to improve performance, you must practice the particular exercise, activity, or skill you want or need to improve. For example, to be good at push-ups you must do push-ups; no other exercise will improve push-up performance as effectively.

The three phases of fitness are *preparatory*, *conditioning*, and *maintenance*. The *preparatory* phase, for poorly conditioned soldiers, helps the CR and muscular systems get used to exercise. The *conditioning* phase includes progressively more strenuous activities aimed at reaching the desired fitness level. The *maintenance* phase sustains a high fitness level achieved in the conditioning phase. The starting phase for individuals and units will vary depending on individual or average age, fitness level, and previous fitness activity. Using individual and average unit APFT scores as a fitness assessment tool will help you determine the phase of your soldiers and unit.

DESIGN AN INDIVIDUAL FITNESS PROGRAM

"Sergeant Smith, I exercise daily and run a lot, but I can't seem to get my PT score above 240. What am I doing wrong?"

Many soldiers do not know how or what to do to increase their physical fitness beyond their present level. This is not because they are uncaring, but because many were never taught how. Many organizations and schools still conduct PT en masse, which normally consists of push-ups, sit-ups, and a run. Additionally, many remedial PT programs are not geared to deficiencies and concentrate instead on running rather than the soldier's weakness.

The following individual PT program was developed for soldiers with little time to devote to PT. It is a modification of a successful PT program found in a light infantry battalion and is based on the principles found in FM 21-20 (FM 3-22-20). This program may help you, the NCO, increase your soldiers' readiness without a major cost in time. It will also help the soldiers individually, both by decreasing their health risk factors and keeping them competitive with their peers. This program is as applicable to reserve components as it is to the active forces.

The program was validated using forty students in an ROTC program. Students exercised three times per week for twenty to twenty-five minutes, not including the run. The following results were achieved: after one month the average score for students increased by 15 to 20 points, from an average of 192 to 212; at the end of three months, students went from their average of 212 to 243; the second three months saw average scores climb to 267, with the low score 242 and the high 300. Since this is an individual program, it is designed to fit every soldier's physical ability. The program takes a soldier gradually to a higher level of physical fitness.

Individual Fitness Program Analysis

Take a look at your last APFT. From your scores, you can determine where your starting point for your Individual Fitness Program should be. If you haven't taken an APFT in the last three to four months, you may want to assess your physical abilities before beginning the program.

To conduct a self assessment, do as many correct push-ups and sit-ups as you can in a one-minute period, and then run as hard as you can for a timed half mile. Multiply your push-up and sit-up scores by 1.25 to find an entry point into the charts. Multiply your half-mile time by four.

The Program

The following, if done correctly, will bring you to muscle failure. This exercise regime is designed to be done every other day, as your muscles need from twenty-four to forty-eight hours to recover from hard usage.

To get your starting numbers of exercises, look at the charts below. The numbers along the top of the charts are the numbers of push-ups or sit-ups that you performed. Follow the number down the column to give you the numbers of repetitions for each exercise that you are to begin with in your individual program. For example, if you did forty push-ups on your last test, your personal fitness improvement program would start with the following repetition each day: sixteen push-ups, eight diamond push-ups, eight wide-arm push-ups, and twelve turn and bounces. You would follow the same procedure for determining sit-up improvement.

PUSH-UP IMPROVEMENT
APFT NUMBER PUSH-UPS

Number	**10**	**15**	**20**	**25**	**30**	**35**	**40**	**45**	**50**	**55**	**60**	**65**	**70**	**75**	**80**	**85**
Push-ups	4	6	8	10	12	14	16	18	20	22	24	26	28	30	32	34
Diamonds	2	3	4	5	6	7	8	9	10	11	12	13	14	15	16	17
Wide-arm	2	3	4	5	6	7	8	9	10	11	12	13	14	15	16	17
Turn & bounce	5	6	7	8	9	10	12	14	16	18	20	22	24	26	28	30

SIT-UP IMPROVEMENT
APFT NUMBER SIT-UPS

Number	**10**	**15**	**20**	**25**	**30**	**35**	**40**	**45**	**50**	**55**	**60**	**65**	**70**	**75**	**80**	**85**
Sit-ups	4	6	8	10	12	14	16	18	20	22	24	26	28	30	32	34
Crunches	4	5	6	7	8	8	9	9	10	10	11	12	13	14	15	16
Flutter kick	5	6	7	8	9	10	12	14	16	18	20	22	24	26	28	30
Leg spreader	5	6	7	8	9	10	12	14	16	18	20	22	24	26	28	30

Sequence of Exercises for Push-up and Sit-up Improvement

1. Regular push-ups. Three sets with one-minute rest between sets. Form is important. If you can't do the push-ups properly, go to your knees and continue until you have finished the sets. After three workouts, add two push-ups to each set. (Example: You start with six push-ups on Wednesday. The next Wednesday you go to eight push-ups.)

2a. Regular sit-ups. Three sets with one-minute rest between sets. If you can't do all of the sit-ups properly, lower the angle of your legs until they are almost parallel to the ground. After three workouts, add two sit-ups to each set. (Example: You start with eight sit-ups on Wednesday. The next Wednesday you go to ten sit-ups.)

2b. Alternate to sit-ups: Crunches. See number five below.

3. Diamond push-ups. Put your hands together under your chest in a diamond shape. Perform the push-ups. Go to your knees if necessary. Add one diamond after every three workouts.
4. Wide-arm push-ups. Place your hands as far apart as possible. Perform the push-ups. Go to your knees if necessary. Add one wide-arm after every three workouts.

5. Crunches. One set equals one repetition of each of the ten crunches; add one repetition every third workout. (Example: You start with six repetitions of the crunches on Wednesday. The next Wednesday you go to seven repetitions.) See the chart on page 162 for crunch positions. Note: If you do exercise 2b instead of sit-ups, do one less repetition of the crunches.
6. Turn and bounce. Arms parallel to the ground, palms facing up. The exercise is an eight-count movement at a slow cadence. Pivot slowly at the waist to the right for four counts and then to the left for four counts. Add two turn and bounces after every three workouts.
7. Flutter kicks. Put your hands under your buttocks. Lift your feet six to eight inches off the ground to start. Begin by lifting legs alternately, raising each six to eighteen inches from starting position. Keep legs slightly bent to reduce the strain on your back. One repetition equals four counts. Add two flutter kicks after every three workouts.
8. Leg spreaders. Put your hands under your buttocks. Lift your feet six to eight inches off the ground to start. Begin by spreading legs eighteen to thirty inches apart, then back together. Keep legs slightly bent to reduce the strain on your back. One repetition equals four counts. Add two leg spreaders after every three workouts.

The Crunch Exercise
Start position is with arms crossed across chest, hands grasping shoulders. Use the stomach muscles to crunch up, not the neck and shoulder. Try not to stop between sets.

Running
The following running chart, if implemented, will both increase your aerobic and anaerobic stamina and better your two-mile run time. Enter the table using your two-mile run time or multiply your half-mile assessment by four. For example, your run time is 26:15. Enter the chart at +26. This program is designed to be run every other day, although there is no harm in running more than three times per week.

Sprint Day. This program will increase your anaerobic ability and decrease your run time. Enter the sprint portion of the chart at your run time row. Do four sprints each of two distances, alternating your sprints between the distances. Begin with the lower distance for your speed. Attempt to beat the time listed. Rest one minute before you run the longer sprint. Rest two minutes between the longer and shorter sprints. If you feel that you are not being properly stressed, and as you develop your wind, decrease the amount of rest time between sprints.

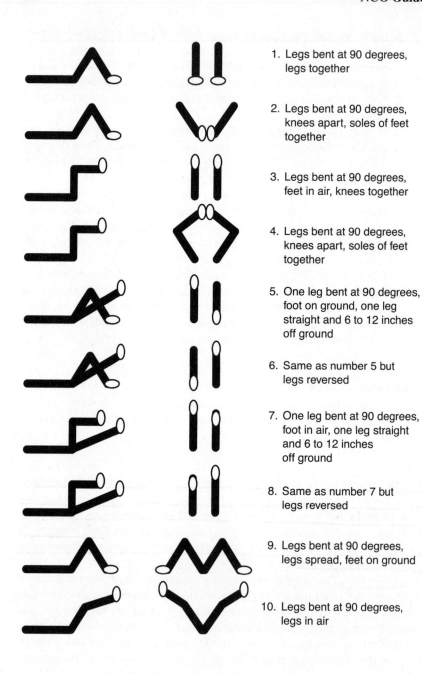

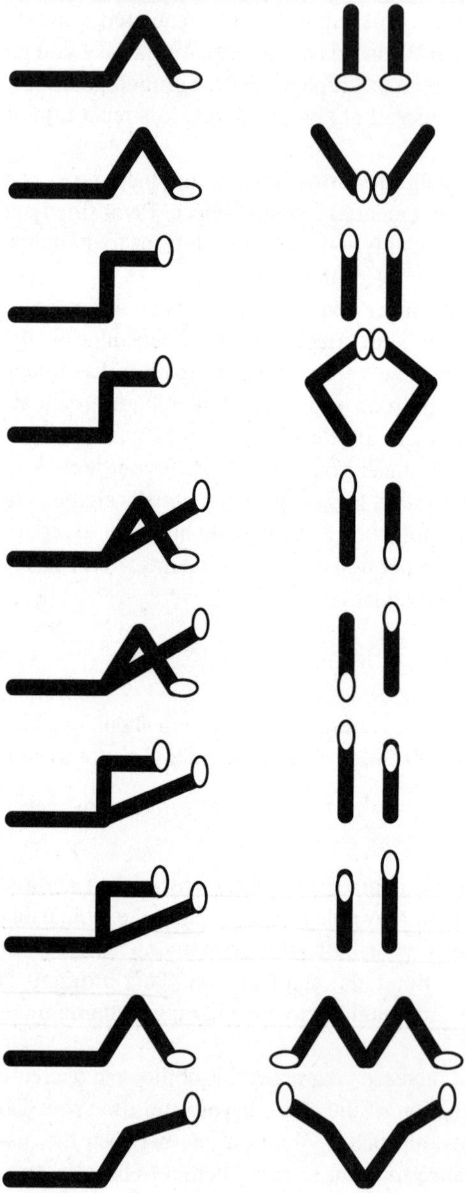

1. Legs bent at 90 degrees, legs together
2. Legs bent at 90 degrees, knees apart, soles of feet together
3. Legs bent at 90 degrees, feet in air, knees together
4. Legs bent at 90 degrees, knees apart, soles of feet together
5. One leg bent at 90 degrees, foot on ground, one leg straight and 6 to 12 inches off ground
6. Same as number 5 but legs reversed
7. One leg bent at 90 degrees, foot in air, one leg straight and 6 to 12 inches off ground
8. Same as number 7 but legs reversed
9. Legs bent at 90 degrees, legs spread, feet on ground
10. Legs bent at 90 degrees, legs in air

Variations of crunches.

For those with run times of +17 to +26, when the one-eighth mile (220) sprint goal is met, move up to the one-quarter mile (440) and one-half mile (880) runs.

Fast Run Day. Begin with the lower distance for your speed. When you beat the time for the distance, move to a longer distance within the same row. When you surpass the time for the distance at the bottom of the row, move one row to the left, maintaining the same distance. When you move one row to the left on the fast run, move your sprint goals to the same row.

RUNNING IMPROVEMENT

Minutes	+12	+13	+14	+15	+16	+17	+18	+19	+20	+21	+22	+23	+24	+25	+26
Sprint															
1/8 mile	—	—	—	—	—	—	:51	:55	:59	1:03	1:07	1:10	1:14	1:18	1:22
1/4 mile	1:07	1:15	1:23	1:30	1:37	1:48	1:52	2:00	2:08	2:15	2:23	2:30	2:37	2:45	3:00
1/2 mile	2:45	3:00	3:15	3:30	3:45	4:00	4:15	4:30	4:45	5:00	5:15	5:30	5:45	6:00	6:15
Fast Run	—	—	—	—	—	1/2 Mi	1/2 Mi	1/2 Mi	1/2 Mi	1/2 Mi	1/2 Mi	1/2 Mi	1/2 Mi	1/2 Mi	1/2 Mi
	—	—	—	—	—	4:00	4:15	4:30	4:45	5:00	5:15	5:30	5:45	6:00	6:15
	—	—	—	—	—	4:00	4:15	4:30	4:45	5:00	5:15	5:30	5:45	6:00	6:15
	—	—	1 Mi	1 Mi	1 Mi	1 Mi	1 Mi	1 Mi	1 Mi	1 Mi	1 Mi	1 Mi	1 Mi	1 Mi	1 Mi
	—	—	6:30	7:00	7:30	8:00	8:30	9:00	9:30	10:00	10:30	11:00	11:30	12:00	12:30
	—	—	6:30	7:00	7:30	8:00	8:30	9:00	9:30	10:00	10:30	11:00	11:30	12:00	12:30
	2 Mi	2 Mi	2 Mi	2 Mi	2 Mi	2 Mi	2 Mi	2 Mi	2 Mi	2 Mi	2 Mi	2 Mi	2 Mi	—	—
	11:30	12:30	13:30	14:30	15:30	16:30	17:30	18:30	19:30	20:30	21:30	22:30	23:30	—	—
	11:30	12:30	—	—	—	—	—	—	—	—	—	—	—	—	—
	2+Mi	2+Mi	—	—	—	—	—	—	—	—	—	—	—	—	—
	14:30	15:30	—	—	—	—	—	—	—	—	—	—	—	—	—
Long Run															

Long and Slow Run. Run at least thirty minutes for a good cardiovascular workout; run for time during this session, not necessarily distance.

The individual PT program is designed to have very little paper overhead. Every soldier is responsible for his or her own pace in the program. This has the additional benefit of exercising the soldiers' self-discipline in that the soldiers regulate themselves. A good time to start the program would be after an APFT or diagnostic test, when each soldier would receive a packet and have the program explained to him or her. Organized PT would still be conducted, but with each soldier doing the amount of exercise determined by his or her specific program. Periodic diagnostic tests could be administered to check progress.

As with any program, results are directly attributable to the amount of effort that we exert. Soldiers who cannot keep up on the battlefield are losses just as much as casualties suffered through enemy action. We, as NCOs, are charged not to let this happen.

THE ARMY PHYSICAL FITNESS TEST (APFT)

Soldiers taking the APFT are encouraged to make a maximum effort to pass and excel. For soldiers on active duty the test is administered a minimum of twice a year with at least four months separating each record test. For guardsmen and reservists in Troop Program Units, the test must be taken at least yearly. Soldiers returning from combat operations/GWOT deployment will take a record APFT no earlier than three months for active components and six months for reserve component soldiers.

Described in detail in chapter 14 of FM 21-20 (FM 3-22-20), the APFT includes timed push-ups, sit-ups, and a two-mile run (or alternate aerobic event in certain circumstances). The push-up event measures the endurance of the chest, shoulder, and triceps muscles. The sit-up event measures the endurance of the abdominal and hip-flexor muscles. The two-mile run or alternate aerobic event measures CR and leg muscle endurance. Instructions for each APFT event in FM 21-20 must be read verbatim before each is administered.

Administering the APFT

The NCO in charge ensures that the APFT is properly administered; gets all necessary equipment and supplies; arranges and lays out the test area (if necessary); trains the event supervisors, scorers, and demonstrators (using Training Videotape 21-191); ensures that events are explained, demonstrated, and scored; and reports results to superiors. Event supervisors administer test events, ensure that necessary equipment is on hand, read test instructions and have events demonstrated, supervise scoring, and rule on questions and scoring errors or disputes. Scorers supervise the testing soldiers' performance, enforce test standards, count aloud the repetitions performed on the push-up and sit-up events, and record raw scores on DA Form 705, the APFT Scorecard, which was revised in 1999 to reflect the new standards. Support personnel handle safety and crowd control.

Test Standards

Standards for the APFT are based on extensive analysis of baseline fitness standards between genders and the need to accommodate new age groups. The current standards are shown on the following charts:

TWO-MILE RUN

Age Group	Male Min.	Male Max.	Female Min.	Female Max.
17–21	15:54	13:00	18:54	15:36
22–26	16:36	13:00	19:36	15:36
27–31	17:00	13:18	20:30	15:48
32–36	17:42	13:18	21:42	15:54
37–41	18:18	13:36	22:42	17:00
42–46	18:42	14:06	23:42	17:24
47–51	19:30	14:24	24:00	17:36
52–56	19:48	14:42	24:24	19:00
57–61	19:54	15:18	24:48	19:42
62+	20:00	15:42	25:00	20:00

PUSH-UPS

Age Group	Male Min.	Male Max.	Female Min.	Female Max.
17–21	42	71	19	42
22–26	40	75	17	46
27–31	39	77	17	50
32–36	36	75	15	45
37–41	34	73	13	40
42–46	30	66	12	37
47–51	25	59	10	34
52–56	20	56	9	31
57–61	18	53	8	28
62+	16	50	7	25

SIT-UPS

Age Group	Male/Female Min.	Male/Female Max.
17–21	53	78
22–26	50	80
27–31	45	82
32–36	42	76
37–41	38	76
42–46	32	72
47–51	30	66
52–56	28	66
57–61	27	64
62+	26	63

The Army Physical Fitness Badge will be awarded to soldiers attaining a score of 90 points in each event for a total of 270 points. Under the current standards, soldiers must score 270 points annually to continue to wear the badge.

Members of the special populations mentioned earlier in this chapter may be unable to take some or all of the APFT events for medical or other authorized or unavoidable reasons. In order to get credit for the APFT, however, the two-mile run or an alternate aerobic event must be taken and passed. Alternate aerobic events include the 800-yard swim, 6.2-mile bicycle ride (in one gear), and 2.5-mile walk. Like the run, the alternate events must be completed unassisted in a prescribed amount of time relative to age and gender. Unlike the run, the alternates are not scored; test-takers get credit for either passing or failing the event. Soldiers who fail any or all of the events must retake the entire test. In case of test failure, commanders may allow soldiers to retake the test as soon as the soldiers and commander feel that the soldiers are ready. Soldiers without a medical profile will be retested not later than three months following the initial APFT failure.

Soldiers in the ranks of sergeant through command sergeant major have their APFT recorded on DA Form 2166-7, the *NCO Evaluation Report* (NCOER). NCOER raters enter "pass," "fail," or "profile" on part IVc of the NCOER. It is also used in determining promotion points for advancement to SGT and SSG, ranging from 50 points for 300 to 10 points for 180. According to AR 623-205, *Enlisted Evaluation Reporting System,* these entries reflect the NCO's status on the date of the most recent APFT administered by the unit within the twelve-month period prior to the last rated day of supervision. As of February 1, 1999, excellent ratings based solely on the APFT require only the bullet "Received the Physical Fitness Badge." Rating of "Needs Improvement" must reflect the actual APFT score. Raters must explain an APFT entry of "fail" or "profile."

Even if not used to demonstrate excellence, annotating the APFT score on the NCOER gives DA selection boards a better picture of the soldier. For example, a soldier in the grade of E4 or E5 consistently scores 270 and above on the APFT. On making SSG, the score drops to 230-240 because he or she no longer receives credit for a high score.

In compliance with Army retention policy, soldiers who have six months or more time in service who fail two consecutive record APFTs must be processed for separation for unsatisfactory performance under chapter 13 of AR 635-200, *Enlisted Personnel.* Receipt of a "Chapter 13" for fitness failure indicates that the soldier is unqualified for further service because he or she will not develop sufficiently to participate in further training or become a satisfactory soldier. It also means that failures would be likely to recur, and the ability of the soldier to perform duties effectively in the future, including potential for advancement or leadership, is unlikely. Entry-level soldiers, those with less than six months' time in service, who repeatedly fail diagnostic and record APFTs may be separated under chapter 11 of the *Enlisted Personnel* regulation. A "Chapter 11" covers inability, lack of reasonable effort, or failure to adapt to the military environment.

Soldiers who score a 270 or above on the APFT are awarded the Army Physical Fitness Badge and for this achievement can receive an excellence block on their NCOER. Fit soldiers also receive verbal commendations and other accolades, are retained in service and selected for advanced military schooling, and can be promoted provided they meet other service-selection criteria, including presenting a sharp military appearance—which requires weight control.

WEIGHT CONTROL

AR 600-9, *The Army Weight Control Program,* states that each soldier (commissioned, warrant, or enlisted) is responsible for meeting service weight control standards. To help soldiers meet their responsibility, height and weight screening tables are published in the weight control regulation. The regulation's proponent agency, the Office of the Deputy Chief of Staff for Personnel (ODCSPER), recommends that soldiers strive to remain at least 5 percent below their individual screening table weight maximum. NCO supervisors should ensure that they and their soldiers practice weight control by individually attaining and maintaining an acceptable weight and body composition through self-motivation or involvement in an official weight control program.

For some, the ODCSPER guidance is easy to follow. Others have a real problem. Whether compliance is easy or not often depends on a number of factors, including the individual's body type—ectomorph (thin), mesomorph (medium to well proportioned), or endomorph (soft, heavier). Each of the body types can meet the standards, and each can fail to comply and exceed the maximum body fat allowable for gender, age, height, and weight. An ectomorph in poor shape who eats a high-fat diet may carry much excess body fat. Conversely, an endomorph on a well-balanced diet, including high fiber, and who exercises regularly may carry little body fat. AR 600-9 (as of C1 March 1994) states that the stringent Department of Defense body fat goal is 20 percent for males, 26 percent for females. Army body fat standards are as follows:

Age Group:	**17–20**	**Age Group:**	**21–27**
Male (% body fat):	20	Male (% body fat):	22
Female (% body fat):	30	Female (% body fat):	32
Age Group:	**28–39**	**Age Group:**	**40 & older**
Male (% body fat):	24	Male (% body fat):	26
Female (% body fat):	34	Female (% body fat):	36

Commanders and NCO supervisors must monitor soldiers under their control to ensure that the soldiers maintain proper weight, body composition (the proportion of lean body mass, including muscle, bone, and essential organ tissue, to body fat), and personal appearance. Soldiers should be coached to select their personal weight goal within or below the 5 percent zone and strive to maintain that weight through adjustment of lifestyle and fitness routines. If a soldier consistently exceeds the personal weight goal, he or she should seek the assistance of a master fitness trainer for advice in proper exercise, and fitness and health-care personnel for a proper dietary program. Soldiers exceeding the screening table weight or identified by the commander or supervisor for a special evaluation will have their body fat measured using the tape test method.

When males are tape tested they must have the abdomen and neck measured; females have the hips, forearm, neck, and wrist measured. All measurements are taken three times and must be to within one quarter of an inch of one another to be considered valid. Valid measurements are recorded on DA Forms 5500-R (males) and 5501-R (females), *Body Fat Content Worksheet.* Recorded measurements are then converted to prescribed body site factors, using site factor tables in AR 600-9. If carefully measured and correctly calculated, the result will fairly accurately show a soldier's body fat percentage. The tape test is not difficult to learn to administer. The male test takes about five minutes, and the female test takes a little longer because more body sites are measured and calculated.

To help soldiers fight fat, NCO supervisors must provide educational and other motivational programs to encourage personnel to attain and maintain proper weight and body fat standards. Programs include nutrition education sessions conducted by qualified health-care personnel, as well as exercise programs. Commanders must enforce body fat standards and monitor, measure, and, if necessary, place individuals into the Army Weight Control Program, then continue to monitor individuals in compliance with AR 600-9. Soldiers entered into the program will not be allowed to reenlist or extend their enlistment, will be considered nonpromotable, and will not be assigned to command positions (e.g., squad leader, platoon sergeant, first sergeant, command sergeant major).

Further, overweight soldiers will be denied attendance at professional military or civilian schooling. AR 351-1, *Individual Military Education and Training,* states that personnel who do not meet body fat standards are not authorized to attend professional military schooling. All soldiers scheduled for attendance at schooling will be screened prior to departing their home station or losing command. Their height and weight will be recorded on their temporary duty orders, DD Form 1610, or on their permanent-change-of-station (PCS) packet. Soldiers exceeding established screening weight will not be allowed to depart their command until the commander has determined that they meet the standards.

WEIGHT FOR HEIGHT TABLE
(SCREENING TABLE WEIGHT)

Height (in inches)	Male Age				Female Age			
	17–20	21–27	28–39	40+	17–20	21–27	28–39	40+
58	—	—	—	109	112	115	119	—
59	—	—	—	113	116	119	123	—
60	132	136	139	141	116	120	123	127
61	136	140	144	146	120	124	127	131
62	141	144	148	150	125	129	132	137
63	145	149	153	155	129	133	137	141
64	150	154	158	160	133	137	141	145
65	155	159	163	165	137	141	145	149
66	160	163	168	170	141	146	150	154
67	165	169	174	176	145	149	154	159
68	170	174	179	181	150	154	159	164
69	175	179	184	186	154	158	163	168
70	180	185	189	192	159	163	168	173
71	185	189	194	197	163	167	172	177
72	190	195	200	203	167	172	177	183
73	195	200	205	208	172	177	182	188
74	201	206	211	214	178	183	189	194
75	206	212	217	220	183	188	194	200
76	212	217	223	226	189	194	200	206
77	218	223	229	232	193	199	205	211
78	223	229	235	238	198	205	210	216
79	229	235	241	244	203	209	215	222
80	234	240	247	250	208	214	220	227

Note: For screening purposes, body fat composition is to be determined in accordance with Appendix B, AR 600-9.

School commandants will take the following action upon determining that a student has arrived for a professional military school exceeding established body fat composition standards. Soldiers arriving at any Department of the Army (DA) board select school or those who PCS to a professional military school but do not meet body fat standards will be processed for disenrollment and removed from the DA board select list. Personnel arriving at professional military schools (other than DA board select or PCS schools) who do not meet body fat composition standards will be denied enrollment and reassigned in accordance with AR 600-9.

Actions to initiate mandatory bars to reenlistment, or initiation of separation proceedings for soldiers who are eliminated for cause from NCOES courses, will be in accordance with AR 601-280, *Army Reenlistment Program,* and AR 635-200, *Enlisted Personnel.* Additionally, soldiers who by the definition in AR 600-9 are considered weight control failures will be processed for separation from the Army.

Soldiers who are entered into the weight control program and then successfully meet their body fat reduction goal will be removed from the program but monitored for a year. Failure to meet the standards at any time during the monitoring period will result in initiation of separation action.

Soldiers who consider themselves too fat—or who come close to qualifying for the Army Weight Control Program—should look at modifying their lifestyles and eating habits for life. Soldiers interested in an improved diet may seek guidance in Appendix C of AR 600-9, "Nutrition Guide to the Weight Control Program."

According to the guide, proper nutrition and regular exercise are necessary to help you lose weight and improve your state of fitness. It says, "Invest in yourself." Here is how:

- Make a decision to lose weight and shape up.
- Get motivated.
- Develop a strategy (diet, exercise routine, lifestyle changes).
- Carry out this strategy and enjoy the payoff—a healthy appearance, an improved self-image, a sense of accomplishment, and a feeling of pride.

Studies show that the average American man eats 2,360 to 2,640 calories per day. The average woman eats between 1,640 and 1,800. Reducing calories taken in leaves fewer calories for the body to burn to lose weight. Research has shown that a healthy man can safely take in as few as 1,500 calories per day, and a healthy woman can consume as few as 1,200.

Vegetables, fruits, and complex carbohydrates, such as whole-grain breads, are "secret weapons" for anyone trying to maintain a healthy diet. They are filling and satisfying because they are high in fiber, but they are generally lower in calories.

PART III

Quick Reference

11

Administration, Logistics, and Maintenance

PERSONNEL ADMINISTRATION

No NCO can function without some knowledge of Army administration. As you rise in rank, your ability to understand and perform administrative tasks becomes more and more important. Squad leaders and platoon sergeants will have to know how to fill out leave forms (DA Form 4187), turn in equipment for repair, initiate requisition actions, plan and conduct convoy operations, and conduct performance ratings on subordinates, among many others.

Most situations that arise in the administration of an Army unit are covered in Army regulations or other publications. Knowing where to look for guidance is almost as important as knowing the answers. The Basic References table will help you find what you are looking for.

Each MOS has a corresponding set of basic reference publications. The effective NCO will know them and what is in them. In addition, the learning resource center and the MOS library are valuable sources for these and other publications.

BASIC REFERENCES

Army Regulations and Publications

Check the U.S. Army Publications Agency (USAPA) website at www.usapa.army.mil/gils/ for on-line regulations and forms.

AR 25-30	*The Army Publishing and Printing Program* (6/2/2004)
AR 25-50	*Preparing and Managing Correspondence* (6/3/2002)
AR 25-400-2	*The Army Records Information Management System* (ARIMS) (11/15/2004)
AR 135-205	*Enlisted Personnel Management* (9/1/1994)
AR 190-11	*Physical Security of Arms, Ammunition, and Explosives* (2/12/1998)

AR 220-1	*Unit Status Reporting* (6/10/2003)
AR 220-15	*Journals and Journal Files* (12/1/1983)
AR 220-45	*Duty Rosters* (11/15/1975)
AR 350-1	*Army Training and Education* (4/9/2003)
AR 350-10	*Management of Army Individual Training Requirements and Resources* (9/14/1990)
AR 350-17	*Noncommissioned Officer Development Program* (5/31/1991)
AR 385-10	*Army Safety Program* (2/29/2000)
AR 600-8-1	*Army Casualty Operations/Assistance/Insurance* (10/20/1994)
AR 600-8-2	*Suspension of Favorable Personnel Actions (Flags)* (12/23/2004)
AR 600-8-6	*Personnel Accounting and Strength Reporting* (9/24/1998)
AR 600-8-7	*Retirement Services Program* (6/1/2000)
AR 600-8-8	*The Total Army Sponsorship Program* (10/21/2004)
AR 600-8-10	*Leaves and Passes* (7/31/2003)
AR 600-8-11	*Reassignment* (10/1/1990)
AR 600-8-14	*Identification Cards for Members of the Uniformed Services, Their Family Members, and Other Eligible Personnel* (12/20/2002)
AR 600-8-19	*Enlisted Promotions and Reductions* (1/25/2005)
AR 600-8-22	*Military Awards* (2/25/1995)
AR 600-8-104	*Military Personnel Information Management/Records* (6/22/2004)
AR 600-9	*The Army Weight Control Program* (6/10/1987)
AR 600-13	*Army Policy for the Assignment of Female Soldiers* (3/27/1992)
AR 600-15	*Indebtedness of Military Personnel* (3/14/1986)
AR 600-20	*Army Command Policy* (5/13/2002)
AR 600-25	*Salutes, Honors, and Visits of Courtesy* (10/24/2004)
AR 600-85	*Army Substance Abuse Program (ASAP)* (10/1/2001)
AR 600-100	*Army Leadership* (9/17/1993)
AR 601-10	*Management and Mobilization of Retired Soldiers of the Army* (11/30/1994)
AR 601-210	*Regular Army and Army Reserve Enlistment Program* (5/16/2005)
AR 601-280	*Army Retention Program* (3/31/1999)
AR 614-30	*Overseas Service* (10/23/2004)
AR 614-200	*Enlisted Assignments and Utilization Management* (9/30/2004)
AR 621-5	*Army Continuing Education System (ACES)* (2/27/2004)

AR 623-205	*Noncommissioned Officer Evaluation Reporting System* (5/15/2002)
AR 635-200	*Active Duty Enlisted Administrative Separations* (6/6/2005)
AR 640-30	*Photographs for Military Personnel Files* (10/1/1991)
AR 670-1	*Wear and Appearance of Army Uniforms and Insignia* (2/3/2005)
AR 710-2	*Inventory Management Supply Policy below the Wholesale Level* (2/25/2004)
AR 750-1	*Army Materiel Maintenance Policy and Retail Maintenance Operations* (8/18/2003)
AR 840-10	*Flags, Guidons, Streamers, Tabards, and Automobile and Aircraft Plates* (11/1/1998)
CMH Pub 70-36	*The NCO—Images of an Army in Action*
CMH Pub 70-37	*Time Honored Professionals*
CMH Pub 70-38	*The Story of the NCO*
CTA 50-900	*Clothing and Individual Equipment*
CTA 50-909	*Field and Garrison Furnishings and Equipment*
CTA 50-970	*Expendable and Durable Items*
DA Form 6	*Duty Roster* (July 1964)
DA Form 2166-8	*Noncommissioned Officer Evaluation Report* (October 2001)
DA Form 2166-8-1	*Noncommissioned Officer Evaluation Checklist* (October 2001)
DA Form 4187	*Personnel Action Request* (January 2000)
MCM 2000	*Manual for Courts-Martial United States* (7/21/2000)
Pam 350-38	*Standards in Weapons Training* (10/1/2002)
Pam 350-59	*Army Correspondence Course Program Catalog* (10/1/2002)
Pam 385-1	*Small Unit Safety Officer/NCO Guide* (11/29/2001)
Pam 600-25	*U.S. Army Noncommissioned Officer Professional Development Guide* (10/15/2002)
Pam 600-35	*Relationships between Soldiers of Different Ranks* (2/21/2000)
Pam 600-60	*A Guide to Protocol and Etiquette for Official Entertainment* (12/11/2001)
Pam 600-67	*Effective Writing for Leaders*
Pam 600-69	*Unit Climate Profile Commanders Handbook* (10/1/1986)
Pam 611-21	*Military Occupational Classification and Structure* (3/31/1999)
Pam 710-2-1	*Using Unit Supply Systems*

Doctrinal Publications

Most Army field manuals are available online at *www.atiam.train.army.mil/soldierPortal/*.

The numbers for the new series are divided into three different categories. This provides a means for the Army and other services to use compatible numbering with the Joint system. In general, there is one number before the dash, reflecting the six basic functional series noted above (the Army has an additional seventh series for Warfighter Support). There are one or two numbers after the dash and/or the "dot." Those FM titles with the word (old) reflect that they still carry the old series number.

New Number	Date	Selected FM Titles	Old Number
	25 Jun 2002	*Battle Drills for the Infantry Rifle Platoon and Squad*	ARTEP 7-8 Drill
JCS PUB 1-02	09 May 2005	*DOD Dictionary of Military and Associated Terms*	
FM 1	14 Jun 2005	*The Army*	FM 100-1
3-0	14 Jun 1993	*Operations*	FM 100-5
5-0	20 Jan 2005	*Army Planning and Orders Preparation*	FM 101-5
1-02	21 Sep 2004	*Operational Terms and Graphics*	FM 101-5-1
4-20.05	14 Apr 2000	*Organizational Supply and Services for Unit Leaders* (old)	FM 10-27-4
4-25.10	21 Jun 2000	*Field Hygiene and Sanitation* (old)	FM 21-10
4-25.12	25 Jan 2002	*Unit Field Sanitation Team*	FM 21-10-1
4-25.11	23 Dec 2002	*First Aid*	FM 21-11
3-25.150	18 Jan 2002	*Combatives*	FM 21-150
3-21.18	01 Jun 1990	*Foot Marches* (old)	FM 21-18
3-22-20	01 Oct 1998	*Physical Fitness Training* (old)	FM 21-20
3-34.31	31 Dec 1968	*Topographic Symbols* (old)	FM 21-31
3-21.60	30 Sep 1987	*Visual Signals* (old)	FM 21-60
3-21.75	03 Aug 1984	*Combat Skills of the Soldier* (old)	FM 21-75
3-05.70	17 May 2002	*Survival*	FM 21-76
6-22	31 Aug 1999	*Army Leadership* (old edition)	FM 22-100
3-21.5	07 Jul 2003	*Drill and Ceremonies*	FM 22-5
3-21.6	15 Jan 1975	*Guard Duty* (old)	FM 22-6
6-22.5	23 Jun 2000	*Combat Stress*	FM 22-9
3-22.23	30 Mar 1973	*Antipersonnel Mine M18A1 and M18 (Claymore)* (old)	FM 23-23
3-22.30	07 Jun 2005	*Grenades and Pyrotechnic Signals*	FM 23-30

New Number	Date	Selected FM Titles	Old Number
3-22.31	13 Feb 2003	*40mm Grenade Launchers M203 and M79*	FM 23-31
3-22.35	25 Jun 2003	*Combat Training with Pistols and Revolvers*	FM 23-35
3-22.68	31 Jan 2003	*Crew Served Machine Guns 5.56-mm and 7.62-mm*	FM 23-14 FM 23-67
3-22.9	24 Apr 2003	*Rifle Marksmanship M16A1, M16A2/3, M16A4, and M4 Carbine*	FM 23-9
7-0	22 Oct 2002	*Training the Force*	FM 25-100
7-1	15 Sep 2003	*Battle-Focused Training*	FM 25-101
7-10.2		*How to Conduct Training Exercises*	FM 25-4
1-04.1	13 Jan 1992	*Legal Guide for Commanders* (old FM)	FM 27-1
1-04.10	18 Jul 1956	*The Law of Land Warfare*	FM 27-10
1-04.14	16 Apr 1991	*Legal Guide for Soldiers*	FM 27-14
1-04.2		*Your Conduct in Combat under the Law of War*	FM 27-2
3-11.7	29 Sep 1994	*NBC Handbook* (old)	FM 3-7
3-21.8	22 Apr 1992	*The Infantry Rifle Platoon and Squad* (old)	FM 7-8
3-21.9	02 Dec 2002	*The SBCT Infantry Rifle Platoon and Squad*	
		Soldier's Manual of Common Tasks	STP 21-24 SMCT
7-27.7	23 Dec 2002	*Army Noncommissioned Officers Guide*	TC 22-6
		Conducting Company Training	TC 25-30
		The Leader Transition	TC 26-10

World Wide Web Sites

Defense Link	*www.defenselink.mil/*
Army Home Page	*www.army.mil*
Army Installations	*www.army.mil/organization/*
Human Resources Command Link	*www.hrc.army.mil/site/active/index2.asp*
Retirement Services	*www.armyg1.army.mil/rso/mission.asp*
PCS	*www.dmdc.osd.mil/sites* (requires a log-in)
Health Affairs Home Page	*www.ha.osd.mil*
Center of Military History	*www.army.mil/cmh-pg*

Duty Rosters

AR 220-45, *Duty Rosters,* clearly states the rules for preparing and maintaining DA Form 6, *Duty Roster*. These rules are logical and easy to understand. Yet accurately putting them into practice requires meticulous attention to detail.

Duty rosters are kept to record the duty performed by each person in an organization. Commanders are authorized to establish procedures that best suit the unit, but they must comply with AR 220-45, the longest off duty, the first on, and impartiality in assignment of duties to individuals.

The "From" date on the roster is always the date immediately following the "To" date on a previous roster and is entered at the time the new roster is prepared. The "To" date is always the date of the last detail made from the roster and is entered when the roster is closed. Intermediate dates are entered as details are made, and no date will be entered for any day that the detail was not made.

Duty rosters contain only the names of those personnel required to perform the duty involved. When a new roster is prepared, all names are entered alphabetically by rank, beginning with the highest-ranking person and using the appropriate grade of rank. Subsequent names are added to the bottom of the roster. Frequently rosters are published in advance, and when absences of personnel already assigned to duty occur, they often occur at the last moment. Many commanders allow personnel to substitute for one another on various details, and in some units, individuals make extra money by selling their services as substitutes. In such cases, the person who maintains the duty roster must be notified of any changes, and recovery of any promised compensation is strictly up to the individuals concerned.

Details of units are made the same as they are for individuals, in turn according to one roster. Commanders are authorized to use other methods, however, providing that equity is maintained.

The diagonal lines in the right corner of any block indicate duty on that date. The numbers in parentheses immediately following a person's name refer to a corresponding explanatory remark on the reverse of the roster. A remark must be made to explain the reason why an individual's name is added to or deleted from a roster, but the authority responsible for the preparation and maintenance of the roster determines the necessity of using an explanatory remark each time an individual is not available.

A number is used with the abbreviation "A" in the column for Feb 14 to indicate the last number charged, as shown on the accompanying duty roster.

The duty roster should be available at all times for inspection by commanders, supervisors, and personnel concerned. If you are charged with the responsibility for maintaining a duty roster, do not feel that your integrity is being impugned when a soldier subject to detail according to the roster asks to see it.

Publish your rosters as far in advance as possible to give all concerned fair warning as to when they are coming up for duty. Be consistent when you publish your rosters. If you post the detail announcements on Monday, always post

DUTY ROSTER		NATURE OF DUTY: Charge of Quarters										ORGANIZATION: Co A 22d Infantry								FROM (Date): 14 Feb		TO (Date)
GRADE	NAME	MONTH: February														March						
		DAY: 14	15	16	17	18	19	20	21	22	23	24	25	26	27	28	1	2	3	4	5	6
SSG	Aldrich	10	11	12	13	6	7	/	1	8	2	3	9	10	4	5	6	7	8	11	12	9
SSG	Ashe	11	12	13	/	5	8	1	2	9	3	4	10	11	5	6	7	8	9	12	13	10
SSG	Fletcher (2)	12	13	/	1	1	9	2	3	10	4	A	A	A	5	6	7	8	9	11	12	11
SSG	Gonyea	13	/	1	2	2	3	3	4	4	5	6	5	6	7	8	9	10	11	7	8	12
SSG	Hall (8)	/	1	2	3	3	4	4	5	5	6	7	6	7	8							
SSG	Hanaburgh	8	9	10	11	16	/	12	13	1	/	1	2	3	2	3	4	5	6	4	5	7
SSG	Hill	6	7	8	9	15	16	10	11	/	12	13	14	15	14	/	1	2	3	/	1	4
SSG	MacDonald (1)	A[7]	A	A	8	/	1	9	10	2	11	12	3	4	13	14	/	1	2	5	6	3
SSG	Spadafora	1	2	3	4	14	15	5	6	1	7	8	2	3	9	10	11	12	13	4	5	14
SGT	Brown	2	3	4	5	13	14	6	7	15	8	9	/	1	10	11	12	13	14	2	3	/
SGT	Clark (7)	3	4	5	6	12	13	7	8	14	8	9	15	/	10	11	U	U	U	U	U	U
SGT	Dawson (4)	4	5	6	7	11	12	8	D	13	/	1	14	15	2	3	4	5	6	16	/	7
SGT	Hamilton	5	6	7	8	10	11	9	10	12	11	12	13	14	13	14	15	/	1	15	16	2
SGT	Nielson (3)	6	7	8	9	9	10	10	A	A	A	A	11	12	11	12	13	14	/	13	14	1
SGT	Richau	7	8	9	10	8	9	11	12	10	13	14	11	12	/	1	2	3	4	13	14	5
SGT	Taunton (6)	8	9	10	11	7	8	12	13	9	14	/	10	11	1	2	A	A	A	A	A	3
CPL	Grady	9	10	11	12	4	5	13	/	6	1	2	7	8	3	4	5	6	7	9	10	8
SSG	Saigh (5)								1	1	2	3	2	3	4	5	6	7	8	4	5	9
CPL	McCallum (5)											1	1	2	2	3	4	5	6	3	4	7

This is a consolidated duty roster. Therefore, 18, 19, 22, 25, and 26 February and 4 and 5 March are holidays

The following remarks go on the back of the roster:
1) Sick in Quarters
2) 72-hour pass (NCO of quarter)
3) Leave 21-24 Feb
4) Special Duty 21 Feb
5) Joined
6) Leave 1-5 Mar
7) AWOL
8) PCS

DA FORM 1 JUL 74 PREVIOUS EDITIONS OF THIS FORM WILL BE USED UNTIL EXHAUSTED

SEE REMARKS ON REVERSE

For use of this form, see AR 220-45, the proponent Agency is the US Army Adjutant General Center them on Mondays. Smart soldiers will always contact the person responsible for the duty roster when making plans, so never discourage personnel from doing this. Thinking ahead benefits everyone.

SAFETY AND RISK MANAGEMENT

The Army Safety Program

The preservation of personnel and materiel resources is critical to maintaining a unit's combat readiness, and every NCO is responsible for ensuring that unsafe acts or unsafe conditions are recognized and steps taken to correct them. By doing this, a unit's ability to operate at maximum combat efficiency will be maintained.

The Army Safety Program includes goals, objectives, policies, and responsibilities. Its safety goals are to reduce and keep to a minimum accidental manpower and monetary losses and provide a safe and healthful environment. Objectives include the following: injury prevention, damage control, accident prevention, regulatory compliance, and liability reduction. Policies of the safety program support the Army mission, make accident prevention a command responsibility, and use available resources on hazards that pose the most immediate threat to safety. Program safety responsibilities are as follows:

- Know and comply with safety policies, regulations, and standard operating procedures (SOPs).
- Conduct inspections to ensure compliance with safety procedures.
- Train your soldiers to avoid unsafe acts and conditions.
- Identify hazards before accidents occur.
- Ensure that soldiers have the ability to safely perform a stated task.
- Provide proper tools and safety equipment.
- Correct unsafe acts and conditions.
- Report unsafe acts and conditions that cannot be corrected.
- Conduct safety meetings.

Safety is a by-product of every successful or completed mission and must receive the highest regard. It is extremely important for you, as a supervisor, to be aware not only of potential hazards that may affect you but also of conditions that may affect those working under your authority.

Risk Management and Risk Assessment

The terms *risk management* and *risk assessment* are often used synonymously, when in fact, they are different. Risk management is a tool that helps leaders make sound logical decisions. When used in a positive command climate, risk management can become a mind-set that governs all unit missions and activities. It enables leaders at all levels to do exactly what the term implies: *manage risk*. Safety risk management is a specific type of risk management and is an extension of the decision-making process that is already ingrained in military leaders.

Risk assessment is part of risk management. It can range from simple to complex, and can be done formally, during the deliberate planning process, or informally, while conducting a hasty plan. A risk assessment allows leaders to identify hazards and threats and place them in perspective relative to the mission or task at hand. Logically, one cannot identify the risk without first determining what the hazards are.

The risk management process consists of five steps: Identify hazards, assess hazards, make risk decisions, implement controls, and supervise.

Identify hazards. Identify the most probable hazards for the mission. Hazards are conditions with the potential of causing injury to personnel, damage to equipment, loss of materiel, or lessening of ability to perform a task or mission. The most probable hazards are those created by readiness shortcomings in the operational environment that impact man and machine. The human error problem areas discussed in the previous section are generic examples of those hazards. When a list of frequently recurring hazards is applied to a specific task or mission, the most probable hazards can be identified.

Assess hazards. Once the most probable hazards are identified, analyze each to determine the probability of its causing an accident and the probable effect of the accident. Also, identify control options to eliminate or reduce the hazard. A tool to use is the Army Standard Risk Assessment Matrix.

Make risk decisions. Weigh the risk against the benefits of performing the operation. Accept no unnecessary risks, and make any residual risk decisions at the proper level of command.

Implement controls. Integrate specific controls into plans, operations orders, SOPs, and rehearsals. Communicate controls down to the individual soldier.

Supervise. Determine the effectiveness of controls in reducing the probability and effect of identified hazards. Ensure that risk control measures are performing as expected. Include follow-up during and after action to ensure that all went according to plan, reevaluating or adjusting the plan as required, and developing lessons learned.

How Can My Soldiers Get Hurt, and What Can I Do about It? Vignette

A low-risk maintenance operation was suddenly turned into a high-risk operation when an NCO parked a 2½-ton truck on a downhill slope about fifteen feet from a Bradley Fighting Vehicle (BFV). It was a normal working day. The battalion had just returned from a lengthy field training exercise (FTX), and the battalion's maintenance shops were full of equipment in need of repair. One crew member was cleaning the engine compartment of the BFV so it could be inspected by a mechanic.

When the driver parked the $2^1/_2$-ton truck on the hill, he set the hand brake, but didn't chock the wheels. He got out to get a cup of coffee, telling the assistant driver not to move the vehicle, but to come get him when the steam cleaner was available. Ignoring the instructions he had received, the unqualified assistant entered the cab and started the vehicle. It lunged forward, pinning the driver of the BFV against the vehicle. The stunned assistant had to be told to back the truck off the BFV crew member, who died as a result of his injuries.

The direct cause of the accident was an unlicensed, untrained driver who disobeyed his NCO's instructions. The NCO himself, however, set the scenario for this tragedy. There are always hazards associated with parking a heavy vehicle on a downhill slope. There are hazards when these vehicles are left unchocked and dependent solely on parking brakes. And there are hazards whenever untrained, unlicensed operators are involved. This leader allowed hazards to pile one on top of another because he did not enforce standards. Unchecked, these hazards were combined with a soldier having a "can-do" attitude and his failure to follow instructions, which turned a seemingly low-risk operation into a high-risk operation.

RULES FOR RISK MANAGEMENT

- Integrate risk management into planning.
- Accept no unnecessary risk.
- Make risk decisions at the proper level.
- Accept risk if benefits outweigh the cost.

NCO SAFETY PROGRAM

More soldiers die in privately owned vehicle (POV) accidents *every year* than were killed by enemy fire in Afghanistan and Iraq. Soldiers survived the combat environment; now we want to be sure that they and their family members survive travel on the highway. Alcohol, speed, fatigue, and failure to use seat belts and airbags are primary factors in POV fatalities. Travel planning is another critical consideration since most individuals/units will have block leave following redeployment.

Safety is an individual task and like other individual tasks is an NCO responsibility. Safety should be a Mission Essential Task List (METL) task. All leaders in a unit should do safety assessments, and update them. Safety guidance should be published and posted in plain view. Units should organize for safety. Leaders should develop long-, short-, and near-term safety education programs. Safety should be part of every quarterly training briefing (attended by the commander and first sergeant). Develop a safety feedback system to remain informed about real and potential hazards. Put safety first when executing missions. Include safety aspects of training in every After Action Review. Reward safety excellence and punish negligence.

Leaders are responsible for the protection of every soldier's life. Safety takes precedence over fairness; safety is a battle-focused concept; safety and performance complement each other; and everyone is a safety officer. Take a look at FM 9-43-1 (FM 4-30.3), *Maintenance Operations and Procedures,* and AR 385-10, *The Army Safety Program,* for detailed guidance. The new Army POV *Risk Management Leader's Guide* will help you keep your soldiers safe.

If you or someone else in your unit is in an accident, you will need to complete DA Form 285, *U.S. Army Accident Report.* If you must complete the report, you can refer to the educational instruction package for the report, available from the U.S. Army Safety Center, ATTN: CSSC-S, Fort Rucker, AL 36362-5363. Or call DSN 558-3842 or commercial (205) 255-3842.

SUPPLY

Everyone in the Army is accountable and responsible for government property; the amount of property for which a soldier is responsible generally increases in value as he or she advances in rank. Safeguarding government property mostly requires lots of good old-fashioned common sense.

Classes of Supply

Supplies are items necessary to equip, maintain, and operate a military command, including food, clothing, arms, ammunition, fuel, materials, and machinery of all kinds. Supplies are divided into ten categories called classes and into lettered subclasses known as material designators (A through T). (For a detailed discussion of supply, see Edwards, *Combat Service Support Guide,* 3rd edition [Stackpole Books, 2000].) For example, Class I C supplies are combat rations.

- Class I—Subsistence, including health and welfare items. Subclassifications include inflight rations, refrigerated subsistence, nonrefrigerated subsistence, and combat rations.
- Class II—Clothing, individual equipment, tentage, organization tool sets and tool kits, hand tools, administrative and housekeeping supplies, and equipment. Subclassifications include weapons, power generators, and textiles.
- Class III—Petroleum, oils, and lubricants.
- Class IV—Construction materials.
- Class V—Ammunition, including chemical, biological, radiological, and special weapons.
- Class VI—Personal demand items, including beverages ("Class VI store" items).

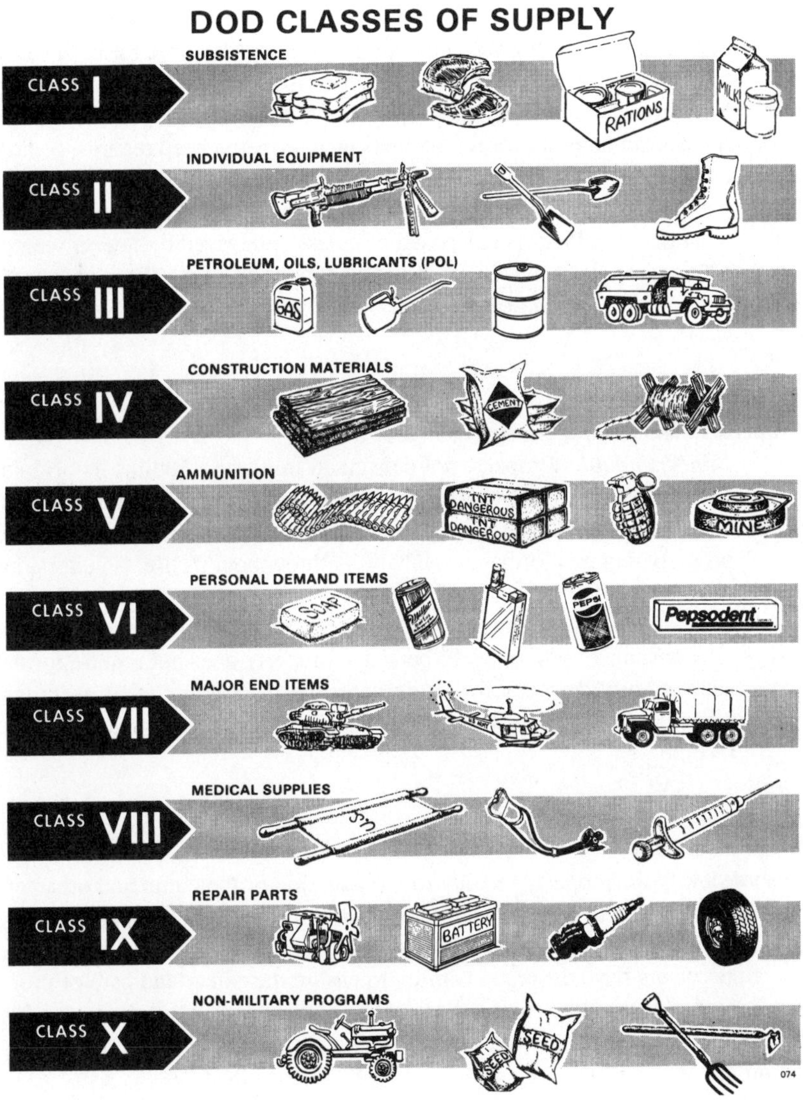

- Class VII—Major end items, such as tanks and helicopters. Subclassifications include bridging and fire fighting equipment, administrative and tactical vehicles, missiles, weapons, and special weapons.
- Class VIII—Medical materials.
- Class IX—Repair parts and components.
- Class X—Material to support nonmilitary programs, such as agricultural and economic development.

Basic Principles

All persons entrusted with government property are responsible for its custody, care, and safekeeping. No commander or supervisor can assign a soldier a duty that would prevent exercising the proper care and custody of property. When you assume accountability for remotely located property, keep records to show the location of the items and the persons charged with safekeeping.

Army property will not be used for private purpose, sold, given as a gift, lent, exchanged, or otherwise disposed of unless authorized by law. Giving or accepting an issue, document, hand receipt, or any form of receipt to cover articles that are missing, or appear to be missing, is prohibited.

Accounting for Property

Property falls into three distinct categories:

- *Nonexpendable.* Property not consumed in use that retains its original identity during the period of use. Includes all serial-numbered items, such as weapons, vehicles, office machines, and so on. Nonexpendable property requires formal accountability throughout its life. A continuous chain of receipts is required if these items pass among different persons.
- *Expendable.* Office supplies, cleaning materials, and other supplies that are consumed upon issue. Expendable property does not require formal accountability except for some sensitive categories, such as drugs.
- *Durable.* Certain kinds of hand tools. Tools must be issued on a hand receipt.

Responsibilities

Responsibility for property results from possession or the command or supervision of others who have possession of Army property. This responsibility may be assigned by appropriate authority in writing or orally.

Supervisors have the responsibility to ensure the safety and care of property issued to or used by their subordinates. Supervisors are also responsible for maintaining the proper atmosphere that leads to supply discipline among subordinates.

Direct responsibility is a formal assignment of property responsibility to a person within the supply chain who has the property within his or her custody but not necessarily in his possession. Accountable officers have direct responsibility unless it has been specifically assigned to another person. An accountable officer maintains formal records that show the balance, conditions, and location of all property assigned to a property account. Enlisted personnel who are sergeants or higher rank, when appointed by proper authority, may serve as accountable officers.

Responsibilities of Hand-Receipt Holders

Signing a hand receipt, including signing for clothing and equipment, is probably the most familiar aspect of the supply system to most soldiers. It carries with it definite responsibilities, and you must follow these simple rules:

- Inventory equipment and supplies receipted to you.
- Have property for which you have signed on hand or accounted for by a receipt, turn-in, or some other type of authorized credit document.
- Prevent loss, damage, or destruction of property under your control.
- When you turn an item in, get a receipt for it.
- Report loss or theft to your superior.
- When you transfer, be sure all property is turned in or passed into the custody of your replacement or whoever succeeds you in custody of the property. You will not be allowed to clear the installation until you have accounted for all the property for which you are responsible.
- Report to your supervisor any circumstances that make the proper security of property or equipment impossible. Failure to do so can result in your being charged for any loss or damage because you knew the facts and did not report them.

Statements of Charges and Reports of Survey

Statements of Charges (DD Form 362) and *Reports of Survey* (DA Form 4697) are unpleasant methods the Army has of getting its money back from soldiers who have been careless or negligent in their duty as property custodians.

A *Statement of Charges* is prepared in the following situations:

- Liability for loss, damage, or destruction of property is admitted.
- The charge does not exceed the monthly basic pay of the person being charged.
- Individuals do not offer cash payment to make good the lost, damaged, or destroyed property. (All military personnel and civilian employees of the Department of the Army who voluntarily admit liability may offer to replace the property through cash purchase.) If the charges levied by a *Statement of Charges* exceed two-thirds of an individual's monthly basic pay, the unit commander will attach a letter requesting that the charges be prorated over a two-month period or longer.

A *Report of Survey* is required to account for lost, damaged, or destroyed property, when it is known that negligence has occurred or misconduct is suspected and liability is not admitted. In addition, a *Report of Survey* is prepared in the following situations:

- A sensitive item is lost or destroyed.
- It is directed by higher authority.
- Property loss is discovered as a result of change of accountability inventory.

- The value of the damages or shortages in occupied government quarters exceeds the responsible person's monthly basic pay.
- A person admits liability, and the loss, damage, or destruction exceeds the individual's monthly basic pay.
- A soldier refuses to admit liability and does not offer repayment.

Senior NCOs may be appointed survey officers. Such investigations are painstakingly thorough. The survey officer is charged with finding out the facts. He or she, based on the facts of the investigation, must recommend whether or not to fix liability upon the subjects.

If you are ever the subject of a *Report of Survey,* remember these guidelines:

- Keep calm, tell the truth, and cooperate with the survey officer.
- The survey officer has a job to do; do not take it personally.
- If the survey officer finds you liable, he or she must show you the report and explain your right to legal counsel and to appeal the recommendation if approved.
- If you appeal, get legal counsel; consult an Army lawyer even if you don't appeal.
- You may request remission of indebtedness or an extension of the collection period if the report is approved.
- Many *Reports of Survey* do not recommend pecuniary liability. If you have taken every reasonable precaution to protect the property in your possession, and you can prove it, you should have nothing to fear. If responsibility is fixed on you and the report is approved, then take your medicine.

Enforcement of Supply Discipline

Various disciplinary and administrative measures are available to a commander to enforce supply discipline and reduce the incidence of lost, damaged, or destroyed government property. When property is lost, damaged, or destroyed by a subordinate, the usual reaction is to reach for AR 735-5 and initiate a report of survey. This action may be appropriate or, in some cases, required.

Military discipline goes hand in hand with supply discipline. Commanders have the following administrative tools available in connection with the report of survey.

- An oral reprimand. In more serious cases, a formal letter of admonition or reprimand may be used and, when appropriate, filed in the soldier's Official Military Personnel File.
- Noting a soldier's inefficiency or negligence in his or her NCOER.
- Article 15 or court-martial in cases of misconduct or neglect resulting in damaged or lost military property.

A *Report of Survey* is not a form of punishment or a deterrent. Nonjudicial punishment, however, is both. Its use in conjunction with a *Report of Survey* may be indicated, depending upon circumstances. Even when no liability is found, the facts may warrant command action. There is little doubt that strong measures should be taken against a supply sergeant whose stocks are found $10,000 short because of his or her misconduct or neglect. But similar action also would be appropriate against supervisors if investigation revealed inadequate supervision, such as if required inventories had never been made or verified.

MAINTENANCE AND THE NCO

The basic document covering maintenance is DA Pam 750-1, *Leader's Unit Level Maintenance Handbook.* As an NCO, you have a direct responsibility and influence on your unit's ability to maintain its equipment. Through your guidance and example, your soldiers will either maintain your unit's equipment or destroy it through neglect. Keep in mind that combat power is a combination of manpower, materiel, and readiness. One cannot survive without the others. With approximately 25 percent of the defense budget being directed toward the maintenance of equipment, each leader must become fully involved in training soldiers to maintain equipment. As a member of the maintenance management team in your unit, ask yourself the following questions:

- Are preventative maintenance checks and services (PMCS) performed on all equipment assigned to my squad/section before, during, and after all periods of operation?
- Have I ever assessed the effectiveness of my maintenance operation?
- Am I personally involved in my unit's maintenance program?
- Do I provide training to my soldiers on maintenance techniques?
- Do I require my soldiers to perform maintenance to the same standards as required when performing other mission tasks?

To demonstrate that maintenance, like training, cuts across all components of the Army, the above was extracted from the *Army National Guard Noncommissioned Officer Handbook.*

12

Assignments

Soldiers who avidly read the *Army Times or Soldiers* magazine for any glimmer of changes to Army personnel policy while waiting for the new regulation updates to arrive in the mail will want to checkout the Internet site at *www.hrc.army.mil/site/Active/enlist/ENLIST.htm.* The enlisted management web page has everything an inquiring soldier wants to know in real time and up to date. Instead of waiting months to find out if your *Personnel Action Request* (DA Form 4187) for reassignment has gone through, call the IVRS, send an e-mail, use the fax, or—even better—sign on to the Assignment Satisfaction Key, all of which are explained below.

COMMUNICATING WITH HUMAN RESOURCES COMMAND

The U.S. Army Human Resources Command (HRC) continues a series of initiatives designed to increase enlisted soldiers' participation in managing their careers. What was once paper-intensive and not very responsive is now, with automation, very responsive to those soldiers who care about their assignments.

To help soldiers communicate better with their career managers, the Enlisted Personnel Management Directorate (EPMD) employs five tools. These initiatives include an Interactive Voice Response Telephone System (IVRS), expanded e-mail capabilities, high-speed fax machines, mail-grams, and a pocket reference information card that lists telephone numbers, e-mail addresses, and other data valuable to soldiers wanting to help manage their careers.

The cornerstone of the new system is the web site on the Internet at *www.hrc.army.mil/indexflash.asp,* although IVRS, which is an automated voice response telephone system that provides soldiers with career information twenty-four hours a day remains available for those without Internet access. Soldiers can activate IVRS by dialing (800) FYI-EPMD or DSN 221-3763. The 800 number is available only in the continental United States. To use IVRS, enter your social security number and then follow the menu options, which will let you know if you are on assignment or scheduled to attend an Army school, or will provide topical information on retention, recruiting, drill sergeant, special forces, ranger, and compassionate reassignments; the Married Army Couples Program; the Exceptional Family Member Program; and separations.

EPMD also encourages you to use e-mail to contact your branch. Inquiries concerning the status of personnel actions, future schooling, or assignments are examples of typical information exchanges that can be conducted twenty-four hours a day.

Soldiers can also correspond with their career managers by using fax machines. Soldiers and personnel service centers can save time by faxing communications directly to the desired career branch within EPMD for processing. The information below contains EPMD e-mail, fax, and mail addresses.

Assignment Satisfaction Key (ASK)

For soldiers who have used ASK—the Soldier Assignment Module (SAM) provides virtually instant capability for your assignment manager and professional development NCO to identify all open requirements you may be eligible for, provides the capabilities to hone in on the most eligible soldiers, and also identifies all volunteers for a specific assignment location.

Accessible from the HRC web site or a soldier's Army Knowledge Online (AKO) account, ASK is the futuristic vision of soldiers making all their own assignments, and it is slowly becoming a reality. This innovation provides soldiers with an automated tool to quickly update their preferences and contact information via the Internet through their respective AKO account. During the "dream sheet" days you had many assignment locations to choose from but little chance of being assigned to where you asked, unless you were able to correspond with your assignment manager. Today the majority of assignment locations are available for you to select, and those who decline to submit a preference will be assigned according to the needs of the Army. Bottom line, the ASK provides soldiers the capability to post assignment preferences directly onto the Total Army Personnel Database. This system is expected one day to eliminate the paper- and labor-intensive DA Form 4187. The Assignment Selection Key is available through the HRC web site at *www.hrc.army.mil/index-flash.asp*. Use your AKO account password to gain access.

Plus-2 Personal Life Cycle Unit Selection System

Plus-2 supports life cycle management and unit focused stability by providing a web-based means for soldiers to volunteer for Units of Action (UA). By using volunteers to maximize soldier/unit cohesion it reduces requirements for nonvolunteer permanent change of station (PCS). The web site is at *www.isdrad16.hoffman.army.mil/HRCSoldierPreferenceWeb/*. As above, log in using your AKO account password.

When you log into the system, you are shown requisitions for which you are eligible. From the list, you select and reserve your unit and duty position.

Although career managers still approve assignment requests based on professional development considerations, indications are that if you are able to make an assignment selection you are virtually assured of your desired assignment.

How to Contact the Enlisted Personnel Management Directorate

Telephone

Interactive Voice Response System (IVRS)
1-800-FYI-EPMD (CONUS)
1-800-394-3763 (CONUS)
(703) 325-3763 (Commercial)
221-2763 Defense Switched Network (DSN)

Mail

U.S. Total Army Personnel Command
Attention: (Your branch office symbol. Column 2 in below table)
2461 Eisenhower Avenue
Alexandria, VA 22331

E-mail

Your branch e-mail ID (column 3 in below table) *@hoffman.army.mil*

Fax

221-XXXX (DSN)
(703) 325-XXXX (Commercial)
Your branch fax extension (column 4 in below table)

Building a base camp with teamwork.

ENLISTED ASSIGNMENT CONTACT INFORMATION

1 Assignment Branch	2 Office Symbol	3 E-mail ID	4 Fax Extension
Infantry	EPK-I	EPINF	4880
Air Defense Artillery	EPK-A	EPADA	4664
Field Artillery	EPK-F	EPFA	4533
Special Forces	EPK-S	EPSF	4510
Armor	EPK-R	EPAR	4683
Engineer	EPL-E	EPENGR	4307
MP	EPL-M	EPMP	4304
MI	EPL-M	EPINTELL	4304
Language	EPL-M	EPLANG	4304
Signal	EPL-S	EPSIG	4306
Aviation	EPL-T	EPAVN	4308
Transportation	EPL-T	EPTRANS	4308
Adjutant General	EPM-A	EPAG	5836
Health Services	EPM-H	EPHS	6402
QM/Chemical	EPM-L	EPQMC	4521
Ordnance	EPM-O	EPORD	6555
CSM/SGM Office	EPZ-E	EPCSMSGM	4694
Retention/Reclass	EPR	TAPCEPR	3565

The Enlisted Personnel Assignment System

The primary goal of the enlisted personnel assignment system is to satisfy the personnel requirements of the Army. Secondary goals are:

- To place soldiers in positions that require skills, knowledge, and abilities as shown by their primary military vehicle specialty (PMOS), secondary military occupational specialty (SMOS), or additionally awarded military occupational specialty (AMOS).
- To provide policies on personnel utilization that will strengthen and broaden MOS qualifications and prepare soldiers for career progression, greater responsibility, and diversity of assignment.

Consistent with Army needs, soldiers remain as long as possible at their CONUS duty stations. The Army's time-on-station (TOS) requirement for

Enlisted Personnel Assignment System

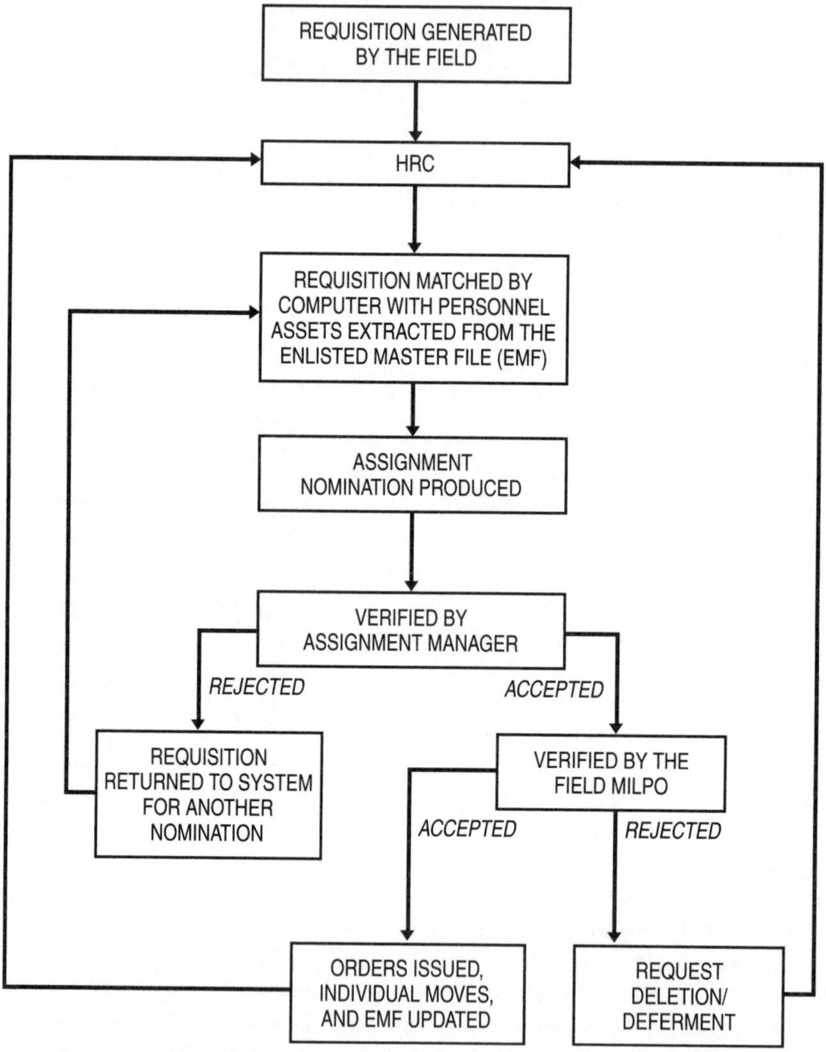

CONUS is forty-eight months; for OCONUS it is the length of the prescribed tour. Soldiers complete the forty-eight-month TOS tour requirement unless operational or training necessities are so overriding that they must be reassigned earlier. There is no statutory limitation on the amount of time soldiers may remain overseas, just as there is no statutory limit as to how long a soldier remains at a CONUS post. Except for CONUS requirements that are filled from OCONUS returnees who are immediately available (IA), qualified volunteers are considered first for all assignments. Soldiers may submit a request for reassignment before completion of TOS requirements, but they must complete minimum TOS requirements at their present duty station before movement. When possible, soldiers will remain on station for the maximum number of years possible consistent with Army requirements.

Enlisted Personnel Management System (EPMS) Manning Priorities:

- Deployed Major Combat Reporting Units (MCRU) Forces (combat battalions, brigade combat teams, and division headquarters)
- Deploying MCRU Forces
- Joint, Major Command Headquarters, and Directed Military Overstrength organizations
- U.S. Army Training and Doctrine Command (TRADOC)
- Forces in Reset
- All other forces

NEW MANNING STRATEGIES

During the next years, the Army will continue combat operations while transitioning to a unit-focused manning strategy. This unit-focused strategy is key to the Army as it transitions to an expeditionary force whose primary objectives are combat readiness and unit cohesion in deploying forces. The primary assumption is that soldiers and units will continue one-year assignments/rotations to Korea, Iraq, Afghanistan, and Kosovo for the near future. The foundation of the strategy is to retain unit integrity for the maximum period possible. Force stabilization will increase unit readiness and deployability by reducing turbulence and increasing stability so soldiers and units can train, deploy, fight, win, and return together.

Soldiers' assignment cycles will be aligned with the operational cycles of their units, making them more deployable and combat ready. The intent under the life cycle manning method is that all soldiers assigned to life cycle–manned units during the reset period will have thirty-six months retainability with an NCO level fill of between 70 and 80 percent with the remaining 20 to 30 percent being filled using grade substitution. Noncommissioned Officer Education System (NCOES) and other leader development opportunities and reenlistment options will occur only during their unit's reset period.

Stabilization

After units redeploy from operational deployments, soldiers will be stabilized for ninety days. Exceptions to the ninety-day period will be minimized and where possible be limited to soldiers volunteering for schools, reassignment, or separating from active service. At the conclusion of their initial stabilization period, unit personnel will begin a formalized reset period of sixty days, during which time they will be refitted and remanned.

The intent during the reset period of a life cycle-manned unit is to bring in new soldiers to replace soldiers scheduled to expiration, time of service (ETS), retire, or permanent change of station (PCS), minimize Headquarters Department of the Army (HQDA) directed departures, and retain as many soldiers already assigned to the unit as possible. Some soldiers with recent combat troop experience, however, will be transferred to fill other high priority assignments. Their knowledge and experience, as lessons learned and promulgated across the Army, will significantly enhance combat operations. Postdeployment assignments will be made with a view to future operations to minimize turbulence and maximize stability and predictability. The intent is to minimize use of Stop Loss/Stop Move for all operational missions. Stabilizing and retaining soldiers in their recently redeployed units is the optimal solution.

Under the individual stabilization concept, soldiers assigned to selected installations in CONUS will serve extended tours at the same duty station. The majority of enlisted soldiers assigned to CONUS installations that house large combat formations—such as BCTs/regiments, divisions, support groups, and corps—can expect to be assigned at the installation for extended periods. Soldiers will be reassigned based on the following prioritized criteria: needs of the Army, leader development, and soldier preference.

Stop Loss

The Stop Loss program is authorized by statute and allows the military services to retain trained, experienced, and skilled manpower by suspending certain laws, regulations, and policies that allow separations from active duty, including retirement. Those affected by the order generally cannot voluntarily retire or leave the service as long as Reserves are called to active duty or until relieved by proper authority. There are two types of Stop Loss that apply to soldiers in the Reserve Components (RC): Unit Stop Loss and Skill-Based Stop Loss. Currently, the only stop loss policy in effect is RC Unit Stop Loss.

Normally, the military personnel office (MILPO), in coordination with the unit, compares authorized and projected positions with current assigned strength and known or projected gains and losses to determine the requirements for assignments. Requisitions are then prepared for these requirements and submitted to Human Resources Command (HRC) in Alexandria, Virginia. On receipt, HRC edits and validates the requisitions. It is the responsibility of the requisitioning unit not to over- or under-requisition and to resolve any discrepancy before submitting the validated requisition for processing. Soldiers become available to be assigned against these requisitions for a variety of reasons. Soldiers who enlist in the Army are available for assignment on completion of training and award of an MOS. Others are available when they have done one of the following:

- Volunteered for reassignment.
- Completed an overseas tour of duty.
- Completed schooling or training.
- Completed a stabilized tour of duty.
- Completed normal time on station in the continental United States for a given MOS ("turnaround time" varies by MOS).

Army Exceptional Family Member Program (AR 608-75)

The Exceptional Family Member Program (EFMP) is based on Public Law 94-142, which entitles handicapped children to free education and all medically related services in pursuit of education. The EFMP includes all family members with special medical and educational needs.

Soldiers enroll through their local Army medical treatment facility. The military sponsor and the attending medical or educational specialist complete enrollment forms. When HRC nominates a soldier enrolled in the EFMP for assignment, the assignment manager coordinates with the gaining command to determine if needed medical services are available. When services are not available, HRC considers alternative assignment locations based on existing assignment priorities or sends the soldier in an unaccompanied status.

Assignment of Women Soldiers

Women soldiers are authorized to serve in all type units except those battalion-size or smaller that have a routine mission to engage in direct combat, or that collocate routinely with units assigned a direct combat mission. Women soldiers are assigned in accordance with Direct Combat Probability Coding (DCPC) and are restricted from filling a position with a DCPC of P1 (men only). All table of organization and equipment (TOE) elements positions are assigned a DCPC code of either P1 (men only) or P2 (open to women). Table of distribution and allowance (TDA) positions are gender neutral.

Homebase and Advance Assignment Program (HAAP) and Deployment Stabilization

HAAP is governed by AR 614-200, chapter 2, section VIII. Participation in the HAAP is optional. The HAAP is designed to reduce permanent change of station (PCS) costs and the number of PCS moves by soldiers and their families. The program has two options. Homebase assignment projects the enlisted soldier to return to the same installation upon completion of a twelve-month dependent-restricted short tour. Advanced assignment projects the enlisted soldier to be assigned to a new duty station upon completion of a twelve-month dependent-restricted short tour.

Only sergeants through master sergeants assigned to twelve-month dependent-restricted short tour areas are authorized to participate in the HAAP. The HAAPs will not be given to enlisted soldiers who voluntarily elect to serve a twelve-month "all others" tour when assigned to an accompanied tour area.

The following primary factors determine HAAP assignments:

- The needs of the Army.
- Assignment preference considerations.
- Professional development.
- Least-cost factors.

Family members who relocate to the advance assignment are not authorized placement on the waiting list for on-post government quarters. Placement begins when the soldier completes the dependent-restricted short tour and signs in at the new duty station. Additionally, after completing a tour in Korea or other dependent-restricted areas, soldiers will be exempt from operational deployment at their new duty station, which will allow soldiers time to become reacquainted with their families.

Compassionate Actions

AR 614-200 establishes specific policies governing individual requests submitted by soldiers for a permanent change of station (PCS) or deletion from assignment instructions. A soldier may submit a request for any of the following reasons:

- Extreme family problem that is temporary and can be resolved in one year.
- Extreme family problem that is not expected to be resolved in one year.
- Sole surviving son or daughter. AR 614-200, paragraphs 5-9, and DA Pamphlet 600-8 apply. The sole surviving son or daughter of a family that has suffered the loss of the father, the mother, or one or more sons or daughters in the military service will not be required to serve in combat. Soldiers who become sole surviving sons or daughters after their enlistment may request discharge under AR 635-200. A soldier may waive entitlement to assignment limitations, whether entitlement was based on his or her own application or the request of his or her immediate family.

Soldiers pending compassionate requests are not exempt from PCS moves or temporary duty (TDY) while waiting for resolution.

Soldiers whose units are ordered to combat zone or hostile fire areas will remain at the home station until reassigned.

Married Army Couples Program

AR 614-200 and AR 614-30 apply. Army requirements and readiness goals are paramount when considering personnel for assignment. Married Army couples desiring joint assignment to establish common household (joint domicile) must request such assignment. The assignment desires of soldiers married to other soldiers are fully considered. Married Army couples must be enrolled in the HQDA Total Army Personnel Database (TAPDB) to be considered for joint assignment. Enrollment is a simple process of verifying that two soldiers are married to one another, and having this information transmitted from the servicing Personnel Service Center (PSC) to the TAPDB. A separate transaction is required for each spouse. Once enrolled, both soldiers will be continuously considered for joint assignments. In 2005, of the 20,000 plus enlisted soldiers enrolled in the program, approximately 75 percent of those enrolled in the Married Army Couples Program (MACP) were serving in joint domicile assignments.

Exchange Assignments

DA Pam 600-8 and AR 614-200, paragraphs 5–8, apply. For mutual convenience, CONUS-assigned soldiers may request an exchange assignment with a soldier within CONUS; a soldier assigned overseas may request an exchange assignment with a soldier within his or her same overseas command.

DA Pam 600-8 contains detailed guidance for preparing and processing requests for an exchange assignment.

CAREER DEVELOPMENT PROGRAM ASSIGNMENTS

A career development program is a system of intensive management of selected MOSs or career management fields (CMFs). Career development programs are established to ensure that there are enough highly trained and experienced soldiers to fill positions that require unique or highly technical skills. To develop soldiers with the required proficiency, career fields within each program often require the following:

- Frequent movement from one job to another to gain required experience.
- An above-average frequency of advanced training.
- Lengthy or frequent training periods.

Unless otherwise stated in AR 614-200, volunteers for a career development program should submit applications on DA Form 4187, using DA Pam 600-8 for detailed application procedures. In applying for career programs and related training, applicants should consider the prerequisites listed in DA Pam 351-4 for the appropriate course of instruction.

Chapter 6, AR 614-200, contains the minimum requirements (subject to change) for each career program. Attaining the prerequisites does not automatically ensure entry into a career program. The appropriate career management branch selects the best-qualified soldiers for a career program.

Waivers are not granted for remaining service requirements for formal training. Waivers for other eligibility requirements or selection standards are considered unless otherwise stated in AR 614-200. Waivers cannot be implied. Each must be specifically requested. In the application for entry into the program or training requested, the applicant must include the reason for the waiver.

Career development programs include the following:

- Intelligence.
- Explosive Ordnance Disposal (EOD) Career Program.
- Technical Escort Training.
- Army Bands Career Program (ABCP).

Assignment to Specific Organizations and Duty Positions

AR 614-200 contains specific policies and procedures for nomination, evaluation, selection, and assignment of enlisted soldiers to the following:

- Presidential support activities.
- Observer controller at combat training centers.
- U.S. Military Entrance Processing Command.
- Enlisted aides to general officers.
- Inspector General positions.
- Drill Sergeant Program.
- Assignment as instructors at uniformed service schools.
- Assignment to international and overseas joint headquarters, U.S. Military Missions, Military Assistance Advisory Groups (MAAGs), and Joint U.S. Military Advisory Groups (JUSMAGs).
- Assignment to certain organizations and agencies: Office of the Secretary of Defense and Office of the Joint Chiefs of Staff; U.S. Central Command; U.S. Readiness Command (USREDCOM) and Joint Deployment Agency; Defense Communications Agency; Defense Intelligence Agency; HQDA, HRC, and HQ TRADOC; U.S. Military Academy, U.S. Army Command and General Staff College, and U.S. Army War College; U.S. Disciplinary Barracks; lst Battalion, 3rd Infantry (The Old Guard), Fort Myer, Virginia; U.S. Army Military District of Washington; U.S. Army Intelligence and Security Command; Office of the Assistant Chief of Staff for Intelligence; U.S. Army Correctional Activity; U.S. Army Courier Service; U.S. Army Service Center for the Armed Forces; U.S. Army Element, Armed Forces Police Department, Washington, D.C.; U.S. Army Criminal Investigation Command; and Defense Logistics Agency.
- Reserve component or Reserve Officer Training Corps (ROTC) duty.
- Food inspection specialists.
- Selection and assignment of first sergeants.

Another question these duties generate is "Will it help me get promoted?" The answer, of course, depends on what you have done up to the point at which you are placed on the special duty. If you have been working in your MOS, have leadership positions commensurate with your rank, and have the right balance of TOE and TDA assignments, then my answer would be yes. These duties are not, however, a quick fix for someone who has neglected his or her

Being a drill sergeant is a rewarding challenge—you teach civillians to be soldiers.

career path. They are tough, demanding jobs. If you qualify and are up to the challenge, then by all means volunteer!

Enlisted Instructors

Soldiers may volunteer or be selected for an instructor or adviser position (AR 614-200, Section II), as appropriate, at the following:

- Combat Training Centers (CTC) and TRADOC schools as project warriors (PW).
- Active Component to Reserve Component (AC to RC) (including full-time manning [FTM] and Reserve Officers' Training Corps [ROTC]).
- Uniformed service schools.
- U.S. Army Sergeants Major Academy (USASMA).

The initial selection criteria for instructor duty are as follow:

- Be a high school graduate or possess the GED equivalent.
- Have no personal habits or character traits that are questionable from a security standpoint. Persons declared rehabilitation successes under the

Army Alcohol and Drug Abuse Prevention and Control Program (ADAPC) Program are not appropriate candidates.

- Possess mature judgment and initiative.
- Have served at least three years of active Federal service in any branch of the Armed Forces.
- Have three years time remaining in-service upon arrival at assignment or be able to reenlist or extend to meet the requirement.
- Have a security clearance consistent with that required to attend the requisite instructor course.
- Meet minimum reading grade level (RGL) and language grade level (LGL) (measured by Test of Adult Basic Education [see AR 350-1]) required for attendance to the requisite instructor course.
- Display good military bearing.
- Meet the body composition requirements in AR 600-9.
- Be able to pass the Army physical fitness test (APFT).
- Be fully qualified in the MOS for which instructor duty is desired.
- Have recently held a leadership assignment.
- Have a demonstrated ability to be an instructor.
- Have no speech impediment.

Drill Sergeant Program

The Drill Sergeant Program (AR 614-200, paragraphs 8-14) is designed to allow highly motivated, well-qualified professionals to serve as cadre at the following:

- U.S. Army Training Centers (USATCs).
- TRADOC training centers.
- U.S. Army Correctional Activity, Fort Riley, Kansas.

To be eligible to enter the Drill Sergeant Program, all candidates must meet the following nonwaiverable prerequisites:

- Be physically fit (maximum profile guide is 111221), meet body composition requirements in AR 600-9, and be able to pass the APFT (no substitution of events) upon arrival at drill sergeant (DS) school.
- Be forty years old or less, or if older have the appropriate medical clearance (see AR 40-501) at the time of request.
- Have no record of emotional instability.
- Have no speech impediment.
- Be a high school graduate or possess the GED equivalent.
- Be a graduate of basic noncommissioned officers' course (BNCOC).
- Display good military bearing.
- Have demonstrated leadership ability during previous tours of duty.
- Have had no court-martial convictions.
- Have no record of disciplinary action or time lost under 10 USC 972 or letter of reprimand filed in OMPF during current enlistment or in last

five years, whichever is longer (does not include Article 15 directed for filing in the restricted portion of the OMPF).

- AA soldiers may not have received EB or selective reenlistment bonus (SRB) for current service obligation if primary military occupational specialty (PMOS) is not among those authorized for DS positions.
- Have a minimum general technical (GT) score of 100. This criterion may be waived by the commander of HRC to not less than 95 on a case-by-case basis.
- Have qualified with M16A2 rifle within last six months.
- Be SSG through SFC (not applicable to USAR/ARNGUS soldiers; not applicable to DS school first sergeant positions).
- Have minimum of four years continuous active Federal service.
- Have a commander's evaluation by a lieutenant colonel (LTC) or higher.
- Have a thorough background screening conducted by HRC. Soldiers with Type I reports of moderate or severe sexual harassment, moderate or severe spouse or child abuse, rape, or indecent acts with minors; incest, bestiality, adultery, sexual activity with subordinate soldiers, or fraternization; conduct in violation of the Army's policy on participation in extremist organizations or activities; any court-martial conviction in the soldier's career, provided it has not been reversed by a higher court or other appropriate authority will be excluded from DS duty permanently. Soldiers with Type II reports of unfavorable information such as DUI, assault, or spouse or child abuse characterized as mild, any drug offense, larceny/theft, or a traffic violation with six points or more assessed, will be excluded for consideration for DS duty for five years from the date of the incident.

Soldiers assigned to drill sergeant duty incur a twenty-four-month obligation for drill sergeant duty after successful completion of Drill Sergeant School and a stabilized tour for twenty-four months with an option to extend an additional six to twelve months. Normally the tour of duty for a drill sergeant will not exceed thirty-six months.

Selection and Assignment of First Sergeants

> The soldier having acquired that degree of confidence of his officers as to be appointed first sergeant of the company, should consider the importance of his office; that the discipline of the company, the conduct of the men, their exactness in obeying orders, and the regularity of their manners, will in great measure depend on his vigilance.
>
> —von Steuben, *Regulations for the Order of the Troops of the United States,* approved by Congress, March 29, 1779

Only the most highly qualified and motivated senior soldiers are selected and assigned to first sergeant positions. He or she is the unit example, encouraging soldiers to "Be like me." This to many is the best assignment, bar none, in the Army. Success as a first sergeant is a real indication of future potential.

Most DA selection boards look closely at a soldier's performance as a first sergeant when selecting for the Sergeants Major Academy and promotion to sergeant major. Sergeants first class and master sergeants are assigned as first sergeants based on outstanding qualities of leadership, dedication to duty, integrity and moral character, professionalism, MOS proficiency, appearance and military bearing, physical fitness, and proven performance or potential for the first sergeant position.

Soldiers who meet the above requirements and who complete the First Sergeant's Course (FSC) are eligible for award of special qualification identifier of M (first sergeant). Soldiers must attend the FSC prior to assuming first sergeant positions. Waiver authority to defer school attendance up to six months rests with the first general officer in the soldier's chain of command.

Command Sergeants Major Assignment Procedures

Command sergeants major (CSMs) are the epitome of the Noncommissioned Officer Corps and must be the best and brightest. Held responsible for the individual and small-unit training of enlisted soldiers, the CSM position at battalion and brigade level must be filled with CSMs who have the career management background relating to that unit. For example, armor battalion must be filled with CSMs who have career management field (CMF) 19 background. The assignment priority for CSMs is as follows:

- Priority of fill for CSM positions is at battalion, brigade, and finally nominative positions.
- Serving CSMs have first priority because they cannot be assigned surplus.
- If a serving CSM is not available, then the second priority is to appoint a CSM (P) who is next on the order of merit list by CMF, regardless of where the vacancy exists or where the individual is stationed.
- The last priority is to accomplish an operational move, i.e., CONUS to CONUS or voluntary/involuntary reassignment within the same overseas command.

Approximately 90 percent of brigade/group/post positions are filled from within at the local level. Every effort is made to assign a CSM to the same level or higher. This does not always happen, however, and a CSM who was once at corps level may be assigned at brigade or battalion level.

Prerequisites for a nominative position (general officer command and certain O-6 commands such as the Sergeants Major Academy) are generally twelve successful months' service at an O-6 level command and achieving the special qualifications specified by the nominative commander.

OVERSEAS SERVICE

Many Americans work very hard all their lives, and then in their declining years, when they at last have the leisure and money to travel, they see the world. Soldiers not only see the world when they are young, but they also have the unique opportunity to live among foreign peoples for extended periods of time and learn about their cultures from firsthand experience.

There are two ways that you can approach your overseas tour. You can go kicking and screaming and spend your time isolated in the American community of some foreign country, never venturing very far outside the cocoon of familiar surroundings, counting the dreary days until you rotate, or you can approach foreign service as a thrilling adventure to be experienced to the fullest, and you can be a goodwill ambassador for the United States of America.

Most major overseas commands operate orientation programs for newly arrived personnel in the command. These courses attempt to expose soldiers to the culture in which they will be living in order to lessen the effect of culture shock that some people experience the first time they encounter a foreign society. When you receive overseas assignment instructions, it would be a very good idea for you (and your spouse, if you have one) to study the language of the country to which you will be going. Some special assignments require extensive formal language training, but most Army installations do provide some language instruction for soldiers and their dependents who are bound overseas. Learning the rudiments of a foreign language can be fun, and speaking a foreign language is a very valuable skill to have once you arrive at your overseas duty station.

Standards of living overseas vary depending on the country. Germany's standard of living is very high, and your money will not go far there; other countries are beset with substantial economic problems, and the standards of living in those places can sometimes be so low that only the very rich can afford luxuries that are considered common in the United States, and you won't be able to afford them at local prices. Be aware that in countries where a status of forces agreement (SOFA) exists between the U.S. government and the foreign government, soldiers may be tried for offenses under the laws of the country concerned.

As with everything else, what you get out of your situation is what you make of it. And remember that your overseas tour will not last forever; sooner or later you must leave to come home. Emotional attachments are very hard to break off, so be warned if you establish any kind of relationship with a foreign man or woman. What usually starts as a casual, fun-filled lark, a pleasant way to pass the time, frequently develops into a serious involvement. If it is not consummated by marriage, its termination can be an emotional trauma that will be very painful for both of you.

Policies

The chief consideration in selecting a soldier for service overseas is that a valid authorization exists for his or her military qualifications. Equitable distribution is made, within a given MOS and grade, of overseas duty assignments, considering both desirable and undesirable locations. All reasonable efforts are made to minimize periods of forced separations and any adverse effects of overseas service encountered by soldiers and their families.

Between overseas tours, with the exception of Hawaii, soldiers are assigned in their sustaining base for at least twelve months on station. Consistent with Army needs, soldiers are retained as long as possible in the continental United States. Among individuals who have previous overseas service, those with the earliest date of return from overseas normally will be selected first. Subject to personnel requirements to short-tour areas, soldiers who have completed a normal overseas service tour in a short-tour area will not be assigned to another short-tour area on their next overseas assignment.

Short-Tour and Long-Tour Eligibility

AR 614-30, chapters 4 and 7, apply. Personnel are assigned to short-tour overseas assignments according to the following priorities:

1. Volunteers who have completed a minimum of twelve months' time on station or are not otherwise stabilized.
2. Intertheater Consecutive Overseas Tour (COT) volunteers after completion of current OCONUS tour.
3. From CONUS.
   a. HQDA approved volunteers.
   b. No previous OCONUS service.
   c. No previous short tour and last OCONUS assignment was a "with-dependents" tour.
   d. Last OCONUS assignment was a "with-dependents" tour in a long-tour area and has previously served a short tour.
   e. Last OCONUS tour was a short tour in accompanied status.
   f. No previous short tour and last assignment was an "all-others" tour.
   g. Serving in a long-tour area of Alaska or Hawaii and completed the prescribed thirty-six month tour.
   h. In CONUS and last OCONUS tour was a short-tour in an unaccompanied status.

Deferments and Deletions

AR 614-30, chapter 3, applies. Because of the possible adverse effect on command operational readiness, granting of deferments for overseas service is strictly controlled and held to an absolute minimum. The needs of the service are the major determining factor in granting deferments.

Normally, once an application has been submitted, the soldier will be retained at the home station, pending a final decision. When a soldier requests deferment and it results in his or her having less remaining time in service than the length of the prescribed tour, the individual will continue on the overseas assignment. Unless he or she voluntarily reenlists or extends to be eligible to complete the prescribed tour, the individual must sign a counseling statement, which is a bar to reenlistment.

Applications are initiated by the individual concerned on DA Form 4187.

The following conditions normally warrant deferments or deletion from overseas assignment:

- A recent severe psychotic episode involving a spouse or child after a soldier receives assignment instructions.
- The soldier's children are being made wards of the court or are being placed in an orphanage or a foster home because of family separation. This separation must be because of military service and not because of neglect or misconduct on the part of the soldier.
- Adoption cases in which the home study (deciding whether a child is to be placed) has been completed and a child is scheduled to be placed in the soldier's home within ninety days.
- Illness of a family member (see AR 614-30 for details).
- Terminal illness of a family member where death is anticipated within one year.
- The death of a soldier's spouse or child, after receipt of assignment instructions.
- Prolonged hospitalization of more than ninety days when the soldier's presence is deemed essential to resolve associated problems.
- Documented rape of the soldier's spouse or child within ninety days of the scheduled movement date, when the soldier's presence is deemed essential to resolve associated problems.
- Selection to attend the Basic or Advanced NCO Course or Officer Candidates School (OCS), where attendance will delay overseas travel more than ninety days.
- Enrollment in the Drug and Alcohol Abuse Residential Rehabilitation Treatment Program.
- Pregnancy or related complications exceeding ninety days.

Change in Overseas Tour Status

Change of tour requests are normally approved, provided the government has not expended funds for shipment of household goods or movement of dependents and the gaining command has concurred with the change. Additionally, a soldier may be required to extend or reenlist to meet tour length requirements. Requests are normally not favorably considered if the government has expended funds for shipment of household goods or movement of family members. Exceptions to policy are considered under extenuating circumstances. Army Regulation 55-46, *Travel of Dependents and Accompanied Military and Civilian Personnel to, from, or between Overseas Areas;* the *Joint Federal Travel Regulation (JFTR);* and AR 614-30, *Overseas Service,* are the applicable regulations.

Consecutive OCONUS Tours

Regulatory guidance pertaining to consecutive overseas tours (COTs) is found in AR 614-30, *Overseas Service,* chapter 4. Soldiers who volunteer to serve two full consecutive OCONUS tours are authorized government-paid travel for themselves and command-sponsored family members to leave locations equal to the distance to the soldier's home of record. Soldiers may travel greater distances provided they pay the additional travel costs. The leave location is not restricted to CONUS and must normally be between the two tours. The government-paid travel is the only benefit associated with a COT; any leave used is chargeable to the soldier.

To be eligible for a COT, soldiers must complete the prescribed tour plus any voluntary extensions and agree to serve another full tour plus leave and travel time between tours. COTs fall into two categories: OCONUS tours that involve a permanent change of station and OCONUS tours that do not involve a PCS.

Curtailment of Tours

AR 614-30, chapter 5, applies. Overseas commanders may curtail overseas tours when military requirements so dictate. They may also disapprove curtailment requests.

When curtailments of more than sixty days are considered, commanders must recommend curtailments and request reassignment instructions from HRC as early as possible but not later than forty-five days before the departure date. Curtailing a tour must not cause an emergency requisition to fill the vacated position.

Overseas commanders may, at any time, curtail the tour of a soldier who has discredited or embarrassed or may discredit or embarrass the United States or jeopardize the commander's mission. They may also curtail tours when family members are moved to the United States because of criminal activity, a health problem, or death in the immediate family living with the sponsor. In exceptional cases, the commander may waive advance HQDA coordination and attach the soldier to the nearest personnel assistance point for issue of Permanent Change of Station (PCS) orders. These exceptions are as follows: potential defectors, extreme personal hardship, and expeditious removal of a soldier in the best interests of the service (for example, when a soldier causes an embarrassment to the command in its relationship with a foreign government).

Pregnant soldiers are not curtailed from their overseas tour solely because of their pregnancy. If noncombatant evacuation is ordered, however, pregnant soldiers who have reached the seventh month of pregnancy will be curtailed and evacuated. Such a curtailment does not, however, preclude the solder being reassigned overseas again after completion of the pregnancy and discharge from inpatient status.

Extension of Tours

Change of tour requests are normally approved, provided the government has not expended funds for shipment of household goods or movement of dependents and the gaining command has concurred with the change. Additionally, a soldier may be required to extend or reenlist to meet tour length requirements.

Requests are normally not favorably considered if the government has expended funds for shipment of household goods or movement of family members. Exceptions to policy are considered under extenuating circumstances.

Kinds of Overseas Tours

Personnel accompanied or joined by their dependents at government expense must have enough remaining service to serve the tour prescribed for those "with dependents."

Army personnel married to each other and serving in the same overseas area serve tours in accordance with AR 614-30. They must extend or reenlist, if necessary, to have enough time in service to serve the tour prescribed by the table before compliance with orders directing movement.

The "all others" tour is served by soldiers who meet the following criteria:

- Elect to serve overseas without dependents.
- Are serving in an area where dependents are not permitted.
- Do not have dependents (this rule does not apply in areas where personnel who have dependents must serve "with dependents" tours).
- Are divorced or legally separated and pay child support.

Tours normally will be the same for all personnel at the same station. Where there are personnel of more than one service, the service having the main interest (normally, the most personnel in the area) develops a recommended tour length that is coordinated with the other services. Tour length may vary within any given country or area, depending on the specific duty station. AR 614-30 lists overseas duty tours for military personnel.

Concurrent and Deferred Travel

Soldiers being transferred overseas should seek command sponsorship of their family members, as well as concurrent or deferred travel for family members. Sponsorship of soldiers' families is dependent upon the availability of government or economy housing, and if housing will be available within 60 days, concurrent travel is normally authorized. If housing will not be available until between 61 and 140 days, deferred travel is normally authorized.

SPONSORSHIP

Every new assignment will raise questions and concerns for the soldier and his or her family. The sponsorship program (AR 600-8-8) assists soldiers and their dependents in establishing themselves at a new duty station and guides soldiers while they adjust to their new work environment.

A "sponsor" is an individual designated by name at a gaining organization to assist incoming members and their families in making a smooth transition into the unit and community environment. Sponsors should be a grade equal to or higher than that of the incoming soldier; be the same sex, marital status, and MOS; be familiar with the surrounding area; and not have received assignment instructions.

Sponsors' duties are varied:

- Forward a welcoming letter to the incoming soldier. It should include the sponsor's duty address and telephone number (and home address and home telephone number, as well, but this is not specifically required by the regulation).
- Try to provide information requested by incoming soldiers.
- Advise the incoming soldier that he or she will be met at the point of arrival in the area or at the aerial port of debarkation.
- Offer to assist in getting temporary housing (guest house or similar accommodations). The sponsor should contact the housing referral office for guidance and information. Sponsors are not required to contract for permanent or temporary housing, but if the sponsor desires to provide this service and the incoming soldier agrees, the sponsor should seek legal advice about the commitments and liabilities involved.
- Accompany the incoming soldier after his or her arrival in the unit while he or she goes through in-processing.
- Acquaint the incoming soldier with the surrounding area and facilities.
- Introduce the incoming soldier to his or her supervisors and immediate chain of command.

Gaining commanders are required to send incoming soldiers welcoming letters. Informality and information sharing are the primary goals of these letters. This letter also responds to any request for specific information appearing in item 42 of DA Form 4787. The welcoming letter and its enclosures should as a minimum contain the gaining unit's address and telephone number and the following information:

- The projected availability of government and economy housing, including when available, rent and utility costs, security deposit, and advance rent requirements.
- The location of the family housing referral office.
- Education facilities available for dependents in both the military and the civilian communities.
- The types of household goods that are essential, optional, or not required at an overseas location.
- The type of climate and recommended clothing.
- Local vehicle registration, safety, emission standards, insurance requirements, and, when available, typical insurance rates.
- The availability of military and civilian medical and dental care facilities.
- Community services and facilities that are available both on post and off post.
- The host nation's culture, customs, and lifestyle.
- Local firearms laws and restrictions.
- Problems that might be encountered when shipping pets to the overseas command.

Commanders are also responsible for ensuring that sponsors are provided enough time from their duties to help new soldiers. In addition, commanders arrange transportation so that sponsors can meet new members and their dependents at the point of arrival and bring them back to the unit (overseas only).

The incoming soldier should answer the sponsor's letter immediately and do the following:

- Inform the sponsor of his or her time, date, and point of arrival (including flight numbers). Any changes to the itinerary should be reported to the sponsor immediately.
- Provide the sponsor a unit mailing address and telephone number (commercial or DSN).
- Inform the sponsor of the expected departure date from the losing duty station.
- If desired, provide the sponsor with leave addresses and telephone numbers.

ORIENTATION PROGRAM

Commanders and supervisors are responsible for conducting a thorough and timely orientation to start new arrivals off properly. These orientations should make the new soldier feel needed and wanted and instill in him or her the motivation to contribute to the unit's mission.

13

Evaluation and Management Systems

THE NCO EVALUATION REPORTING SYSTEM

The NCO Evaluation Reporting System is designed to strengthen the ability of the NCO Corps to meet its professional duties. It enables the best NCOs to serve in positions of increasing responsibility by providing information on individual NCO performance and potential from raters and senior raters to promotion and selection boards. AR 623-205, *Noncommissioned Officer Evaluation Reporting System,* provides detailed information. Evaluations are based on two forms, DA Form 2166-8-1, *NCO Counseling Checklist/Record,* which is used when counseling NCOs, and DA Form 2166-8, *NCO Evaluation Report,* (NCOER). These two forms are used to evaluate all NCOs except those command sergeants major serving at three- and four-star nominative positions.

Study the NCOER carefully! It states very clearly what the Army expects of its noncommissioned officers. The current Army NCOER emphasizes Army values, NCO responsibilities, and counseling duties, as well as your skills, values, attributes, and current and potential performance.

Performance Counseling/Checklist

Performance counseling is personal counseling; it informs soldiers face-to-face about their jobs and expected performance standards. It also provides performance feedback. The goal of this part of the system is to help NCOs be successful and meet applicable standards. Although past performance must be acknowledged, the best counseling looks ahead to the future and what can be improved.

Counseling takes place within thirty days of each rating period and at least quarterly thereafter. The first session tells the rated NCO what is expected, and the quarterly sessions (for active-duty NCOs) tell what he or she has done well and what could be done better. After initial counseling, Army National Guard (ARNG) and U.S. Army Reserve (USAR) soldiers are counseled semiannually.

NCO EVALUATION REPORT
For use of this form, see AR 623-205; the proponent agency is ODCSPER

SEE PRIVACY ACT STATEMENT IN AR 623-205, APPENDIX C.

PART I - ADMINISTRATIVE DATA

a. NAME *(Last, First, Middle Initial)* | b. SSN | c. RANK | d. DATE OF RANK | e. PMOSC

f. UNIT, ORG., STATION, ZIP CODE OR APO, MAJOR COMMAND | g. REASON FOR SUBMISSION

h. PERIOD COVERED: FROM (YYYY MM) THRU (YYYY MM) | i. RATED MONTHS | j. NON-RATED CODES | k. NO. OF ENCL | l. RATED NCO COPY *(Check one and Date)*: 1. Given to NCO; 2. Forwarded to NCO; *Date* | m. PSC Initials | n. CMD CODE | o. PSB CODE

PART II - AUTHENTICATION

a. NAME OF RATER *(Last, First, Middle Initial)* | SSN | SIGNATURE

RANK, PMOSC/BRANCH, ORGANIZATION, DUTY ASSIGNMENT | DATE

b. NAME OF SENIOR RATER *(Last, First, Middle Initial)* | SSN | SIGNATURE

RANK, PMOSC/BRANCH, ORGANIZATION, DUTY ASSIGNMENT | DATE

c. RATED NCO: I understand my signature does not constitute agreement or disagreement with the evaluations of the rater and senior rater. I further understand my signature verifies that the administrative data in Part I, the rating officials in Part II, the duty description to include the counseling dates in Part III, and the APFT and height/weight entries in Part IVc are correct. I have seen the report completed through Part V, except Parts IId and IIe. I am aware of the appeals process of AR 623-205. | SIGNATURE | DATE

d. NAME OF REVIEWER *(Last, First, Middle Initial)* | SSN | SIGNATURE

RANK, PMOSC/BRANCH, ORGANIZATION, DUTY ASSIGNMENT | DATE

e. ☐ CONCUR WITH RATER AND SENIOR RATER EVALUATIONS ☐ NONCONCUR WITH RATER AND/OR SENIOR RATER EVAL *(See attached comments)*

PART III - DUTY DESCRIPTION *(Rater)*

a. PRINCIPAL DUTY TITLE | b. DUTY MOSC

c. DAILY DUTIES AND SCOPE *(To include, as appropriate, people, equipment, facilities and dollars)*

d. AREAS OF SPECIAL EMPHASIS

e. APPOINTED DUTIES

f. COUNSELING DATES | INITIAL | LATER | LATER | LATER

PART IV - ARMY VALUES/ATTRIBUTES/SKILLS/ACTIONS *(Rater)*

a. ARMY VALUES. Check either "YES" or "NO". *Comments are mandatory for "No" entries; optional for "Yes" entries.*		YES	NO
V A L U E S Loyalty Duty Respect Selfless-Service Honor Integrity Personal Courage	1. LOYALTY: Bears true faith and allegiance to the U. S. Constitution, the Army, the unit, and other soldiers.		
	2. DUTY: Fulfills their obligations.		
	3. RESPECT/EO/EEO: Treats people as they should be treated.		
	4. SELFLESS-SERVICE: Puts the welfare of the nation, the Army, and subordinates before their own.		
	5. HONOR: Lives up to all the Army values.		
	6. INTEGRITY: Does what is right - legally and morally.		
	7. PERSONAL COURAGE: Faces fear, danger, or adversity (physical and moral).		
	Bullet comments		

DA FORM 2166-8, OCT 2001 REPLACES DA FORM 2166-7, SEP 87, WHICH IS OBSOLETE USAPA V1.01

RATED NCO'S NAME *(Last, First, Middle Initial)* | SSN | THRU DATE

PART IV *(Rater)* - VALUES/NCO RESPONSIBILITIES

Specific Bullet examples of "EXCELLENCE" or "NEEDS IMPROVEMENT" are mandatory.
Specific Bullet examples of "SUCCESS" are optional.

b. COMPETENCE
- o Duty proficiency; MOS competency
- o Technical & tactical; knowledge, skills, and abilities
- o Sound judgment
- o Seeking self-improvement; always learning
- o Accomplishing tasks to the fullest capacity; committed to excellence

EXCELLENCE *(Exceeds std)* **SUCCESS** *(Meets std)* **NEEDS IMPROVEMENT** *(Some)* *(Much)*

c. PHYSICAL FITNESS & MILITARY BEARING
- o Mental and physical toughness
- o Endurance and stamina to go the distance
- o Displaying confidence and enthusiasm; looks like a soldier

APFT | HEIGHT/WEIGHT

EXCELLENCE *(Exceeds std)* **SUCCESS** *(Meets std)* **NEEDS IMPROVEMENT** *(Some)* *(Much)*

d. LEADERSHIP
- o Mission first
- o Genuine concern for soldiers
- o Instilling the spirit to achieve and win
- o Setting the example; Be, Know, Do

EXCELLENCE *(Exceeds std)* **SUCCESS** *(Meets std)* **NEEDS IMPROVEMENT** *(Some)* *(Much)*

e. TRAINING
- o Individual and team
- o Mission focused; performance oriented
- o Teaching soldiers how; common tasks, duty-related skills
- o Sharing knowledge and experience to fight, survive and win

EXCELLENCE *(Exceeds std)* **SUCCESS** *(Meets std)* **NEEDS IMPROVEMENT** *(Some)* *(Much)*

f. RESPONSIBILITY & ACCOUNTABILITY
- o Care and maintenance of equipment/facilities
- o Soldier and equipment safety
- o Conservation of supplies and funds
- o Encouraging soldiers to learn and grow
- o Responsible for good, bad, right & wrong

EXCELLENCE *(Exceeds std)* **SUCCESS** *(Meets std)* **NEEDS IMPROVEMENT** *(Some)* *(Much)*

PART V - OVERALL PERFORMANCE AND POTENTIAL

a. RATER. Overall potential for promotion and/or service in positions of greater responsibility.

AMONG THE BEST | FULLY CAPABLE | MARGINAL

b. RATER. List 3 positions in which the rated NCO could best serve the Army at his/her current or next higher grade.

e. SENIOR RATER BULLET COMMENTS

c. SENIOR RATER. Overall performance

1 2 3 Successful | 4 Fair | 5 Poor

d. SENIOR RATER. Overall potential for promotion and/or service in positions of greater responsibility.

1 2 3 Superior | 4 Fair | 5 Poor

DA FORM 2166-8, OCT 2001 USAPA V1.01

The *NCO Counseling Checklist/Record* is designed to be used with the NCOER as the only counseling support document. It includes the information needed to assist you in preparing and conducting a counseling session. It also provides a section to record counseling results. After a counseling session, the rater maintains the checklist until the next session or the end of the rating period. The counseling form includes reference material related to counseling, Army values, and NCO responsibilities.

Types of NCOers

Only the following reports, authorized by AR 623-205, may be submitted.

Annual Reports. Annual reports are submitted twelve months after the ending month of the last report. If twelve months have elapsed since the ending month of the last report, but the required three-month minimum rating period or rater qualification criteria have not been met, the annual report period is extended until the minimum requirements are satisfied. Annual reports should not be signed before the first day of the month following the ending month.

Change-of-Rater Reports. Providing that minimum rater qualifications are met and no other reports have been submitted in the preceding three months, change-of-rater reports are rendered when there has been a normal change of the designated rater, the individual has been on extended temporary duty (TDY), the rater has left the Army, or the rater is relieved or incapacitated. Change-of-rater reports may be signed at any time during the closing or following month of the report.

Temporary Duty, Special Duty, or Compassionate Reassignment Reports. Provided minimum rater qualifications are met, change-of-rater-reports for both the NCO and their eligible subordinates will be submitted prior to departure when an NCO departs on temporary duty (TDY) or special duty (SD) to attend training scheduled for ninety calendar days or more at a service school, to attend a civilian academic or training institution on a full-time basis for a period of ninety calendar days or more, or to perform duties not related to his or her primary functions in his or her parent unit under a different immediate supervisor for ninety days or more. NCOs on TDY or SD who are not responsible to rating officials in their parent organization will be rated by the TDY or SD supervisor. NCOs attached to organizations pending a compassionate reassignment remain responsible to their parent unit and will not receive an evaluation report from the organization to which they are attached.

Complete-the-Record Reports. At the option of the rater, a complete-the-record report may be submitted on a soldier who is to be considered by a DA centralized board for promotion, school, or command sergeant major (CSM) selection provided the soldier is in the zone of consideration, has been in the current duty assignment under the same rater for at least ninety days, and has not had a previous report for the current duty assignment.

Senior Rater Option Reports. Provided minimum rater qualifications are met, when a change in senior rater occurs, the senior rater may direct that a report be made on any NCO for whom he or she is the senior rater if the senior rater has served in that position for at least sixty rated days and the rated NCO has not received a report in the preceding ninety rated days. The senior rater will submit a senior rater option report in instances where the senior rater's departure would result in a report submitted without a senior rater evaluation.

Sixty-Day Short-Tour Option Report. Provided minimum rater qualifications are met, at the rater's option, the rater may prepare a sixty-day option report on a rated NCO, who must be serving in an overseas designated short tour for a period of fourteen months or less. The senior rater must meet the minimum time-in-position requirements to evaluate (sixty rated days) and must approve or disapprove submission of the report. If disapproved, the rater will inform the rated NCO that the report has been disapproved and will destroy the report.

Relief-for-Cause Reports. Relief-for-cause is the early release of a soldier from a specific duty or assignment, directed by superior authority, and based on a decision that the soldier has failed in his or her duty performance through inefficiency or misconduct. The reasons for relief must be clearly explained by the rating official in his narrative portion of DA Form 2166-7, along with a statement that the soldier concerned has been informed of the reasons for the relief. When the relief is directed by someone not on the designated rating chain, that official describes the reasons for the relief in an enclosure to the report. The minimum rating period for these kinds of reports is normally thirty days, but a general officer in the chain of command (or the general court-martial convening authority) may waive this requirement and authorize the relief report to be written in clear-cut cases of misconduct. Relief-for-cause reports are signed at any time during the closing or following month of the report. Regardless of who directs the relief, the rater will enter the bullet "the rated NCO has been notified of the reason for the relief" in part IV.f.

Restrictions

A number of restrictions apply to the type of material that may be included in an efficiency report:

- The zeal with which a soldier performs his or her duty as a member of a court-martial, counsel for an accused, or an Equal Opportunity NCO cannot be referred to in an efficiency report.
- No reference may be made to unproven derogatory information in a report. This prohibition prevents allegations from being included in reports and excludes information that would be unjustly prejudicial.
- Although incidents caused by alcohol or drug abuse should be taken into account by rating officials, a soldier's voluntary participation in the Army Substance Abuse Program (ASAP) is not normally mentioned.

Although paragraph 3-22, AR 623-205, authorizes raters to mention a soldier's voluntary entry into the ASAP and successful rehabilitation "as a factor to the rated soldier's credit," this kind of information should not be included in a report unless previous reports cited problems arising from substance abuse.

Commander's Inquiry

When a commander learns that a report made by a subordinate or a member of a subordinate command may have been illegal or unjust or may have violated the provisions of AR 623-205, he or she must investigate. The commander does not have the authority to direct that an evaluation be changed and may not use command influence to alter the honest evaluation of an NCO by the rating official. He or she may, however, provide results of a commander's inquiry to the rating chain.

When a report has been corrected under the circumstances mentioned above, it is forwarded with no reference to action taken by the commander.

Rater Qualifications and Responsibilities

With few exceptions, the rater must be the first-line supervisor of the rated soldier for a minimum of ninety rated days, and senior to the rated soldier either by grade or by date of rank. Members of other U.S. military services who meet these qualifications may also be raters.

Commanders may appoint U.S. government civilian raters GS-6 and above when a first-line military supervisor is not available and when the civilian supervisor is in the best position to accurately evaluate the soldier's performance. The civilian rater must be officially designated on a published rating scheme established by the local commander. Members of the allied forces are not authorized to be raters.

Raters must counsel the rated soldier and assess his or her performance, using all reasonable means to do so, and then prepare a fair, correct report. Without a doubt, you will find NCOER counseling of good soldiers a pleasant experience. Counseling bad soldiers is a difficult experience, yet you must face up to it if you are to be a good leader.

Ensure that you keep the counseling record, DA Form 2166-8-1, up-to-date and fulfill your rating duties by properly counseling your soldiers.

Senior Rater Qualifications and Responsibilities

The senior rater must be in the direct line of supervision of the rated soldier for a minimum period of sixty rated days, and senior to the rater in grade or date of rank.

Members of other U.S. military services who meet these qualifications may be senior raters, and civilians may be appointed as senior raters provided that they are the supervisors in the best position to evaluate the soldier's performance and that their appointments are published in a rating scheme established by the local commander. Members of allied forces are not authorized to be senior raters. A senior rater is not required when the rater is a general officer or equivalent.

The senior rater uses his or her position and experience to evaluate the rated NCO from a broad organizational perspective. His or her evaluation is the link between the day-to-day observation of the rated NCO's performance by the rater and the longer-term evaluation of the rated NCO's potential by DA selection boards. A senior rater fulfills his or her responsibility by using all reasonable means to become familiar with the rated NCO's duty performance throughout the rating period so that he or she can render a fair, accurate, and correct report that evaluates the rated NCO's duty performance, professionalism, and potential.

The senior rater dates and signs the report in part II.b; obtains the rated NCO's signature in part II of the NCOER; ensures that the rated NCO is aware that his or her signature does not constitute agreement or disagreement with the evaluations of the rater and senior rater; ensures that the specific bullet examples support the appropriate ratings in part IV.b-f; and ensures that the bullet statement "senior rater does not meet minimum qualifications" is entered in part V.e when the senior rater does not meet the minimum time requirement for evaluating the rated NCO.

Reviewer Qualifications and Responsibilities

The reviewer must be a commissioned or warrant officer, command sergeant major, or sergeant major in the direct line of supervision, and senior in grade or date of rank to both the rater and the senior rater. There is no minimum time period requirement for reviewer qualification.

- Commanders may appoint officers of other U.S. military services as reviewers when the grade and line-of-supervision requirements listed above are met and when either the rater or senior rater is a uniformed Army official.
- In cases in which both the rater and the senior rater are other than uniformed Army rating officials, and no uniformed Army reviewer is available, the report is reviewed by an officer in the rated soldier's military personnel office.
- Commanders may appoint U.S. civilians GS-6 and above or other civilian pay grades when the grade and line-of-supervision requirements are met and either the rater or senior rater is a uniformed Army official.
- Members of allied forces are not authorized to be reviewers, and a reviewer is not required when the rater or the senior rater is a general officer or equivalent.
- The reviewer ensures that the proper rater and senior rater complete the report, examines the evaluations, and resolves discrepancies and incon-

sistencies. The reviewer also ensures compliance with the provisions for change-of-rater and relief-for-cause reports.

- The reviewer ensures, too, that required comments have been made to explain low ratings on the NCOER and that allegations of injustice or illegality are resolved or brought to the attention of the commander. The reviewer is responsible for ensuring that the rated soldier, rater, and senior rater's *army.mil* e-mail addresses are placed on the NCOER and for forwarding the report to the military personnel office.

Responsibilities of Commanders

Commanders ensure that official rating schemes are published, by name or duty position, and are posted in the unit so that each soldier knows his or her rater, senior rater, and reviewer.

Commanders are also responsible for ensuring the following:

- Each rating official is fully qualified and knows whom he or she is responsible to rate.
- Reports are prepared by the designated individuals.
- Rating officials give timely counseling.
- Each rated soldier is provided a copy of his or her completed evaluation report.
- Soldiers receive assistance in preparing and submitting appeals.
- Reports are prepared properly and submitted in time to reach the U.S. Army Enlisted Records and Evaluation Center (EREC) not later than sixty days after the ending month of the report.

Responsibilities of the Military Personnel Office

The military personnel office (MILPO) initiates the report and forwards it to the rated soldier's commander for proper control. Returned reports are reviewed at the MILPO for completeness and administrative accuracy. The MILPO makes copies of the report and forwards one to the rated soldier and one to the EREC, and assists soldiers who appeal.

EVALUATION REPORT REDRESS PROGRAM (APPEALS)

The Redress Program protects the Army's interests and ensures fairness to the NCO. At the same time, it avoids impugning the integrity or judgment of the rating officials without sufficient cause. Commander's inquiries and appeals for redress are separate actions. Rated NCOs may seek an initial means of redress through a commander's inquiry; however, a commander's inquiry is not a prerequisite for submission of an appeal.

The burden of proof rests with the soldier making an appeal. Once NCOERs are filed in the soldier's Official Military Personnel File (OMPF), they are presumed to be administratively correct, to have been prepared by the proper officials, and to represent the considered opinions and impartial judgments of rating officials.

The allegation of error or injustice does not constitute proof. Clear and convincing evidence must be submitted to cause alteration, replacement, or withdrawal of a report in the OMPF. The decision to appeal should not be made lightly. Frequently, sound evidence may be difficult to obtain, and in most cases, the appellant may be unable to analyze his or her own case objectively.

Normally, appeals are originated by the rated soldier, but in cases in which an appeal is originated by someone other than the rated soldier, it is not processed unless the rated soldier has been notified in person or in writing (by certified mail) and given the opportunity to submit statements pertaining to the case. Rating officials who claim "second thoughts" about ratings previously made have no grounds for submitting an appeal on behalf of the rated soldier.

Appeals alleging bias, prejudice, unjust ratings, or any matter other than administrative error will be adjudicated by the Army Enlisted Special Review Board. The board's determination is final.

To be considered, substantive appeals must be received at EREC within five years of the date of the rated soldier's authentication or the MILPO's certification, if the soldier refused to sign the report. Appeals that do not meet this time restriction may be submitted to the Army Board for Correction of Military Records, in accordance with AR 15-185. Once the decision has been made to appeal an evaluation report, the following steps should be taken:

- Begin reading chapter 6, AR 623-205, "Evaluation Redress Program."
- Write down clearly and specifically what will be appealed and why it should be.
- Identify what evidence should be obtained to substantiate the appeal.
- Determine what evidence can be obtained.
- Obtain the evidence. If statements from persons are necessary, make sure the statements clearly identify their roles at the time of the contested report and ensure that the statements make specific, not general, comments. Seek statements from senior personnel who have specific knowledge of the facts; avoid statements from subordinates or persons whose knowledge of the facts may be limited. Obtain sworn statements, if possible.
- Documentary evidence, if not original, should be in certified true copies.
- Prepare the appeal in military letter format.

THE QUALITATIVE MANAGEMENT PROGRAM (QMP)

The QMP was established in 1971 with the intended purpose of barring nonproductive NCOs from further service in the Army. The QMP consists of two subprograms: *qualitative retention* and *qualitative screening*.

Qualitative Retention Subprogram

The Qualitative Retention Subprogram consists of the use of reenlistment ineligibility points for each grade. Based on years of service, the reenlistment ineligibility point is the maximum number of years of active federal service authorized for a soldier in a specific grade.

As of March 2006, the retention control points are:

Rank	Total Active Service
SPC, CPL	10 years
SPC, CPL (P)	15 years
SGT	15 years
SGT (P)	20 years
SSG	22 years
SSG (P)	24 years
SFC	24 years
SFC (P)	26 years
1SG, MSG	26 years
1SG, MSG (P)	30 years
CSM, SGM	30 years

Specialists, corporals, and sergeants who are on a local order of merit promotion list will be considered for reenlistment under the criteria of the rank to which they will be promoted. Staff sergeants, sergeants first class, and first and master sergeants selected for promotion by Headquarters, Department of the Army, may voluntarily continue on active duty if they are not beyond the reenlistment ineligibility point for the grade to which they will be promoted. Those who are beyond the point for the grade to which they will be promoted will not be considered for extension.

NCOs who are in DA-announced primary zones of consideration for promotion and who have reached or are beyond the reenlistment point may be voluntarily extended beyond their expiration of term of service (ETS). Those with more than twenty years' service who have not received a waiver to reenlist and who were not selected will be retired by the third month after the promotion list is published.

Soldiers who apply for retirement before the announced zone of consideration will not be considered for promotion.

Extensions apply only to soldiers affected by the *qualitative retention.* They do not apply to those who have a DA bar to reenlistment imposed by *qualitative screening.*

Qualitative Screening Subprogram

This is the DA bar to reenlistment aspect of the Qualitative Management Program (QMP). The screening subprogram applies to enlisted members who are staff sergeants or above. It does not apply to members who have completed twenty-eight years of active federal service or to command sergeants major, regardless of time in service. Selection for elimination under this program results in an administrative discharge.

NCOs who cannot or will not meet minimum standards of service, or who exhibit moral or ethical misconduct, or who have not demonstrated the potential for continued service, are legitimate targets of the QMP. That is it.

QMP screening is performed as an adjunct to DA level promotion boards. Board members are told that the program is *qualitative,* not *quantitative.* No minimum quotas or select goals are preestablished. QMP is not a force reduction tool, nor should it be used as such. The boards look at the whole record of a soldier being considered for elimination from the ranks. They are therefore able to spot downward or cyclical performance trends based on a greater period of time and more information than is available to NCOER raters and senior raters in the field. QMP does not apply to soldiers in the rank of SGT and below; those who have requested or received an approved retirement prior to the date of the QMP letter; or those who have over twenty-eight years active federal service (AFS).

Records are screened as follows:

For sergeant major	By DA Command Sergeants Major Selection Board
For staff sergeant, sergeant first class, master sergeant, and first sergeant	HQDA promotion selection boards

The Qualitative Screening subprogram is based on the premise that reenlistment is a privilege for those whose performance, conduct, attitude, and potential for advancement meet Army standards. The program is applied equally to all personnel. The only soldiers who have anything to fear from the QMP are the poor performers.

Bars to Reenlistment

Bars to reenlistment for those identified by the qualitative screening program selection boards and approved by the Deputy Chief of Staff for Personnel (DCSPER) are imposed as directed by the Commanding General, Human Resources Command (HRC).

Soldiers selected for a bar are informed by letter. Copies of documents in the individual's OMPF that contributed to the board's decision are attached as an enclosure to the letter. These documents are privileged information and must be treated with the utmost discretion.

Letters are forwarded through the chain of command to the individual's commander (lieutenant colonel and above). They are not delivered to soldiers who have retirement applications approved or pending.

The individual's commander (lieutenant colonel and above) may, within seven days after receipt of the notification letter, request withdrawal of the bar if it was improperly imposed or based on material error in the soldier's OMPF when reviewed by the board. A commander's request to withdraw the bar must provide specific information to refute the board's action.

The individual's commander must interview the soldier and give him or her the letter, enclosures, and endorsement. He must also ensure that the soldier understands the impact of the bar and available options. The commander must also ensure that the soldier completes DA Form 4941-R, *Statement of Option,* within seven days of receipt and returns it through the chain of command to HRC.

NCOs receiving QMP notices have the following options:

- Submit an appeal within sixty days of notification.
- Do not submit an appeal.
- Request immediate discharge.
- Request immediate retirement, if eligible.
- Soldiers with at least seventeen years, nine months of active federal service may request an extension to attain retirement eligibility.

A soldier may appeal. An appeal must arrive at HRC not later than twelve months after the date of the bar letter. The soldier must understand that this appeal is the only one he or she may submit, although this does not preclude the commander's submitting an appeal on the soldier's behalf.

The appeal should address the basis for the bar and actions taken by the soldier to improve his or her performance to overcome noted deficiencies. Documents that demonstrate improved performance or the resolution of a deficiency military personnel office [MILPO]-authorized NCOER, award orders, revocation of a court-martial, and removal of disciplinary data) should be attached to the appeal.

If the appeal is denied, the soldier's commander must reevaluate the soldier to determine whether there has been a demonstrated marked improvement in performance and potential.

For a soldier who has less than eighteen months remaining until estimated time of separation (ETS) at the date of the bar and who was not granted an extension to provide for the eighteen months, no reevaluation is required. If the commander desires to reevaluate the soldier, an extension for the amount of time originally required to allow the eighteen-month period may be granted. For a soldier who has more than eighteen months remaining until ETS on the date of the bar or for a soldier who was granted an extension to provide for the eighteen months, the commander must reevaluate the soldier not less than ninety days before ETS.

Staff sergeants cannot be extended past twenty years. A soldier who has completed eighteen or more years' service on the effective date of the DA bar letter may be extended to reach retirement eligibility.

Indefinite Enlistment Status

Indefinite enlistment status is mandatory for all Regular Army soldiers in the rank of staff sergeant to command sergeant major who are eligible for reenlistment and have at least ten or more years of active federal service (AFS) on the date of reenlistment. From that point on, whenever the soldier is promoted, the expiration of term of service will be updated to reflect the retention control point for the new rank. After reenlisting for the indefinite program, a soldier may request voluntary separation or retirement at any time, provided all remaining service requirements have been fulfilled, in a manner similar to officers.

14

Promotion and Reduction

THE SYSTEM

All soldiers hope to get promoted, but not all are. Many times this is through neglect on their part; sometimes it's through their leaders' neglect. One of our responsibilities as noncommissioned leaders is to take care of our soldiers. A large measure of the success we achieve is through the success of our subordinates. We know we have done well when we watch a young specialist whom we have raised from private get the stripes of sergeant pinned on.

Soldiers should be counseled on their opportunities for advancement just as we expect to be counseled. Understand what it takes to be competitive in your field—for troop unit soldiers, it is troop leading at the crew, squad, or platoon levels; for someone working in an office, it may be additional civilian education.

Soldiers are recommended for promotion only after they develop the skills, knowledge, and behavior to perform the duties and assume the responsibility of the next higher grade. Generally, if soldiers do well in their present grades, they will work well in the next higher grade.

The Army promotion system has the following objectives:

- Fill authorized enlisted spaces with qualified soldiers.
- Provide for career progression and rank that is in line with potential.
- Recognize the best-qualified soldier to attract and retain the highest-caliber soldier for a career in the Army.
- Preclude promoting the soldier who is not productive or not best qualified.
- Provide an equitable system for all soldiers.

By using standard promotion scoring forms with predetermined promotion point factors, corporals, specialists, and sergeants can measure how well they qualify for promotion. They can set goals to increase their promotion potential. Staff sergeants, sergeants first class, first sergeants, and master sergeants can judge their qualifications when compared with other soldiers in their MOS. The Army promotes soldiers who are qualified and who will accept Army-wide assignments.

Commanders at the grades indicated may promote soldiers, subject to authority and delegation of responsibility by higher commanders.

- *Specialist (SPC) and below.* Unit commanders may advance or promote assigned soldiers to private (PV2), private first class (PFC), and SPC. When soldiers are fully eligible, promotions to PV2, PFC, and SPC are automatic unless the commander submits a DA Form 4187 blocking the promotion no later than the twentieth of the preceding month.
- *SGT and SSG.* Lieutenant colonel or higher-ranking commanders may promote soldiers attached or assigned or on temporary duty (TDY) to their command or installation.
- *SFC and above.* Headquarters, Department of the Army.
- *Hospitalized soldiers.* Commanders of medical facilities may promote hospitalized soldiers to SSG and below.
- *Students.* Commandants and commanders of training installations and activities.
- *Posthumous promotion.* Headquarters, Department of the Army.

Promotion of Private to Private First Class

Active Army personnel are advanced to the rank of private E-2 when they have completed six months of active federal service, unless it is stopped by the commander. ARNG and USAR personnel on initial active-duty training are advanced to private E-2 when they complete six months of service from the day of entry, unless it is stopped by the commander. To recognize outstanding performance, local commanders may advance to private E-2 a limited number of soldiers who have at least four but less than six months' active service.

Unit commanders may advance a soldier to private first class with twelve months' time in service and four months' time in grade. To recognize outstanding performance, unit commanders may advance a soldier to PFC who has a minimum of six months' time in service and two months' time in grade.

Promotion to Specialist or Corporal

Normally, commanders may advance to specialist or corporal those soldiers who meet the following qualifications:

- Twenty-six months in service.
- Six months' time in grade.
- Security clearance appropriate for the MOS in which promoted; advancement may be based on granting an interim security clearance.

To recognize outstanding performance, commanders may advance soldiers on an accelerated basis, providing advancements do not cause more than 20 percent of the total number of assigned specialists and corporals to have less than twenty-four months' time in service, and providing that soldiers meet the following qualifications:

- Eighteen months in service.
- Three months' time in grade.
- Security clearance required for the MOS in which advanced; may be based on an interim clearance.

Unused waivers that are computed at unit level (not consolidated) may be returned to higher command for redistribution, providing that computation of the higher command's strength will allow additional promotions. For example, suppose that four companies in a battalion have ten promotion authorizations but use only eight. Computation of battalion strength indicates that twelve promotions would have been authorized if consolidated. Thus the two unused authorizations may be redistributed.

Commanders with zero waiver authorizations may promote any soldier with eighteen or more months' time in grade. Commanders may use all waiver authorizations to promote soldiers with eighteen or more months' time in grade. In such cases, any remaining soldier with eighteen or more months' time in grade also may be promoted.

Promotion to Sergeant and Staff Sergeant

Field commanders and Department of the Army both have a hand in promotions to sergeant (SGT) and staff sergeant (SSG). The process begins with a recommendation by the soldier's noncommissioned officers through the chain of command to the unit commander, who then submits it to the O-5 promotion authority who conducts the local promotion board. The unit commander's recommendation states that the soldier meets the promotion criteria established for promotion to the specific grade for which the soldier is competing. To recommend or not recommend a soldier for promotion is the sole prerogative of the unit commander.

The normal sequence from recommendation to promotion to sergeant and staff sergeant follows.

1. *The soldier meets requirements.* The time-in-service requirement for attaining eligibility for promotion to SGT is thirty-six months' active federal service for the primary zone and eighteen months for the secondary zone. The time-in-grade requirement for attaining eligibility for promotion to SGT is eight months as a corporal (CPL) or SPC, waiverable to four months for those recommended in the secondary zone. Soldiers in the secondary zone may be boarded with sixteen months' time in service and four months' time in grade as of the first day of the board month.

   The time-in-service requirement for attaining eligibility for promotion to SSG is eighty-four months' active federal service for the primary zone and forty-eight months for the secondary zone. The time-in-grade requirement for attaining eligibility for promotion to SSG is ten months as a SGT, waiverable to five months for those recommended in the secondary zone. Soldiers in the secondary zone may be boarded with forty-six months' time in service and five months' time in grade as of the first day of the board month.

Once a soldier reaches primary zone eligibility, commanders either must recommend that she or he appear before a promotion board or, if a soldier is fully eligible but not recommended, must complete DA Form 3355 and counseling documents and forward them to the promotion authority for a final decision. From that point until the soldier is recommended for promotion or is no longer eligible, unit commanders must provide copies of the soldier's (at least quarterly) counseling to the promotion authority. After forty-eight months service and twelve months in the grade of E4, soldiers are automatically put on the promotion list unless denied by the commander (see Directed Automatic Promotion List Integration below).

Soldiers competing for promotion to SGT or SSG must possess either a high school diploma, GED equivalency, or an associate or higher degree. Soldiers competing for promotion to SSG must be graduates of the Primary Leadership Development Course (PLDC) before being recommended for promotion.

2. *Soldier's chain of command recommends promotion.* Soldiers may only compete for promotion in their career progression military occupational specialty (CPMOS) as outlined in AR 611-201. Eligible CPLs or SPCs and SGTs compete Army-wide by a three-character MOS, and their relative standing is determined by the points attained on an 800-point system. If a soldier is in the primary zone for promotion and not selected for appearance before the board, then he or she must be counseled in writing about why he or she was not selected to appear.
3. *Administrative points computed* (400 points available). See table on pages 228–229.
4. *Battalion commander convenes promotion board.* Although AR 600-8-19, *Enlisted Promotions,* states that officers may serve as members of the promotion board with an officer as president, in most cases the board is composed of senior noncommissioned officers with the battalion command sergeant major sitting as president. If a command sergeant major is not available, then a serving sergeant major may sit as president. Rules for conduct of the promotion board are found in AR 600-8-19.
5. *Board recommends soldier for promotion* (150 points available). See table on pages 228–229. Based on the soldier's personal appearance, self-confidence, bearing, oral expression and conversational skill, knowledge of world affairs, awareness of military programs, and knowledge of basic soldiering and attitude, the board awards up to 150 promotion points.

6. *Total promotion points computed* (800 total points available). The minimum promotion point score for attaining recommended list status for promotion to SGT is 350. The minimum score for attaining recommended list status for promotion to SSG is 450. Upon being recommended for promotion, obtain copies of all source documents used for promotion points (if not sure, ask). Soldiers should turn one set in with their initial promotion point worksheet and maintain a second set with a copy of their promotion board proceedings and each DA Form 3355 (initial evaluation and reevaluations). Promotion points cannot be backdated. Soldiers must understand that the Enlisted Distribution and Assignment System (EDAS) generates the promotion points' year/month/date to accurately determine promotions by MOS and grade. EDAS uses the points that are on file at HQDA. Following input to the Total Army Personnel Database (TAPDB) via EDAS input, promotion points are effective for promotion eligibility purposes on the first day of the third month after input.
7. *Education requirements met.* Effective October 1, 1992, soldiers must be a graduate of the Basic NCO Course (BNCOC) in order to be unconditionally promoted to SSG. Soldiers competing for promotion to SSG must be graduates of the Primary Leadership Development Course (PLDC) prior to being recommended for promotion. Soldiers competing for promotion to SGT must be graduates of PLDC before being promoted. Conditional promotions may be made for soldiers who lack the education requirements through no fault of their own. Those soldiers who accept a conditional promotion and are subsequently denied enrollment, declared a no-show, become academic failures, or otherwise do not meet graduation requirements will have their promotions revoked and be administratively removed from the promotion list.
8. *DA sets monthly promotion points.* Each month the Department of the Army establishes the total number of soldiers to be promoted based on budgetary and strength constraints. The number of promotions are allocated by primary military occupational speciality (PMOS) within these constraints. Department of the Army promotion cutoff scores are announced monthly. (See the section on cutoff scores in this chapter.)
9. *Soldiers' points meet or exceed DA established points.* After three months on the waiting list, soldiers who meet or exceed the announced cutoff score are promoted if otherwise eligible. Each soldier promoted to SSG must have a minimum of twelve months' active federal service remaining at the time of promotion. For SGT, there is no service obligation.

Congratulations!

YOUR KEY TO SUCCESS

Become familiar with AR 600-8-19, chapters 1 and 3, the Monthly Cutoff Score and Junior Enlisted Issues memorandums, and applicable military personnel (MILPER) messages (which are available at the BNS1, Personnel Service Battalion/Military Personnel Division (PSB/MPD) promotion section and on HRC on-line at *www.198.97.189.85/HRC_edit/Active/index2.asp).*

Promotable soldiers must monthly review and initial the recommended list. This is the most important document you have to refer to after undergoing any type of promotion board or point adjustment action. If you disagree with the promotion points and/or promotion points date data reflected on the EDAS C10, bring it to the attention of your first sergeant and battalion adjutant (BNS1), and be prepared to document all promotion related requests.

WHERE THE POINTS COME FROM (CHAPTER 3, AR 600-8-19)

Performance Evaluation and Military Training Points	Maximum Allowable	How Achieved	Individual Points
Duty Performance	150	Unit Commander	
a. Competence			30
b. Military Bearing			30
c. Leadership			30
d. Training			30
e. Responsibility and Accountability			30
Weapons Qualification	50	Score ranges from 50 to 14 dependent upon number of targets hit.	
Physical Readiness Test	50	Score ranges from 50 to 5 dependent upon APFT Score.	
Administrative Points			
Awards:	100		
Soldier's Medal or higher award			35
Bronze Star Medal (BSM); Purple Heart			30
Defense Meritorious Service; Medal Meritorious Service Medal (MSM)			25
Air Medal; Joint Service Commendation Medal; Army Commendation Medal (ARCOM)			20
Joint Service Achievement Medal; Army Achievement Medal (AAM)			15
Good Conduct Medal; Army Reserve Component Achievement Medal			10
Combat Infantry Badge; Combat Field Medical Badge, Combat Action Badge			15
Expert Infantry Badge; Expert Field Medical Badge; Basic U.S. Army Recruiter Badge (additional badges 5 each); Ranger Tab; Special Forces Tab; Drill Sergeant Identification Badge			10

Parachutist Badge; Air Assault Badge; Parachute Rigger Badge; Divers Badge; Explosive Ordnance Disposal Badge; Pathfinder Badge; Aircraft Crewman Badge; Nuclear Reactor Operator Badge; Awards of higher skill badge count as subsequent awards and will receive points (senior parachutist, master diver, additional recruiting badges); Driver and Mechanic Badge (maximum 5 points); Tomb Guard Identification Badge		5
Soldiers receiving incentive pay for parachute duty. Parachutist		20
Senior		25
Master		30
Campaign Service Star		5
Southwest Asia Medal (maximum 12 points)		3
Soldier/NCO of the Quarter—BDE Level		10
Soldier/NCO of the Quarter—Installation/Division		15
Soldier/NCO of the Year—Major Army Command (MACOM)		25
Distinguished Honor Graduate		15
Distinguished Leadership Award		10
Commandants List		5
Certificate of Achievement awarded by commanders/deputy commanders serving in positions authorized the grade of lieutenant colonel (LTC) or higher, or any general officer or CSM at the brigade or higher level		5 (maximum 20)
Military Education	200	
Active Component Primary Leadership Development Course (AC PLDC)		16
PLDC Equivalency (as approved by Human Resources Command-Alexandria [HRC-A])		TBD
AC BNCOC		40
Additional completed BNCOC (per week)		4
Ranger School		32
Special Forces Qualification Course		60
Battalion level or higher training certified by a DA Form 87, *Certificate of Training,* signed by an LTC or above (per week)		4
Completion of military correspondence, extension, or nonresident subcourses (per five hours)		1
Other courses of at least one week duration (forty hours)		4
Civilian education	100	
For each semester hour earned of business/trade school/college		1.5
Any soldier completing a degree while on active duty		10
CLEP Tests (for each semester hour earned)		1.5
Promotion Board	150	
Personal Appearance		25
Oral Expression		25
Awareness World Affairs		25
Knowledge of Military Programs		25
Basic Soldiering		25
Soldier's Attitude		25
Total Possible Points	**800**	

Records Check

The total elimination of the Military Personnel Records Jacket (MPRJ) is fast approaching. Soldiers are responsible for maintaining individual personnel documents that have a direct impact on their career. These documents are essential to the promotion process establishing promotion points for SGT/SSG and for establishing the Official Military Personnel File (OMPF). Ultimately, the soldier, along with the chain of command are responsible for accuracy of promotion paperwork and follow up of action requests.

You may now review your OMPF online by logging on to the Human Resources Command Enlisted Records and Evaluation Center website at *www.hrc.army.mil/site/erec/index.htm,* using your Army Knowledge Online (AKO) user ID and password.

Recommended List

After completion of all promotion actions during the month, a recommended list is published. It lists all soldiers of the organization who have been selected but not yet promoted. Names are listed by grade and zone in ascending MOS and descending promotion point score order.

Soldiers are promoted from the current recommended list by MOS. Promotions are made on the first calendar day of the month in which they are authorized. Promotion orders may be published with future effective dates.

Soldiers are eligible for promotion on the first day of the second month following the date of selection; for example, a soldier recommended in January 2003 becomes eligible for promotion on March 1, 2003.

A soldier's name on the secondary zone list for promotion to sergeant is transferred to the primary zone list on the first day of the month in which he completes thirty-three months of active service. He or she becomes eligible for promotion in the primary zone on the first day of the month in which he or she completes thirty-six months' active service.

A soldier's name on the secondary zone list for promotion to staff sergeant is transferred to the primary zone on the first day of the month in which he completes eighty-one months of active service. He or she becomes eligible for promotion in the primary zone on the first day of the month in which he or she completes eighty-four months of active service.

Cutoff Scores

When a soldier's number of promotion points is known, many wonder why he or she cannot be promoted immediately if the cutoff is low enough. In the first place, soldiers may be selected for promotion three months before they have the required time in service.

Second, reports from the field reflecting the number of soldiers on promotion lists, their number of points, and their zones and MOSs arrive at HQDA about the middle of the month following the month in which the soldier appeared before the promotion board.

At this point, MOS and grade vacancies are computed. The total number of promotions for a particular grade (regardless of MOS) is determined by comparing the number of personnel projected to be in that grade against the number allowed in the Army budget for the month in which promotions are to be made. This projection includes losses, those promoted in and out of the grade, and reductions. Available promotions are distributed to MOSs based on the percentage of fill.

Promotions go to those MOSs with the greatest need first. Secondary zone (waiver) promotions are limited, so they go to MOSs with the greatest need after the primary zone (no waiver) promotions are distributed. At this time—which is one to two months after the soldier appears before the promotion board—the soldier's number of promotion points comes into the process. For example, if vacancies and budget permit the promotion of a hundred soldiers from the primary zone of a particular MOS, a promotion cutoff score is established by going down the scores until the hundred limit is reached. That is, if the top hundred sergeants in an MOS have 716 or more points, the cutoff score would be 716. If the top hundred have 796 or more, the cutoff would be 796.

Directed Automatic Promotion List Integration (ALI)

This policy is designed to assist the Army in filling vacant sergeant authorizations. Each month, soldiers meeting the established criteria for list integration will be added to the recommended list with a minimum of 350 promotion points, unless previously denied. Commanders may block automatic integration by informing their supporting personnel support battalion/military police investigations (PSB/MPD) which soldiers not to integrate.

Soldiers in the rank of CPL/SPC not earlier recommended for promotion will be automatically integrated onto the SGT recommended list upon meeting the following criteria.

- Forty-eight months time in service.
- Twelve months time in grade.
- Not denied integration by the commander.
- Otherwise not ineligible (AR 600-8-19).

The existing rules provide for an SPC to be fully eligible for promotion recommendation upon the attainment of thirty-four months' service and six months in grade—with promotion eligibility at three years in service. This allows the chain of command one full year past the fully eligible point to recommend a soldier under the existing means—that is by board appearance.

The only avenue for soldiers automatically integrated onto the list to increase their promotion points is to appear before the promotion board. Soldiers are only promoted from the Automatic List Integration to SGT when their score meets the announced cutoff score and they have seniority over others within their PMOS listed on the ALI.

REEVALUATION

You may request an administrative reevaluation using a memorandum or total reevaluation by using the DA Form 3355. Dropping off source documents at the unit or battalion adjutant (BNS1) does not constitute a request for reevaluation. You must be proactive and follow up on all action requests.

Total Reevaluation

A soldier on the current recommended list for six months may ask to be reevaluated at that time and each six months thereafter if he or she is still promotable. A soldier reevaluated is not immediately eligible for promotion based on his (or her) new score. He will continue to be eligible for promotion based on the promotion point score he held immediately before reevaluation. Eligibility under the old score continues until the reevaluated score becomes effective. The new score becomes effective two months from the date of reevaluation because of the three-month reporting time.

After the request for reevaluation is approved, the soldier appears before the organization's next regularly scheduled promotion board. His promotion list status is then based on the number of points he attains. If he remains on the list, his original selection date is adjusted to the date on which the promotion authority approves the board report. This gives the soldier a chance to improve his total score. He also runs the risk of lowering his standing if he makes a poor showing before the board.

Loss of recommended list status through reevaluation does not, however, preclude promotion consideration by future boards. Such consideration is not a vested right. Those being considered to regain recommended list status are subject to the provisions of chapter 3, AR 600-8-19, and the recommendations of their commanders.

Administrative Reevaluations

Soldiers believing they have twenty or more points to add to their promotion score may request an administration revaluation of their points by submitting DA Form 4187, *Personnel Action Request*. With the commander's approval, the promotions clerk will recalculate the promotion point worksheet and increase or decrease, as applicable, the duty performance points and erroneous points. The personnel support battalion (PSB) will evaluate the new promotion points and those of the recomputed worksheet. If there is a promotion point increase of twenty points or more, the PSB will enter the new score into the appropriate database.

Revalidation

What this means is that soldiers can no longer stay on a promotion list without revalidating their scores. Within two years of the board appearance, soldiers who have fewer than 700 promotion points must either validate their list standing through the administrative reevaluation process when they have twenty points or more; or do a total reevaluation, which includes a board reappearance, to stay on the list if they have not gained enough points to initiate an administrative reevaluation. Failure to validate list standing results in the soldier being administratively removed from the recommended list on the first day of the twenty-fifth month from the year-month current points by the promotions work center. The only exception to an administrative recomputation with less than twenty points is when a soldier has a current point score of 781 or higher and increases the current score by at least one-third of the remaining point total to achieve 800 points.

REMOVAL FROM PROMOTION LIST

Soldiers may be removed from promotions lists for the following reasons:

- Failure to qualify, for cause, for the security clearance required for the MOS in which the soldier is recommended. Those who fail to qualify for a security clearance through no adverse reason are reclassified and remain on the list in the new MOS.
- Failure to reenlist or extend to meet a service-remaining obligation.
- Being barred to reenlist.
- Reclassification from an MOS because of inefficiency or misconduct.
- Erroneous listing due to not meeting the criteria for promotion.
- Enrollment in the weight-control program.
- Failure to pass reclassification training.
- Reduction in grade after being placed on the recommended list.

A removal board is convened when required to determine whether a soldier should be removed from a recommended list. The board will be constituted as for promotion boards. The soldier being considered for removal has certain rights. The soldier may choose to do the following:

- Appear before the board.
- Challenge any member of the board for cause.
- Request an available witness whose testimony is pertinent to his case.
- Elect to remain silent, to make an unsworn statement, to make a sworn statement, or to be verbally examined by the board.
- Question any witness appearing before the board.
- Present written affidavits and depositions of witnesses.

Failure on the part of a soldier to exercise these rights is not a bar to the board proceedings or its findings and recommendations. The promotion authority is the final approval or disapproval authority on the board's recommendations. This action is final.

A soldier removed from a list and later exonerated is reinstated to the current local recommended list as soon as possible but not more than ten days after being completely exonerated.

PERSONNEL ON TEMPORARY DUTY

Commanders must ensure that soldiers are considered for promotion before they are placed on temporary duty, in isolated areas, or on special duty or assignment. Promotion authorities must ensure that they are kept informed of the duty performance of soldiers on temporary duty.

REASSIGNMENT BEFORE PROMOTION

When a soldier is processing for transfer, the promotion packet and a copy of the current recommended list must be sealed in an envelope and filed in the action-pending section of the soldier's Military Records Personnel Jacket (MPRJ). The gaining promotion authority should then put the soldier's name on his or her current recommended list on the reporting date as stated in the orders.

Newly assigned soldiers who are on a recommended list from a previous command are added to the current recommended list of the gaining command effective on the reporting date stated in reassignment orders.

No soldier who is on a recommended list should depart a unit (or be permitted to depart) until his or her promotion packet has been prepared and its presence in the MPRJ has been verified.

RECLASSIFICATION OF PMOS

A soldier on a recommended list who is voluntarily or involuntarily reclassified for reasons other than inefficiency or misconduct may compete against the announced DA promotion cutoff scores in the newly awarded MOS and be promoted in the new PMOS on the first day of the month following reclassification, if eligible.

SENIOR NCO/DA SELECTION BOARDS

Much of the following information comes from the Human Resources Command Enlisted Personnel Management Directorate (EPMD) web page at *www.hrc.army.mil/site/Active/enlist/ENLIST.htm.* No one could better define the centralized promotion system and how to prepare for the board than the proponent. The DA centralized promotion system described here is used for promotion to grades E-7, E-8, and E-9.

Board Operation

Headquarters, Department of the Army (HQDA), convenes Enlisted Centralized Selection Boards at the Enlisted Records and Evaluation Center (EREC), Indianapolis, Indiana. EREC is a subordinate command of the Human Resources Command. About four months before the convening date of each selection board, HQDA establishes and announces the zones of consideration for each board. These zones define the date of rank (DOR) requirements for consideration by the board for both primary zone (PZ) and secondary zone (SZ) selection.

The PZ consists of all soldiers of a specified grade whose DOR falls within the announced zone of consideration and who meet the requirements of AR 600-8-19, chapter 4. The SZ provides outstanding soldiers with later DOR an opportunity to compete for advancement ahead of their contemporaries.

The following general criteria must be met before the board convenes to qualify a soldier for inclusion in a zone of consideration.

- Meet the announced date of rank requirements and other criteria prescribed by HQDA.
- Have the required cumulative enlisted service creditable in computing basic pay for promotion to master sergeant or above.
- Be on active duty on the convening date of the board.

Teaching, mentoring, listening, learning.

- Have a high school diploma or GED equivalent or an associate's or higher degree.
- Not be barred from or denied reenlistment.
- For promotion to sergeant first class, a soldier must have the security clearance required for the MOS in which promoted. For master sergeant and above, the soldier must have a favorable National Agency Check (NAC) completed or have a final secret security clearance or higher.
- Promotion to sergeant first class and master sergeant requires completion of the Advanced NCO Course (soldiers selected for sergeant first class who are not graduates are automatically selected for attendance). Promotion to sergeant major and command sergeant major requires the Sergeants Major Course.

Soldiers compete for promotion/school selection against all other eligible soldiers in their primary MOS and zone. The number of NCOs selected for promotion in both zones is based on the Army's projected requirements in each MOS and grade. These requirements are determined by Human Resources Command (HRC) and approved by the Office of the Deputy Chief of Staff for Personnel (G1), HQDA.

The Human Resources Command nominates, and the G1 approves, the individuals who sit on the board. Each board consists of officers and noncommissioned officers, with a general officer serving as board president. Nine to eleven panels compose each board, with at least four members on each panel. Panels are organized by the career management field (CMF), and the panel size varies in proportion to the number of records it must consider. Each panel has a nonvoting administrative NCO who controls the flow of records.

Prior to looking at or reviewing any file, EREC provides board members with a comprehensive orientation on the board process, evaluations reports, and detailed written guidance from the Army Deputy Chief of Staff, G-1 and the various branch proponents. The G-1's Memorandum of Instruction (MOI) gives them specific guidance on how to conduct themselves during the board process. The proponents provide specific guidance on the unique qualifications soldiers should possess to be the most competitive for selection. NCOs may wish to review a previously published MOI to better prepare themselves for an upcoming board.

During the selection board proceedings, each board member considers the soldier's entire career. This process ensures that no one success or failure, by itself, will be an overriding factor in determining the soldier's standing in relation to his or her peers. The primary areas that boards consider are performance and potential, military and civilian education, awards, APFT and height/weight trends, and any misconduct reflected in the record.

The most important document in the promotion file is the Official Military Personnel File (OMPF), which is stored at EREC. Within the OMPF, board members look primarily at each evaluation report, i.e., enlisted evaluation reports (EERs), academic evaluation reports (AERs), and NCOERs. They generally review all reports and place emphasis on the current grade or the last five years. The board also has access to the official photo, the Promotion Enlisted Record Brief (ERB), a synopsis of previous assignments, and whatever correspondence the Soldier forwards to the board president.

Three board members vote each file using a numerical score. Scores range from 1 to 6, with "+" or "-" used to further rank the files. The scoring system with a typical word picture appears below:

SCORE	WORD	PICTURE
6 +/-	Exceptional performer	Select Now
5 +/-	Excellent	Definitely Select
4 +/-	Strong	Should Select
3 +/-	Successful	Select if Room
2 +/-	Acceptable	Retain in grade
1 +1	Substandard	QMP referral

Each voter places his or her score on a separate vote sheet. The other two voting members do not see that vote score. Board members may request additional information pertaining to the individual soldier before casting their independent vote. Also, board members are not told how many NCOs are authorized to be promoted until all records are voted, and the scores are entered into the computer.

After all records are voted, the board identifies all primary zone soldiers whom they believe are "fully qualified"—those who meet the basic prerequisites for possible promotion to the next higher grade or attendance to a particular school. The fully qualified soldiers in each MOS are rank ordered based on the numerical scores given by the voting members. The panel selects those receiving the highest scores as "best qualified" based on specific select objectives for each MOS, which are determined by the projected needs of the Army. The same procedure is followed for selecting soldiers from the secondary zone. There are separate select objectives for the primary and secondary zones.

The board also performs a qualitative screening of soldiers whose overall records are unsatisfactory and warrant a bar to reenlistment. Soldiers identified and selected as unsatisfactory performers under the provisions of the Qualitative Management Program (QMP) receive an HQDA "Bar to Reenlistment."

Preparing for DA Selection Boards

Assume that you are eligible for consideration by a DA Selection Board. How can you best present yourself to the board?

The centralized selection system relies on information contained in your OMPF, your official photograph, and your Enlisted Record Brief (ERB). These documents must portray an accurate profile of your ability and potential. Although the OMPF is used for other personnel management actions throughout your career, you must realize that the accuracy of the information on the OMPF may determine whether or not a board selects you for promotion.

The results of any selection board can be no more valid than the information upon which the board bases its judgment. For that reason, it is important for you to personally ensure that your file is current and accurate before a selection board reviews it. If you prepare your records with the same attention to detail as you would if you were preparing to appear in person, you will greatly enhance your chance for selection. Board members have the following items to review: your OMPF, Promotion ERB, Correspondence to the President of the Board, and Official Photograph as well as a data summary of all of your evaluations.

Records Review

You have a responsibility to ensure your records are up to date and ready for review by the selection board. If they aren't right, you are to blame. With the latest tool, OMPF On-line, the task of getting a copy of your OMPF has been eliminated. Now you can go on-line and see your actual file, real time. All you need is an AKO account and password to access the OMPF On-line web site. Go to *www.hrc.army.mil,* click on HRC Indianapolis, and then click on the OMPF On-line link. Look at it and compare it to your personal paper files. If it is incomplete, then get the missing documents to EREC either through digital senders located in many PSB's or the most expeditious means possible. EREC posts the documents that they receive to the OMPF within twenty-four to forty-eight hours of receipt. See *www.hrc.army.mil/site/EREC/index.htm.*

Review your evaluation reports. Check to see if they are all there. The NCOER is without question the most important document in your file! Missing reports reduce critical information available to selection board members. If an evaluation report is missing from your OMPF but you have a copy in your personal file, submit it to EREC as above. If you do not have a copy in your personal records, then you should try to locate your rater for that time period or get your personnel service branch (PSB) or current commander to contact the rater, asking him or her to prepare a report for you. You should have the dates that you served under him or her, and you should remind him or her of your significant accomplishments during that rating period. The same steps can be taken with the senior rater and reviewer. If only one rater is located, that is better than a nonrated period. Remember, the purpose of an evaluation report is to provide information on the types of jobs you have held, your duty performance, and your demonstrated potential.

Review commendatory and disciplinary data included in your OMPF. These data include certificates of achievement, awards and decorations, Articles 15, etc. If you have any commendatory items that are not in your file, you may send documentation directly to EREC at the above address, or your PSB will do it for you. Caution: If you want to keep the original, most can be scanned and sent in digitized form. Memorandums of appreciation/commendation are no longer authorized for file in the OMPF, except in exceptional cases. Make sure that any document sent to EREC contains your Social Security number.

Correct erroneous records. During the review of your OMPF, if you find an evaluation report that you successfully appealed, an Article 15 that was wholly set aside, or any erroneous/misfiled document(s), then you must contact your PSB. They will advise you on the steps to take to correct your record.

Enlisted Record Brief (ERB)

The ERB is the data information counterpart to the OMPF. You should review and authenticate your promotion ERB prior to every board. Look carefully at each item on the ERB to ensure the data is there and accurate. Once you are confident that it is correct, then validate it and keep a copy for your records. When you are in the zone of consideration for a board, you can view and validate your promotion ERB on-line at the EREC web site.

Place special emphasis on the accuracy of the following information: NAME, SSN, GRADE, DOR, PMOS, SMOS, Mil Ed, Civ Ed, DOB, and basic active service date (BASD). Your servicing PSB/MPD must process update transactions to the Total Army Personnel Data Base (TAPDB) (HRC).

Jobs matter; boards look for NCOs who are successful in hard assignments (platoon sergeant, 1SG, drill sergeant, recruiter, etc.) for twenty-four or more months. These NCOs are generally rewarded. Muddy boots time also counts. Make sure your assignment history accurately reflects the job you held, as well as your current duty title.

Correspondence to the President of the Board

Memorandums to the president of the selection board are seen by voting members of the board. You may write to the board president to call attention to any matter that you feel is important to your consideration. The memorandum should not include information already in your file. The memorandum should be very brief, well written, and carefully proofread.

Official Photograph

The official photo is not part of the performance fiche. All selection boards are provided a hard-copy photograph, if available. The photograph represents the soldier appearing before the board and is used in the decision-making process of the board members. Many board members have said that the photograph is the soldier's personal statement of professionalism to the board.

Although the regulation (AR 640-30) requires a photograph every five years, there is no prohibition against having one made sooner. If you have lost weight, been promoted, have new awards and/or decorations, or have a better-fitting uniform since your last photograph, you may want to have a new one made. Ensure that the photograph is current and sharp, that your image does not blend with the background, and that you assemble the menu board accurately. A sloppy appearance, unauthorized awards and decorations, not wearing the chevrons of your current grade, or appearing to be overweight could affect your opportunity for selection. A missing photograph may also mislead board members to believe that you are apathetic or are trying to hide something (being overweight?).

Discrepancies

The following are some common discrepancies found by DA Enlisted Selection Boards in the Official Military Personnel Files of soldiers. These are not inclusive of every discrepancy. They are offered simply as a tool to use when reviewing your files.

1. Missing/outdated photographs.
2. Missing or incomplete ERB data.
3. Missing NCOER.
4. Height and weight differences—getting taller as you gain weight.
5. Blank or incorrect PMOS/SMOS/BASD/DOR.
6. P3 profile with no MOS/Medical Retention Board (MMRB).
7. Blank or incorrect military/civilian education entries.
8. Wearing of unauthorized badges, tabs, awards, and decorations.

Interactive Voice Response Telephone System (IVRS)

The IVRS is an automated system used in conjunction with touch-tone telephones that allows for the retrieval of information about photo dates, NCOER end dates, OMPF microfiche requests, and upcoming DA Enlisted Centralized Selection Board data (which includes Personnel Qualification Record (PQR) data, declination/acceptance statements, and memos to the board president). To use the IVRS and PSB, individuals can call (on a touch-tone telephone only) DSN 221-EREC (3732) or commercial (703) 325-EREC (3732).

Summary

At least six months before your records are to appear before a DA selection board, you should begin getting your records in order. Your file is appearing before the board in your place; take your time, and make sure it is complete and accurate. Three parts of your file—your photograph, your OMPF, and your Promotion ERB—contain over 95 percent of the information that the selection board members will use to decide whether or not to select you for promotion, school attendance, or QMP. You must not ignore the importance of that fact. *Review your file!*

ADDITIONAL INFORMATION

Acceptance

Unless a soldier declines promotion, it is accepted as of the effective date of the announcing order. Letters of declination must be sent through command channels to the military personnel office (MILPO) not later than thirty days after the effective date of the promotion given in the orders. Soldiers who decline promotion will be considered by the next regularly constituted board, providing they are otherwise eligible.

Soldiers promoted to sergeant first class and above incur a two-year service obligation; the obligation begins from the effective date of the promotion.

Frocking

When a soldier is frocked, he or she assumes the insignia of a higher grade so that his or her title is commensurate with the duty position, although no pay or allowances are authorized in the higher grade. Sergeants first class (promotable) to first sergeants, master sergeants (promotable) to sergeants major in certain assignments, and command sergeants major (designate) may be frocked.

Enlisted Standby Advisory Board (STAB)

This board considers the following records:

- Those from a primary and secondary zone not reviewed by a regular board.
- Those from a primary zone that were not properly constituted due to a material error when reviewed by the regular board. The deputy chief of staff for personnel or designee will approve cases for referral to a STAB upon declaring invalid, in whole or in part, an adverse NCO Evaluation Report or academic evaluation report that was reviewed by a promotion board, providing that with the absence of this report, or portions thereof, there is a reasonable chance that the soldier would have been recommended for promotion. An error is major when, had it not existed, the soldier would clearly have been more competitive and his or her qualifications appear to have been scored to equal those of others who were selected.
- Those of recommended soldiers on whom derogatory information has developed that may warrant removal from a recommended list.

Only those soldiers who were not selected from a primary zone of consideration will be reconsidered for promotion. Soldiers who were considered in a secondary zone are not reconsidered.

Removal from a Recommended List

Commanders may recommend that a soldier's name be removed from a DA recommended list at any time. The recommendation for the removal must be fully documented and justified. HQDA makes the final decision on the removal based on the results and recommendation of the DA Enlisted Standby Advisory Board.

Removal may be recommended for a number of reasons, including the following:

- Failure to make progress in the weight-control program.
- Reprimand, admonition, censure, and other nonpunitive measures, including for substandard duty performance over a period of time.
- Misconduct.

Before forwarding a recommendation for removal, the initiator must send it in writing to the soldier. All documents must be included. The soldier must be allowed to respond to the proposed action and may submit a rebuttal within fifteen days after receipt of the written notice. The commander initiating the removal may extend this time only for unusual circumstances beyond the soldier's control. A soldier who elects not to rebut must send a signed statement saying that he or she has reviewed the proposed action and elects not to submit a rebuttal.

Removal from a DA promotion recommended list has far-reaching, long-lasting effects on the soldier. The probability for subsequent selection for promotion is extremely unlikely.

REDUCTIONS IN GRADE

Commanders at the grades indicated may administratively reduce the grade of assigned soldiers:

- Specialist or corporal and below—company, troop, battery, and separate detachment commanders.
- Sergeant and staff sergeant—field-grade commanders of any organization that is authorized a lieutenant colonel or higher-grade commander. For separate detachments, companies, or battalions, reduction authority is the next senior headquarters within the chain of command authorized a lieutenant colonel or higher-grade commander.
- Sergeant first class and above—commanders or organizations that are authorized a colonel or higher-grade commander. For separate detachments, companies, or battalions, reduction authority is the next senior headquarters within the chain of command authorized a colonel or higher-grade commander.

Erroneous Enlistment Grades

Soldiers in higher grades than authorized upon enlistment or reenlistment in the Regular Army or Army Reserve will be reduced to the one to which they are entitled. Authorized grades are prescribed in AR 601-210, AR 140-11, and AR 140-158.

Misconduct

For reductions imposed by court-martial, see the *Manual for Courts-Martial*. Sergeants first class and above cannot be reduced under the provision of Article 15, Uniform Code of Military Justice (UCMJ).

Inefficiency

Inefficiency is defined as "demonstration of characteristics which show that the person cannot perform the duties and responsibilities of the grade and MOS" (AR 600-8-19, chapter 7). It may include any act or conduct that shows a lack of abilities and qualities required and expected of a person of that grade and experience. Commanders may consider misconduct, including conviction by civil court, as bearing on efficiency.

A soldier may be reduced under the authority of chapter 7, AR 600-8-19, for long-standing unpaid personal debts that he or she has not made a reasonable attempt to pay.

An assigned soldier who has served in the same unit for at least ninety days may be reduced one grade for inefficiency. The commander starting the reduction action will document the soldier's inefficiency. The documents should establish a pattern of inefficiency rather than identify a specific incident.

The commander reducing a soldier will inform him or her, in writing, of the action contemplated and the reasons. The soldier must acknowledge receipt of the letter, by endorsement, and may submit any pertinent matters in rebuttal. Sergeants and above may request to appear before a reduction board. If appearance is declined, it must be done in writing and will be considered as acceptance of the reduction action. A reduction board, when required, must be convened within thirty days after the individual is notified in writing.

Reduction Boards

When required, reduction boards are convened to determine whether an enlisted soldier's grade should be reduced. This convening authority must ensure that the following conditions exist:

- The board consists of officers and enlisted personnel of mature judgment and senior in grade to the person being considered for reduction.
- For inefficiency cases, at least one member must be thoroughly familiar with the soldier's specialty.
- The board must consist of at least three voting members and will comprise both officer and enlisted voting members.

- The board has an officer or senior enlisted member (or both) of the same sex as the soldier being considered for reduction.
- The composition of the board represents the ethnic population of soldiers under its jurisdiction.
- No soldier with direct knowledge of the case is appointed to the board.
- A soldier who is to appear before the board will be given at least fifteen working days' written notice before the date of the hearing so that the soldier or his or her counsel has time to prepare the case.

The convening authority may approve or disapprove any portion of the recommendation of the board, but her or his action cannot increase the severity of the board's recommendation. If she or he approves a recommended reduction, she or he may direct it. When the board recommends a reduction and the convening authority approves it, the soldier will be reduced without regard to any action taken to appeal the reduction.

The soldier has the right to the following:

- Decline, in writing, to appear before the board.
- Have a military counsel of his or her own choosing, if reasonably available, or may employ a civilian counsel at own expense, or both.
- Appear in person, with or without counsel, at all open proceedings of the board.
- If the soldier appears before the board without counsel, have the president counsel him or her on the action being contemplated, the effect of such action on his or her future in the Army, and the right to request counsel.
- Challenge (dismiss) any member of the board for cause.
- Request any reasonably available witness whose testimony the soldier believes to be pertinent to the case. When requested, the soldier must tell the nature of the information the witness will provide.
- Submit to the board written affidavits and depositions of witnesses who are unable to appear before the board.
- Employ the provisions of Article 31, UCMJ (prohibition against compulsory self-incrimination), or submit to an examination by the board.
- Have his or her counsel question any witness appearing before the board.

Failure of the soldier to exercise his or her rights is not a bar to the board proceedings or its findings and recommendations.

Appeals

Appeals from reduction for misconduct are governed by Article 15, UCMJ; paragraph 135, MC; and AR 27-10.

Appeals based on reduction for failure to complete training will not be accepted.

Appeals from staff sergeants and below based on reduction for inefficiency or conviction by civil court are allowed. They must be submitted in writing within thirty workdays from the date of reduction. The officer having general court-martial jurisdiction, or the next higher authority, may approve, disapprove, or change the reduction if he or she determines that the reduction was without sufficient basis, should be changed, or was proper. His or her action is final.

Written appeals from sergeants first class and above based on reduction for inefficiency or conviction by civil court must also be submitted within thirty days of the date of reduction. A copy of all correspondence and the appeal are furnished to the authority next above the officer who reduced the soldier. This officer, if a general, will take final action on the appeal. If not reviewed at the appellate level by a general officer, the file is then sent to the first general officer next in the chain of command above the officer who acted on the appeal for final review and action. This authority personally reviews the file, including action taken on the appeal, and makes final corrections where indicated.

Other Reasons for Reductions

When a separation authority determines that a soldier is to be discharged from the service under other than honorable conditions, he or she will be reduced to the lowest enlisted grade. Board action is not required for such actions. Also, soldiers appointed to a higher grade on entering or while attending a service or civilian school and who fail to complete the course successfully may be reduced.

Restoration to Former Grades

Grade restoration may result from setting aside, mitigation, or suspension of nonjudicial punishment; when a court-martial sentence is set aside or disapproved; when a conviction by a civil court is reversed; or when officers—taking final appeal or review action after reduction—direct that the soldier be restored to his or her former grade or any intermediate grade, on determining that reduction was without sufficient basis.

15

Pay and Entitlements

This chapter explains the basic facts about your Army pay and benefits and provides a quick reference for questions that may come up in your day-to-day duties.

The soldier who enlists in the Army for the money is in the wrong business. Relatively substantial paychecks do not begin until a soldier reaches the senior noncommissioned ranks with twenty to twenty-six years of service, although service overseas in a combat zone does increase take-home pay substantially. That said, if pay and benefits were the only inducement to a military career, then we would have no Army. Unlike first term soldiers, soldiers who reenlist understand the "score" and accept the challenges and rewards of being a soldier.

PAY AND ALLOWANCES

Military pay consists of basic pay, special and incentive pay, and allowances. Pay is computed on the basis of a thirty-day month, and soldiers may elect to be paid once a month (at the end of the month) or twice a month (on the fifteenth and the thirtieth of each month).

In order to change your pay option, contact your local finance and accounting office to execute DA Form 3685, *JUMPS–Army Pay Elections.* Which option you select depends upon how you budget your money. Some soldiers find that they can get along quite well with one lump-sum payment at the end of the month; others prefer to get paid twice a month. Read the pay elections form carefully before filling it out. Submit your options to the finance officer as early in the month as possible to give the finance center enough time to process your request so that your new option will be reflected during the next pay period.

Report discrepancies in your pay immediately. To do so, you must know what you are authorized.

Leave and Earnings Statement (LES)

The LES is a computerized monthly statement of each soldier's pay account. The LES shows all entitlements earned, collections affected, and payments made during the period covered by the statement. In addition, this statement

DEFENSE FINANCE AND ACCOUNTING SERVICE MILITARY LEAVE AND EARNINGS STATEMENT

ID	NAME (LAST, FIRST, MI)	SOC. SEC. NO.	GRADE	PAY DATE	YRS SVC	ETS	BRANCH	ADSN/DSSN	PERIOD COVERED
	1	2	3	4	5	6	7	8	9

	ENTITLEMENTS		DEDUCTIONS		ALLOTMENTS		SUMMARY	
	TYPE	AMOUNT	TYPE	AMOUNT	TYPE	AMOUNT	+ AMT FWD	13
A B C D E F G H I J K L M N O	10		11		12		+ TOT ENT	14
							- TOT DED	15
							- TOT ALMT	16
							= NET AMT	17
							- CR FWD	18
							= EOM PAY	19
							DIEMS	RET PLAN
	TOTAL	20		21		22	23	24

LEAVE	BF BAL	ERND	USED	CR BAL	ETS BAL	LV LOST	LV PAID	USE\LOSE
	25	26	27	28	29	30	31	32

FED TAXES	WAGE PERIOD	WAGE YTD	M/S	EX	ADD'L TAX	TAX YTD
	33	34	35	36	37	38

FICA TAXES	WAGE PERIOD	SOC WAGE YTD	SOC TAX YTD	MED WAGE YTD	MED TAX YTD
	39	40	41	42	43

STATE TAXES	ST	WAGE PERIOD	WAGE YTD	M/S	EX	TAX YTD
	44	45	46	47	48	49

PAY DATA	BAQ TYPE	BAQ DEPN	VHA ZIP	RENT AMT	SHARE	STAT	JFTR	DEPNS	2D JFTR	BAS TYPE	CHARITY YTD	TPC	PACIDN
	50	51	52	53	54	55	56	57	58	59	60	61	62

Thrift Savings Plan (TSP)	BASE PAY RATE	BASE PAY CURRENT	SPEC PAY RATE	SPEC PAY CURRENT	INC PAY RATE	INC PAY CURRENT	BONUS PAY RATE	BONUS PAY CURRENT
	63	64	65	66	67	68	69	70

Thrift Savings Plan (TSP)	CURRENTLY NOT USED	TSP YTD DEDUCTIONS	DEFERRED	EXEMPT	CURRENTLY NOT USED
	71	72	73	74	75

REMARKS **YTD ENTITLE**__________ **YTD DEDUCT** __________

76 77 78

www.dfas.mil

DFAS Form 702, Jan 02

provides the soldier a complete record of transactions that affect his or her leave account for the period of the statement. It also serves as the official leave record. You may also access your LES at the MyPay web site listed below.

Changes to the LES

In 2002, the LES changed to reflect a soldier's involvement in the Thrift Savings Plan (TSP). The new blocks are located directly above the "Remarks" area of the LES. The four entitlement categories are Base Pay (blocks 63 and 64 on the sample), Special Pay (blocks 65 and 66), Incentive Pay (blocks 67 and 68), and Bonus Pay (blocks 69 and 70). There are two new blocks for each of four entitlement categories. The blocks containing the word "Rate" reflect the percentage rate of the monthly entitlement that the servicemember elects to contribute to TSP. The blocks that contain the word "Current" reflect the dollar amount designated by the servicemember. The "TSP YTD [year-to-date] Deductions" block (72) is simply what a soldier has contributed to date. The "Deferred" block (73) will contain the amount of TSP YTD contributions that are tax deferred. There is a yearly maximum for tax-deferred contributions, and once a soldier reaches the yearly maximum the system generates a stop transaction and creates a remark with a stop date. The "Exempt" block (74) contains the amount of YTD tax-exempt TSP contributions. Deductions for TSP contributions and loan payments appear in the "Deductions" block (11) of the LES. If a soldier receives a TSP loan payment and any TSP contribution refund, the "Entitlements" block (10) of the LES will denote the amount.

Additionally, two new blocks advise the soldier on his or her retirement status. These blocks are located on the far right side of the document, under the "EOM Pay" block. The "DIEMS (date initially entered military service) block" (23) reflects the date used to establish the soldier's retirement plan. The "RET Plan" block (24) indicates the retirement plan a soldier is under, based on the DIEMS date shown in the preceding block.

Study your LES very carefully. Should you discover any item you believe to be in error or should there be an entry recorded thereon that you do not understand, consult with your local finance office immediately. If, during a routine audit of your pay record, it should be discovered that you have been overpaid at some time in the past, the government will collect what is due.

On-line Finance

The Defense Finance and Accounting Service (DFAS) My Pay web site at *www.mypay.dfas.mil/mypay.aspx* allows soldiers to access their pay record and update certain payroll information directly, without having to fill out any paper forms. The E/MSS allows you access to your financial records at either your home or office through the Internet using a personal computer or through an Interactive Voice Response Telephone System (IVRS) using a touch-tone telephone. MyPay allows you to review or make changes to your federal and state tax information, financial allotments, home or correspondence address, savings bonds, and direct deposit or electronic funds transfer (EFT) information without the problems involved with paperwork. When you make a change, the system saves the transaction and sends it to the payroll system the next day for update. This system also allows you to view and print your Leave and Earnings Statement on line.

Basic Pay

Basic pay is established by law and is that pay a soldier receives, based on grade and length of service, exclusive of any special or incentive pay or allowances.

Reserve Drill Pay

Reserve drill pay, like basic pay, is established by law. And like basic pay, reserve drill pay is pay a soldier receives based on grade and length of service. Unlike monthly basic pay, however, reserve drill pay is computed and paid for the number of days' service rendered. It is comparable to basic pay.

Collections of Erroneous Payments

Overpayments for two months in a row are collected from the next month's pay. If these payments are two or more months old, collection is delayed to allow time for unit commanders to arrange for prorated collection, if necessary, before computer collection action is initiated.

Normally, the amount deducted for any period will not exceed an amount equal to two-thirds of a soldier's pay. Monthly installments may be increased or decreased to reflect changes in pay.

Soldiers may appeal the validity of a debt, the amount, or the rate of payment. If an enlisted soldier's appeal is denied, the chief of personnel operations, Department of the Army, may consider his or her case for remission or cancellation of the indebtedness.

Advance Payments

An advance of pay is authorized upon permanent change of station to provide a soldier funds for expenses, such as transportation, temporary storage of household goods, packing and shipping costs, and securing new living quarters. Advance payments are limited to no more than one month's advance pay of basic pay less deductions or, if warranted, not more than three months' basic pay less deductions at the old station, en route, or within sixty days after reporting to a new station.

Requests for advance pay from enlisted personnel in pay grades E-1 through E-4 must be approved by their commander, and this approval must be indicated in the *Pay Inquiry Form* (DA Form 2142), together with a statement

MONTHLY BASIC PAY (Effective 1 January 2006)

Years of Service

Grade	<2	2	3	4	6	8	10	12	14	16	18	20	22	24	26
Commissioned officers															
O-10	0.00	0.00	0.00	0.00	0.00	0.00	0.00	0.00	0.00	0.00	0.00	13,365.00	13,430.40	13,709.70	14,196.30
O-9	0.00	0.00	0.00	0.00	0.00	0.00	0.00	0.00	0.00	0.00	0.00	11,689.50	11,857.50	12,101.10	12,525.60
O-8	8,271.00	8,541.90	8,721.60	8,772.00	8,996.10	9,371.10	9,458.10	9,814.20	9,916.20	10,222.80	10,666.20	11,075.40	11,348.70	11,348.70	11,348.70
O-7	6,872.70	7,191.90	7,339.80	7,457.10	7,669.80	7,879.50	8,122.50	8,364.90	8,607.90	9,371.10	10,015.80	10,015.80	10,015.80	10,015.80	10,066.50
O-6	5,094.00	5,596.20	5,963.40	5,963.40	5,985.90	6,242.70	6,276.60	6,276.60	6,633.30	7,263.90	7,634.10	8,004.00	8,214.60	8,427.60	8,841.30
O-5	4,246.50	4,783.50	5,115.00	5,177.10	5,383.50	5,507.40	5,779.20	5,978.70	6,236.10	6,630.60	6,818.10	7,003.80	7,214.40	7,214.40	7,214.40
O-4	3,663.90	4,241.40	4,524.30	4,587.60	4,850.10	5,131.80	5,482.20	5,755.80	5,945.40	6,054.30	6,117.60	6,117.60	6,117.60	6,117.60	6,117.60
O-3	3,221.40	3,651.90	3,941.70	4,297.50	4,503.00	4,728.90	4,875.30	5,115.90	5,240.70	5,240.70	5,240.70	5,240.70	5,240.70	5,240.70	5,240.70
O-2	2,783.10	3,170.10	3,651.00	3,774.30	3,852.00	3,852.00	3,852.00	3,852.00	3,852.00	3,852.00	3,852.00	3,852.00	3,852.00	3,852.00	3,852.00
O-1	2,416.20	2,514.60	3,039.60	3,039.60	3,039.60	3,039.60	3,039.60	3,039.60	3,039.60	3,039.60	3,039.60	3,039.60	3,039.60	3,039.60	3,039.60
Officers with more than 4 years' active duty as enlisted or warrant officer															
O-3E	0.00	0.00	0.00	4,297.50	4,503.00	4,728.90	4,875.30	5,115.90	5,318.40	5,434.50	5,592.90	5,592.90	5,592.90	5,592.90	5,592.90
O-2E	0.00	0.00	0.00	3,774.30	3,852.00	3,974.70	4,181.40	4,341.60	4,460.70	4,460.70	4,460.70	4,460.70	4,460.70	4,460.70	4,460.70
O-1E	0.00	0.00	0.00	3,039.60	3,246.30	3,366.00	3,488.70	3,609.30	3,774.30	3,774.30	3,774.30	3,774.30	3,774.30	3,774.30	3,774.30
Warrant officers															
W-5	0.00	0.00	0.00	0.00	0.00	0.00	0.00	0.00	0.00	0.00	0.00	5,720.10	5,916.30	6,113.10	6,311.10
W-4	3,328.80	3,581.10	3,684.00	3,785.10	3,959.40	4,131.30	4,305.90	4,475.70	4,651.50	4,927.20	5,103.60	5,276.10	5,454.90	5,631.00	5,811.00
W-3	3,039.90	3,166.80	3,296.40	3,339.30	3,475.50	3,631.50	3,837.30	4,040.40	4,256.40	4,418.40	4,579.80	4,649.10	4,720.80	4,876.80	5,032.50
W-2	2,673.90	2,826.60	2,960.40	3,057.30	3,140.70	3,369.60	3,544.50	3,674.40	3,801.30	3,888.30	3,961.50	4,100.70	4,239.00	4,379.10	4,379.10
W-1	2,361.30	2,554.50	2,683.80	2,767.50	2,990.40	3,124.80	3,243.90	3,376.80	3,465.00	3,544.80	3,674.70	3,773.10	3,773.10	3,773.10	3,773.10
Enlisted members															
E-9	0.00	0.00	0.00	0.00	0.00	0.00	4,022.10	4,113.30	4,228.20	4,363.50	4,499.40	4,717.80	4,902.30	5,097.00	5,394.00
E-8	0.00	0.00	0.00	0.00	0.00	3,292.50	3,438.30	3,528.30	3,636.30	3,753.30	3,964.50	4,071.60	4,253.70	4,354.80	4,603.50
E-7	2,288.70	2,498.10	2,593.80	2,720.70	2,819.40	2,989.50	3,084.90	3,180.30	3,350.40	3,435.60	3,516.30	3,565.80	3,732.60	3,840.60	4,113.60
E-6	1,979.70	2,178.00	2,274.30	2,367.60	2,465.10	2,685.00	2,770.50	2,865.30	2,948.70	2,978.10	2,998.50	2,998.50	2,998.50	2,998.50	2,998.50
E-5	1,814.10	1,935.30	2,028.60	2,124.60	2,273.70	2,402.10	2,496.60	2,526.60	2,526.60	2,526.60	2,526.60	2,526.60	2,526.60	2,526.60	2,526.60
E-4	1,662.90	1,748.10	1,842.60	1,935.90	2,018.40	2,018.40	2,018.40	2,018.40	2,018.40	2,018.40	2,018.40	2,018.40	2,018.40	2,018.40	2,018.40
E-3	1,501.20	1,595.70	1,692.00	1,692.00	1,692.00	1,692.00	1,692.00	1,692.00	1,692.00	1,692.00	1,692.00	1,692.00	1,692.00	1,692.00	1,692.00
E-2	1,427.40	1,427.40	1,427.40	1,427.40	1,427.40	1,427.40	1,427.40	1,427.40	1,427.40	1,427.40	1,427.40	1,427.40	1,427.40	1,427.40	1,427.40
E-1	1,273.50	1,273.50	1,273.50	1,273.50	1,273.50	1,273.50	1,273.50	1,273.50	1,273.50	1,273.50	1,273.50	1,273.50	1,273.50	1,273.50	1,273.50

E-1<four months: 1,178.10

RESERVE DRILL PAY (Four Drills) (Effective 1 January 2006)

	Years of Service														
Grade	***<2***	***2***	***3***	***4***	***6***	***8***	***10***	***12***	***14***	***16***	***18***	***20***	***22***	***24***	***26***
Commissioned officers															
O-7	916.36	958.92	978.64	994.28	1,022.64	1,050.60	1,083.00	1,115.32	1,147.72	1,249.48	1,335.44	1,335.44	1,335.44	1,335.44	1,342.20
O-6	679.20	746.16	795.12	795.12	798.12	832.36	836.88	836.88	884.44	968.52	1,017.88	1,067.20	1,095.28	1,123.68	1,178.84
O-5	566.20	637.80	682.00	690.28	717.80	734.32	770.56	797.16	831.48	884.08	909.08	933.84	961.92	961.92	961.92
O-4	488.52	565.52	603.24	611.68	646.68	684.24	730.96	767.44	792.72	807.24	815.68	815.68	815.68	815.68	815.68
O-3	429.52	486.92	525.56	573.00	600.40	630.52	650.04	682.12	698.76	698.76	698.76	698.76	698.76	698.76	698.76
O-2	371.08	422.68	486.80	503.24	513.60	513.60	513.60	513.60	513.60	513.60	513.60	513.60	513.60	513.60	513.60
O-1	322.16	335.28	405.28	405.28	405.28	405.28	405.28	405.28	405.28	405.28	405.28	405.28	405.28	405.28	405.28
Commissioned officers with more than 4 years' active duty as enlisted or warrant officer															
O-3E	0.00	0.00	0.00	573.00	600.40	630.52	650.04	682.12	709.12	724.60	745.72	745.72	745.72	745.72	745.72
O-2E	0.00	0.00	0.00	503.24	513.60	529.96	557.52	578.88	594.76	594.76	594.76	594.76	594.76	594.76	594.76
O-1E	0.00	0.00	0.00	405.28	432.84	448.80	465.16	481.24	503.24	503.24	503.24	503.24	503.24	503.24	503.24
Warrant officers															
W-5	0.00	0.00	0.00	0.00	0.00	0.00	0.00	0.00	0.00	0.00	0.00	762.68	788.84	815.08	841.48
W-4	443.84	477.48	491.20	504.68	527.92	550.84	574.12	596.76	620.20	656.96	680.48	703.48	727.32	750.80	774.80
W-3	405.32	422.24	439.52	445.24	463.40	484.20	511.64	538.72	567.52	589.12	610.64	619.88	629.44	650.24	671.00
W-2	356.52	376.88	394.72	407.64	418.76	449.28	472.60	489.92	506.84	518.44	528.20	546.76	565.20	583.88	583.88
W-1	314.84	340.60	357.84	369.00	398.72	416.64	432.52	450.24	462.00	472.64	489.96	503.08	503.08	503.08	503.08
Enlisted members															
E-9	0.00	0.00	0.00	0.00	0.00	0.00	536.28	548.44	563.76	581.80	599.92	629.04	653.64	679.60	719.20
E-8	0.00	0.00	0.00	0.00	0.00	439.00	458.44	470.44	484.84	500.44	528.60	542.88	567.16	580.64	613.80
E-7	305.16	333.08	345.84	362.76	375.92	398.60	411.32	424.04	446.72	458.08	468.84	475.44	497.68	512.08	548.48
E-6	263.96	290.40	303.24	315.68	328.68	358.00	369.40	382.04	393.16	397.08	399.80	399.80	399.80	399.80	399.80
E-5	241.88	258.04	270.48	283.28	303.16	320.28	332.88	336.88	336.88	336.88	336.88	336.88	336.88	336.88	336.88
E-4	221.72	233.08	245.68	258.12	269.12	269.12	269.12	269.12	269.12	269.12	269.12	269.12	269.12	269.12	269.12
E-3	200.16	212.76	225.60	225.60	225.60	225.60	225.60	225.60	225.60	225.60	225.60	225.60	225.60	225.60	225.60
E-2	190.32	190.32	190.32	190.32	190.32	190.32	190.32	190.32	190.32	190.32	190.32	190.32	190.32	190.32	190.32
E-1	169.80	169.80	169.80	169.80	169.80	169.80	169.80	169.80	169.80	169.80	169.80	169.80	169.80	169.80	169.80

that the circumstances in the individual's case warrant advancing the amount requested and that advancing a lesser amount would result in hardship to the soldier or his or her family.

The commander's approval for an advance of pay is not required for enlisted personnel in pay grades E-5 through E-9, but advances are not made to senior-grade personnel when it is apparent that the tour of duty (obligated service) will terminate before completion of the scheduled repayment of the advance.

Lump-Sum Payments

A lump-sum payment is made to pay bonuses and accrued leave paid on immediate reenlistments. These payments are made by cash or check through the use of a local payment. Lump-sum payments are always made in even dollar amounts. The maximum amount that may be paid is the gross amount of the enlistment minus the estimate of federal and, when applicable, state taxes. When the computation results in a new amount due in dollars and cents, the amount to be paid may either be the lesser full dollar amount or be rounded to the next higher dollar.

OTHER PAY

Duty in a Combat Zone

As an enlisted member, if you serve in a combat zone for any part of a month, all of your military pay for that month is excluded from your income tax. You also can exclude military pay earned while you are hospitalized as a result of wounds, disease, or injury incurred in the combat zone. The exclusion of your military pay while you are in hospital extends to two years past the termination of hostilities in the designated combat zone. Your hospitalization does not have to be in the combat zone.

Assignment Incentive Pay

Assignment Incentive Pay is used to voluntarily fill hard-to-fill assignments and is taxable unless in a combat zone. In Iraq and Afghanistan soldiers can receive $300 per month for a three-month extension, $600 per month for a six-month extension, and $900 per month for a twelve-month extension. In South Korea, soldiers extending their twelve-month tours for an additional year receive $300 in assignment incentive pay.

Reserve component soldiers assigned in Iraq or Afghanistan who have completed twenty-two months of mobilization and volunteer (for ARNG with the consent of the governor) to extend on active duty beyond twenty-four months of cumulative mobilization time will be offered the opportunity to contract for Assignment Incentive Pay (AIP). Soldiers will be offered $1,000 per month for extended duty beyond completion of their twenty-second month of mobilization. The AIP terminates when the soldier leaves the Central Command area of operations.

Experimental Stress Pay

Experimental stress duty pay is authorized for all Army personnel who, on or after July 1, 1965, participate as human experimental subjects in duties utilizing acceleration/deceleration experimental devices, in thermal stress experiments, and in low-pressure or high-pressure chamber duty.

Foreign Duty Pay

All enlisted personnel assigned to an area outside the contiguous forty-eight states and the District of Columbia where an "accompanied by dependents" tour of duty is not authorized have entitlement to foreign duty or "overseas pay." Chapter 6, part 1, *DOD Pay Manual,* lists the places where foreign duty pay is authorized.

Hardship Duty Pay (HDP)

Hardship duty pay is payable to members entitled to basic pay, at a monthly rate not to exceed $300, while such members are performing specified hardship duty. HDP is paid to members (a) for performing specific missions or (b) when assigned to designated locations. Except for certain restrictions, HDP is payable in addition to all other pay and allowances. Hardship duty pay for mission assignment (HDP-M) is payable to members, both officer and enlisted, for performing designated hardship mission. HDP-M is payable at the full monthly rate, without prorating or reduction, for each month during any part of which the member performs a specified mission. Hardship duty pay for location assignment (HDP-L) is payable only to enlisted members when they are assigned to duty in designated locations.

Hostile Fire Pay

Hostile fire pay is paid to soldiers permanently assigned to units performing duty in designated hostile fire areas or to soldiers assigned to temporary duty in such areas. Hostile fire pay is authorized on a monthly basis or one-time basis, depending upon the soldier's period of exposure to enemy fire. While drawing hostile fire pay, soldiers are exempt from federal and state taxes.

Diving Pay

To qualify for special pay for diving duty, a soldier must be a rated diver in accordance with AR 611-75 and be assigned to a table of organization and equipment (TOE) or a table of distribution and allowances (TDA) position of MOS 00B, or to a position that has been designated diving duty by the assistant chief of staff for force development, Department of the Army.

Soldiers, such as these in Iraq, earn Hostile Fire Pay while on duty in regions designated by the Secretary of Defense.

Demolition Pay

A soldier is entitled to receive incentive pay for demolition duty for any month or portion of a month in which he or she was assigned and performed duty in a primary duty assignment.

Flight Pay

Flight pay is authorized for enlisted crew members.

Parachute Pay

Soldiers who have received a designation as a parachutist or parachute rigger or are undergoing training for such designations, and who are required to engage in parachute jumping from an aircraft in aerial flight and actually perform the specified minimum jump of once per three months, are authorized parachute duty pay. In imminent danger areas, however, the commanding officer may determine a soldier cannot meet the minimum requirements due to the absence of jump equipment, aircraft, or military operations. In this situation the soldier may perform the required four jumps anytime in the twelve-month period. An additional amount is authorized for parachutists who are assigned to positions requiring high-altitude, low-opening (HALO) jump status.

Special Duty Assignment Pay

Special duty pay is authorized on a graduated scale for enlisted members in designated specialties who are required to perform extremely demanding duties or duties demanding an unusual degree of responsibility. Qualifying jobs include career counselor, recruiter, and drill sergeant.

ALLOWANCES

Basic Allowance for Subsistence (BAS)

Upon entitlement to BAS (separate rations) a soldier's unit commander forwards to the finance officer DA Form 4187, *Personnel Action Request* (see chapter 8, DA Pamphlet 600-8), in duplicate, showing the effective date and hour of entitlement to BAS. When a soldier ceases to be entitled to BAS, the unit commander will forward to the finance officer a DA Form 4187 showing date and hour of termination.

The BAS rate for enlisted personnel is $267.18 as of January 1, 2005.

Entitlement to BAS terminates automatically upon permanent change of station (PCS). Care should be taken during in-processing at a new duty station that entitlement is revalidated for personnel authorized separate rations.

Basic Allowance for Housing (BAH)

The basic allowance for housing combines the two older allowances Basic Allowance for Quarters (BAQ) and Variable Housing Allowance (VHA) into one single payment based on rank, with or without dependents. The new rates are based on housing costs for civilians with comparable income levels in the same area. Under this system, the annual growth in the housing allowance will be indexed in the national average monthly housing cost.

BAH terminates for married personnel when they occupy government quarters or when dependency terminates. Dependency is verified by the local finance and accounting officer. The documentary evidence that must be submitted to substantiate dependence includes the original or certified copy of a marriage certificate, the individual's signed statement (when called to active duty or active duty for training for ninety days or less), birth certificate, or a public church record of marriage issued over the signature of the custodian of the church or public records, and, if applicable, a divorce decree. Entitlements must be recertified upon permanent change of station.

Reserve Component (RC)-mobilized soldiers are entitled to BAH based on their primary residence, however, they are not authorized *to change* the BAH from which they were ordered to active duty, regardless of whether or not their primary residence changes.

Family Separation Allowance (FSA)

The Family Separation Allowance is paid to a soldier who has dependents and is serving in an overseas location where dependents are not permitted. It is in the amount of $250.00 per month.

Soldiers in a Temporary Change of Station (TCS) status may be authorized FSA Type II (T) at the rate of $250 per month when they are away from their Permanent Duty Station (PDS) (for mobilized RC personnel this is their home of residence) continuously for a period of thirty days, and the soldiers' dependents are not residing at or near the TCS. Army/service married couples who were living together prior to and immediately before the deployment and single soldiers with authorized primary dependents may be paid Family Separation Allowance for Temporary Duty (FSA-T). Relocation of dependents at government expense is not authorized.

Station Allowances

A list of areas where station allowances are authorized is in chapter 4, part 3, *DOD Pay Manual,* and chapter 4, part G, volume 1, *Joint Travel Regulations.* These allowances are paid to offset the high cost of living in certain geographical areas (overseas and in the United States). They consist of housing (HOUS) and cost of living allowances (COLA). A temporary lodging allowance (TLA) and interim housing allowance (IHA) may also be paid in certain cases.

RC-mobilized soldiers may receive COLA based on the location of their residence when ordered to active duty. CONUS COLA is normally determined by the zip code of the soldier's residence. Regular active duty soldiers located in CONUS or OCONUS areas, who are authorized COLA, will continue to draw COLA as determined by the area to which they are assigned.

Clothing Maintenance Allowance

Clothing maintenance allowance is paid at two different rates:

- Basic, which covers replacement of unique military items that would normally require replacement during the first three years of service.
- Standard, which covers the replacement of unique military items after the first three years of service.

Female personnel are also authorized an initial cash allowance established by AR 700-84 for the purchase of undergarments, dress shoes, and stockings.

A soldier receives the clothing maintenance allowance annually, on the last day of the month in which the soldier's anniversary date of enlistment falls.

Civilian Clothing Allowance

When duty assignments require soldiers to wear civilian clothing, they receive lump-sum payments under the following circumstances:

- Permanent duty requiring civilian clothing.
- Temporary Duty in graduations of fifteen to thirty days and over thirty days.

Temporary Lodging Allowance (TLA)

TLA is the allowance received when arriving at an overseas base that offsets some of the expense of temporary housing and meals. The amount of the TLA depends on variables that include family size, the cost, and cooking/dining facilities of quarters, as well as other allowances the family is receiving.

Temporary Lodging Expense (TLE)

TLE is the allowance received when arriving at a CONUS base that offsets some of the expense of temporary housing and meals. The TLE is up to $110 per day and can last up to ten days. It applies to stateside base arrivals from both CONUS and OCONUS bases.

BONUSES

The enlistment bonus is an enlistment incentive offered to those enlisting in the Regular Army for duty in a specific MOS. The objective of the bonus is to increase the number of enlistments in MOSs that are critical and have inadequate first-term manning levels. Section A, chapter 9, part 1, of the DOD Pay Manual gives basic conditions of entitlement, amount of the bonus, time of payment, and reduction and termination of the award.

Selective Reenlistment Bonus (SRB)

The SRB is a retention incentive paid to soldiers in certain selected MOSs who reenlist or voluntarily extend their enlistment for additional obligated service. The objective of the SRB is to increase the number of reenlistments or extensions in critical MOSs that do not have adequate retention levels to man the career force.

The SRB is established in three zones: zone A consists of those reenlistments falling between twenty-one months and six years of active service; zones B and C consist of those reenlistments or extensions of enlistments falling between six and fourteen years of service.

Payments are based on multiples, not to exceed six, of a soldier's monthly basic pay at the time of discharge or release from active duty or the day before the beginning of extension, multiplied by years of additional obligated service.

The SRB is paid by installments. Up to 50 percent of the total bonus may be paid as the first installment, with the remaining portion paid in equal annual amounts over the remainder of the enlistment period.

A list of the MOSs designated for award of SRB and enlistment bonuses is in the DA Circular 611 series, *Announcement of Proficiency Pay/Selective Reenlistment Bonus/Enlistment Bonus/Comparable MOS for Bonus Recipients.* Periodic program changes are announced by Headquarters, Department of the Army.

BENEFITS AND ENTITLEMENTS

Allotments

An allotment is a specified amount of money withheld from military pay, normally upon the soldier's authorization, for a specific purpose. Payment is made by government check and mailed to the payee.

Allotments are made by filling out DD Form 2558, *Authorization to Start, Stop, or Change an Allotment for Active Duty or Retired Personnel.* These forms are prepared by the individual's military personnel office, unit personnel office, or finance office, and by Army Emergency Relief and the American Red Cross. Preparation of allotment documents in the finance office, rather than in the personnel office, is intended to eliminate delays of one or more days. When there is a delay near the end of the processing month, the effective date of an allotment may be delayed a full month. Commanders may have DD Form 2558 prepared in the unit personnel office, if it will conserve time and assure that there will be no delays in transmission to the finance office.

Repayment of Army Emergency Relief (AER) Loans. These allotments are authorized in multiples. AER allotments are established for a definite term of not less than three months (although this provision may be waived in certain cases).

Combined Federal Campaign (CFC) Contributions. This allotment is authorized to be in effect one at a time only. CFC allotments are made for a period of twelve months, beginning in January and ending in December. Military personnel who execute the *Payroll Withholding Authorization for Voluntary Charitable Contributions* (a Civil Service form) may do so in lieu of DA Form 1341.

Payment to a Dependent (SPT-V). This kind of allotment is authorized in multiples. This voluntary allotment is paid to a soldier's dependent without regard to whether the soldier is already receiving BAH. In addition, involuntary SPT-V allotments can be administratively established. Normally, the amount of these allotments is not permitted to exceed 80 percent of a soldier's pay. Not more than one SPT-V allotment may be made to the same person.

Payment to a Financial Institution for Credit to a Member's Account (FININ). Only two of these allotments are authorized to be in effect at any one time. FININ allotments are for payment to a financial organization for credit to the allotter's savings, checking, or trust accounts. The FININ allotment may be established for an indefinite term and for any amount the soldier designates, provided he or she has sufficient pay to satisfy the deduction of the allotment.

Payment for Indebtedness to the United States (FED). FED allotments are for the purpose of payment of delinquent federal, state, and local taxes and/or indebtedness to the United States. A separate allotment is required for each debt or overpayment to be repaid.

Payment of Home Loans (HOME). Only one HOME allotment is authorized to be in effect at any one time. This allotment is authorized for repayment of loans for the purchase of a house, mobile home, or house trailer. A HOME allotment is established for an indefinite term and for any amount designated provided the soldier's pay credit is sufficient to satisfy the deduction of the allotment.

Payment of Commercial Life Insurance Premiums (INS). These allotments are authorized in multiples. INS allotments must be made payable to a commercial life insurance firm. INS allotments are not authorized for payment of insurance on the life of a soldier's spouse or children except under a family group contract or for health, accident, or hospitalization insurance. INS allotments are established for an indefinite period and in the amount of the monthly premium, as indicated by the number on DA Form 1341.

Repayment of American Red Cross Loans (REDCR). REDCR allotments are authorized in multiples.

Educational Savings Allotment (EDSAV). This allotment is authorized to allow soldiers entering service after December 13, 1976 (except those who enlisted under the Delayed Entry Program before January 1, 1977) to participate in the Veterans Educational Assistance Program (VEAP). Only one such allotment is authorized. The EDSAV allotment is established with no discontinuance date. The soldier may stop it at any time after one year of participation.

Class X Allotments. A Class X allotment is paid locally and is authorized in emergency circumstances when other classes of allotments are impracticable. This instance applies overseas only. Class X allotments may be ordered by a commander as a standby allotment when adequate provision for the financial support of a soldier's dependents has not been made.

Thrift Savings Plan (TSP)

The purpose of the TSP is to provide retirement income. It offers soldiers the same type of savings and tax benefits that many private corporations offer their employees under so-called 401(k) plans. Under the plan, soldiers save a portion of their pay in a special retirement account administered by the Federal Retirement Thrift Investment Board. The total amount contributed generally cannot exceed 9 percent of your basic pay plus up to 100 percent of any bonus or incentive pay you may receive up to the limits established by the Internal Revenue Service. Contributions from pay earned in a combat zone do not count against the ceiling.

Participation in the TSP is neither optional nor automatic. You must sign up through your finance office to participate. Soldiers have two "open seasons" per year in which to enroll. (Open seasons are currently May 15 through July 31 and November 15 through January 31.) You contribute to the TSP from your own pay on a pretax basis, and the amount you contribute and the earnings attributable to your contributions belong to you. They are yours to keep even if you do not serve the twenty years ordinarily necessary to receive military retired pay.

While you are a member of the uniformed services, any tax-deferred money withdrawn before the age of fifty-nine-and-a-half as a result of financial hardship is subject to the IRS 10 percent early withdrawal penalty, as well as regular income tax. With respect to postseparation withdrawals, if you separate from the service during or after the year in which you turn age fifty-five, your withdrawals are not subject to the early withdrawal penalty. If you separate before the year you reach age fifty-five, you can transfer your TSP account to an IRA or other eligible retirement plan (e.g., 401(k) plan, your civilian TSP account) or begin receiving annuity payments without penalty.

Transportation of Household Goods

Transportation of household goods at government expense is authorized for soldiers in accordance with the table on this page. For information on authorized weight limitations for other grades, see the Joint Federal Travel Regulations (JFTR).

PCS WEIGHT ALLOWANCE (POUNDS)

Pay Grade	With Dependents	Without Dependents
E-9	14,500	12,000
E-8	13,500	11,000
E-7	12,500	10,500
E-6	11,000	8,000
E-5	9,000	7,000
E-4 (over 2 years' service)	8,000	7,000
E-4 (2 years' service or less)	7,000	3,500
E-3	5,000	2,000
E-2, E-1	5,000	1,500

Government Quarters

Bachelor accommodations for enlisted personnel range from the fairly austere communal living conditions offered junior enlisted personnel in troop units to the small but private and well-appointed quarters offered senior NCOs in bachelor enlisted quarters (BEQ). During the course of an Army career, you will see them all if you do not marry at a young age.

Modern troop billets are dormitory-style facilities with central air conditioning and heating; two-, three-, or four-person rooms; recreational facilities; and convenience facilities. Less than a generation ago, the bulk of the Army's bachelor enlisted personnel were living in one- and two-story wooden World War II barracks that were hot in the summer, cold in the winter, a real effort to keep clean, and generally overcrowded. Older soldiers remember very well living in large troop bays, double-bunked, with only a small wooden footlocker and a metal wall locker to use for the storage of their uniforms and personal clothing.

Family housing—where it is available—ranges in style from detached single-family housing to high-rise apartment-style buildings accommodating scores of families. In some cases, the quarters you are assigned will be in excellent condition and will require little maintenance to keep them that way; others will cause you constant maintenance headaches.

When reporting to some new duty stations, you will find pleasant family housing waiting for you; at other stations, you will have to wait weeks or even months to get any kind of quarters. In some areas, the waiting list for government housing is so long that you might find it necessary to buy or rent off the post. Your family housing officer will be of great assistance to you if you should decide to occupy off-post quarters. Each installation and each major overseas command has a different family housing situation.

Because of your rank, you may very well find yourself either the senior occupant of a multiple dwelling or responsible for a number of families in a stairwell of such a dwelling. These assignments are necessary, and you should consider them as part of your obligation as an NCO to the military community in which you live. You should discharge them with the same dedication and enthusiasm that you devote to your primary duties, but be prepared for many headaches, and expect that from time to time your patience will be tested.

Occupancy of family quarters carries the responsibility for doing "handyman work." The facilities engineer performs all maintenance and repairs other than those that are within the capabilities of the occupants. Emergency work or work beyond your individual capabilities can be obtained by making a service call or submitting a job order request to the installation repair and utilities office. Do not, however, expect the engineers to drop everything and run to your quarters, no matter how severe the emergency.

If you are fortunate enough to be assigned to a single-family dwelling, you will be expected to perform that type of self-help maintenance that is done by any prudent homeowner to conserve funds and preserve the premises, such as minor carpentry, maintenance of hardware (door hinges, and so forth), touch-up and partial interior painting, caulking around doors and windows, repair of screens, repair of simple plumbing malfunctions (minor leaking, defective washers, simple drainage stoppages), and so forth. Accumulate a set of tools that you can use around the house or apartment for this minor maintenance work.

No matter where you live—family quarters or the barracks—you are expected to conserve energy and utilities. Soldiers are among the most flagrant violators of good energy conservation, wasting water and electricity and fuel as if there were no tomorrow. Remind yourself and others to be conservation conscious.

Your quarters will be inspected by someone from the housing office before you are cleared to vacate your quarters. This inspection can be very rigorous. The specific details will be furnished to you by the housing officer. Some people prefer to hire a civilian contractor to do the work for them. You can avoid this unnecessary expense if you and your family take proper care of your quarters while you are living in them. For example, use rugs on the floors, keep the walls clean and in good repair, and keep your appliances clean.

Commissary and Post Exchange Services

The price you pay for a grocery item in the commissary is the same price the government pays for it: If an item is sold to the government for eighty-five cents, then that is its cost to you. Even the commissary surcharge and tipping do not add as much to the cost of an item as do the standard markups found on similar items in civilian retail outlets.

The commissary surcharge pays for operating supplies, equipment, utilities, facility alterations, and new construction.

The Post Exchange Service was designated the Army and Air Force Exchange Service (AAFES) in 1948. What originally began as an outlet "to supply troops at reasonable prices with articles of ordinary use . . . not supplied by the Government . . . to afford them the means of rational recreation and amusement" has since become a multibillion-dollar enterprise that spans the globe. Many post exchange stores are actually department stores designed for family shoppers, although single soldiers can buy all the necessities of barracks life. Some stores even permit personnel in uniform to be waited on first during certain hours of the day, such as the lunch hour.

Several hundred military exchanges are operated throughout the world by the Department of Defense. (AAFES, headquartered in Dallas and headed by a general officer, operates outlets worldwide.) At a minimum, AAFES customers save the state sales tax, which is not charged.

IDENTIFICATION CARDS

Your DD Form 2A, *U.S. Armed Forces Identification Card* (green, active duty, and reserve duty), is possibly the most important military document you possess. DD Form 1173, *Uniformed Services Identification and Privilege Card,* is equally important to military dependents. These cards identify the bearers as persons who are entitled to the wide range of entitlements, privileges, and benefits authorized for military personnel and their dependents.

DD Form 2A (green) is issued to the following:

- All military personnel on active duty for more than thirty days.
- Members of the Army National Guard and the U.S. Army Reserve.
- Cadets of the U.S. Military Academy.

DD Form 2A (red) is issued to inactive reserves who are not yet entitled to receive retired pay at age sixty and to ROTC college program students in their last two years of training or in receipt of a full service scholarship.

DD Form 2A (retired—blue) is issued to retired personnel of the uniformed services who are entitled to retirement pay. The DD Form 2A (retired) is also issued to persons who retired from ARNG or USAR at age sixty after completing federal service under Section 1331, Title 10, U.S. Code, and personnel permanently retired for physical disability.

All ID cards are the property of the U.S. government. They are not transferable. The individual (or sponsor) to whom the card is issued must turn in cards in the following circumstances:

- Expiration of the card.
- Change in eligibility status (such as change in grade or rank and changes caused by disciplinary action, discharge, death, retirement, reenlistment, age, marriage, or release to inactive duty of the sponsor).
- Replacement by another card.
- Request from competent authority.
- Demand of the installation commander, verifying activity, or issuing activity.
- Recovery of a lost card after a replacement has been issued.
- Request by the installation commander for temporary safekeeping while an individual is taking part in recreation and gymnastic activities.
- Official placement of a sponsor in a deserter status.
- Change in the status of a sponsor if it terminates or modifies the right to any benefit for which the card may be used.

A lost ID card must be reported promptly to military law enforcement authorities or to ID card issuing authorities. DD Form 1172, *Application for Uniformed Services Identification and Privilege Card,* is used for this purpose. The form also becomes the application for a new card, provided the individual continues to be eligible to receive it. DD Form 1172 must contain a statement of the circumstances of the loss, what was done to recover the card, and the card number, if known.

Any NCO who is performing his or her official duties may confiscate an ID card that is expired, mutilated, used fraudulently, or presented by a person not entitled to use it. Managers and employees of benefit and privilege activities may confiscate any expired or obviously altered ID card or document.

COMMISSARY CARDS

In 2004, Congress authorized unlimited commissary access for members of the Ready Reserve (which includes members of the Selected Reserve, Individual Ready Reserve, and Inactive National Guard) and members of the Retired Reserve who possess a Uniformed Services Identification Card.

Former members eligible for retired pay at age sixty but who have not yet attained the age of sixty and who possess a Department of Defense Civilian Identification Card are also eligible. Dependents of the members described above who have a Uniformed Services Identification Card or who have a distinct identification card used as an authorization card for benefits and privileges administered by the Uniformed Services also have access.

DEPENDENT ID CARDS

DD Form 1173 is used throughout the Department of Defense to identify persons, other than active-duty or retired military personnel, who are eligible for benefits and privileges offered by the armed forces.

Dependent ID cards are authorized for issue to lawful spouses; unremarried former spouses married to the member or former member for a period of at least twenty years, during which period the member or former member performed at least twenty years of service; children (adopted, legitimized, stepchildren, wards); parents (in special cases); and surviving spouses of active-duty or retired members. See AR 640-3 for specific details.

Generally, DD Forms 1173 are replaced for the same reasons that govern replacement of military ID cards.

To verify initial eligibility for issue of a dependent ID card and entry into the Defense Enrollment Eligibility Reporting System (DEERS), sponsors must be prepared to show marriage certificates, birth certificates, death certificates (in the case of unremarried widows or widowers), or any other documentation prescribed by AR 640-3 required to establish dependency.

ABUSE OF PRIVILEGES

All DD Forms 2, DD Form 1173, and other authorized identification documents issued to Army members and their dependents may be confiscated and overstamped for abuse of privileges in Army facilities. Medical benefits, however, cannot be suspended for these reasons.

Abuse of privileges includes the following:

- Unauthorized resale of commodities bought in Army activities to unauthorized persons, whether or not to make a profit (customary personal gifts are permissible).
- Shoplifting.
- Unauthorized access to activities.
- Misuse of a privilege (such as allowing an unauthorized person to use an otherwise valid ID card to gain access to a facility).
- Issuing dishonored checks in Army facilities.

Penalties for abuse of privileges in an appropriated or nonappropriated fund facility are a warning letter, temporary suspension of privileges, and indefinite suspension of privileges.

LEAVES AND PASSES

Leave

AR 600-8-10 governs leaves and passes. All members of the Army serving on active duty are entitled to leave with pay and allowances at the rate of two and one-half calendar days each month of active duty or active duty for training, including the following:

- Members of the Army serving in active military service, including members of the Army National Guard and the Army Reserve serving on active duty for a period of thirty days or more.
- Members of the Army National Guard and reserve who are serving on initial active duty for training or active duty for training for a period of thirty days or more and for which they are entitled to pay.
- Members of the Army National Guard who are serving on full-time training duty for a period of thirty days or more and for which they are entitled to pay.

The following circumstances do not qualify as periods of earned leave:

- AWOL.
- Confinement as a result of a sentence of court-martial; confinement for more than one day while awaiting court-martial (providing the court-martial results in a conviction).
- When in excess leave.
- Unauthorized absence as a result of detention by civil authorities.
- Absence due to misconduct.

The total accumulation of accrued leave (earned leave) at the end of a fiscal year (September 30) cannot exceed sixty days. Leave accumulated after that date is forfeited. The single exception to this policy applies to personnel who were prohibited from taking leave during the latter part of the fiscal year due to assignment or deployment to hostile fire or imminent danger pay areas. Eligible members can accumulate up to 30 additional days in excess of 60 but cannot carry over more than 120 days into the next fiscal year. Leave that begins in one fiscal year and is completed in another is apportioned to the fiscal year in which each portion falls. Upon discharge and immediate reenlistment, separation at expiration of term of service (ETS), or retirement, soldiers are authorized to settle their leave accounts for a lump-sum cash payment at the rate of one day of basic pay for each day of earned leave, up to 60 days. Public Law 94-212, February 9, 1976, limited settlement for accrued leave during a military career to a maximum of 60 days.

The following types of leave are authorized:

- *Advance leave.* Leave granted before its actual accrual, based on a reasonable expectation that it will be earned by the soldier during the remaining period of active duty.
- *Annual leave.* Leave granted in execution of a command's leave program, chargeable to the soldier's leave account. Also called "ordinary leave," as distinguished from emergency leave and special leave.
- *Convalescent leave.* A period of authorized absence granted to soldiers under medical treatment that is prescribed for recuperation and convalescence for sickness or wounds. Also called "sick leave," convalescent leave is not chargeable. Soldiers who sustain illness or injury while eligible for hostile fire pay are entitled to funded transportation per *Joint Federal Travel Regulation* (JFTR), paragraph U7210. Reference AR 600-8-10, paragraph 5-5.
- *Emergency leave.* Leave granted for a bona fide personal or family emergency requiring the soldier's presence. Emergency leave is chargeable.
- *Environmental and morale leave.* Leave granted in conjunction with an environmental and morale leave program established at overseas installations where adverse environmental conditions exist that offset the full benefit of annual leave programs. This leave is chargeable.
- *Excess leave.* This leave is in excess of accrued and/or advance leave, granted without pay and allowances.
- *Graduation leave.* A period of authorized absence granted, as a delay in reporting to the first permanent duty station, to graduates of the U.S. Military Academy who are appointed as commissioned officers. Not chargeable, providing it is taken within three months of graduation.
- *Leave awaiting orders.* This is an authorized absence, chargeable to accrued leave and in excess of maximum leave accrual, taken while awaiting further orders and disposition in connection with disability separation proceedings under the provisions of AR 635-40.
- *Reenlistment leave.* This leave is granted to enlisted personnel as a result of reenlistment. May be either advance leave or leave accrued or a combination thereof; chargeable against the soldier's leave account.

- *Rest and recuperation (R&R)—extensions of overseas tours.* This is a nonchargeable increment of R&R leave authorized for enlisted soldiers in certain specialties who voluntarily extend their overseas tours. It is authorized in lieu of $50 per month special pay. The tour extension must be for a period of at least twelve months. Options under this program include nonchargeable leaves of fifteen or thirty days.
- *Rest and recuperation leave.* This leave is granted in conjunction with rest and recuperation programs established in those areas designated for hostile fire pay, when operational military considerations preclude the full execution of ordinary annual leave programs. R&R leave is chargeable to the normal leave account; however, the Army pays for transportation to and from the leave destination. Currently, soldiers, active or reserve, assigned to a twelve-month tour of duty within the U.S. Central Command area of operations (USCENTCOM AOR) in support of the Global War on Terror (GWOT) may take up to fifteen days of leave during their deployment with leave beginning the day the soldier arrives at the leave destination and ends the day before travel begins to return to the theater of operations. The commander determines priority for personnel who are eligible for R&R leave based on the criteria above, as well as operational, safety, and security requirements.
- *Special leave.* This is leave accrual that is authorized in excess of sixty days at the end of a fiscal year for soldiers assigned to hostile fire/imminent danger areas or certain deployable ships, mobile units, or other duty.
- *Terminal leave.* This leave is granted in connection with separation, including retirement, upon the request of the individual.

When possible, soldiers should be encouraged to take at least one annual leave period of about fourteen consecutive days or longer (paragraph 203b, AR 630-5). Personnel who refuse to take leave when the opportunity is afforded them should be counseled and informed that such refusal may result in the loss of earned leave at a later date.

Leave is requested on part I, DA Form 31, *Request and Authority for Leave.* Requests for leave must be processed through the individual's immediate supervisor, although this step may be waived where supervisory approval or disapproval is inappropriate. This approval authority (generally, the soldier's commanding officer) ascertains that the individual has sufficient leave accrued to cover the entire period of absence requested.

Personnel should be physically present when DA Form 31 is authenticated and when commencing and terminating leave. Commanders may, at their discretion, authorize telephonic confirmation of departure and return.

Pass

A pass is an authorized absence not chargeable as leave, granted for short periods to provide respite from the working environment or for other specific reasons, at the end of which the soldier is actually at his or her place of duty or in the location from which he or she regularly commutes to work. This provision includes both regular and special passes.

Regular passes are granted to deserving military personnel for those periods when they are not required to be physically present with their unit for the performance of assigned duties. Normally, regular passes are valid only during specified off-duty hours, not more than seventy-two hours, except for public holiday weekends and holiday periods which, by discretion of the president, are extended to the commencement of working hours on the next working day.

Special passes are granted for periods of three or four days (seventy-two to ninety-six hours) to deserving personnel on special occasions or in special circumstances for the following reasons: as special recognition for exceptional performance of duty, such as soldier of the month or year; to attend spiritual retreats or to observe other major religious events; to alleviate personal problems incident to military service; to vote; or as compensatory time off for long or arduous duty away from the home station or for duty in an isolated location where a normal pass is inadequate.

Passes may not be issued to soldiers so that two or more are effective in succession or used in a series, through reissue immediately after return to duty.

Extension of a pass is authorized provided the total absence does not exceed seventy-two hours for a regular pass, seventy-two hours for a special three-day pass, and ninety-six hours for a special four-day pass. Special passes will not be extended by combination with public holiday periods or other off-duty hours in cases in which the combined total will exceed the maximum limits of a three-day or four-day pass. Passes may not be taken in conjunction with leave, and extensions beyond the authorized maximum are chargeable to leave (AR 600-8-10).

16

Uniforms, Insignia, and Personal Appearance

WEARING THE UNIFORM

Your Army uniform is the outward evidence of your profession, your standing in that profession, and a prime indicator of the degree of respect with which you regard your service to the United States of America and the Army. The condition of your uniform and the way you wear it are also a reflection of your own self-respect.

One of the basic responsibilities of every NCO is to know the composition of the Army uniforms and how to wear them properly. This is not to say that a good NCO will fly into a huff every time he or she spots a soldier whose personal appearance is less than recruiting-poster sharp, but no NCO should tolerate negligence when it comes to good grooming or ignorance when it comes to wearing the Army uniform.

Occasions When the Uniform Is Required to Be Worn

The Army uniform is worn by all personnel when on duty unless Headquarters, Department of the Army (HQDA), has authorized the wearing of civilian clothes. The following general rules apply:

- Installation commanders may prescribe the uniforms to be worn in formations; duty uniforms are generally prescribed by local commanders or heads of agencies, activities, or installations.
- The wearing of combinations of uniform items not prescribed in AR 670-1 is prohibited.
- Uniform items changed in design or material may continue to be worn until wear-out date unless specifically prohibited by Headquarters, Department of the Army.

Occasions When the Uniform May Not Be Worn

The wearing of the Army uniform is prohibited for all Army personnel under the following circumstances:

- In connection with the promotion of any political interests or when engaged in off-duty civilian employment.
- Except as authorized by competent authority, when participating in public speeches, interviews, picket lines, marches, rallies, or public demonstrations.
- When wearing the uniform would bring discredit upon the Army.
- When specifically prohibited by Army regulations.

WEARING OF HEADGEAR

The Army uniform is not complete unless the proper form of hat, cap, or beret is worn with it. Headgear is worn when outdoors and when indoors under arms.

Soldiers are exempt from wearing headgear to evening social events (after retreat). The appropriate headgear is, however, worn when wearing these uniforms on all other occasions.

Headgear is not required to be worn when it would interfere with the safe operation of military vehicles. Military headgear is not required to be worn in privately owned or commercial vehicles.

Berets

The black beret is the Army standard headgear and is worn by those soldiers not currently wearing the green, maroon, or tan beret. Soldiers will wear the beret with the utility and service uniforms in garrison environments only and will wear the patrol cap (formerly called the [battle dress uniform] BDU cap) in the field when authorized to remove their helmets. Commanders may authorize the wear of the patrol cap on work details or in other situations when wear of the beret is impractical.

New soldiers receive the black beret at their first permanent duty assignment after the completion of initial entry training or officer/warrant officer basic courses. Soldiers who are not issued or who do not wear the black beret will wear the patrol cap with utility uniforms and the garrison cap with service uniforms.

For enlisted soldiers, the crest of the unit assigned is worn centered on the blue Army flash on the black beret. Soldiers wear the beret so that the headband is straight on the head, one inch above the eyebrows, with the flash over the left eye and the excess material draped over to the right, down to at least the top of the ear, but no lower than the middle of the ear. A dip is formed in the wool, just behind the flash stiffener, and a slight fold is formed to the right front of the beret, next to the flash. Soldiers will tie off the adjusting ribbon into a nonslip knot, cut off the excess adjusting ribbon as close to the knot as possible, and tuck the knot into the edge binding at the back of the beret. The beret is formfitting to the head when worn properly; therefore, soldiers may not wear hairstyles that distort the beret.

The blue and white service caps remain the prescribed headgear for the blue and white dress and mess dress uniforms.

UNIFORM APPEARANCE

The word "uniform" as used in this context means "conforming to the same standard or rule." Although absolute uniformity of appearance by all soldiers at all times cannot reasonably be expected as long as armies are composed of so many various individuals, uniformed soldiers should project a military image that leaves no doubt that they live by a common standard.

One important rule of uniformity is that, when worn, items of the uniform should be kept buttoned, zippered, and snapped; metallic devices (such as collar brass insignia) should be kept in proper luster; and shoes should be cleaned and shined. In instances where boots are worn with uniforms, soldiers will not blouse boots any lower than the third eyelet from the top.

Lapels and sleeves of coats and jackets for both male and female personnel should be roll pressed (without creasing). Trousers, slacks, and sleeves of shirts and blouses should be creased.

Care and Maintenance of the Uniform

All solid brass items (belt buckles, belt-buckle tips, collar brass insignia) should be maintained in a high state of luster at all times. These items come coated with a lacquer, and if their surfaces are kept protected and gently rubbed clean with a soft clean cloth, they will keep their shine for a long time. But when the lacquer coating becomes scratched, the item can be kept shined only by completely removing the lacquer surface. The safest and most reliable method for removing the coating from brass items is to use Brasso polish applied with thumb and forefinger or a cloth.

Spit-shining does make shoes, boots, and equipment look sharp, but it dries out the leather.

Replace heels on shoes and boots after wear of seven-sixteenths of an inch or more. To check your soldiers' footgear, attempt to role a pencil under the heel.

Pay attention to the removal of stains from your clothing.

Never press dirty clothing, and be careful when you do press clothing that the iron is not too hot. Use a damp cloth between the iron and the fabric when pressing wool items, dampen the surface of cotton clothing before applying the iron, and observe the various fabric settings on the iron when pressing synthetic fabric.

Frequent cleaning of uniform items will increase their longevity and maintain the neat soldierly appearance that the uniform is designed to project. Rotating items of clothing, such as shoes and boots, will contribute to their longer life.

Fitting of Uniforms

Uniform items purchased in the Clothing Sales Store are fitted (or should be fitted) before they are taken off the premises. Personnel who purchase uniform items through the post exchange or from commercial sources should pay close attention to the proper fit of the items before wearing them. An NCO should be able to tell at a glance whether a soldier (male or female) is wearing a properly fitted uniform. Fitting instructions and alterations of uniforms are made in accordance with AR 700-84 and TM 10-227, *Fitting of Army Uniforms and Footwear.*

The Clothing Allowance System

Clothing allowances are provided so that each soldier may maintain the initial clothing issue. Monthly clothing allowances provide for the cost of replacement and purchase of new items or the purchase of additional clothing items, not cleaning, laundering, and pressing. The basic allowance begins on the soldier's 181st day of active duty and is paid each month for the remainder of the first three-year period. The standard allowance begins the day after the soldier completes thirty-six months on active duty. The clothing allowance accrues monthly and is paid annually during the month of the soldier's basic active service date.

CLASSIFICATION OF SERVICE AND UTILITY FIELD UNIFORMS

Class A Service Uniform. For men: consists of the Army green AG 489 coat and trousers, a short-sleeved or long-sleeved AG 415 shirt with pleated pockets, a black four-in-hand tie (tied in a slip knot with the ends left hanging), and other accessories. For women: consists of the appropriate Army green coat and skirt or slacks of the Army green classic uniform, a short-sleeved or long-sleeved AG 415 shirt, a black neck tab, and authorized accessories. The Army green maternity uniform (slacks or skirt) is also a Class A service uniform when the tunic is worn.

Class B Service Uniform. For men: consists of the same as for the Class A except that the service coat is not worn. The black tie is required when wearing the long-sleeved AG 415 shirt and is optional with the short-sleeved shirt. For women: consists of the same as for the Class A except that the service coat and the maternity tunic are not worn. The black neck tab is required when wearing the long-sleeved AG 415 shirt and the long-sleeved maternity shirt. It is optional with the short-sleeved version of both shirts.

Class C Uniforms. These are utility, field, and other organizational uniforms, such as the battle dress (BDU), hospital duty, and food service uniforms.

Optional Dress Uniforms. The Army blue uniform, white uniform, blue mess uniform, and white mess uniform are available for optional purchase by enlisted soldiers. The Army blue uniform is issued to soldiers when required as a duty uniform, such as when assigned to the Old Guard at Arlington Cemetery.

MEN'S ARMY GREEN UNIFORM

The Army green uniform Class A and Class B variations may be worn by male personnel when on duty, off duty, or during travel. These uniforms are also acceptable for informal social functions after retreat, unless other uniforms are prescribed by the host.

Men's Class A Uniform

The Army green uniform (Class A) consists of the Army green AG shade 489 coat and trousers, worn with either the new long-sleeved or short-sleeved AG 415 pleated pocket shirt and a black four-in-hand necktie.

The coat should fit with a slight drape in both the front and the back. No pronounced tightness at the waist or flare below the waist is authorized. The length of the coat will extend to below the crotch.

Matching Army green uniform trousers are straight-legged and will reach the top of the instep and be cut on a diagonal line to reach a point approximately midway between the top of the heel and the top of the standard shoe in the back. The trousers may have a slight break in the front.

Accessories (Class A)

The U.S. insignia disk is worn on the right lapel collar approximately one inch above the notch. The branch insignia disk is worn on the left lapel collar approximately one inch above the notch. Both are centered on the lapel collar so as to be parallel with the inside of the lapel.

Distinctive unit insignia (unit crests) of the currently assigned unit are worn centered on both shoulder loops (epaulets) of the coat between the outside edge of the shoulder loop button and the seam of the loop.

The current organization shoulder sleeve insignia (patch) is sewn on the left sleeve one-half inch down from the shoulder seam and centered. When the Ranger, Special Forces, Sappers, or President's Hundred Tab is worn, the tab will be placed one-half inch below the shoulder seam, other tabs one-eighth inch below it, and the current organization shoulder patch worn one-quarter inch below the bottom of the lowest tab. A shoulder patch for a former wartime organization may be worn on the right sleeve one-half inch below the shoulder seam.

With the Class A Army green uniform, rank insignia is sewn on the sleeve halfway between the elbow and the shoulder seam of the coat.

When awarded, sew-on service stripes (hash marks) are placed four inches above the bottom of the left sleeve and centered on the sleeve. Overseas bars are placed four inches above the bottom of the right sleeve.

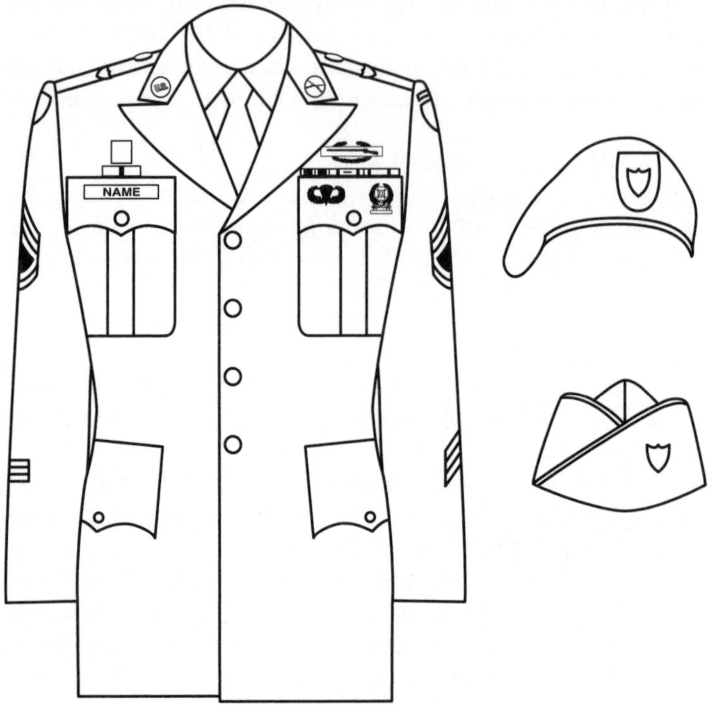

Class A uniform for men.

The nameplate is worn on the right breast pocket of the coat, centered between the top of the button and the top of the pocket. Unit awards, such as the Presidential Unit Citation, Joint Meritorious Unit Award, and so forth, are worn one-eighth inch above the right breast pocket.

Individual decorations and service ribbons are worn one-eighth inch above the left breast pocket of the coat. When combat and special skill badges are worn, they are centered one-quarter inch above the ribbons. When more than one badge is worn above the ribbons, badges will be stacked one-half inch apart and may be aligned to the left to present a better appearance.

Marksmanship badges are worn on the left breast pocket flap one-eighth inch below the top seam of the pocket. If more than one badge is worn, they are spaced one inch apart and centered in relation to the bottom edge of the ribbons and the pocket button. When special skill badges, e.g., driver's badge, are worn on the pocket flap, they are placed to the right of the marksmanship badges.

The Army black beret, organizational berets, and drill sergeant hats are authorized for wear with the Class A and Class B uniforms.

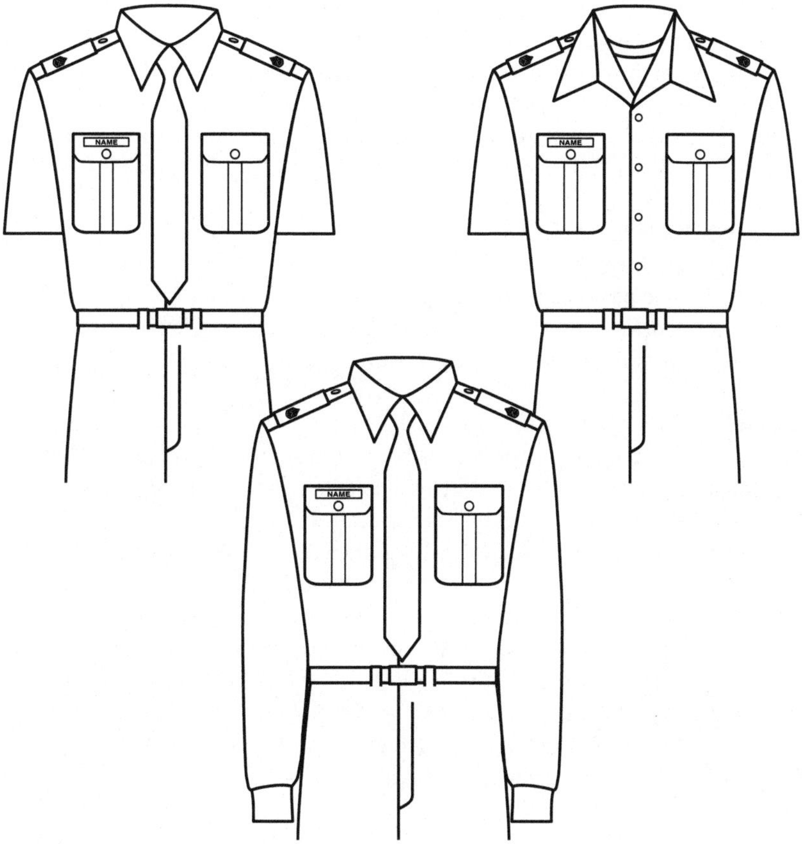

Class B uniforms for men.

Men's Army Green Dress Uniform

The men's Army green dress uniform consists of the Army green coat and trousers, with a commercially purchased long-sleeved white shirt and black bow tie. The dress uniform is restricted to formal social functions, private or official, and transit to and from such functions. It cannot be worn for duty or travel. Boots, berets, or organizational items, such as brassards or Military Police (MP) accessories, are not used with the green dress uniform.

Men's Class B Uniform

The men's Class B uniform merely omits the coat. It consists of the long-sleeved or short-sleeved AG 415 shirt and AG 489 trousers with black web belt and brass buckle. The black four-in-hand necktie must be worn with the long-sleeved shirt and is optional for the short-sleeved shirt. Soldiers are required to have one long-sleeved and two short-sleeved AG 415 pleated pocket shirts.

Individual awards and decorations are authorized to be worn on the Class B uniform shirts. Their placement is as on the coat. Check AR 670-1 for additional details. Rank insignia is worn on the Class B uniform shirt on shoulder marks for NCOs and on the shirt collars for non-NCO enlisted grades.

WOMEN'S ARMY GREEN UNIFORM

The women's Army green uniform Class A and Class B variations may be worn by female personnel when on duty, off duty, or during travel. These uniforms are also acceptable for informal social functions after retreat, unless other uniforms are prescribed by the host.

Women's Class A Uniform

The women's Class A uniform consists of the Army green classic coat and either the Army green classic skirt or slacks, a new AG 415 short-sleeved or long-sleeved tuck-in shirt, and a black neck tab. The short-sleeved and long-sleeved tuck-in shirts replace the long-sleeved and short-sleeved AG 415 overblouses, which are now an optional purchase item.

The women's coat is a hip-length, single-breasted coat with four buttons and button-down shoulder loops. The Army green classic skirt has a waistband and side zipper closure. The skirt length will not be more than one inch above or two inches below the crease in the back of the knee. Women now wear the new AG 489 green slacks which have belt loops and are worn with a one-inch black web belt and matching brass buckle.

Accessories (Class A)

Specifications for wear of the organizational shoulder sleeve insignia (patch), unit crests, rank insignia, service stripes, overseas bars, and regimental crests are the same for the women's Class A uniform as they are for the men's Class A uniform and are described above. There are, however, some differences.

The U.S. insignia disk is centered on the right collar of the coat approximately five-eighths inch up from the notch, with the center line of the insignia parallel to the inside edge of the lapel. The branch insignia disk is centered in the same manner on the left collar.

The key to the alignment of accessories on the women's Class A uniform is the placement of the plastic nameplate. The nameplate can be adjusted to conform to individual figure differences.

The nameplate is centered horizontally on the right side between one and two inches above the top button of the coat. Individual and service ribbons are aligned on the left side parallel to the bottom edge of the nameplate. Other badges are aligned on the nameplate or the ribbons in the same manner as on the men's Class A uniform.

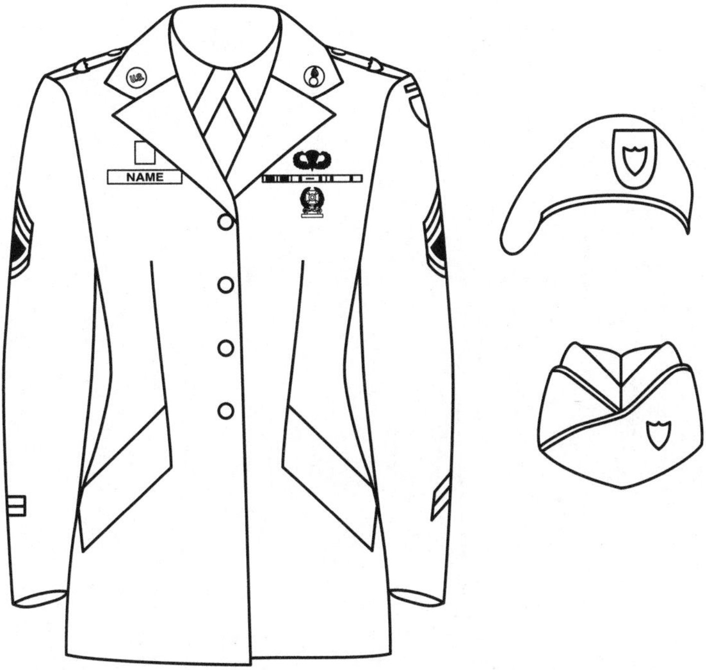

Class A uniform for women.

The Army black beret, organizational berets, and drill sergeant hats are authorized for wear with the Class A and Class B uniforms. No hair should show on the forehead below the front bottom edge of the beret or hat, which should be situated approximately one inch above the eyebrows.

Women's Army Green Dress Uniform

The women's Army green dress uniform consists of the Army green coat and skirt or slacks, with a commercially purchased long-sleeved white shirt. The Army black neck tab is worn. The dress uniform is restricted to formal social functions, private or official, and transit to and from such functions. It cannot be worn for duty or travel. Boots, berets, or organizational items, such as brassards or MP accessories, are not used with the women's green dress uniform.

Women's Class B Uniforms

The women's Class B uniform merely omits the coat. It consists of the long-sleeved or short-sleeved AG 415 shirt, which is worn with either the AG 489 slacks, black web belt, and brass buckle, or the AG 489 classic skirt. The black

Class B uniforms for women.

neck tab must be worn with the long-sleeved shirt and is optional for the short-sleeved shirt. Soldiers are required to have one long-sleeved and two short-sleeved AG 415 tuck-in shirts. Women soldiers must also possess two pairs of AG 489 slacks with belt loops.

Individual awards and decorations are authorized to be worn on the Class B uniform shirts. Their placement is as on the coat. Check AR 670-1 for additional details. Shoulder mark rank insignia is worn on the Class B uniform shirt for all NCOs and on the shirt collars for non-NCO enlisted grades.

Green Maternity Uniform

The pregnant soldier has been provided with a special uniform with considerable flexibility. The ensemble of components can be combined to form both a Class A and a Class B uniform. The Class A uniform is composed of a green maternity tunic, matching maternity slacks or skirt, a long-sleeved or short-sleeved AG 415 maternity shirt, and a black neck tab.

Accessories, insignia, awards, badges, and accoutrements for the maternity uniforms follow the same regulations as those for the servicewomen's Class A, Class B, and green dress uniforms.

WORK AND DUTY UNIFORMS

Army Combat Uniform (ACU)

Three different versions of the ACU have been developed, and fielding to the total Army should be complete by December 2007. There are currently twenty changes to the uniform, including removing the color black and adapting the digital print from the Marine Corps uniform. The bottom pockets on the jacket were removed and placed on the shoulder sleeves so soldiers can have access to them while wearing body armor. The pockets were also tilted forward so that they are easily accessible. Buttons were replaced with zippers that open from the top and bottom to provide comfort while wearing armor. Patches and tabs are affixed to the uniform with Velcro to give the wearer more flexibility. The ACU consists of a jacket, trousers, moisture wicking T-shirt, and the brown combat boots. It will replace both versions of the BDU and the desert camouflage uniform. The black beret will be the normal headgear for the ACU, but there is a matching patrol cap to be worn at the commander's discretion.

Temperate and Enhanced Hot Weather Battle Dress Uniforms (EHWBDU)

The temperate, hot-weather (HW), and enhanced hot-weather (EHW) battle dress uniforms (BDUs) remain authorized for year-round wear by all personnel when prescribed by the commander.

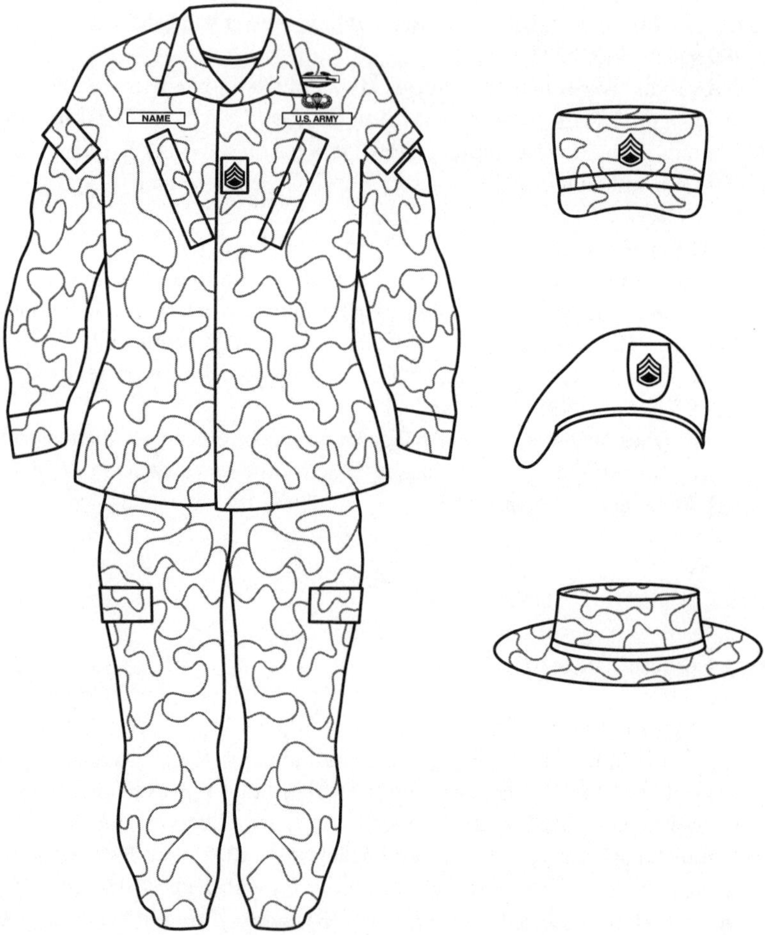

Army Combat Uniform (ACU).

Maternity Work Uniform

This uniform is authorized for year-round on-duty wear by pregnant soldiers. It is not intended as a travel uniform, but it may be worn in transit between the individual's quarters and duty station.

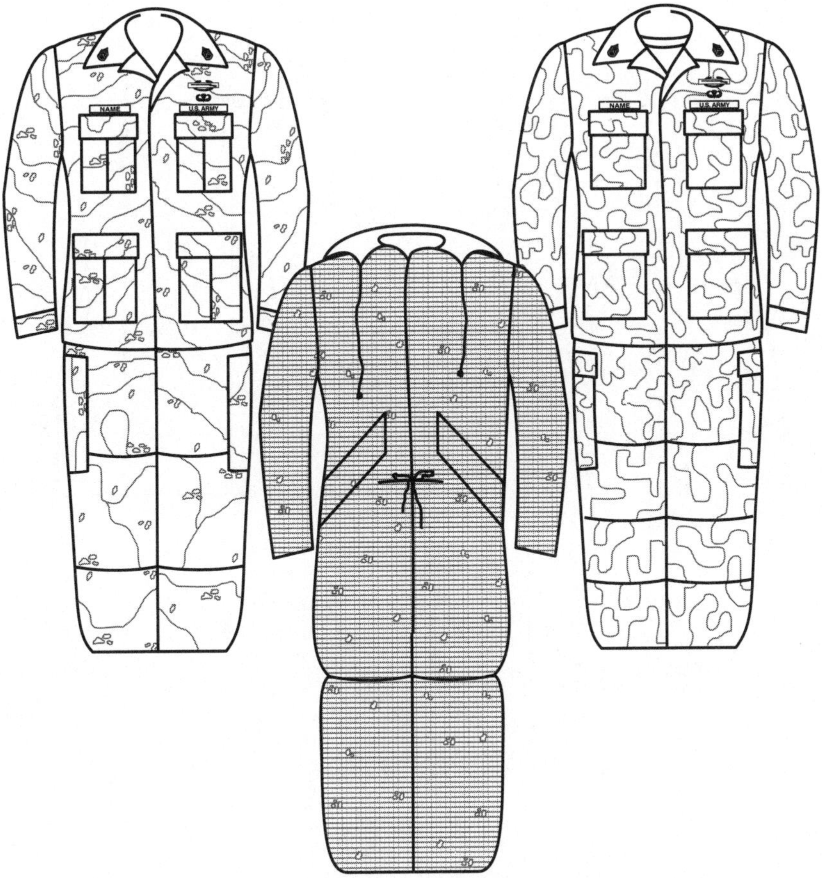

Desert BDU, night desert coverall, temperate and enhanced hot weather BDU.

Desert Battle Dress Uniform (DBDU)

These uniforms are issued as organizational utility, field, training, or combat uniforms, and they are not intended for wear as all-purpose uniforms when other uniforms are more appropriate.

Personnel wear the DBDU on duty when prescribed by the commander. Soldiers may wear the DBDU off post, unless prohibited by the commander, but may not wear DBDUs for commercial travel, unless authorized. Personnel

Hospital duty uniforms.

may not wear DBDUs in establishments that primarily sell alcohol. If the establishment sells alcohol and food, soldiers may not wear utility uniforms if their activities in the establishment center on drinking alcohol only.

Cold Weather Uniform

The OG 108 cold weather uniform is designed for year-round wear by all personnel when issued as organizational clothing and prescribed by the commander. It is not authorized for travel or wear off military installations except in transit. Components of this uniform may be worn with utility and other organi-

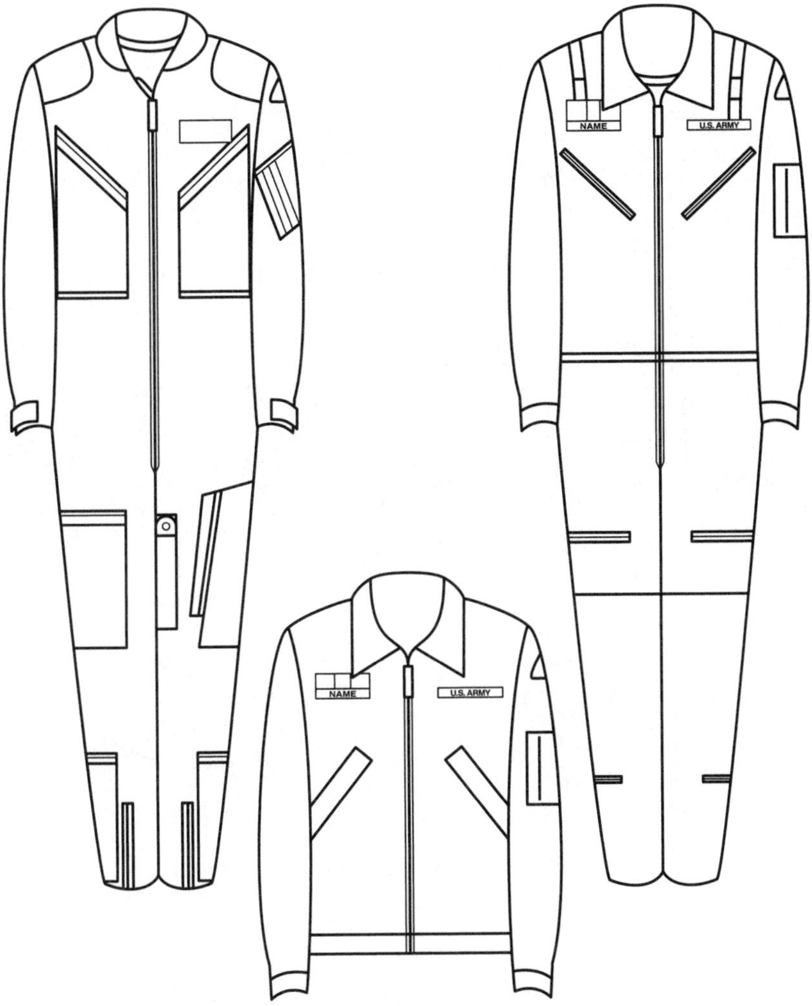

Flight uniform and combat vehicle crewman uniform.

zation uniforms as part of a cold weather ensemble when issued and prescribed by the commander.

Hospital Duty Uniform (Male)

This year-round duty uniform for all male soldiers in the Army Medical Specialist Corps and those in medical, dental, or veterinary MOSs is worn in medical healthcare facilities as prescribed by the medical commander. The

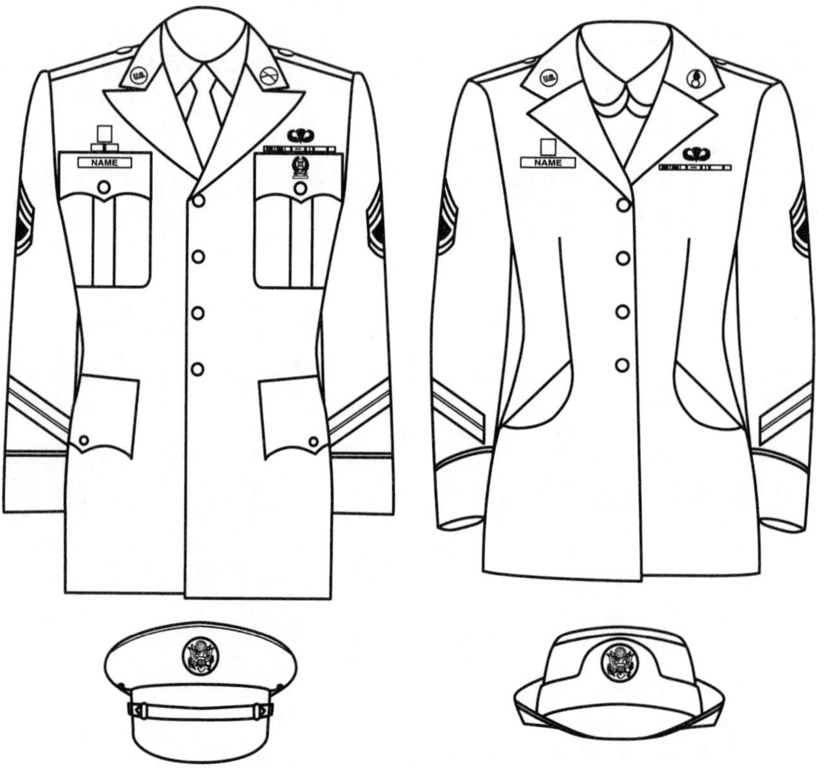

Army blue uniform for men and women, respectively.

commander may authorize the wear of this uniform in a civilian community when in support of civilian activities.

Hospital Duty and Maternity Uniform

This authorized year-round uniform is worn by Army Medical Specialist Corps personnel and enlisted women with medical, dental, or veterinary MOSs.

Flight Uniform

This uniform is authorized for year-round wear when on duty in a flying or standby-awaiting-flight status. Commanders may direct exceptions to wear policy.

Combat Vehicle Crewman (CVC) Uniform

The CVC is a year-round duty uniform for combat vehicle crewmen when on duty or as directed by the commander. This uniform is not for travel.

OPTIONAL UNIFORMS

Army Blue Uniform (Male and Female)

This uniform is authorized for optional wear by enlisted personnel. Although primarily a uniform for social functions of a general or official nature before or after retreat, it may be worn on duty if prescribed by the commander.

Other Authorized Uniforms

- Army white uniform for both male and female soldiers.
- Army blue mess uniform.
- Army white mess uniform.

DISTINCTIVE UNIFORM ITEMS

The following uniform items are distinctive and should not be sold to or worn by unauthorized personnel: all Army headgear, badges, decorations, service medals, awards, tabs, service ribbons, appurtenances, and insignia of any design or color that have been adopted by the Department of the Army.

Headgear

The following items of headgear are authorized for Army personnel:

Item	Female Version*
Beret, black	
Beret, green (Special Forces)	
Beret, maroon (Airborne)	
Beret, tan (Ranger)	
Cap, cold weather (AG 344)	
Cap, cold weather, utility	
Cap, food handler's, white, paper	
Cap, garrison, green (AG 489)	Cap, garrison (AG 489)
Cap, hot weather	
Cap, service, blue	Hat, service, blue
Cap, service, white	Hat, service, white
Hat, camouflage, desert	
Hat, drill sergeant	Hat, drill sergeant

* These are distinctively female items. Other items of headgear listed may be worn by female soldiers, as prescribed in AR 670-1.

Leader Identification Insignia

The Leader Identification insignia is a green cloth loop, one and five-eighths inches wide, worn in the middle of both shoulder loops of the Army green and cold weather coats. Personnel cease to wear them when reassigned from a command position. Leaders in all units (Active Army, Army National Guard, and Army Reserves), regardless of unit category Modification Table of Organization and Equipment (MTOE) or Table of Distribution and Allowances (TDA), will wear the leader's identification (LI) insignia. The specific leaders in units authorized to wear the LI are: commanders, deputy commanders, platoon leaders, command sergeants major, first sergeants, platoon sergeants, section leaders (when designated in TOE), squad leaders and tank commanders, and rifle squad fire team leaders.

Unit Insignia and Heraldic Items

Distinctive unit insignia (DUI) are made of metal or metal and enamel and are usually based on elements of the design of the coat of arms or historic badge approved for a specific unit. Sometimes erroneously referred to as "unit crests," distinctive unit insignia are subject to the approval of the Institute of Heraldry, U.S. Army, and, like shoulder sleeve insignia, are authorized for wear on the uniform as a means of promoting esprit de corps.

When authorized, these insignia are worn by all assigned personnel of an organization, except general officers. A complete set of insignia consists of three pieces: one for each shoulder loop and one for headgear (garrison, utility, cold weather caps, or berets).

Regimental Insignia

Regimental DUI are worn by all personnel affiliated with a regiment. The "crest" of the affiliated regiment is worn centered and one-eighth inch above the pocket seam or one-half inch above unit and foreign awards, if worn, on the Army green, white, and blue uniforms. The DUI worn on the shoulder loops of the Army green, white, and blue (enlisted men only) coats and jackets are always the unit of assignment. If assigned and affiliated to the same regiment, then all three crests are the same.

Distinctive Items—Infantry

Infantry personnel are authorized to wear the following distinctive items:

- A shoulder cord of infantry blue formed by a series of interlocking square knots around a center cord. The cord is worn on the right shoulder of the Army green, blue, and white uniform coats and shirts, passed under the arm and through the shoulder loop and secured to the button on the shoulder loop.
- A plastic infantry blue disk, one and one-quarter inches in diameter, is worn by enlisted personnel of the infantry, secured beneath the branch of

Adjutant General's Corps

Air Defense Artillery

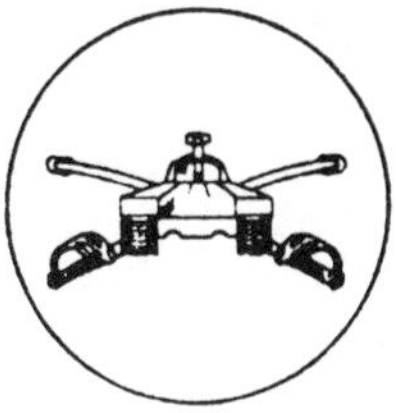

Armor

Branch Immaterial

Aviation

Cavalry

Chaplain Assistant

Chemical Corps

Civil Affairs

Corps of Engineers

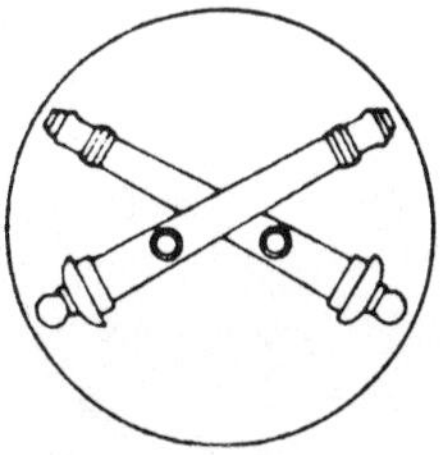

Field Artillery

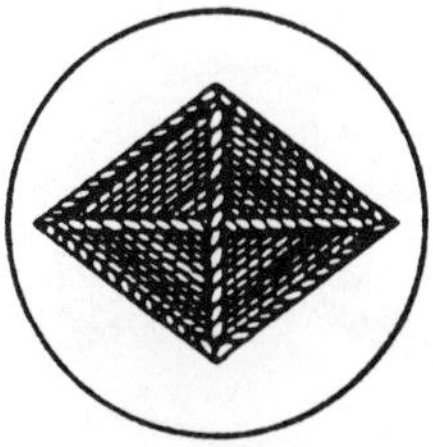

Finance

Enlisted branch insignia.

Infantry

Inspector General

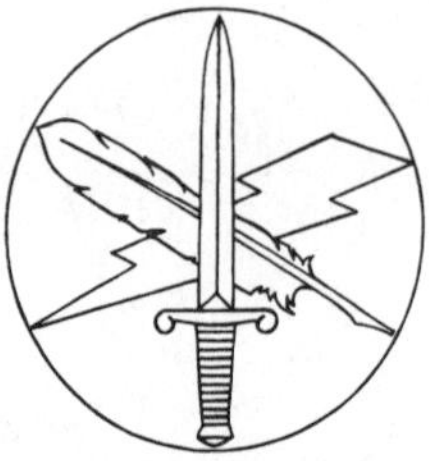
Public Affairs

Judge
Advocate General

Medical Corps

Military Intelligence

Military Police Corps

Ordnance Corps

Quartermaster Corps

Signal Corps

Special Forces

Transportation Corps

The Sergeant Major
of the Army

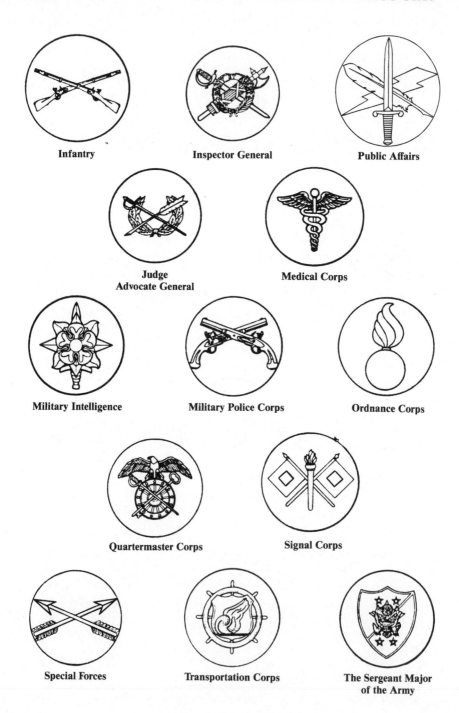

Enlisted branch insignia.

the service and the U.S. insignia, with a one-eighth-inch border around the insignia. It is authorized to be worn on the Army green, blue, and white uniforms.

- An insignia disk, service cap, of infantry blue plastic, one and three-quarter inches in diameter. This disk is worn secured beneath the insignia on the service cap. Criteria for wear are the same as those for the infantry blue insignia disk.

Organizational Flash

This shield-shaped embroidered patch with a semicircular bottom approximately two and one-quarter inches long and one and seven-eighths inches wide is worn centered on the stiffener of the beret by personnel authorized to wear one of the organizational berets (Ranger, Special Forces, and Airborne).

Airborne Background Trimming

Background trimming is authorized for wear with the parachutist or air assault badge. When authorized, such background will be worn by all personnel of an airborne-designated organization who have been awarded one of the parachute badges or by personnel in an organization designated air assault who have been awarded the air assault badge.

PERSONAL APPEARANCE

A vital ingredient of the Army's strength and military effectiveness is the pride and discipline that soldiers bring to their service. It is the responsibility of noncommissioned officers to assure that the military personnel under their supervision present a neat and soldierly appearance. It is the duty of each individual soldier to always take pride in his or her appearance.

Standards for All

Dreadlocks are prohibited. Hair color must look natural on the soldier. No tinted or color contact lenses. Fingernails must be neatly trimmed: males to the tip of the finger, females one-fourth inch from the tip. Tattoos or brands anywhere on the head, face, and neck above the class A uniform collar are prohibited. Tattoos regardless of location on the body that are extremist, indecent, sexist, or racist are prohibited as they are prejudicial to good order and discipline within units.

Standards for Men

Many hairstyles are acceptable in the Army. The hair must be neatly groomed, and the length and bulk of the hair must not be excessive or present a ragged, unkempt, or extreme appearance. Hair must present a tapered appearance and, when combed, must not fall over the ears or eyebrows or touch the collar. Block cuts are permitted in moderate degree, but in all cases the bulk and length of hair may not interfere with the normal wear of headgear or protective mask.

A soldier's face should be clean shaven, except that Army regulations do permit mustaches. No portion of a mustache is permitted to cover the upper lip line or extend beyond the crease of the upper and lower lips. Handlebar mustaches, goatees, and beards are not authorized. Where beard growth is prescribed by appropriate medical authority, as is sometimes necessary in the treatment of different types of skin disorders, the length required for medical treatment should be specified: "A neatly trimmed beard is authorized. The length will not exceed one-quarter inch," for example. If you should have such a soldier under your authority, follow his medical progress closely and be sure he keeps his exemption slip handy at all times when in uniform.

Men may shave their heads bald. Men are not authorized to wear nail polish.

Standards for Women

The principle that soldiers should always maintain a neat and well-groomed personal appearance applies equally to men and to women, though the specific grooming standard for each reflects the traditional differences in appearance between the sexes.

Hair must be neatly groomed. The length and/or bulk of the hair should not be excessive or present a ragged, unkempt, or extreme appearance. Females may wear braids and cornrows. Hair may not fall over the eyebrows or extend below the bottom edge of the collar. Hairstyles may not interfere with the proper wearing of military headgear or protective masks.

Cosmetics shall be applied conservatively and in good taste. Two-tone or multitone manicures and nail designs are prohibited. Prohibited nail polish colors include bright fire-engine red, khaki or camouflage, purple, gold, blue, black, white, and neon.

Wearing of Civilian Jewelry

The wearing of a personal wristwatch, identification wrist bracelet, and not more than two rings is authorized with the Army uniform as long as they are not prohibited for safety reasons and the style is conservative and in good taste. The wearing of a purely religious medal on a chain around the neck is authorized, provided that neither the medal nor the chain is exposed.

No jewelry, watch chains, or similar civilian items, including pens or pencils, should be allowed to appear exposed on the uniform. Exceptions are that a conservative tie tack or tie clasp may be worn with the black four-in-hand necktie, and a pen or pencil may appear exposed on the hospital duty and food service uniforms.

Soldiers, in and out of uniform, are prohibited from displaying pierced body parts while on military installations worldwide—except for females with pierced ears. Female soldiers may wear screw-on or post-type earrings with the service, dress, or mess uniforms. Earrings may not be worn with Class C utility uniforms (utility, field, or organization, including hospital duty and food service uniforms). Earrings should be small in diameter, six millimeters or one-quarter inch; gold, silver, or white pearl; unadorned; and spherical. When worn, they must fit snugly against the ear and must be worn as a matched pair with only one in each earlobe.

One electronic device is authorized for wear on the uniform in official duties. It must be black in color and measure no larger than four by two by one inches. Items that do not comply must be carried elsewhere.

Wearing of Civilian Clothing

Civilian clothing is authorized for wear off duty unless the wear is prohibited by the installation commander within CONUS or the major command overseas. When on duty in civilian clothes, soldiers will conform to the appearance standards of AR 670-1, unless specifically authorized for mission requirements.

Security Badges

Security identification badges are worn in restricted areas as prescribed by local commanders. They are usually laminated plastic identification badges worn suspended from clips. They should never be worn outside the secure area for which they authorize an individual access. To prevent the possibility of losing them, some personnel suspend them from a chain worn around the neck and, when in public, under their outer garments.

SOURCES

AR 600-8-22, *Military Awards.*
AR 670-1, *Wear and Appearance of Army Uniforms and Insignia.*
AR 700-84, *Issue and Sale of Personal Clothing.*
FM 21-15 (3-21-15), *Care and Use of Individual Clothing and Equipment.*

17

Awards and Decorations

The Army's awards and decorations program provides tangible recognition for acts of combat valor, and noncombat exceptional service or achievement, special skills or qualifications, and acts of heroism not involving actual combat.

RECOMMENDATIONS

It is the responsibility of any soldier having personal knowledge of an act, an achievement, or a service believed to warrant the award of a decoration to submit a formal recommendation for consideration.

And yes, it is possible that a private may recommend a captain for a decoration, but usually the system works the other way. As an NCO, you must be alert for service or acts that warrant special recognition. The only consideration that should be used is this one: Does the person's act or service warrant an award?

CRITERIA

Award recommendations must be factual and specific, and they must clearly demonstrate that the person being recommended deserves recognition. If your narrative does not support award of a decoration—if you use clichés in place of straightforward and factual prose narrative writing—your recommendation likely will be disapproved.

Time Limitation

Awards for meritorious service should be anticipated, and your recommendation should be submitted far enough in advance to ensure that the award is ready in time to be presented to the individual before his or her departure.

Another reason for acting quickly is that the closer you are to the act or service for which an individual is being recommended, the fresher the details will be in your memory. In any event, each recommendation for an award of a military decoration must be entered into military channels within two years of the act, achievement, or service to be honored. No recommendation except the Purple Heart is awarded more than three years after the act or period of service to be honored (with the exception of lost recommendations or those circumstances covered in paragraph 1-14c, AR 600-8-22). If a soldier under your supervision deserves an award, let him or her know that you've submitted a recommendation. If the recommendation is not approved, at least the soldier will know you tried and will respect you for it.

PRECEDENCE

Decorations, the Good Conduct Medal, and service medals are ranked in the following order of precedence when worn or displayed:

U.S. military decorations.
U.S. unit awards.
U.S. nonmilitary decorations.
U.S. service (campaign) medals, and service and training ribbons.
U.S. Merchant Marine awards.
U.S. nonmilitary unit awards.
Foreign military decorations.
Foreign unit awards.
Non-U.S. service awards.
State awards for ARNG soldiers.

U.S. military decorations are ranked in the following order of precedence when worn or displayed:

Medal of Honor (Army, Navy, Air Force).
Distinguished Service Cross.
Navy Cross.
Air Force Cross.
Defense Distinguished Service Medal.
Distinguished Service Medal (Army, Navy, Air Force, Coast Guard).
Silver Star.
Defense Superior Service Medal.
Legion of Merit.
Distinguished Flying Cross.
Soldier's Medal.
Navy and Marine Corps Medal.
Airman's Medal.
Coast Guard Medal.
Bronze Star Medal.
Purple Heart.
Defense Meritorious Service Medal.
Meritorious Service Medal.
Air Medal.

Aerial Achievement Medal
Joint Service Commendation Medal.
Army Commendation Medal.
Navy Commendation Medal.
Air Force Commendation Medal.
Coast Guard Commendation Medal.
Joint Service Achievement Medal.
Army Achievement Medal.
Navy Achievement Medal.
Air Force Achievement Medal.
Coast Guard Achievement Medal.
Combat Action Ribbon.
Prisoner of War Medal.
Good Conduct Medal.

Good Conduct Medals from the other services follow the Army Good Conduct Medal in order of precedence. The Army reserve components' Achievement Medal and equivalents awarded by other Service reserve components follow the Army Good Conduct Medal and Good Conduct Medals from the other U.S. Services, in order of precedence.

U.S. service (campaign) medals, and service and training ribbons authorized for wear on the uniform are listed below, in their order of precedence:

Army of Occupation Medal.
Medal for Humane Action.
National Defense Service Medal.
Korean Service Medal.
Antarctica Service Medal.
Armed Forces Expeditionary Medal.
Vietnam Service Medal.
Southwest Asia Service Medal.
Kosovo Campaign Medal.
Afghanistan Campaign Medal.
Iraq Campaign Medal.
Global War on Terrorism Expeditionary Medal.
Global War on Terrorism Service Medal.
Korean Defense Service Medal.
Armed Forces Service Medal.
Humanitarian Service Medal.
Military Outstanding Volunteer Service Medal.
Armed Forces Reserve Medal.
NCO Professional Development Ribbon.
Army Service Ribbon.

Overseas Service Ribbon.
Army Reserve Components Overseas Training Ribbon.
Coast Guard Special Operations Service Ribbon.
Air Force Combat Readiness Medal.
Navy Sea Service Deployment Ribbon.

Personnel may wear service medals and service and training ribbons awarded by other U.S. Services on the Army uniform, except for the Air Force Longevity Service Award ribbon and Air Force, Navy, and Coast Guard marksmanship medals and ribbons. Personnel will wear service and training medals and ribbons awarded by other U.S. Services after U.S. Army service and training ribbons, and before foreign awards.

U.S. unit awards are given to an operating unit and are worn by members of that unit who participated in the cited action. Personnel who did not participate in the cited action, but who are assigned in the cited unit, are authorized temporary wear of some unit awards. U.S. unit awards authorized for wear on Army uniforms are listed below in their order of precedence:

Presidential Unit Citation (Army, Air Force).
Presidential Unit Citation (Navy).
Joint Meritorious Unit Award.
Valorous Unit Award.
Meritorious Unit Commendation (Army).
Navy Unit Commendation.
Air Force Outstanding Unit Award.
Coast Guard Unit Commendation.
Army Superior Unit Award.
Meritorious Unit Commendation (Navy).
Navy "E" Ribbon.
Air Force Organizational Excellence Award.
Coast Guard Meritorious Unit Commendation.

WEARING OF MEDALS AND RIBBONS

All individual U.S. decorations and service medals (full-size medals, miniature medals, and ribbons) are worn above the left breast pocket or centered on the left side of the coat or jacket of the prescribed uniform (with the exception of the Medal of Honor, which may be worn suspended around the neck). Decorations are worn with the highest displayed above and to the wearer's right of the others.

Full-size decorations and service medals may be worn on the Army blue, white, and green uniforms when worn for social functions or when directed. They are worn in order of precedence from the wearer's right to left, in one or more lines, without overlapping within a line, with one-eighth-inch space

Ribbons Representing Decorations and Service Medals

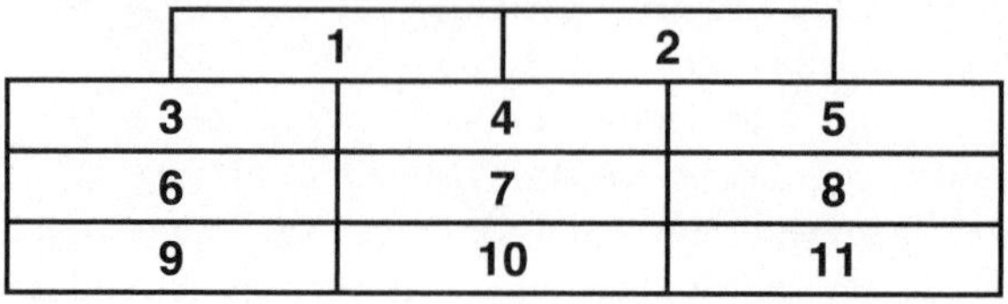

1. Medal of Honor
2. Distinguished Service Cross
3. Distinguished Service Medal
4. Silver Star
5. Legion of Merit
6. Distinguished Flying Cross
7. Soldier's Medal
8. Bronze Star Medal
9. Purple Heart
10. Meritorious Service Medal
11. Air Medal

between lines. No line will contain fewer medals than the one above it. The Medal of Honor is worn with the neckband ribbon around the neck, outside the shirt collar and inside the coat collar, with the medal hanging over the necktie.

Miniature decorations and service medals are authorized for wear on the mess and evening mess uniforms only. They may be worn side by side or overlapped, but the overlap will not exceed 50 percent and will be equal for all. There are no miniature medals authorized for the Medal of Honor.

Service ribbons are worn in the order of precedence from the wearer's right to left in one or more lines either without a space between rows or with a one-eighth-inch space. No row should contain more than four service ribbons. Male and female personnel are authorized to wear them on the Army green, white, and blue uniforms.

Retired personnel and former soldiers may wear either full-size or miniature medals on appropriate civilian clothing on Veterans Day, Memorial Day, and Armed Forces Day, and at formal occasions of ceremony and social functions of a military nature.

Unauthorized Wearing of Decorations and Badges

Federal law prescribes stiff penalties for the unauthorized wearing of U.S. decorations, badges, appurtenances, and unit awards:

> Whoever knowingly wears . . . any decoration or medal authorized by Congress for the Armed Forces of the United States or any of the service medals or badges awarded to the members of such forces, or

> the ribbon, button, or rosette of any such badge, decoration or medal, or any colorable imitation thereof, except when authorized under regulations made pursuant to law, shall be fined not more than $250 or imprisoned not more than six months, or both.
>
> —62 Stat. 732, June 25, 1948, as amended 18 U.S.C. 704

The U.S. Code (18 U.S.C. 703) further prescribes:

> Whoever, within the jurisdiction of the United States, with intent to deceive or mislead, wears any naval, military, police, or other official uniform, decoration, or regalia of any foreign state, nation, or government with which the United States is at peace, or anything so nearly resembling the same as to be calculated to deceive, shall be fined not more than $250 or imprisoned not more than six months or both.

The Medal of Honor

The Army and Air Force version of the Medal of Honor (MOH) is the highest award for the risk of life "above and beyond the call of duty" involving actual conflict with an enemy; the Navy version can and has been awarded to noncombatants in peacetime, and Congress has similarly awarded special medals to honor individual exploits during peacetime.

The Medal of Honor is designed in the form of a five-pointed star, made of silver and heavily electroplated in gold. In the center of the star appears the head of Minerva—the Roman goddess whose name is associated with wisdom and righteousness in war—surrounded by the words "United States of America." An open laurel wreath, enameled in green, encircles the star, and the oak leaves at the bases of the prongs of the star are likewise enameled. The medal is suspended by a blue silk ribbon, spangled with thirteen white stars (representing the thirteen original states), and attached to an eagle supported by a horizontal bar upon which is engraved the word "Valor."

The reverse of the medal is plain so that the name of the recipient may be engraved thereon; the reverse of the bar is stamped "The Congress to . . . "

On December 21, 1861, President Lincoln approved the Medal of Honor for enlisted men of the Navy and Marine Corps; a similar medal was established for the Army on July 12, 1862, further amended by legislation enacted on March 3, 1863, to include officers and making the provisions retroactive to the beginning of the Civil War. The first Army Medals were awarded on March 25, 1863. The Medal of Honor is awarded only to U.S. citizens. The Army Medal may be awarded only to military personnel on active federal service (paragraph 3.6, AR 600-8-22).

Distinguished Service Cross

Established by legislation on July 9, 1918 (as amended July 25, 1963), the Distinguished Service Cross (DSC) evolved from the Certificate of Merit of 1847. The DSC is the second highest decoration for valor in war and is bestowed to recognize extraordinary heroism in connection with military operations in time of war. Unlike the Medal of Honor, however, the DSC may be awarded for heroism involving several acts over a short period of time that need not have been performed in actual conflict with an enemy but must have involved extraordinary risk of life. Successive awards are denoted by oak-leaf clusters (paragraph 3.7, AR 600-8-22).

Defense Distinguished Service Medal

Established by Executive Order 11545, July 9, 1970, the Defense Distinguished Service Medal (DDSM) is awarded to any military officer who, while assigned to joint staffs and other joint activities of the Department of Defense, distinguishes himself or herself by exceptionally meritorious service in a position of unique and great responsibility. It is not awarded for a period of service for which a Distinguished Service Medal or similar decoration is awarded. Subsequent awards are denoted by oak-leaf clusters (paragraph 2.3, AR 600-8-22).

Distinguished Service Medal

Established by an act of Congress of July 9, 1918, the Distinguished Service Medal (DSM) is awarded to any person who, while serving in any capacity with the U.S. Army, has distinguished himself or herself by exceptionally meritorious service in a duty of great responsibility. Awards may be made to persons other than members of the armed forces of the United States for wartime services only, and then only under exceptional circumstances with the approval of the president. Successive awards are denoted by oak-leaf clusters (paragraph 3.8, AR 600-8-22).

Silver Star

Established by an act of Congress of July 9, 1918 (as amended by an act of July 25, 1963), the Silver Star (SS) is the third-ranking U.S. decoration for heroism in wartime.

When first established, the SS was worn in the form of a small silver star, three-sixteenths inch in diameter, upon the respective service medal and ribbon to indicate each separate citation for gallantry in action earned during the campaign for which the service medal was authorized. These stars were known as "citation stars."

The current version of the SS is gilt bronze in the shape of a star one and one-quarter inches across. On the obverse is a laurel wreath, within which is a silver star three-sixteenths inch in diameter; on the reverse are inscribed the words "For Gallantry in Action." The SS may be awarded by any commander who has the authority to award the DSC, and the SS, like the DSC, may be awarded for acts of heroism that take place over a period of time. Successive awards are denoted by oak-leaf clusters (paragraph 3.9, AR 600-8-22).

Defense Superior Service Medal

Established by Executive Order 11904, February 6, 1976, the Defense Superior Service Medal (DSSM) may be awarded to U.S. personnel who give superior meritorious service in a position of significant responsibility. It is not awarded to any individual for a period of service for which a Legion of Merit or similar decoration is awarded. Successive awards are denoted by oak-leaf clusters (paragraph 2.4, AR 600-8-22).

Legion of Merit

Established by an act of Congress of July 20, 1942, the Legion of Merit (LM) is awarded to any member of the armed forces of the United States or a friendly foreign country who distinguishes himself or herself by outstanding meritorious conduct in the performance of outstanding services. Successive awards are denoted by oak-leaf clusters (paragraph 3.10, AR 600-8-22).

Distinguished Flying Cross

Established by an act of Congress of July 2, 1926, the Distinguished Flying Cross (DFC) may be awarded, in war or peace, to U.S. military personnel who distinguish themselves by heroism or extraordinary achievement while participating in aerial flight. Such awards are made only to recognize single acts of heroism or extraordinary achievement that are not sustained operational activities against an armed enemy. An act of heroism must be evidenced by voluntary action above and beyond the call of duty. Achievement awards must have resulted in an accomplishment so exceptional and outstanding as to clearly set the individual apart from other persons in similar circumstances. Awards to foreign personnel serving with the U.S. armed forces may be made only in connection with actual wartime operations. Successive awards are denoted by oak-leaf clusters (paragraph 3.11, AR 600-8-22).

Soldier's Medal

Established by an act of Congress of July 2, 1926, the Soldier's Medal (SM) is awarded to U.S. and foreign military personnel in recognition of heroism not involving actual conflict with an enemy. The performance must have involved personal hazard or danger and voluntary risk of life of approximately the same degree as that required for award of the Distinguished Flying Cross, but awards of the SM are not made solely on the basis of having saved a life. Subsequent awards of this decoration are denoted by oak-leaf clusters (paragraph 3.12, AR 600-8-22).

Bronze Star Medal

Originally established by Executive Order 9419 of February 4, 1944 (superseded by Executive Order 11046 of August 26, 1962), the Bronze Star Medal (BSM) can be awarded to U.S. and foreign personnel, both military and civilian, for acts that display heroism, meritorious achievement, or service performed in connection with military operations against an armed force. A bronze V device is worn to denote awards for heroism, and successive awards are denoted by oak-leaf clusters (paragraph 3.13, AR 600-8-22).

Purple Heart

Originally established by Gen. George Washington on August 7, 1782, the Purple Heart (PH) is the oldest U.S. military decoration. The PH is awarded in the name of the president to any member of the armed forces or any civilian of the United States who, while serving under competent authority in any capacity with one of the U.S. armed services after April 5, 1917, has been wounded or killed or who has died or may die after being wounded.

A "wound" is defined as any injury (not necessarily one that breaks the skin) caused by an outside force or agent. Multiple injuries suffered at the same moment from the same agent are considered as one wound. Specific examples of injuries that would be authorized the award of the PH are those incurred while making a parachute landing from an aircraft that had been brought down by enemy fire, or injuries received as the result of a vehicle accident caused by enemy fire. Subsequent awards of the PH are denoted by oak-leaf clusters (paragraph 2-8, AR 600-8-22).

Defense Meritorious Service Medal

Established by Executive Order 12019 of November 3, 1977, the Defense Meritorious Service Medal (DMSM) is awarded in the name of the Secretary of Defense to any member of the armed forces who, while serving in any joint activity of the Department of Defense on or after November 3, 1977, for a period of sixty days or more, demonstrates incontestably exceptional service or achievement of a magnitude that clearly places him or her above his or her peers. Subsequent awards of the DMSM are denoted by oak-leaf clusters (paragraph 2-5, AR 600-8-22).

Meritorious Service Medal

Established by Executive Order 1144.8 on January 16, 1969, the Meritorious Service Medal (MSM) is awarded to any member of the armed forces of the United States who, while serving in a noncombat area after January 16, 1969, has distinguished himself or herself by outstanding meritorious achievement or service. The achievement or service must have been comparable to that required for the Legion of Merit but in a position of lesser, though considerable, responsibility. This decoration is the equivalent of the Bronze Star Medal for recognition of outstanding meritorious noncombat achievement or service and takes precedence with, but after, the BSM when both are worn on the uniform. This decoration is not awarded to foreign personnel. Subsequent awards are denoted by oak-leaf clusters (paragraph 3-14, AR 600-8-22).

Air Medal

Established by Executive Order 9242-A, September 11, 1942, the Air Medal (AM) is awarded to any person who, while serving in any capacity in or with the Army, shall have distinguished himself by meritorious achievement while participating in aerial flight. Awards may be made in recognition of single acts of merit or heroism or for meritorious service. A system of denoting successive awards of the medal was devised using bronze arabic numerals instead of oak-leaf clusters. Therefore, an individual holding fifteen awards of the AM wears the numeral "14" on the suspension ribbon and service ribbon (paragraph 3-15, AR 600-8-22).

Joint Service Commendation Medal

The Joint Service Commendation Medal (JSCM) is awarded to any member of the armed forces who distinguishes himself or herself by meritorious achievement or service while serving in any joint assignment. Awards made for acts or services involving direct participation in combat operations on or after June 25, 1963, may be denoted by the bronze V device. Subsequent awards of the JSCM are denoted by oak-leaf clusters (paragraph 2-6, AR 600-8-22).

Army Commendation Medal

The Army Commendation Medal (ARCOM) is awarded to any member of the armed forces who distinguishes himself or herself by heroism, meritorious achievement, or meritorious service. The ARCOM may also be awarded to a member of the armed forces of a friendly foreign nation who distinguishes himself or herself by an act of heroism, extraordinary achievement, or meritorious service that has been of mutual benefit to a friendly nation and the United States. Awards of the ARCOM may be made for acts of valor performed under circumstances described above that are of lesser degree than those required for award of the Bronze Star Medal and may include acts that involve aerial flight. Awards may also be made for noncombat acts of heroism that do not meet the requirements for award of the Soldier's Medal. This decoration is primarily awarded to company-grade officers, warrant officers, and enlisted personnel (paragraph 3.16, AR 600-8-22).

Joint Service Achievement Medal

The Joint Service Achievement Medal (JSAM) is awarded to any member of the armed forces of the United States, below the grade of full colonel, who distinguishes himself or herself by meritorious achievement or service while serving in any joint activity after August 3, 1983. Military personnel on temporary duty to a joint activity for at least sixty days are also eligible.

The required achievement or service, while of lesser degree than that required for award of the Joint Service Commendation Medal, must have been accomplished with distinction. Subsequent awards are designated by oak-leaf clusters (paragraph 2.7, AR 600-8-22).

Army Achievement Medal

The Army Achievement Medal (AAM) is awarded to any member of the armed forces of the United States, or to any member of the armed forces of a friendly foreign nation, who, while serving in any capacity with the Army in a noncombat area on or after August 1, 1981, distinguishes himself or herself by meritorious service or achievement of a lesser degree than that required for award of the Army Commendation Medal. Subsequent awards are designated by oak-leaf clusters (paragraph 3.7, AR 600-8-22).

Prisoner of War Medal

The Prisoner of War Medal (POWM) is authorized for all U.S. military personnel who were taken prisoner of war after April 6, 1917, during an armed conflict and who served honorably during the period of captivity (paragraph 2.9, AR 600-8-22).

Good Conduct Medal

The Good Conduct Medal (GCM) is awarded to enlisted personnel for exemplary behavior, efficiency, and fidelity to active federal military service. Generally, the qualifying period is three years of continuous active service completed on or after August 26, 1940. Exceptions are for those who are separated from the service by reason of physical disability incurred in the line of duty, who died or were killed before completing one year of service, or who separated after more than one year but less than three years (draftees). Those exceptions apply only to the first award.

Isolated examples of nonjudicial punishment are not necessarily automatically disqualifying but must be considered on the basis of the soldier's whole record; consideration as to the nature of the infraction, the circumstances under which it occurred, and when it occurred must be duly weighed by the individual's commander. Conviction by court-martial terminates a period of qualifying service; a new period begins following the completion of the sentence imposed by court-martial.

Successive awards of the GCM are identified by clasps, or bars one-eighth inch by one and three-eighths inches, of bronze, silver, or gold, with loops (also called knots) that indicate each period of service for which the medal is authorized. The first award is the actual medal itself. Successive awards are indicated with clasps with loops (chapter 4, section 1, AR 600-8-22).

Army Reserve Components Achievement Medal

The Army Reserve Components Achievement Medal (ARCAM) may be awarded upon recommendation of the unit commander for four years of honest and faithful service on or after March 3, 1972. Service must have been consecutive, in the grade of colonel or below, and in accordance with the standards of conduct, courage, and duty required by law and customs of the service of an active-duty member of the same grade. The reverse of this medal is struck in two designs for award to personnel whose service has been primarily in the Army Reserve or primarily in the National Guard (chapter 4, section 111, AR 600-8-22).

U.S. ARMY AND DEPARTMENT OF DEFENSE UNIT AWARDS

Unit awards are authorized in recognition of group heroism or meritorious service, usually during a war, as a means of promoting esprit de corps. They are of the following categories: unit decorations, infantry and medical streamers, campaign streamers, war service streamers, and campaign silver bands.

U.S. unit decorations, in order of precedence listed in this section, have been established to recognize outstanding heroism or exceptionally meritorious conduct in the performance of outstanding services. These awards may be worn permanently by those who served with the unit during the cited period. The Presidential Unit Citation (Army), the Valorous Unit Award, the Meritorious Unit Commendation, and the Army Superior Unit Award may be worn temporarily by those serving with the unit subsequent to the cited period.

Presidential Unit Citation

The Presidential Unit Citation is awarded to units of the armed forces of the United States and cobelligerent nations for extraordinary heroism in action against an armed enemy occurring on or after December 7, 1941. The unit must display such gallantry, determination, and esprit de corps in accomplishing its mission under extremely difficult and hazardous conditions as to set it apart from and above other units participating in the same campaign. The degree of heroism required is the same as that which would warrant award of a Distinguished Service Cross to an individual. The Presidential Unit Emblem (Army) is a blue ribbon set in a gold-colored metal frame of laurel leaves (paragraph 7.13, AR 600-8-22).

Joint Meritorious Unit Award

The Joint Meritorious Unit Award is awarded to joint activities of the Department of Defense for meritorious achievement or service, superior to that normally expected, during combat with an armed enemy of the United States, during a declared national emergency, or under extraordinary circumstances that involve the national interest (paragraph 7.15, AR 600-8-22).

Valorous Unit Award

Criteria for the Valorous Unit Award are the same as those for the Presidential Unit Citation except that the degree of valor required is that which would merit award of the Silver Star to an individual. The emblem is a scarlet ribbon with the Silver Star color design superimposed in the center, set in a gold-colored metal frame with laurel leaves (paragraph 7.14, AR 600-8-22).

Meritorious Unit Commendation

The Meritorious Unit Commendation is awarded for at least six months of exceptionally meritorious conduct in support of military operations to service and support units of the armed forces of the United States and cobelligerent nations. The degree of achievement is that which would merit the award of the Legion of Merit to an individual. The emblem is a scarlet ribbon set in a gold-colored metal frame with laurel leaves (paragraph 7.15, AR 600-8-22).

Army Superior Unit Award

The Army Superior Unit Award is given for outstanding meritorious performance of a difficult and challenging mission under extraordinary circumstances by a unit during peacetime. The emblem is a scarlet ribbon with a vertical green stripe in the center, on each side of which is a narrow yellow stripe, set in a gold-colored metal frame with laurel leaves (paragraph 7.16, AR 600-8-22).

U.S. SERVICE MEDALS

Service or campaign medals denote honorable performance of military duty within specified limited dates in specified geographical areas. With the exception of the Humanitarian Service Medal, the Armed Forces Reserve Medal, the Army Reserve Component Achievement Medal, the Army Service Ribbon, and the NCO Professional Development Ribbon, they are awarded only for active federal military service.

Service medals are worn in order by the date when the person became eligible for the award, not by the date of entry in the records or the date upon which the award was established. Foreign military service medals are worn following authorized U.S. decorations. Not more than one service medal is awarded for service involving identical or overlapping periods of time, except that each of the following groups of service medals may be awarded to an individual provided he or she meets the criteria prescribed by chapter 5, AR 600-8-22. For information concerning the criteria for the award of any service medal not listed below, see chapter 5, AR 600-8-22.

Army of Occupation Medal

Established by the War Department General Orders 32, 1946, this medal is awarded for service for thirty consecutive days at a normal post of duty with

DECORATIONS, AWARDS, AND SERVICE MEDALS

U.S. ARMY AND DEPARTMENT OF DEFENSE MILITARY DECORATIONS

Medal of Honor
(Army)

Distinguished Service Cross (Army)

Defense Distinguished Service Medal

Distinguished Service Medal (Army)

Silver Star

Defense Superior Service Medal

Legion of Merit

Distinguished Flying Cross

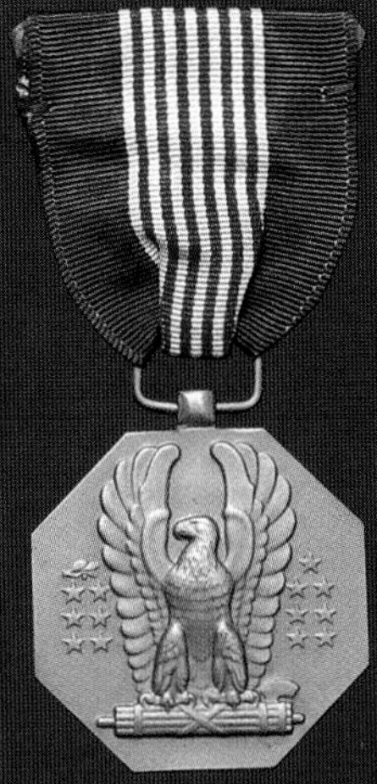

Soldier's Medal (Army)

Bronze Star Medal

Purple Heart

Defense Meritorious Service Medal

Meritorious Service Medal

Air Medal

Joint Service Commendation Medal

Army Commendation Medal

Joint Service Achievement Medal

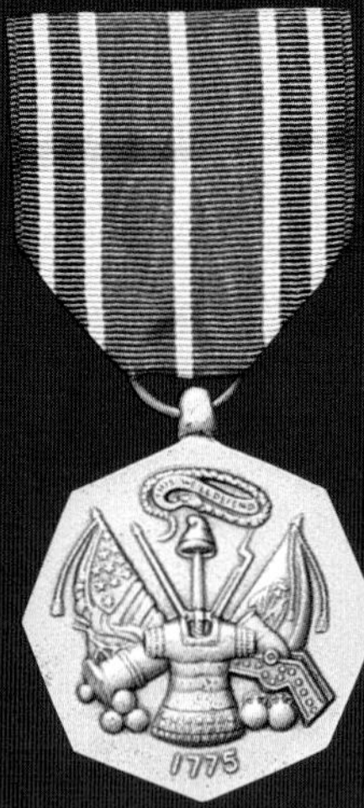

Army Achievement Medal

Prisoner of War Medal

Good Conduct Medal (Army)

Army Reserve Components Achievement Medal

National Defense Service Medal

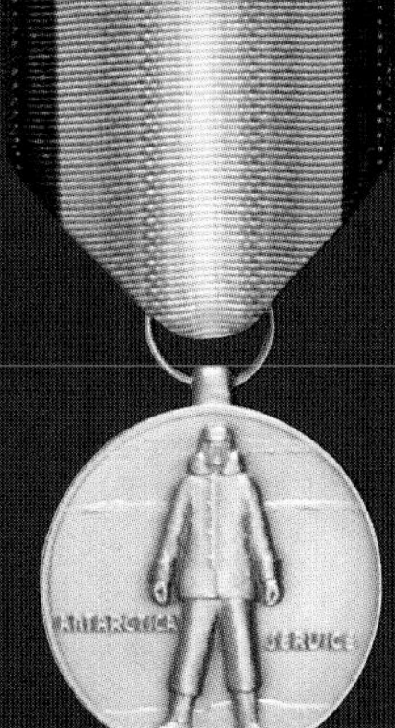

Antarctica Service Medal

Armed Forces Expeditionary Medal

Vietnam Service Medal

Southwest Asia Service Medal

Kosovo Campaign Medal

Afghanistan Campaign Medal

Iraq Campaign Medal

Global War on Terrorism Expeditionary Medal

Global War on Terrorism Service Medal

Korean Defense Service Medal

Armed Forces Service Medal

Humanitarian Service Medal

Military Outstanding Volunteer Service Medal

Armed Forces Reserve Medal

U.S. ARMY SERVICE AND TRAINING RIBBONS

NCO Professional Development Ribbon

Army Service Ribbon

Overseas Service Ribbon (Army)

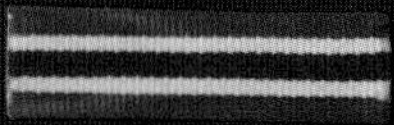

Army Reserve Components Overseas Training Ribbon

NON-U.S. SERVICE MEDALS

United Nations Medal

NATO Medal

Multinational Force and Observers Medal

Republic of Vietnam Campaign Medal

Kuwait Liberation Medal (Kingdom of *Saudi Arabia*)

Kuwait Liberation Medal (Government of *Kuwait*)

U.S. ARMY AND DEPARTMENT OF DEFENSE UNIT AWARDS

Presidential Unit Citation (Army)

Joint Meritorious Unit Award

Valorous Unit Award

Meritorious Unit Commendation (Army)

Army Superior Unit Award

U.S. ARMY BADGES AND TABS

Combat and Special Skill Badges

Combat Infantryman Badge
1st Award

Combat Medical Badge
1st Award

Combat Infantryman Badge
2nd Award

Combat Medical Badge
2nd Award

Combat Infantryman Badge
3rd Award

Combat Medical Badge
3rd Award

Expert Infantryman Badge

Expert Field Medical Badge

Combat Action Badge

Master Astronaut Badge

Basic Astronaut Badge

Senior Astronaut Badge

Master Aviator Badge

Basic Aviator Badge

Senior Aviator Badge

Master Flight Surgeon Badge

Basic Flight Surgeon Badge

Senior Flight Surgeon Badge

Master Aircraft Crewman Badge

Basic Aircraft Crewman Badge

Senior Aircraft Crewman Badge

Master Parachutist Badge

Basic Parachutist Badge

Senior Parachutist Badge

Combat Parachutist Badge (1 Jump)

Combat Parachutist Badge (2 Jumps)

Combat Parachutist Badge (3 Jumps)

Combat Parachutist Badge (4 Jumps)

Combat Parachutist Badge (5 Jumps)

Air Assault Badge

Glider Badge

Special Forces Tab (Metal Replica)

Ranger Tab (Metal Replica)

Sapper Tab

Pathfinder Badge

Salvage Diver Badge

Second Class Diver Badge

Master Diver Badge

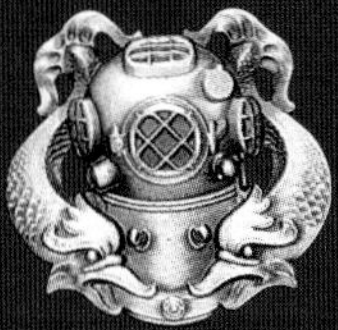

First Class Diver Badge

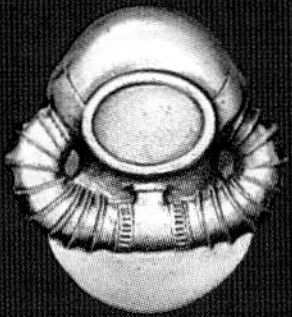

Scuba Diver Badge

Master Explosive Ordnance Disposal Badge

Basic Explosive Ordnance Disposal Badge

Senior Explosive Ordnance Disposal Badge

Nuclear Reactor
Operator Badge
(Basic)

Nuclear Reactor
Operator Badge
(Second Class)

Nuclear Reactor
Operator Badge
(First Class)

Nuclear Reactor
Operator Badge
(Shift Supervisor)

Parachute Rigger
Badge

Driver and Mechanic
Badge

Marksmanship Badges

Marksman

Sharpshooter

Expert

Identification Badges

Presidential Service

Vice-Presidential Service

Secretary of Defense

Joint Chiefs of Staff

Army Staff

Guard,
Tomb of the Unknown Soldier

Drill Sergeant

U.S. Army Recruiter
(Active Army)

U.S. Army Recruiter
(Army National Guard)

U.S. Army Recruiter
(U.S. Army Reserve)

the Army of Occupation of Berlin during the period 1945–1990. This medal was previously authorized for post–World War II occupation duty in Germany, Austria, Italy, Japan, and Korea (see paragraph 5.1, AR 600-8-21). Berlin service does not authorize the wearing of a clasp on either the service medal or the service ribbon.

National Defense Service Medal (NDSM)

This medal is awarded for honorable active service for any period between the periods June 27, 1950, to July 27, 1954; January 1, 1961, to August 14, 1974; August 2, 1990, to November 30, 1995, and September 11, 2001, to a date to be later determined. Subsequent award of the NDSM is denoted by a bronze service star (paragraph 2.10, AR 600-8-22).

Antarctica Service Medal

Any member of the Armed Forces of the United States who participates in or has participated in scientific, direct support, or exploratory operations in Antarctica under sponsorship and approval of the U.S. Government is eligible for this medal. This included flights as a member of the crew of an aircraft flying to or from the Antarctic Continent or as a member of a U.S. ship operating south of latitude 60 degrees south in support of U.S. Programs in Antarctica. (paragraph 2.11, AR 600-8-22).

Armed Forces Expeditionary Medal

The Armed Forces Expeditionary Medal is authorized for U.S. military operations, U.S. operations in direct support of the United Nations, and U.S. operations of assistance for friendly foreign nations. Operations are defined as military actions or the carrying out of strategic, tactical, service, training, or administrative military missions and the process of carrying on combat, including movement, supply, attack, defense, and maneuvers needed to gain the objectives of any battle or campaign.

Designated areas and dates of service for eligibility are in AR 600-8-22. Subsequent awards of this medal are denoted by bronze service stars (paragraph 2.12, AR 600-8-22).

Vietnam Service Medal

The Vietnam Service Medal is awarded to all members of the armed forces who served in Vietnam and contiguous waters or airspace there after July 3, 1965, and through March 28, 1973. Members of the armed forces in Thailand, Laos, or Cambodia or the airspace thereover who during the same period served in direct support of operations in Vietnam are also eligible. See AR 600-8-22, Appendix B, for authorized campaigns and dates. One bronze service star (or a combination of bronze and silver stars, as applicable) may be worn on the suspension ribbon and bar representing this medal (paragraph 2.13, AR 600-8-22).

Southwest Asia Service Medal (SWASM)
The Southwest Asia Service Medal is awarded to U.S. military personnel who have served in the Persian Gulf area since August 2, 1990, through November 30, 1995. Subsequent awards of the SWASM are denoted by service stars affixed to the medal (paragraph 2.14, AR 600-8-22).

Kosovo Campaign Medal
The Kosovo Campaign Medal is to recognize the accomplishments of military servicemembers who participated in, or were in direct support of, the conflict in Kosovo. Members authorized the Kosovo Campaign Medal must have participated in or served in direct support of the Kosovo operation after March 24, 1999. Servicemembers must be bona fide members of a unit participating in, or engaged in direct support of, the operation for thirty consecutive days in the area of eligibility, or for sixty nonconsecutive days provided this support involves entering the area of eligibility. One bronze service star is worn on the suspension and service ribbon of the Kosovo Campaign Medal for qualified participation during the campaign period. Meeting the qualification in each of the two campaigns would warrant the medal and two bronze service stars.

Afghanistan Campaign Medal
The Afghanistan Campaign Medal is awarded to soldiers who deploy to Afghanistan in direct support of Operation Enduring Freedom (OEF) on or after October 24, 2001, to a date to be determined or the cessation of OEF. The area of eligibility encompasses all land area of the country of Afghanistan and all air spaces above the land.

Iraq Campaign Medal
The Iraq medal is awarded to soldiers who deploy to Iraq in direct support of Operation Iraqi Freedom (OIF) on or after March 19, 2003, to a date to be determined or the cessation of OIF. The area of eligibility encompasses all land area of the country of Iraq and the contiguous water area out to twelve nautical miles, and all air spaces above the land area of Iraq and above the contiguous water area out to twelve nautical miles.

Global War on Terrorism Expeditionary Medal
The Global War on Terrorism Expeditionary Medal (GWOTEM) is awarded to servicemembers who serve in military expeditions to combat terrorism on or after September 11, 2001. Beginning April 30, 2005, the Global War on Terrorism Expeditionary Medal is no longer authorized to be awarded for service in Afghanistan and/or Iraq. The GWOTEM is still authorized for service in the other geographical areas of eligibility.

The Global War on Terrorism Service Medal (GWOTSM)

The Global War on Terrorism Service Medal is awarded to servicemembers who have participated in or served in support of Global War on Terrorism Operations outside the designated areas of eligibility (AOE) for the Global War on Terrorism Expeditionary Medal, on or after September 11, 2001, to a date to be determined. All soldiers serving on active duty between September 11, 2001, and March 2004 are all authorized the GWOTSM. After March 2004, battalion commanders, the award approval authority, must determine if a soldier serving on active duty has qualified for the GWOTSM.

Soldiers will not receive more than one of the following medals for the same act, time period or service: Afghanistan Campaign Medal, Iraq Campaign Medal, Global War on Terrorism Expeditionary Medal, or Armed Forces Expeditionary Medal.

Korea Defense Service Medal

The Korea Defense Service Medal (KDSM) is authorized to members of the armed forces who have served on active duty in support of the defense of the Republic of Korea from July 28, 1954, to a date to be determined. The area of eligibility encompasses all land area of the Republic of Korea, and the contiguous water out to twelve nautical miles, and all air spaces above the land and water areas. Effective February 3, 2004, the Overseas Service Ribbon (OSR) is no longer authorized for overseas tours in the Republic of Korea.

Armed Forces Service Medal

Awarded to members of the armed forces, who as of June 1, 1992, are participating, or have participated, as members of U.S. military units in a U.S. military operation that is deemed to be a significant activity, and are encountering, or have encountered, no foreign armed opposition or imminent threat of hostile action.

Servicemembers must be bona fide members of a unit participating for one or more days in the operation or engaged in direct support in the area of eligibility, or for sixty nonconsecutive days provided this support involves entering the area of eligibility or participating as a regularly assigned aircrew member of an aircraft flying into, out of, within, or over the area of eligibility in support of the operation. Second and subsequent awards will be denoted by bronze service stars (Milper msg 96-098, March 11, 1996).

Humanitarian Service Medal

The Humanitarian Service Medal is authorized to be awarded to any armed forces personnel who directly participated in a Department of Defense-approved humanitarian act or operation, except when a by-name eligibility list is published. No more than one award of this medal may be made for the same act or operation. Subsequent awards are designated by bronze numerals. Operations for which award of the Humanitarian Service Medal have thus far been approved are listed in Appendix C, AR 600-8-22 (paragraph 2.15, AR 600-8-22).

Military Outstanding Volunteer Service Medal

Received by members of the armed forces of the United States who subsequent to December 31, 1992, perform outstanding volunteer community service of a sustained, direct, and consequential nature. To be eligible, an individual's service must (1) be to the civilian community, including the military family community; (2) be significant in nature and produce tangible results; (3) reflect favorably on the military service and the Department of Defense; and (4) be of a sustained and direct nature.

The Military Outstanding Volunteer Service Medal (MOVSM) is intended to recognize exceptional community support over time and not a single act or achievement. Further, it is intended to honor direct support of community activities (paragraph 2.16, AR 600-8-72).

Armed Forces Reserve Medal

Awarded for honorable and satisfactory service as a member of one or more of the reserve components of the armed forces of the United States for a period of ten years within a twelve-year period. Subsequent ten-year awards are denoted by a bronze hourglass. A gold hourglass is awarded on completion of the fourth ten-year period.

Awarded for mobilization on or after August 1, 1990, to members called to active duty in support of U.S. military operations or contingencies designated by the Secretary of Defense. The "M" device is worn to indicate mobilization. Subsequent mobilizations are denoted by the wearing of a number to indicate the number of times mobilized. No hourglass is worn unless authorized as explained above (paragraph 5.7, AR 600-8-22, and Milper msg 96-196).

NCO Professional Development Ribbon

Established by the secretary of the Army on April 10, 1981, and effective August 1, 1981, the NCO Professional Development Ribbon is awarded to members of the U.S. Army, Army National Guard, and Army Reserve for successful completion of designated NCO professional development courses. The ribbon is awarded for four levels of professional development: (1) Primary; (2) Basic; (3) Advanced; and (4) the Sergeants Major Academy (paragraph 5.6, AR 600-8-22).

Army Service Ribbon

Established by the secretary of the Army on April 10, 1981, and effective August 1, 1981, the Army Service Ribbon is awarded to members of the U.S.

Army, Army National Guard, and Army Reserve who have successfully completed initial entry training. Enlisted persons are eligible upon completion of initial MOS-producing courses. For those enlisted persons assigned an MOS based on civilian or other-service acquired skills, it is awarded after four months of honorable active service (paragraph 5.5, AR 600-8-22).

Overseas Service Ribbon

Established by the secretary of the Army on April 10, 1981, and effective August 1, 1981, the Overseas Service Ribbon is awarded to all members of the U.S. Army, Army National Guard, and Army Reserve credited with a normal overseas tour completed in accordance with AR 614-30. A soldier who has overseas service credited by another armed service is also eligible for this ribbon. The ribbon is not authorized for completion of an overseas tour of duty for which a service medal has been authorized (paragraph 5.4, AR 600-8-22).

Army Reserve Components Overseas Training Ribbon

Established by the secretary of the Army on July 11, 1984, the ribbon is awarded to members of the U.S. Army Reserve components for successful completion of annual training or active-duty training for a period of not less than ten days on foreign soil (paragraph 5.3, AR 600-8-22).

NON-U.S. SERVICE MEDALS

United Nations Medal

This medal may be awarded to personnel who have been in the service of the United Nations for a period of not less than six months with one of the units designated in paragraph 9.17, AR 688-8-2. The United Nations has, to date, cast medals for eleven different operations. Effective October 13, 1995, soldiers awarded any of these medals may wear the first medal and ribbon for which they qualify. Not more than one UN Medal may be worn. Award of a medal in a different UN mission is denoted by a bronze service star on the one UN Medal.

NATO Medal

Qualifying periods of service for the NATO medal are either thirty days (continuous or accumulated) in the territory and airspace of the former Republic of Yugoslavia and the Adriatic Sea, or ninety days (continuous or accumulated) in the area of operations outside the former Republic of Yugoslavia and the Adriatic Sea between July 1, 1992, and a date to be determined.

Multinational Force and Observers Medal

To qualify for this medal, a soldier must have served with the Multinational Force and Observers at least ninety days after August 3, 1981. Subsequent awards for each completed six-month tour are indicated by an appropriate numeral, starting with numeral "1" (paragraph 9.18, AR 600-8-22).

Republic of Vietnam Campaign Medal

Authorized for acceptance by Department of Defense instructions 1348.17, January 31, 1974, by members of the armed forces who meet the following criteria:

- Have served in the Republic of Vietnam for six months during the period March 1, 1961, to March 28, 1973, inclusive.
- Have served outside the geographical limits of the Republic of Vietnam and contributed direct combat support to the Republic of Vietnam Armed Forces for six months. Such persons must meet the criteria established for the Armed Forces Expeditionary Medal (Vietnam) or the Vietnam Service Medal during the period of service required to qualify for the Republic of Vietnam Campaign Medal.
- Have served under the above conditions for less than six months but have been wounded by hostile forces, captured, or killed in action or otherwise in the line of duty (paragraph 9.19, AR 600-8-22).

Kuwait Liberation Medal (Kingdom of Saudi Arabia)

Awarded by the kingdom of Saudi Arabia to members of the armed forces of the United States who served within the designated war zone of Operation Desert Storm during the period January 17, 1991, through February 28, 1991.

Kuwait Liberation Medal (Government of Kuwait)

Awarded by the government of Kuwait to U.S. military personnel who were assigned to one of several designated areas in and around Kuwait from August 2, 1990, to August 31, 1993. To be eligible, personnel must have been attached to, or regularly served for one day or more, with an organization participating in ground and/or shore operations; with a naval vessel directly supporting military operations; or as a crew member in one or more aerial flights that directly supported military operations in the designated areas. Temporary duty for thirty or sixty nonconsecutive days supporting such operations during the designated period also qualifies for award of the medal. The time requirement may be waived for temporary duty (TDY) soldiers who actually participated in combat operations (paragraph 9.20, AR 600-8-22).

FOREIGN INDIVIDUAL AWARDS

Decorations received from a foreign government in recognition of active field service in connection with combat operations or for outstanding or unusually meritorious performance may be accepted and worn upon approval of the Department of the Army. Without this approval, they become the property of the United States and must be deposited with the Department of the Army for use or disposal.

Qualification and special skill badges may be accepted if awarded in recognition of meeting the criteria, as established by the awarding foreign government, for the specific award.

Foreign badges are authorized for wear only on service and dress uniforms. The German marksmanship award (Schützenschur) may be worn only by enlisted personnel, on the right side of the uniform with the upper portion attached under the center of the shoulder loop and the bottom portion attached under the lapel.

U.S. ARMY BADGES AND TABS

Badges and tabs are appurtenances of the uniform. In the eyes of their wearers, several badges have a significance equal to or greater than all but the highest decorations. There is no established precedence with badges as there is with decorations and service medals or ribbons. The badges are of three types: combat and special skill badges, marksmanship badges and tabs, and identification badges. Badges are awarded in recognition of attaining a high standard of proficiency in certain military skills. Subdued combat and special skill badges and the Ranger and Special Forces tabs are authorized on field uniforms.

COMBAT AND SPECIAL SKILL BADGES

The following badges are awarded to denote excellence in performance of duties under hazardous conditions and circumstances of extraordinary hardship as well as for special qualifications and successful completion of prescribed courses of training. (See chapter 8, AR 600-8-22, for details.)

Combat Infantryman Badge (CIB). Awarded to infantry personnel in the grade of colonel or below who, after December 6, 1941, satisfactorily perform duty while assigned or attached as a member of an infantry brigade, regiment, or smaller unit during any period that such unit is engaged in active ground combat. Members of attached Ranger companies are also eligible (paragraph 8.6, AR 600-8-22).

Combat Medical Badge (CMB). Awarded to medical personnel assigned or attached by appropriate orders to an infantry unit of brigade, regimental, or smaller size, or to a medical unit of company or smaller size, organic to an infantry unit of brigade or smaller size, during any period the infantry unit is engaged in actual ground combat, provided they are personally present and under fire during such ground combat: For the Global War on Terror, requirements are for medical personnel assigned or attached to or under operational control of any ground combat arms units (not to include members assigned or attached to aviation units) of brigade or smaller size, who satisfactorily perform medical duties while the unit is engaged in active ground combat, provided they are personally present and under fire. Retroactive awards are not authorized for service prior to September 18, 2001 (paragraph 8.7, AR 600-8-22).

Combat Action Badge. Awarded to any soldier performing assigned duties in an area where hostile fire pay or imminent danger pay is authorized, who is personally present and actively engaging or being engaged by the enemy, and performing satisfactorily in accordance with the prescribed rules of engagement, according to its authorizing language. Lastly, the soldier must not be assigned/attached to a unit that would qualify the soldier for the CIB/CMB.

Stars for Combat Infantryman Badge, Combat Medical Badge, and Combat Action Badge. The second and succeeding awards of the Combat Infantryman, the Combat Medical, and the Combat Action Badges, made to recognize participation and qualification in additional declared wars, are indicated by the addition of stars to the basic badges.

Expert Infantryman Badge. Awarded to infantry personnel of the active Army, ARNG, and USAR who satisfactorily complete prescribed proficiency tests (paragraph 8.8, AR 600-8-22).

Expert Field Medical Badge. Awarded to Army Medical Service personnel who satisfactorily complete prescribed proficiency tests (paragraph 8.9, AR 600-8-22).

Army Astronaut Badge. The Army Astronaut Badge has been added to the authorized special skill badges, but the requirements for award of this badge are not stated in the regulations. These badges are awarded in three degrees: basic, senior, and master.

Army Aviation Badges. There are nine badges relating to Army aviation—three each for Army aviators, flight surgeons, and aircraft crewmen—in the degrees of basic, senior, and master.

The *Master Army Aviator Badge,* the *Senior Army Aviator Badge,* and the *Army Aviator Badge* are awarded upon satisfactory completion of prescribed training and proficiency tests as outlined in AR 600-105.

The *Master Aircraft Crewman Badge,* the *Senior Aircraft Crewman Badge,* and the *Aircraft Crewman Badge* are authorized for award to enlisted personnel who meet the prescribed requirements (paragraph 8.24, AR 688-8-22.).

Glider Badge. This badge is no longer awarded but is still authorized for wear by individuals who were previously awarded the badge (paragraph 8.29, AR 600-8-22).

Parachutist Badges. To be awarded the *Master Parachutist Badge*, an individual must meet the following criteria: have participated in sixty-five jumps, twenty-five with combat equipment, four at night, and five mass tactical jumps; have graduated as jumpmaster or served as jumpmaster on one or more combat jumps or on thirty-three noncombat jumps; have been rated excellent in character and efficiency; and have served on jump status for not less than thirty-six months (paragraph 8.13, AR 600-8-22).

For the *Senior Parachutist Badge,* an individual must meet the following criteria: have been rated excellent in character and efficiency with participation in thirty jumps, including fifteen jumps made with combat equipment, two night jumps, and two mass tactical jumps; have graduated from a jumpmaster course or served as jumpmaster on one or more combat jumps or fifteen non-combat jumps; and have served on jump status for not less than twenty-four months (paragraph 8.12, AR 600-8-22).

The *Parachutist Badge* is awarded for satisfactory completion of the course given by the Airborne Department of the Infantry School or while assigned or attached to an airborne unit or for participation in at least one combat jump (paragraph 8.11, AR 600-8-22).

Combat Parachutist Badge. Participation in a combat parachute jump entitles the individual to wear a bronze star, or stars, affixed to the Parachutist Badge.

Pathfinder Badge. Awarded upon successful completion of the Pathfinder course conducted at the Infantry School (paragraph 8.22, AR 600-8-22).

Air Assault Badge. Awarded to personnel who have satisfactorily completed either the Training and Doctrine Command (TRADOC) prescribed training course or the standard air assault course while assigned or attached to the 101st Air Assault Division since April 1, 1974 (paragraph 8.23, AR 600-8-23).

Diver Badge. Awarded after satisfactory completion of prescribed proficiency tests (AR 611-75). Five badges are authorized for enlisted personnel (paragraph 8.17, AR 600-8-22).

Driver and Mechanic Badge. Awarded only to enlisted personnel to denote a high degree of skill in the operation and maintenance of motor vehicles (paragraph 8.28, AR 600-8-22).

Explosive Ordnance Disposal Badges. There are three badges under this heading, any of which may be awarded to soldiers: *Master Explosive Ordnance Disposal Badge, Senior Explosive Ordnance Disposal Badge,* and *Explosive Ordnance Disposal Badge.* They are awarded to individuals assigned to duties involving the removal and disposition of explosive ammunition under hazardous conditions (paragraph 8.18, AR 600-8-22). This is now a Group 3 badge.

Nuclear Reactor Operator Badges. The *Shift Supervisor Badge,* the *Operator First Class Badge,* and the *Operator Basic Badge* were awarded upon completing the Nuclear Power Plant Operators Course or equivalent training and after operating nuclear power plants for specific periods. These badges are no longer awarded but are still authorized for wear by individuals to whom they were previously awarded (paragraph 8.30, AR 600-8-22).

Parachute Rigger Badge. Awarded to any individual who successfully completes the Parachute Rigger Course conducted by the U.S. Army Quartermaster School and who holds a Parachute Rigger MOS or skill identifier (paragraph 8.14, AR 600-8-22).

Physical Fitness Training Badge. This badge is awarded to soldiers who obtain a minimum score of 270 on the Army Physical Fitness Test (APFT) and who meet the weight-control requirements of AR 600-9 (paragraph 8.48, AR 600-8-22).

Special Forces Tab. The Commander, U.S. Army John F. Kennedy Special Warfare Center (USAJFKSWC), Fort Bragg, NC 28307-5000, may award the Special Forces Tab to any individual who has successfully completed the Special Forces Qualification Course or the Special Forces Officer Course. The Special Forces Tab may be awarded to any person on active duty, active status in the reserve components, in retired status, or honorably discharged who meets the appropriate criteria listed in AR 600-8-22.

Ranger Tab. Awarded to any person who successfully completes a Ranger course conducted by the Infantry School or who was awarded the CIB while serving during WWII as a member of the 1st through 6th Ranger Battalions or the 5307th Composite Group (paragraph 8.46, AR 600-8-22).

Special Forces Tab. Awarded to any person who successfully completes the Special Forces Qualification Course conducted by the Special Forces School of the Special Warfare Center. This tab also may be awarded for former wartime service (paragraph 8.47, AR 600-8-22).

Sapper Tab. After successful completion of a Sapper leaders course conducted by the U.S. Army Engineer School or retroactively, the Sapper tab may be awarded to any person successfully completing the Sapper Leaders Course on or after June 14, 1985.

MARKSMANSHIP BADGES AND TABS

These badges and tabs include basic marksmanship qualification badges, excellence in competition badges, distinguished designation badges, the *U.S. Distinguished International Shooter Badge,* and the *President's Hundred Tab.*

Only members of the armed forces of the United States and civilian citizens of the United States are eligible for these qualification badges. Qualification badges for marksmanship are of three types: basic qualification, excellence in competition, and distinguished designation. *Basic Qualification Badges* (including *Expert, Sharpshooter,* and *Marksman Badges*) are awarded to those individuals who attain the qualification score prescribed in the appropriate field manual for the weapon concerned. *Excellence in Competition Badges* are awarded to individuals in recognition of an eminent degree of achievement in firing the rifle or pistol. *Distinguished Designation Badges* are awarded to individuals in recognition of a preeminent degree of achievement in target practice firing with the military service rifle or pistol (paragraph 8.44, AR 600-8-22).

The *Distinguished International Shooter Badge* is awarded to military or civilian personnel in recognition of an outstanding degree of achievement in international competition (paragraph 8.50, AR 600-8-22).

A *President's Hundred Tab* is awarded each person who qualifies among the top one hundred contestants in the President's Match held annually at the National Rifle Matches (paragraph 8.51, AR 600-8-22).

IDENTIFICATION BADGES

Identification badges are worn to signify special duties.

Presidential Service Identification Badge. The Presidential Service Certificate and the Presidential Service Badge were established by Executive Order 11174, September 1, 1964. The Presidential Service Certificate is awarded in the name of the president of the United States as public evidence of deserved honor and distinction to members of the armed forces who have been assigned duty in the White House for at least one year after January 20, 1961. It is awarded to Army members by the Secretary of the Army upon recommendation of the military aide to the president. The Presidential Service Badge is issued to members of the armed forces who have been awarded the Presidential Service Certificate. Once this badge is awarded, it may be worn as a permanent part of the uniform (paragraph 8.32, AR 600-8-22).

Vice Presidential Service Identification Badge. The Vice Presidential Service Badge was established by Executive Order 11544, July 8, 1970. It may be awarded upon recommendation of the military assistant to the vice president and may be worn as a permanent part of the uniform (paragraph 8.33, AR 600-8-22).

Secretary of Defense Identification Badge. Military personnel who have been assigned to duty and have served not less than one year after January 13, 1961, in the office of the secretary of defense are eligible for this badge. Once awarded, it may be worn as a permanent part of the uniform. It also is authorized for temporary wear by personnel assigned to specified offices of the Secretary of Defense (paragraph 8.34, AR 600-8-22).

Joint Chiefs of Staff Identification Badge. This badge may be awarded to military personnel who have been assigned to duty and who have served not less than one year after January 16, 1961, in a position of responsibility under the direct cognizance of the Joint Chiefs of Staff. Once awarded, the badge may be worn as a permanent part of the uniform (paragraph 8.35, AR 600-8-22).

Army Staff Identification Badge. This badge has been awarded by the Army since 1920 and is the oldest of the five types of identification badges now authorized for officers. It was instituted to give a permanent means of identification to those commissioned officers who had been selected for duty on the War Department General Staff, with recommendation for award based upon performance of duty. It has been continued under the present departmental organization.

Between September 30, 1979, and May 28, 1985, the badge could be awarded to the sergeant major of the Army and to other senior NCOs (SGM

E-9) assigned to duty with the same staff units. Effective May 28, 1985, qualifying service must be of at least one year while assigned to permanent duty on the Army General Staff or assigned to the Office of the Secretary of the Army. Once awarded, this badge may be worn as a permanent part of the uniform (paragraph 8.36, AR 600-8-22).

Guard, Tomb of the Unknown Soldier Identification Badge (paragraph 8.37, AR 600-8-22).

Army ROTC Nurse Cadet Program Identification Badge (paragraph 8.38, AR 600-8-22).

Drill Sergeant Identification Badge (paragraph 8.39, AR 600-8-22).

U.S. Army Recruiter Identification Badge (paragraph 8.40, AR 600-8-22).

Army National Guard Recruiter Identification Badge (paragraph 8.42, AR 600-8-22).

U.S. Army Reserve Recruiter Identification Badge (paragraph 8.43, AR 600-8-22).

Career Counselor Badge (paragraph 8.41, AR 600-8-22).

APPURTENANCES

Appurtenances are devices affixed to service or suspension ribbons or worn in place of medals or ribbons. They are worn to denote additional awards, participation in a specific event, or other distinguished characteristics of the award.

Oak-Leaf Cluster

A bronze or silver twig of four oak leaves with three acorns on the stem, thirteen thirty-seconds inch in length for the suspension ribbon and five-sixteenths inch in length for the service ribbon, is issued in lieu of a decoration for second or succeeding awards of decorations (other than the Air Medal) and service medals. A silver oak-leaf cluster is issued to be worn in lieu of five bronze clusters. Five one-sixteenth-inch oak-leaf clusters, joined together in series of two, three, and four clusters, are authorized for optional purchase and wear on service ribbons.

Numerals

Arabic numerals three-thirteenths inch high are issued in lieu of a medal or ribbon for second and succeeding awards of the Air Medal, the Humanitarian Service Medal, the Multinational Force and Observers Medal, the Army Reserve Components Overseas Training Ribbon, and the Overseas Service Ribbon. The numeral worn on the NCO Professional Development Ribbon denotes the highest completed level of NCO development. The numerals are worn centered on the suspension ribbon of the medal or the ribbon bar.

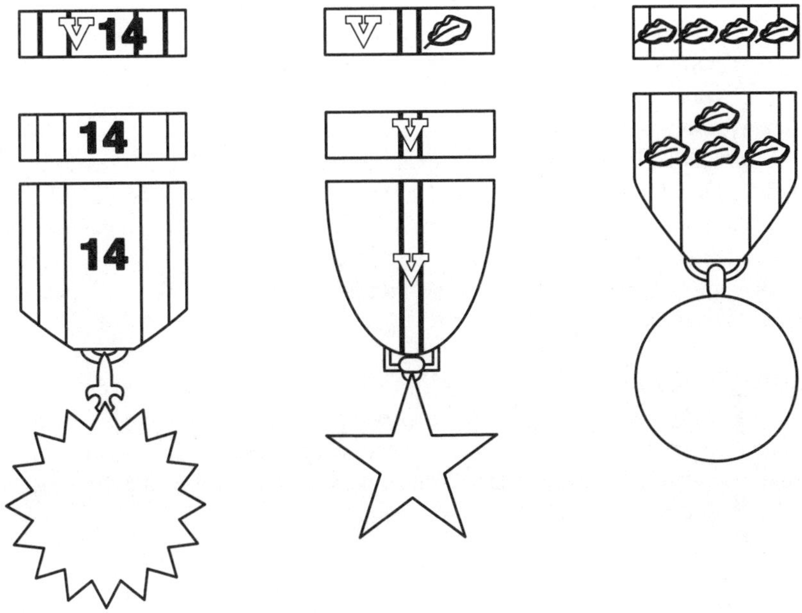

Appurtenances of medals and ribbons.

V Device

The V Device is a bronze letter V, one-quarter inch high with serifs at the top of the members (that is, the little strokes at the tops of the arms of the V that look like little rectangles). The V Device denotes awards of a medal for heroism and may be awarded with the Bronze Star Medal, the Air Medal, the Joint Service Commendation Medal (when the award is for acts or services involving direct participation in combat operations), and the Army Commendation Medal.

Clasps

Clasps are authorized to be worn on the Good Conduct Medal, the Army of Occupation Medal, and the Antarctic Service Medal.

Service Stars

The service star is a bronze or silver five-pointed star three-sixteenths inch in diameter. Three-sixteenths-inch service stars joined together in a series of two, three, and four stars are authorized for optional purchase and wear on service ribbons. Service stars, signifying participation in a combat campaign, are authorized for wear on the Armed Forces Expeditionary Medal and the Vietnam Service Medal. (Note: Bronze and silver stars are worn on U.S. Navy decorations in the same manner as oak-leaf clusters are worn on Army and Air Force decorations.)

Arrowhead

The arrowhead is a bronze replica of an Indian arrowhead, one-quarter inch high. It denotes participation in a combat parachute jump, combat glider landing, or amphibious assault landing, while assigned or attached as a member of an organized force carrying out an assigned tactical mission. It is worn on the service and suspension ribbons of the Vietnam Service Medal and the Armed Forces Expeditionary Medal.

SERVICE RIBBONS

Service ribbons are identical to the suspension ribbons of the medals they represent and are mounted on bars equipped with attaching devices; they are issued for wear in place of medals. The service ribbon for the Medal of Honor is the same color as the neck band, showing five stars in the form of a letter M.

MINIATURE MEDALS

Miniature replicas of all medals except the Medal of Honor are authorized for wear on specified uniforms, such as the blue and white mess uniforms, in lieu of the issued medals. Miniatures of decorations are issued only to foreign nationals. Awards issued by the secretary of defense include miniature medals.

LAPEL BUTTONS

Lapel buttons are authorized for wear on the left lapel of civilian clothing only. They are available for service ribbons and other decorations and badges. Included in this category are the Army Lapel Button, which is awarded to any soldier (except retirees) who completed nine months' honorable active federal service after April 1, 1984, and the U.S. Army Retired Lapel Button.

CERTIFICATES AND LETTERS

As a senior NCO, you may write and sign letters of appreciation and commendation for other enlisted personnel. Frequently, soldiers will ask for these accolades, but you should be constantly alert to any circumstances that may authorize a letter of appreciation or commendation for a deserving individual. When writing these letters, you should give them your best effort and put as much into composing them as you would into the writing of a recommendation for a decoration. Remember that a letter or certificate from an overseas commander or brigade or higher CSM is worth five promotion points.

An important responsibility is to see that your commander is aware of those deeds that deserve special recognition, and you should not be hesitant to recommend personnel for consideration. But do the commander a favor: Prepare a draft citation or letter and offer it along with your verbal recommendations. The CO may sign the final product, but if the person being recommended is one of your soldiers, you should write the original draft—you know your soldiers better than the commander does.

Certificates and letters may be nothing more than pats on the back. Nevertheless, they go a long way toward boosting the morale of most recipients, and their judicious use is a good way to recognize faithful and competent service.

Certificate of Achievement

Commanders may recognize periods of faithful service, acts, or achievements that do meet the standards required for decorations by issuing to individual military personnel a *Certificate of Achievement,* DA Form 2442.

Certificates of achievement are awarded under local criteria and may be used for awarding the Good Conduct Medal, for participation in the Department of the Army Suggestion Program, or to recognize meritorious acts or service.

Letters of Commendation and Appreciation

Acts or services that do not meet the criteria for decorations or a certificate of achievement may be recognized by written expressions of commendation or appreciation. These letters are typed on letterhead stationery and do not contain formalized printing, seals, or other distinguishing features that depart from normal letter form.

18

Military and Social Customs

The customs of the service make up the unwritten "common law" of the Army. Customs are rich in tradition, and knowing what they are and observing them should be second nature.

Of course, times are changing. Today, hardly anyone remembers the ancient taboos against soldiers carrying packages or pushing baby carriages while in uniform. But customs that are still accepted should be observed, and the soldier who flouts them should be made to understand just how important it is to maintain customs and tradition.

Following are some customs observed today:

- Men do not carry an umbrella while in uniform. AR 670-1 does not authorize an umbrella as part of the male uniform. Women may carry and use umbrellas.
- Never sit on another soldier's bed or bunk in the barracks without permission.
- Never criticize a subordinate NCO in front of his or her troops.
- Never criticize the Army in front of civilians.
- Never accept gifts from subordinates.
- Never go over the heads of superiors.
- Never offer excuses.
- Act upon the commander's "desires" or "suggestions" as if they were orders (which they are, really, but politely phrased).
- Never "wear" a superior's rank by saying something like, "The commander wants this done right away." Phrase the request as your own.
- Never turn and walk the other way to avoid giving the hand salute.
- Never run indoors to avoid standing reveille or retreat.
- With the exception of on-the-spot corrections of military courtesy and discipline breaches, give orders to another NCO's troops only when absolutely necessary for mission accomplishment.
- Never appear in uniform while under the influence of alcohol.
- Treat others with the same dignity and respect as you expect to be treated.

Remember these two responses to questions or orders from your superiors, and you will never go wrong: "I don't know, sir, but I'll find out," and "I'll do it or have it done."

ETIQUETTE

Etiquette is the set of rules or forms for manners and ceremonies established as acceptable or required in professional or official life. As a professional NCO, you must know these rules as they pertain to official social events. Guidance set forth in this section goes hand in hand with courtesy, and if you take courtesy to others as your guiding principle, no matter what the situation, you can never go wrong. Your soldiers look to you to set the example both on duty and off and will follow your lead, whether you realize it or not.

Proper Speech

You should make every effort to develop and maintain good speech habits.

Speech begins with a good vocabulary and an understanding of grammar and pronunciation. Constantly misusing and mispronouncing words in front of your soldiers will undermine your authority and cause you to lose their respect. Lighten up on the profanity. A few well-chosen words are much more effective than a daily dose of four-letter words. A good speaker is listened to and understood.

Being able to converse in an interesting, intelligent, and entertaining manner is a social asset that will reflect favorably upon you. Never discuss your personal or business affairs at social gatherings. Never gossip, criticize others, boast, or engage in arguments.

Telephone Etiquette

Observe proper telephone courtesy at all times.

When answering the phone, identify your unit or office first and then give your rank and name in a clear and normal tone of voice. If you are the first sergeant of Alpha Company, do not simply bellow your rank into the telephone, but give the caller the same courtesy you demand of your troops when they answer the telephone.

Pay attention to the caller's rank, title, and name, and use them, wherever appropriate, during the conversation. If the person being called is not in, offer to take a message or refer the caller to another party who may be able to help. Listen patiently and politely. Speak distinctly and with confidence.

When calling someone else, give your rank and name first. If you should reach discourteous or bewildered people on the other end of the line, bear with them. It does no good for you to lose your patience. Should you dial a wrong number, it is impolite to hang up without saying anything. The proper procedure is to excuse yourself for the interruption and then check the number you have dialed. Never ask, "What number is this?" but say "Have I reached 979-9383?"

Never let a telephone ring endlessly because you happen to be talking to someone on another line. Ensure that all calls are answered within four rings. If a phone near you is not answered by then, pick it up yourself.

Etiquette in the Workplace

Good manners are never out of place. Never sit with your feet on your desk. Never sit at your desk reading non-job-related materials. The worst impression you can give a visitor is to be seen reading a novel with your feet propped up on the desk.

When a superior who is not your immediate supervisor enters your work area, you are obliged to stand. And when someone comes to see you, on business or just calling, you should stand and greet that person. If you cannot stand—for example, if you are on the telephone—indicate by a nod of the head or a gesture with a free hand that the visitor should be seated. Never keep a person standing unless he or she is to be disciplined.

If coffee or tea is available, offer it to your visitor. This may not always be appropriate, as when an NCO from another staff section drops by to deliver a report, but if the person is a friend or well known to you, make the offer a standard part of your greeting. Never lean or sit on another person's desk. If the person you are visiting is thoughtless enough not to offer you a seat, remain standing.

You should consider that a visit in person takes precedence over a telephone call. If you happen to be on the telephone when a visitor arrives, finish your conversation quickly and call the other party back later.

It is best not to eat where you work. Give yourself a break. Find a few minutes to step outside your work area, find a quiet spot, and eat your lunch there.

Be tolerant. At work certain people just do not get along, generally for the most frivolous reasons. Over a period of time, minor problems can turn into animosity. Set the example. If you encounter someone you dislike, suppress your intolerance. Allowing other people to annoy you is evidence of your own lack of self-discipline.

SALUTING

The hand salute is a formal sign of courtesy between soldiers. It is both recognition of rank and authority and a greeting exchanged between members of a unique professional organization with special rules and codes of conduct. Precisely whom to salute is defined in AR 600-25, *Salutes, Honors, and Visits of Courtesy.* But the best rule to follow when saluting is "When in doubt, whip it out." The salute is a recognized form of greeting, and no soldier should feel embarrassment because he or she may have saluted someone who is not strictly entitled to it by AR 600-25.

All soldiers in uniform are required to salute when they meet and recognize persons entitled to the salute. Salutes are exchanged between officers (commissioned and warrant) and enlisted personnel. Salutes are exchanged with personnel of the Army, Navy, Air Force, Marine Corps, and Coast Guard entitled to the salute. It is customary to salute officers of friendly foreign nations as well. Civilians may be saluted by persons in uniform when appropriate, but the uniform hat or cap should not be raised as a form of salutation. Salutes are not required if either the senior or subordinate or both are in civilian attire.

Soldiers under arms give the salute prescribed for the weapon with which they are armed. The practice of saluting others in official vehicles is appropriate and should be observed. Salutes are not required to be given by or to personnel who are driving or riding in privately owned vehicles except by gate guards.

Don't salute when driving any type of vehicle. Salutes are not required in public areas, such as theaters, outdoor athletic facilities, or other situations when the act would be inappropriate or impractical.

Accompanying the hand salute with an appropriate greeting, such as "Good morning, sir," or "Good morning, ma'am," is proper. Personnel do not salute indoors except when reporting to a superior officer.

The salute is given when the person approaching or being approached is recognized as being authorized a salute, usually at six paces. The officer is obliged to return the salute.

If a superior remains in your area but does not engage in conversation, he is saluted only once, upon the initial greeting; should a superior engage you in conversation, however, then you must salute when he finishes talking to you and departs.

Always salute with precision and enthusiasm. Never salute with anything in your hands or mouth. Never duck your head when you salute, but always keep your chin up and your back straight. Give a greeting clearly, in a normal tone of voice. You should not greet people in the same tone of voice you use when shouting out commands on the drill field.

Do not salute when in the following situations:

- A prisoner.
- Marching; the officer or NCO in charge salutes for everyone.
- Indoors, except when reporting or on guard duty.
- Carrying articles or occupied so that saluting would be awkward.
- When it is inappropriate to do so, such as when assisting a superior who is injured.
- In ranks; the officer or NCO in charge will salute for the whole formation.
- Engaged in athletics or sports.
- In places of public assembly or conveyance.
- Maneuvering against a hostile force or participating in field training.

"Outdoors" may actually be indoors, such as in gymnasium buildings used for drill halls and other roofed structures commonly used for drilling and exercising. Theater marquees and covered walkways open on both sides are considered outdoors, and it is appropriate to salute when underneath them.

Saluting in Groups

Individuals in formations never salute except at the command *present arms.* The officer or NCO in charge does the saluting for the entire group. If the troops are not at attention when it becomes necessary to salute a senior, the person in charge calls them to attention before saluting.

A soldier in formation, not standing at attention, comes to the position of attention when spoken to by a senior.

When a group not in formation is approached by a superior, the first person seeing him or her calls *attention,* and all come to attention and salute, unless they are at work or engaged in organized athletics.

Saluting on Guard

In garrison, guards armed with a rifle halt and face toward the music when the national anthem or "To the Color" is played, or face toward the person or the colors to be saluted, and present arms. When challenging, the first salute is given when the officer has been recognized and advanced.

A sentinel armed with a pistol gives the hand salute, except when challenging, and then the weapon is held at the raise *pistol position* and kept there until the challenged party departs.

If the officer to whom a sentinel may be talking salutes a senior, the sentinel also salutes. Wherever he is posted, indoors or outdoors, a guard or a sentinel salutes all officers, except when saluting would endanger the officers or interfere with duty performance.

Reporting

If you are reporting to your commander, salute and formally report. If you are told to report to a senior officer to discuss an ongoing project, whether you salute depends on the protocol considered acceptable on the particular staff and the frequency with which you visit.

When reporting to a commander, a salute is always given at the report and again when dismissed. When reporting indoors and without arms, first remove your hat and then knock on the commander's door. When given permission to enter, advance to within two paces from the commander's desk, halt, salute, and make your report: "Sir [or Ma'am], Sergeant Smith reporting as directed." Hold the salute until it is returned. After stating your business, salute again, and exit the room.

When reporting while under arms, never remove your hat. If carrying a rifle, enter with the weapon at the trail and give the rifle salute at *order arms.* Otherwise, give the hand salute. Outdoors, a soldier may approach an officer with the weapon at either trail or right shoulder arms and execute the rifle salute at order or right shoulder arms.

FORMS OF ADDRESS

Either the rank or title "sir" or "ma'am" should be used when addressing an officer or a civilian.

Privates and privates first class are addressed as "private." Corporals and specialists are called "corporal" and "specialist" respectively. Sergeants through the rank of master sergeant are referred to as "sergeant," except first sergeants, who are called "first sergeant." Likewise, sergeants major and command sergeants major (including the sergeant major of the Army) are called "sergeant major."

BUGLE CALLS

These signals to the troops are transmitted on the bugle. Traditionally, Army bugle calls have been divided into four major categories:

- Alarm ("Fire," "To Horse").
- Formation ("Adjutant's Call," "Assembly").
- Service ("Church Call," "Fatigue," "First Sergeant's Call," "Mess Call," "Officer's Call," "Recall," "Retreat," "Reveille," "School Call," "Sick Call," "Taps," "Tattoo," "To the Color").
- Warning ("Boots and Saddles," "Drill Call," "First Call," "Guard Call," "Stable Call," "To Quarters").

Bugle calls help order the activities of soldiers throughout the day. At most installations, the few calls that are used are played from recordings on a public address system, although a live bugler is sometimes used to sound retreat and reveille.

Following are brief explanations of some of the more common calls in the normal order they are sounded. The music for Army bugle calls can be found in *The 1863 U.S. Infantry Tactics* (Stackpole Books, 2002).

First Call

This call is actually the first bugle call of the day. It is given as a warning that reveille is to take place within a few minutes.

Reveille

The word "reveille" is originally from the Latin *evigilare,* to watch or to wake. The custom of sounding some sort of call to signify the beginning of the day is very ancient. The British adopted the practice from the French and were calling it "revelly" as early as 1644. Although "First Call" is actually the initial bugle call of the Army day, reveille has come into our vocabulary as the word for the bugle call that signifies to awake.

Mess Call

In former days, this call was affectionately dubbed "Soupy."

Retreat

The term "retreat" is taken from the French word *retraite* and refers to the evening ceremony. The bugle call sounded at retreat was first used in the French army and dates back to the Crusades. Retreat was sounded at sunset to notify sentries to start challenging until sunrise and to tell the rank and file to go to their quarters. Retreat is a ceremony in which the unit honors the U.S. flag when it is lowered in the evening.

To the Color

This call is the bugle call played immediately after retreat. The first note of "To the Color" signals that the flag is to be lowered. While this call is being sounded, military personnel in uniform give the appropriate salute. On many posts, the interval between the end of retreat and the beginning of "To the Color" is used to fire a salute cannon. This call was adopted by the U.S. Army in 1835, replacing the cavalry "To the Standard."

Tattoo

This call is usually played at or very near 2100 hours, and it signifies that lights should be off within fifteen minutes. It is the longest bugle call in the U.S. Army—twenty-eight bars. The first eight bars are from the French *"L'extinction des feux"* ("Lights Out") and the following twenty bars are a British Army infantry tattoo.

The commonly accepted origin of the taptoo is from the practice in seventeenth-century armies of provost marshals visiting the civilian inns and taverns at night, informing the proprietors when it was time for the troops to return to garrison. Eventually, that custom gave way to a party of drummers parading around a garrison at the same time each night, beating a signal to inform soldiers it was time for them to return to quarters. The first beat of the drum as the musicians fell in was known as "first post," the final beat as "last post." "Last post" is sometimes used today as another name for a military obituary.

Taps

This call is the last bugle call of the military day. "Taps" is also traditionally played at military funerals. Originally, the U.S. Army used the French *"L'extinction des feux"* to end the day. The music for "Taps" was written by Maj. Gen. Daniel Butterfield in July 1862 at Harrison's Landing, Virginia, when he was a member of the Army of the Potomac during the Peninsular campaign of the Civil War.

SOCIAL FUNCTIONS

Entertaining is part of military life, and over your career you will attend a variety of social functions, from the very casual to the very formal. Protocol is designed to let us know what to expect in a given situation. For most of us it is a combination of military traditions, etiquette, and common sense. Knowing some of these guidelines will help you feel more comfortable in any given situation. When in doubt, take your cue from what someone senior is doing. They might not always be right, but at least you will be in good company.

In the course of your military life and especially as you become more senior, you will receive many invitations to social events, both military and civilian. Keeping a few main points in mind will help you avoid misunderstandings and hurt feelings. At times you will find that an invitation will conflict with another obligation or interest. When it comes to deciding which function to attend, put your family first. Hail and farewells are usually held monthly and probably will be your next priority. These get-togethers are opportunities for you to get to know other people in the company or battalion.

If you are invited to dinner at the sergeant major's house, remember that he and his wife have been entertaining many more years than you have. Over their years in the military, they have developed a style that is comfortable for them. Do not be afraid to reciprocate with an invitation because your "picnic in the backyard with the kids" might fall short. Your leadership will be happy for the chance to get to know you better in any setting.

R.S.V.P.

"R.S.V.P." means "please respond" and "let us know if you are coming." If you receive an invitation to an event, answer yes or no within forty-eight hours after receiving an invitation. If you are having trouble giving a response within this time frame, call the host to regret and explain your situation. Do not wait for your host to call you to see if you received an invitation or to ask if you are coming.

A small gift is always appreciated when visiting someone's home. This does not have to be expensive. A batch of muffins, homemade cookies, jellies, a bottle of wine, and flowers are all appropriate. It sends the message that you appreciate the invitation. A phone call or short "thank you" note afterwards thanking the hosts is always appropriate and sure to be appreciated.

TYPES OF FUNCTIONS

Cocktail Parties

Cocktails are usually served from 5:00 P.M. or 6:00 P.M. until 7:00 P.M. or 8:00 P.M. They are usually about two hours long. Hors d'oeuvres or appetizers are served. Plan for dressy attire for women and coat and tie for men unless special dress is requested on the invitation (Texas casual, aloha, beach).

Open House

This literally means the home is open to guests between set hours. Guests are free to arrive and depart between those hours. Check the invitation for dress.

Buffets

A buffet supper is a dinner party served buffet style. It is a convenient way to serve guests, especially a number of guests in a limited space. At a buffet supper, the plates, silverware, napkins, and platters of food are arranged on the dining room table or buffet table, and guests serve themselves. You also might be invited to someone's home for "heavy hors d'oeuvres," which is very similar to the buffet dinner. There is no need to eat before you go. At these functions, a variety of hors d'oeuvres will be served—from dips, to meats on small rolls, to desserts. Again, dress should be indicated on your invitation and could range from casual to informal.

Seated Dinners

These dinners may range from the very casual family style to the very formal, with place cards and many courses. Check your invitation for dress.

Hail and Farewells

Unit members and guests share the cost and planning of these get-togethers. They range from dinners at local restaurants, to picnics and barbecues, to treasure hunts. This is a time to welcome incoming members and farewell members who are leaving the unit. These get-togethers build unit spirit and camaraderie, and are successful only if everyone supports them and participates in them.

Promotion Party

A time-honored tradition is the promotion party, which is given by an officer or NCO or a group of people with similar dates of rank, shortly after the promotion. It does not have to be a fancy affair, but it provides a chance to invite friends and their spouses to share the good fortune.

Dining-In

The dining-in is an old military tradition that has been passed down from the British. As the most formal of events, a dining-in allows officers and NCOs of a unit to celebrate unit successes and to enjoy its traditions and heritage. It is strictly an officer/NCO affair. Dress for soldiers is usually dress blues or greens with a white shirt and bow tie.

Dining-Out

When spouses are invited to a dining-in, it becomes a dining-out. Dress for spouses is formal gowns or tuxedos; for soldiers, dress blues or greens with a white shirt and bow tie. All stand for the posting and retiring of the colors and for the invocation and toasts. Men and women stand and drink for all toasts, except women sit to the toast "to the ladies." If you do not drink alcoholic beverages, toast with the beverage of your choice or simply lift your glass as a token. You may also stand if the guest speaker receives a standing ovation.

Receptions

A reception is usually held in honor of a special guest or guests, or after a change of command. There may or may not be a receiving line. Guests should mingle and visit with other guests. Before departing, be sure to thank the hostess and host and bid good-bye to the guest of honor.

Receiving Lines

At official functions ranging from a change of command to a unit social, you may be invited to greet the host, hostess, or guest of honor in a receiving line. A receiving line is a formal way for the host and/or hostess to greet guests and to introduce other dignitaries in the line. It is especially important to be punctual, as sometimes units go through the line together. Keep these few pointers in mind. Set your drink and/or cigarette aside before going through the line. Except for receiving lines at the White House, diplomatic corps, and Air Force functions, the lady goes before the gentleman. The unit adjutant will look to you to give them your name. Do not shake this person's hand. Simply state your name. This person will turn to the guest of honor and pass your name along. You will shake hands with the rest of the people in the receiving line. You can greet them, welcome them, and wish them well in their new assignment. Do not talk long, even if you know the guest(s) of honor.

FLAGS, FLAG CUSTOMS, AND FLAG CEREMONIES

A "flag" is a general descriptive term for a cloth device with a distinguishing color or design that has a special meaning or serves as a signal. The flag of the United States, the white flag of truce, and weather flags are examples.

In the military service, the *color* is a flag of a dismounted unit; an *ensign* is a national flag; a *pennant* is a small triangular flag, usually flown for identification of a unit; a *standard* is a flag of a mounted unit; and a *guidon* is a swallow-tailed flag carried by Army units for identification, especially in drills and ceremonies.

The Flag of the United States

The flag of the United States is displayed at all Army installations. It represents the Union—the fifty stars on a field of blue. The field is always to the left of the observer because it is the "field of honor."

The flag should never be used as part of a costume or dress, or on a vehicle or float unless it is attached to a staff, nor should it be displayed as drapery. Bunting—strips of cloth in the colors of the flag—is used for draping and decoration. No lettering or any other kind of object should ever be placed on the flag, and its use in advertising is discouraged.

Soiled, torn, or weathered flags should be burned, privately.

Three different sizes of U.S. flags are flown on Army installations:

- *Post flag*. Flown in fair weather, except on those occasions when the garrison flag is prescribed. Its dimensions are nineteen feet fly by ten feet hoist.
- *Garrison flag*. Flown on holidays and important occasions. Its dimensions are thirty-eight feet fly by twenty feet hoist.
- *Storm flag*. Flown in lieu of the post flag in inclement weather. It is also used to drape caskets at a military funeral. Its dimensions are nine and one-fourth feet fly by five feet hoist.

Flag Displays

Officers look to NCOs for flag protocol, as they should; and the more senior an NCO becomes, the more AR 840-10, *Flags, Guidons, Streamers, Tabards, and Automobile and Aircraft Plates,* becomes a part of daily life. Although the regulation covers in depth the use and etiquette for flags, some commonsense rules need to be emphasized.

When displayed in a line, flags may be set up in one of two ways: from the flag's right to left (the most common method) or with the highest precedence flag in the center if no foreign national colors are present. When set up from right to left, the highest precedence flag always goes on the right of all other flags, but if you look at the flag display from the audience, the highest precedence flag (normally the U.S. flag) is on your far left; other flags extend to your right in descending precedence. When set up with the highest precedence flag in the center, other flags are placed, in descending precedence, first to the right, then to the left, alternating back and forth (see AR 840-10, figure 2-3).

Remember the following when displaying flags:

1. When the U.S. flag is displayed with foreign national flags, all flags will be comparable in size. The flagstaffs or flagpoles on which they are flown will be of equal height. The tops of all flags should be of equal distance from the ground (AR 840-10, paragraph 2-4b).
2. The flagstaff head (finial) is the decorative ornament at the top of a flagstaff. The only finials authorized on the flag by Army organizations are the
   a. Eagle (presidential flagstaffs)
   b. Spearhead (the only device used with Army flags)
   c. Acorn (markers and marking pennants flagstaffs)
   d. Ball (outdoor wall mounted for advertising or recruiting)
3. When displaying the Army flag, the Army's first and last streamers (Lexington 1775 is first) are always positioned at the center facing forward (AR 840-10, paragraph 6). Remember that the Army flag and all other organizational colors are not complete without their streamers.

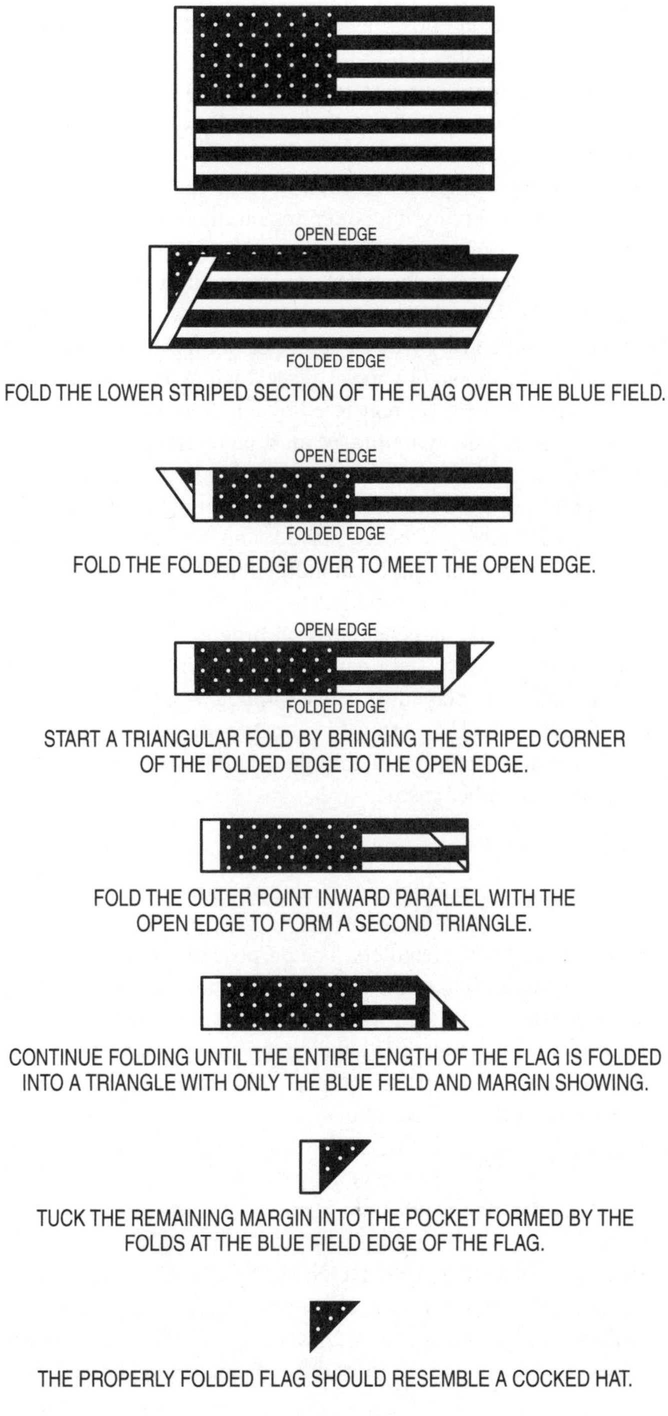

OPEN EDGE
FOLDED EDGE
FOLD THE LOWER STRIPED SECTION OF THE FLAG OVER THE BLUE FIELD.
OPEN EDGE
FOLDED EDGE
FOLD THE FOLDED EDGE OVER TO MEET THE OPEN EDGE.
OPEN EDGE
FOLDED EDGE
START A TRIANGULAR FOLD BY BRINGING THE STRIPED CORNER OF THE FOLDED EDGE TO THE OPEN EDGE.
FOLD THE OUTER POINT INWARD PARALLEL WITH THE OPEN EDGE TO FORM A SECOND TRIANGLE.
CONTINUE FOLDING UNTIL THE ENTIRE LENGTH OF THE FLAG IS FOLDED INTO A TRIANGLE WITH ONLY THE BLUE FIELD AND MARGIN SHOWING.
TUCK THE REMAINING MARGIN INTO THE POCKET FORMED BY THE FOLDS AT THE BLUE FIELD EDGE OF THE FLAG.
THE PROPERLY FOLDED FLAG SHOULD RESEMBLE A COCKED HAT.

Folding the U.S. flag.

4. Ensure all finials are positioned in the same direction. For most Army flags, this means that the flat portion of the finial is facing forward.
5. Ensure that general officer personal flags are hung on the staff right side up. When properly hung, the point of the star(s) will point to the right as the flag is viewed.
6. When using spreaders (horizontal devices that allow the flag to flair slightly, thereby giving it a better appearance) to display flags, ensure that the flag is draped across the spreader from the flag's left to right.

Remember also the following when rendering honors:

- The flag of the United States, the national color, and the national standard are not dipped by way of salute or compliment. An exception to this is the rule followed by naval vessels when, upon receiving a salute of this type from a vessel registered by a nation formally recognized by the United States, the compliment must be returned.
- The organizational color or standard may be dipped in salute in all military ceremonies while the U.S. national anthem, "To the Color," or a foreign national anthem is being played, and when giving honors to the organizational commander or an individual of higher grade, including a foreign dignitary of higher grade, but not otherwise.
- The U.S. Army flag is considered an organizational color and is also dipped when the U.S. national anthem, "To the Color," or a foreign national anthem is played. It is also dipped when giving honors to the chief of staff of the U.S. Army, his direct representative, or an individual of higher grade, including a foreign dignitary of equivalent or higher grade, but in no other case.

Flag Detail

Generally, a flag detail responsible for raising and lowering the national colors consists of one noncommissioned officer in charge (NCOIC), two halyard pullers, and two to eight flag handlers. The purpose of the handlers is to ensure correct folding and unfolding of the flag and to ensure that it does not touch the ground. Two handlers are needed when raising or lowering the storm flag, six handlers for the post flag, and eight handlers for the garrison flag.

Members of the flag detail are equipped according to local standing operating procedure and letter of instructions.

During the ceremony, the NCOIC subtly gives necessary commands or directives to ensure proper performance by the flag detail. On windy days, the NCOIC may assist the flag handlers in securing or folding the flag.

SURVIVOR ASSISTANCE AND HONORING THE DEAD

Chances are that at some point in your military career you will be detailed to act as a casualty notifier, survivor assistance officer (SAO), or body escort. You will find the experience one of the most difficult and trying duties you will ever face. Performing these duties well brings great satisfaction to you and comfort to the bereaved family.

Notification of Next of Kin

As a casualty notifier, you represent the secretary of the Army. You are expected to be courteous, helpful, and sympathetic. Your presence should soften the blow, if possible, and demonstrate the Army's concern.

Department of the Army policy is to make personal notification of the next of kin of all deceased and missing soldiers. The deceased soldier's desires for notification of next of kin listed on DD Form 93, *Record of Emergency Data,* will be followed.

Paragraph 5-4, AR 600-8-1, prescribes that enlisted personnel in the senior grades may be used as notifiers providing that an officer is not available and the grade of the enlisted person used is equal to or higher than that of the deceased.

If the person to be notified is not fluent in English, a qualified interpreter should accompany you. The linguist should interpret only what is spoken between you and the next of kin. Contact your installation personnel officer in cases that require a linguist.

Be prepared for an adverse reaction on the part of the person being notified. If you know beforehand that the next of kin has a medical problem, consult the family doctor. If one cannot be identified, consult any physician in the area where notification is to be made. If you feel it is best, get the doctor to go with you when you make notification. You might find it helpful to have with you the telephone numbers for a local hospital, ambulance service, and fire department rescue squad.

If the person being notified suffers medically as a result of the news, you must keep your casualty commander notified. Additionally, all personal notifications must be confirmed promptly by commercial telegram. These details are set forth in Army Regulation 600-8-1, *Army Casualty Operations/Assistance/-Insurance.*

Be careful to observe the following basic guidelines:

- Present the best possible military appearance. Be in a Class A uniform.
- Make your visit promptly after receiving casualty information, but only during the hours from 0600 to 2200, unless otherwise directed.
- Be natural in speech, manner, and method of delivery. What you say is of the utmost importance.
- If the next of kin is alone at the time of your visit, offer to call someone or ask a neighbor to step in.
- You may inform the next of kin that survivor's assistance will be rendered, but do not specify date or time on which such a visit will be made.
- Advise the next of kin that a confirmation of your visit will be sent by telegram.

- In cases of death, if the remains have been recovered, tell the next of kin that a message on the disposition of the remains will be coming. If the remains have not been recovered, tell the next of kin how memorial services are conducted (see AR 600-8-1).
- If the next of kin are not at home when you visit, make an effort to locate them, using neighbors or local authorities, as necessary. Be most discreet so as not to compromise the purpose of your visit, especially if you deal with friends or neighbors. Should the next of kin be on vacation and too far away for you to carry out your visit, redirect action at once by telephone through the casualty reporting chain of command.
- Once you begin notification action, you must continue to completion.
- You may inform the primary next of kin that personal notification will be made to the secondary next of kin if required. When notifying the secondary kin, you may inform that the primary kin have already been notified.
- Inform the next of kin that a letter from the soldier's commander will give more complete details (see chapter 6, AR 600-8-1).

Be careful to observe the following prohibitions:

- DO NOT notify by telephone, unless there are indications the family will receive the information through unofficial sources.
- DO NOT call for an appointment before making the visit.
- DO NOT hold notes or a prepared speech in your hand when approaching the residence of the next of kin.
- DO NOT disclose the purpose of your visit or the contents of your message except to the next of kin.
- DO NOT leave word with neighbors or others to have the next of kin contact you, should you find them away from home.
- DO NOT speak hurriedly.
- DO NOT pass on any gory or embarrassing details.
- DO NOT use military jargon when speaking with the next of kin.
- DO NOT touch the next of kin unless there is extreme shock or fainting.
- DO NOT discuss entitlements. Advise that the SAO will be in touch.
- DO NOT discuss disposition of remains or personal effects.
- DO NOT inform the secondary kin that they will receive an SAO visit.
- DO NOT commit either your organization or the Department of the Army to carrying out any action or obtaining any information by a given time.
- DO NOT, under ANY circumstances, "fortify" yourself with alcohol or any other substance before making the visit.

Survivor Assistance

As a survivor assistance officer (SAO), you are charged by the Secretary of the Army to render assistance necessary to settle the personal affairs of a deceased soldier. Keep the thoughts and feelings of the next of kin uppermost in your mind at all times. Above all, be prepared. Nothing can reflect more adversely upon you than to demonstrate ignorance or indecision when dealing with the next of kin. Should you be asked questions for which you do not know the answers, remain cool and assure the next of kin that you will get the answers. A thorough study of the references given to you by your local casualty office should ensure that you are not caught unprepared for any contingency.

Your point of contact as an SAO is the local casualty section. You may receive assistance from the staff judge advocate, surgeon, provost marshal, public affairs officer, and finance, housing, and transportation officers. You are expected to make contacts with these officers, as required, without referral by the casualty section.

The casualty branch of your local adjutant general office should furnish you a complete packet relating to your duties as notifier/SAO at the time you receive a case for action. This packet should contain details pertaining to the services available to you locally to assist you in the completion of your duties. The details should include a telephone directory of those services, as well as most of the information sources listed below:

AR 37-104-3, *Military Pay and Allowances Procedures: Joint Uniform Military Pay System (JUMPS—Army).*

AR 40-121, *Uniformed Services Health Care Benefits Program.*

AR 600-8-1, *Army Casualty and Memorial Affairs and Line of Duty Investigations.*

AR 600-8-22, *Military Awards.*

AR 600-25, *Salutes, Honors, and Visits of Courtesy.*

AR 608-2, *Servicemen's Group Life Insurance (SGLI); Veterans Group Life Insurance (VGLI).*

AR 608-50, *Legal Assistance.*

AR 640-3, *Personnel Records and Identification of Individuals, Identification Cards, Tags, and Badges.*

DA Pam 55-2, *Personal Property Shipping Information; It's Your Move.*

DOD Military Pay and Allowances Entitlements Manual.

BODY ESCORT DETAIL

Body escort detail is an extremely important duty. Soldiers selected to act as escort represent the Army and the United States. The escort's mission is to see that the remains of the deceased reach the final destination chosen by the next of kin and that they are treated with honor, respect, and dignity during transport.

Maintaining a correct state of personal appearance is of primary importance. The uniform for this duty is the Army green uniform. Neatness and cleanliness of your person are a part of the respect shown for the dead.

You will receive a package containing papers necessary to your assignment, including VA Form 40-1330, *Application for Headstone or Marker,* and DD

Form 1375, *Request for Payment of Funeral and/or Interment Expenses.* You will also receive a statement of condition of remains (a locally reproduced form) and the deceased's death certificate, which you should give to the funeral director when you arrive at your destination.

You are responsible for the remains from the time you sign for them to the time you obtain a receipt for them from the funeral director at your destination. The statement of the condition of the remains serves as your receipt.

When remains are to be transported in a casket, they may be sent by air or by rail, although the latter is used less often than air transportation. But regardless of how the remains are being shipped, you should be at the terminal well before the time of departure. Determine at that time where you should go to make sure that the casket has arrived. Examine the casket and check the label at the head of the casket that shows the deceased's name and Social Security number. Sign your name on the label to show that you have checked it. Be sure that no cargo is placed on the casket.

When the casket is placed in the cargo compartment of the airplane, it is moved in a feet-first position. On the aircraft, the body should be placed in a head-first position, with the head toward the nose of the aircraft. The airline employees should be reminded of this. In a railcar, the remains are placed feet-first.

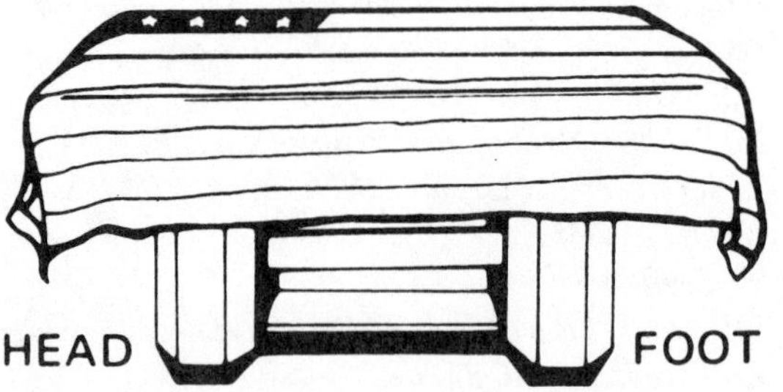

Draping the flag over a closed casket or shipping case.

Salute the casket while it is being loaded on the carrier.

When traveling by airplane, tell the flight attendant that you are escorting a deceased person and wish to be the first to leave after landing. When the casket is being moved, you should accompany it to ensure proper handling and to make sure that the remains do not become separated from you.

If any emergency or unavoidable delay occurs, notify the receiving funeral home by telephone. Also call the mortuary officer at the shipping installation. You may call this officer collect. Be sure to include the new arrival time and flight number of the airplane.

When you reach your destination, go immediately to watch the casket being unloaded. As soon as the remains arrive in the terminal, drape the flag over the casket with the blue-starred field above the left shoulder of the deceased. The remainder of the flag should be draped evenly over the casket. Secure the flag on the shipping case with the elastic flag band. If the casket was shipped by rail, remove the baggage tag and turn it in at the baggage room.

The funeral director will meet you at the terminal. The remains will be loaded into a hearse for transfer to the funeral home. The casket should be moved feet-first.

Honoring our fallen comrades.

Salute the remains before the door of the hearse is closed.

Cremated remains are shipped in an urn placed inside a shipping box that you hand-carry and keep in your possession at all times. You will also carry along the flag, folded and in a plastic case; you do not place or drape the flag on the shipping box.

When you arrive at your destination, remove the urn from the shipping box. During the interment service, the flag may be taken out of its case, folded to resemble a cocked hat, and placed in front of the urn. At the end of the service, it is put back into its case and presented to the next of kin.

When escorting cremated remains, you will obtain from the funeral director a receipt for the remains instead of a statement on the condition of the remains. In all other aspects, the details of escort duty for cremated remains are the same as for escorting a body in a casket.

Ordinarily, the family of the deceased will not be present at the terminal when you arrive, and your first contact with them will not occur until you have reached the funeral home. But should they be present at the terminal, be sure to introduce yourself to them at that time. Should there be an SAO present, be sure to make yourself known. He or she may be of great help to you if you should need assistance.

You should accompany the funeral director in the hearse. Use this opportunity to find out all you can about the next of kin and the other relatives of the deceased whom you will meet at the funeral home. Try to find out their attitude and any other facts that will help to make your assignment easier.

When you arrive at the funeral home, salute the casket as it is being unloaded.

Once at the funeral home, you and the funeral director will fold the flag that has been draped over the casket. The funeral director will inspect the casket to see that it has not been damaged during shipment. If the remains are to be viewed, he or she also opens the casket for inspection. You are responsible for inspecting the uniform and decorations of the deceased. If the casket is to be closed, arrange the flag as you did at the terminal (see picture on page 336).

When you and the funeral director have completed these steps, he or she will prepare the statement of the condition of the remains and sign it. You are responsible for returning the statement to the supervisor of mortuary operations at the installation that prepared the remains. You will also give the funeral director the certificate of death, which will have been included in your packet.

If there is an SAO present, he or she will handle all matters pertaining to insurance, back pay, casualty information, awards, military funeral arrangements, and such. If an SAO is not present, offer the family your assistance and sympathy, but remain quiet, tactful, and dignified. Offer to remain for the funeral services. If the family wants you to stay, you are required to do so.

If burial is to be made in a private cemetery, show the family VA Form 40-1330 and DD Form 1375. If the remains are consigned to a funeral director before interment in a government or national cemetery, show the family DD Form 1375. Explain to the next of kin that the forms should be filled in as soon as possible and mailed to the military activity listed on the form.

When you have completed your assignment, you are to return to your duty station. After your return, you are required to submit a short report in letter form concerning your escort duty. Be sure to include any problems you encountered during your escort duty and how they were resolved.

19

Military Justice

A fact of military life is that, despite the availability of information on the subject and the effort of commanders to keep their soldiers informed, many individuals simply do not know very much about the military justice system. Specific provisions pertaining to administration of the military justice system are in the *Manual for Courts-Martial* and AR 27-10, *Military Justice*. It is the noncommissioned officer's business to know nonjudicial punishment thoroughly—as thoroughly as any commander—and, inasmuch as it is the noncommissioned officers who first become aware of the offenses referred to commanders for punishment, it would be very good to consider that "prevention is the best cure."

NONJUDICIAL PUNISHMENT

Article 15 of the Uniform Code of Military Justice (UCMJ) provides commanding officers the authority and procedures to impose disciplinary punishments for minor offenses without a court-martial. Such punishments may be in addition to or in lieu of admonition or reprimand. Unless the accused is embarked on a vessel, Article 15 punishment may not be imposed if the accused demands trial by court-martial.

Punishments authorized under Article 15 are less severe than court-martial punishments. Unlike a special or general court-martial, Article 15 is not considered a federal conviction for a criminal offense. Article 15 is intended to provide a swift, efficient, and relatively easy method for punishing those committing minor offenses, for maintaining discipline, and for deterring future offenses. Under Article 15, commanders have wide latitude in punishments that may be imposed, ranging from oral reprimand to reduction in pay grades, fines, restriction, extra duty, or a combination of these. Article 15 is the most likely contact that NCOs will have with the military justice system.

It is a mistake to disregard the effect of an Article 15 on a soldier's career. For a noncommissioned officer, an Article 15 usually means that the soldier's career will be limited to the lower NCO grades, whether that was the intent or not. The original copy of DA Form 2617, *Record of Proceedings under Article 15, UCMJ,* may be filed in either the Official Military Personnel File performance portion or the restricted portion of the permanent record. Records of Article 15 punishments can be used in a wide variety of personnel decisions and can lead to an involuntary administrative discharge.

Article 15 is not a legal process. Legal rules of evidence do not apply, and providing defense counsel at the hearing is not mandatory. Nevertheless, the accused does have protection against arbitrary use of Article 15. In addition to the right to demand trial in lieu of Article 15 punishment, the accused has the right to consult with counsel to decide whether to accept the punishment; if the accused accepts Article 15 and considers the punishment too harsh, he or she may appeal it. Other rights include the right to remain silent, to fully present his or her case in the presence of the imposing commander, to call witnesses, to present evidence, to be accompanied by a spokesperson, to request an open hearing, and to examine available evidence.

In order to find the soldier guilty, the commander must be convinced beyond a reasonable doubt that the soldier committed the offense. The maximum punishment depends on the rank of the commander imposing punishment and the rank of the soldier being punished.

Persons Subject to Nonjudicial Punishment

Punishment may be imposed under Article 15 by a commanding officer upon commissioned and warrant officers and enlisted military personnel, except that punishment may not be imposed under Article 15 upon cadets of the U.S. Military Academy.

Nonjudicial punishment may not be imposed on an individual by a commanding officer after the person ceases to be in his or her command. The commander who has instituted the proceedings may, in the case of such a change in status, forward the record of proceedings to the gaining commander for appropriate disposition.

Purposes of Nonjudicial Punishment

Nonjudicial punishment may be imposed in appropriate cases for the following purposes:

- To correct, educate, and reform offenders who have shown that they cannot benefit by less stringent measures.
- To preserve, in appropriate cases, an offender's record of service from unnecessary stigmatization by record of court-martial conviction.
- To further military efficiency by disposing of minor offenses in a manner requiring less time and personnel than trial by court-martial.

Generally, the term *minor offenses* includes misconduct not involving any greater degree of criminality than is involved in the average offense tried by summary court-martial.

Nonpunitive measures usually deal with misconduct resulting from simple neglect, forgetfulness, laziness, inattention to instructions, sloppy habits, immaturity, difficulty in adjusting to disciplined military life, and similar deficiencies. These measures are primarily tools for teaching proper standards of conduct and performance and do not constitute punishment. Included are denial of pass or other privileges, counseling, administrative reduction in grade, extra training, bar to reenlistment, and MOS reclassification. Certain commanders have the authority, apart from any under Article 15, to reduce enlisted persons administratively for inefficiency or other reasons. *Nonpunitive measures and nonjudicial punishment should not be confused.*

A written admonition or reprimand should contain a statement indicating that it has been imposed merely as an administrative measure and not as punishment under Article 15. On the other hand, admonitions and reprimands that are imposed as punishment under Article 15 should be clearly stated to have been imposed as punishment under that article.

Commanding officers also have the authority to impose restraints or restrictions upon a soldier for administrative purposes, such as to ensure the soldier's presence within the command. This authority exists apart from the authority to impose restriction as nonjudicial punishment. These nonpunitive measures may also include, subject to any applicable regulation, administrative withholding of privileges.

Extra training or instruction is one of the most effective nonpunitive measures available to a commander. It is used when a soldier's duty performance has been substandard or deficient. For example, a soldier who fails to maintain proper attire may be required to attend classes on the wearing of the uniform and stand inspection until the deficiency is corrected.

Summarized Proceedings

Summarized Proceedings under Article 15 may be used if, after a preliminary inquiry, a commander determines that the punishment for an offense should not exceed extra duty or restriction for fourteen days; oral reprimand or admonition; or any combination of these punishments. The record of these proceedings is made on DA Form 2627-1. Generally, Summarized Proceedings are conducted as they are for more serious cases prosecuted under nonjudicial punishment except that the individual normally is allowed twenty-four hours to decide whether to demand trial by court-martial and to gather matters in defense, extenuation, and/or mitigation. Because of the limited nature of the punishments imposed under these proceedings, the soldier has neither the right to consult with legally qualified counsel nor the right to a spokesperson.

MAXIMUM PUNISHMENTS FOR ENLISTED MEMBERS UNDER ARTICLE 15*

*Note: The maximum punishment imposable by any commander under Summarized Proceedings cannot exceed extra duty for fourteen days, restriction for fourteen days, oral reprimand, or any combination thereof.

Punishment	Imposed by Company-Grade Officers	Imposed by Field-Grade or General Officers
Admonition/Reprimand	Yes	Yes
and		
Extra Duties[1]	14 days	45 days
and		
Restriction	14 days	60 days
or		
Correctional Custody[2] (PVT1 to PFC)	7 days	30 days
or		
Restricted Diet Confinement (PVT1 to PFC attached or embarked on a vessel)	3 days	3 days
and		
Reduction (CPL E4 to PVT E1)	One grade	One grade or more
(SGT and SSG)		One grade in peacetime[3]
and		
Forfeiture[4]	7 days' pay	Half of one month's pay for 2 months

[1] Combinations of extra duties and restriction cannot exceed the maximum allowed for extra duty.

[2] Subject to limitations imposed by superior authority and presence of adequate facilities. If punishment includes reduction to private first class or below, reduction must be unsuspended.

[3] Only if imposed by a field-grade commander of a unit authorized to have a commander who is a lieutenant colonel or higher.

[4] Amount of forfeiture is computed at the reduced grade, even if suspended, if reduction is part of punishment.

Nature of Punishments

Nonjudicial punishments include the following actions:

- *Admonition and reprimand.* An admonition or reprimand may be imposed in lieu of or combined with Article 15 punishments.
- *Restriction.* The severity of this type of restraint is dependent upon its duration and geographical limits specified when punishment is imposed. A soldier undergoing restriction may be required to report to a designated place at specified times if it is considered reasonably necessary to ensure that the punishment is being properly executed.
- *Extra duties.* This form involves the performance of duties in addition to those normally assigned to the person undergoing the punishment. Extra duties may include fatigue duties. In general, extra duties that would demean his or her position as a noncommissioned officer may not be assigned a corporal or above.
- *Reduction in grade.* This form involves these considerations:
  —Promotion authority. The grade from which a soldier is reduced must be within the promotion authority of the imposing commander or the officer to whom authority to punish under Article 15 has been delegated.
  —Lateral appointments or reductions of corporal to specialist are not authorized. An NCO may be reduced to a lower pay grade provided the lower grade is authorized in his or her primary MOS.
  —Date of rank. When a soldier is reduced in grade as a result of unsuspended reduction, the date of rank in the grade to which reduced is the date the punishment of reduction was imposed.
  —Entitlement to pay. When a soldier is restored to a higher pay grade because of a suspension or when a reduction is mitigated to a forfeiture, entitlement to pay at the higher grade is effective on the date of the suspension or mitigation.
  —Senior noncommissioned officers. Sergeants first class and above may not be reduced under the authority of Article 15.
- *Forfeiture of pay.* Pay refers to basic pay of the individual plus any foreign duty pay. Forfeitures imposed by a company-grade commander may not be applied for more than one month, while those imposed by a field-grade commander may not be applied for more than two months. The maximum forfeiture of pay to which a soldier is subject during a given month, because of one or more actions under Article 15, is one half of his or her pay per month. Article 15 forfeitures cannot deprive a soldier of more than two-thirds of his or her pay per month.

Combination and Apportionment

No two or more punishments involving deprivation of liberty may be combined in the same nonjudicial punishment to run either consecutively or concurrently, but other punishments may be combined. Restriction and extra duty may be combined in any manner to run for a period not in excess of the maximum duration imposable for extra duty by the imposing commander.

FORFEITURES OF PAY AUTHORIZED UNDER ARTICLE 15

Maximum monthly authorized forfeitures of pay under Article 15, UCMJ, may be computed using the applicable formula below:

1. Upon enlisted persons:

$$\frac{(\text{monthly basic pay}^{1,2} + \text{foreign pay}^{1,3})}{2} = \text{maximum forfeiture per month if imposed by major or above}$$

$$\frac{(\text{monthly basic pay}^{1,2} + \text{foreign pay}^{1,3}) \times 7}{30} = \text{maximum forfeiture if imposed by captain or below}$$

2. Upon commissioned and warrant officers when imposed by an officer with general court-martial jurisdiction or by a general officer in command:

$$\frac{(\text{monthly basic pay}^{2})}{2} = \text{maximum authorized forfeiture per month}$$

[1] Amount of forfeiture is computed at the reduced grade, even if suspended, if reduction is part of the punishment imposed.
[2] At the time punishment is imposed.
[3] If applicable.

Suspension, Mitigation, Remission, and Setting Aside

Suspension. The purpose of suspending nonjudicial punishment is to grant a deserving soldier a probational period during which the individual may show that he or she deserves a remission of the suspended portion of his or her nonjudicial punishment. If, because of further misconduct within this period, it is determined that remission of the suspended punishment is not warranted, the suspension may be vacated and the suspended portion of the punishment executed.

Mitigation. Often there are factors other than the facts and circumstances of the offense that show that the accused should receive a light punishment.

Examples include lack of past criminal record, good duty performance, and family hardship.

Remission. Remission can cancel any portion of the unexecuted punishment. Remission is appropriate under the same circumstances as mitigation.

Setting Aside and Restoration. Under this action, the punishment or any part or amount thereof, whether executed or unexecuted, is set aside, and any property, privileges, or rights affected by the portion of the punishment set aside are restored. The basis for this action is ordinarily a determination that, under all the circumstances of the case, the punishment has resulted in a clear injustice.

Notification and Explanation of Rights

The imposing commander must ensure that the soldier is notified of the intention to dispose of the matter under Article 15. The imposing commander may delegate notification authority to another officer, warrant officer, or NCO (sergeant first class and above), providing that person outranks the person being notified. If an NCO is selected, that person should normally be the unit first sergeant or another NCO who is the senior enlisted person in the command in which the accused is serving.

The soldier must be given a "reasonable time" to consult with counsel, including time off from duty, if necessary, to decide whether to demand trial. The amount of time granted is normally forty-eight hours.

Before deciding to demand trial, the accused is not entitled to be informed of the type or amount of punishment he or she will receive if nonjudicial punishment is imposed. The imposing commander will inform the soldier of the maximum punishment allowable under Article 15 and the maximum allowable for the offense if the case proceeds to a trial by court-martial and conviction for the offense.

Right to Demand Trial

The demand for trial may be made at any time before imposition of punishment. The soldier will be told that if trial is demanded, it could be by summary, special, or general court-martial. The soldier will also be told that he or she may object to trial by summary court-martial and that at a special or general court-martial he or she would be entitled to be represented by qualified military counsel or by civilian counsel obtained at the soldier's expense.

Appeals

Only one appeal is permitted under Article 15 proceedings. An appeal not made within a "reasonable time" may be rejected as untimely by the superior authority. The definition of what constitutes a "reasonable time" varies according to the situation. Generally, an appeal, including all documentary matters, submitted more than five calendar days (including weekends and holidays) after punishment is imposed will be presumed to be untimely. If, at the time of imposition of punishment, the soldier indicates a desire not to appeal, the superior authority may reject a subsequent election to appeal, even if it is made within the five-day period.

Appeals are made on DA Form 2627 or DA Form 2627-1 and forwarded through the imposing commander or successor-in-command to the superior authority. The superior must act on the appeal unless otherwise directed by competent authority. A soldier is not required to state the reasons for the appeal, but he or she may present evidence or arguments proving innocence or why the sentence should be mitigated or suspended. Unless an appeal is voluntarily withdrawn, it must be forwarded to the appropriate superior authority. A timely appeal does not terminate because a soldier is discharged from the service but will be processed to completion.

Announcement of Punishment

The punishment may be announced at the next unit formation after punishment is imposed or, if appealed, after the decision. It also may be posted on the unit bulletin board. The purpose of announcing the results is to avert the perception of unfairness of punishment and to deter similar misconduct by others.

Records of Punishment

DA Forms 2627 are prepared in an original and five copies. What happens to those copies, especially the original, is of the utmost importance to soldiers who receive punishment under nonjudicial proceedings.

Original. For enlisted soldiers, the original copy is forwarded to the U.S. Army Enlisted Records and Evaluation Center, Indianapolis, Indiana. The decision on where in the punished soldier's Official Military Personnel File (OMPF) this copy will be placed is determined by the imposing commander at the time punishment is imposed and is final. The imposing commander will decide if it is to be filed in the performance fiche or the restricted fiche of the individual's OMPF.

Copy One. For those Articles 15 filed in the performance fiche of the OMPF, copy one is placed into the permanent section of the Military Personnel Records Jacket (MPRJ) unless the original is transferred from the performance to the restricted fiche, at which time it is destroyed. Otherwise, it is kept in the unit personnel files and destroyed two years from the date of punishment or on the soldier's transfer, whichever occurs first. Copies two through four are used variously as prescribed by AR 27-10, depending on whether forfeiture of pay is involved and whether the punished soldier appeals. Copy five is given to the individual.

Transfer or Removal of Records

Staff sergeants and above and commissioned and warrant officers may request the transfer of a record of nonjudicial punishment from the performance to the restricted fiche of their OMPF. To support such a request, the individual must submit substantive evidence that the purpose of the Article 15 has been served and that transfer of the record is in the best interests of the Army. The request must be made in writing to the Department of the Army Suitability Evaluation Board: President, DA Suitability Evaluation Board, HQDA (DAPE-MPC-E), Washington, DC 20310.

Soldiers may also apply to the Army Board for Correction of Military Records (ABCMR) for the correction of military records by the secretary of the Army. AR 15-185, *Army Board for Correction of Military Records,* contains policies and procedures for making such applications.

COURTS-MARTIAL

Courts-martial are the agencies through which Army magistrates try personnel accused of violations of the punitive articles of the UCMJ. These are Articles 77 through 134 of the UCMJ and are designed to provide punishment of three broad groups of crimes and offenses:

- Crimes common to both the military and civilian law, such as murder, rape, sodomy, arson, burglary, larceny, and frauds against the United States.
- Crimes and offenses peculiar to the military services, such as desertion, disobedience, misbehavior before the enemy, and sleeping on post.
- General offenses that are prosecuted under Article 134, the General Article, which covers "all disorders and neglects to the prejudice of good order and discipline in the armed forces, all conduct of a nature to bring discredit upon the armed forces, and crimes and offenses not capital."

During peacetime, courts-martial may impose sentences ranging from simple forfeiture of pay to confinement and forfeiture of all pay and allowances to death. (See Appendix 12, *Manual for Courts-Martial,* for the Maximum Punishment Chart.) During time of war, a general court-martial may impose any penalty authorized by law, including death.

Who May Prefer Charges

Charges are initiated by anyone bringing to the attention of the military authorities information concerning an offense suspected to have been committed by a person subject to the UCMJ. This information may be received from anyone, whether subject to the UCMJ or not.

Action by Immediate Commander

Upon receipt of information that an offense has been committed, the commander exercising immediate jurisdiction over the accused under Article 15, UCMJ, must make a preliminary inquiry into the charges in order to permit an intelligent disposition of them.

Based on the outcome of the preliminary inquiry, a commander may decide that all or some of the charges do not warrant further action, and those charges may be dismissed. The commander may also decide, based upon the preliminary investigation, that the offenses committed warrant punishment under Article 15, UCMJ, or he or she may refer more serious charges to higher authority for trial by courts-martial.

Preparation of Charge Sheets

Rule 307 and Appendix 4, *Manual for Courts-Martial,* contain specific instructions on the preparation of charge sheets, together with specimen forms for charges and specifications under the punitive articles of the Uniform Code of Military Justice. If you're not a legal clerk, it's important to get help from your Judge Advocate General (JAG) officer.

Composition of Courts-Martial

General courts-martial consist of a military judge and not fewer than five members, or of a military judge alone. *Special courts-martial* consist of not fewer than three members or, if so detailed, a military judge and not less than three members, or a military judge alone. *Summary courts-martial* consist of one commissioned officer.

Any commissioned officer on active duty with the armed forces is eligible to serve on courts-martial. Any warrant officer on active duty with the armed forces is eligible to serve on general and special courts-martial for the trial of any person other than a commissioned officer. Any enlisted person on active duty with the armed forces who is not a member of the same unit as the accused is eligible to serve on general and special courts-martial for the trial of any enlisted person who has personally requested in writing before assembly that enlisted members serve on the court.

Convening Authorities

General courts-martial may be convened by the president of the United States; the secretary of the Army; the commander of a territorial department, army group, army, army corps, division, separate brigade, or corresponding unit; or any other commander designated by the Secretary of the Army or empowered by the president to convene such courts-martial. It is unlawful for any commander who is an accuser to convene a general court-martial for the trial of the person so accused.

Special courts-martial may be convened by any person who may convene a general court-martial or the commanding officer of a district, garrison, fort, camp, station, or other place where members of the Army are on duty.

Summary courts-martial may be convened by any person who may also convene a general or special court-martial; the commander of a detached company or other detachment of the Army, as well as any other officer empowered by the secretary of the Army may convene such a court-martial. When only one commissioned officer is present with a command or detachment, that officer is the summary court-martial authority of that command or detachment and hears and determines all summary court cases.

Challenges

The military judge and members of a general or special court-martial may be challenged by the accused or the trial counsel for cause stated to the court. The military judge, or, if none, the court, determines the relevancy and validity of challenges for cause. Challenges by the trial counsel are ordinarily presented and decided before those by the accused are offered.

Each accused and the trial counsel is entitled to one preemptory challenge, meaning the accused may challenge any member of the court to sit on his trial without offering any reasons for the challenge.

Appeals

At the close of a trial or soon thereafter, if the accused is found guilty, the defense counsel should prepare a recommendation for clemency setting forth any matters as to clemency he or she desires to have considered by the members of the court of the reviewing authority. If the accused is convicted, the defense counsel advises him or her of appellate rights.

The Court of Military Review. The Judge Advocate General (JAG) refers to a court of military review the record in every case of trial by court-martial in which the sentence, as approved, extends to death, dishonorable or bad-conduct discharge, or confinement for one year or more.

In a case referred to it, the court of military review may act only with respect to the findings and sentence as approved by the convening authority. If the court sets aside the findings and sentence, it may, except where the setting aside is based on lack of sufficient evidence, order a rehearing. If it sets aside the findings and sentence and does not order a rehearing, it orders that the charges be dismissed.

The Court of Military Appeals. The U.S. Court of Military Appeals, established under Article I of the Constitution, reviews the record in all of the following cases:

- Those in which the sentence, as affirmed by a court of military review, extends to death.

- Those reviewed by a court of military review that the Judge Advocate General orders sent to the Court of Military Appeals for review.
- Those reviewed by a court of military review in which the Court of Military Appeals has granted a review. Reviewed cases may be forwarded to the U.S. Supreme Court.

Remission and Suspension of Sentences

The secretary of the Army or his designated representative may remit or suspend any amount of the unexecuted part of any sentence, including all uncollected forfeitures other than a sentence approved by the president. The secretary of the Army may, for cause, substitute an administrative form of discharge for a discharge or dismissal executed in accordance with the sentence of a court-martial. The convening authority may suspend the execution of any sentence, except a death sentence.

Effective Dates of Sentences

Whenever a sentence includes a forfeiture of pay or allowances in addition to confinement, the forfeiture applies to pay or allowances becoming due on or after the date the sentence is approved by the convening authority.

Confinement included in a sentence begins to run from the date of sentencing by the court-martial. Reductions are effective on the date the sentence is approved. All other sentences of courts-martial are effective on the date ordered executed.

NCO Responsibilities

If you should be appointed to serve on a general or special court-martial as a member of the court, your duties and responsibilities will be very carefully explained to you before the court convenes and as the trial proceeds. If a soldier should seek your advice regarding what he or she should do in the event that charges are brought against the individual, advise the person concerned to seek assistance from an officer of the Judge Advocate General's Corps.

Unless you are a legal clerk, your acquaintance with the military justice system will probably be only a superficial one. Your closest contact with the military justice system will come through your commander's exercise of judicial authority under Article 15 of the UCMJ, and you should be intimately familiar with every aspect of that part of the system. But you are neither an expert in military law nor a lawyer, and you should never take upon yourself the duties of counsel.

The *Manual for Courts-Martial* is an important text. Every soldier should know what it contains and how to use it to answer questions on the military justice system. Do not, however, use that acquaintance to practice law.

SOURCES

AR 27-10, *Military Justice,* 1989.

FM 27-1 (FM 1-04.1), *Legal Guide for Commanders,* 1987.

FM 27-14 (FM 1-04.14), *Legal Guide for Soldiers,* 1986.

Manual for Courts-Martial, 1984.

Servicemember's Legal Guide, 5th edition, by Lt. Col. Jonathan P. Tomes, USA (Ret.). Mechanicsburg, PA: Stackpole Books, 2005.

20

Personal Affairs

Busy NCOs often allow their personal needs to pile up under more pressing professional matters. Doing so can be costly to you and to your loved ones.

Consider, for example, that neglecting to get life insurance and a last will and testament can cause surviving family members to get left out in the cold, financially and otherwise. Consider, too, that medical bills for unforeseen illnesses and injuries can devastate your financial future. What can you do about portions of major bills disallowed by TRICARE or the Dependent Dental Plan? Do you really understand your family's medical and dental benefits and how and under what circumstances TRICARE supplements are strongly recommended?

Suppose you're the kind of NCO who takes pride in hitting the ground running when assigned to a new job. What happens, for example, when you go to work in a new job overseas and your spouse and children remain behind in local quarters? Do your family members have what they need to achieve a decent quality of life and standard of living in their new environment? Where can they turn for help when associated problems arise?

What if, for some reason beyond your control, your end-of-month Leave and Earnings Statement reads "No pay due" and you must pay rent and meet other living expenses? Who can help to fully or partially defray necessary payments to landlords, banks, and other creditors until your pay is sorted out?

Are your personal affairs in order? To what extent? Do you keep records? Where are they? Who else knows where your vital records are kept? Does your spouse or other next of kin know important account numbers and first and supplemental points of contact?

You must make the effort to consider and take charge of your personal affairs. It is your responsibility to plan for your personal needs and those of your family. Commanders, sergeants major, first sergeants, and other leaders frown on NCOs who are unable or unwilling to ensure that they are fully deployable. Deployability includes personal readiness.

IMPORTANT PERSONAL RECORDS

The simplest way to keep your survivors informed about arrangements you have made for them is to prepare a record of your personal affairs. At the minimum, be sure that they know the location of the following:

- Your birth certificate and those of all members of your immediate family.
- Your marriage certificate.
- Divorce papers or previous spouse's death certificate, if applicable.
- Your life insurance policies.

If you put the original of your will and other key documents in a safe-deposit box, be sure that your spouse or executor has access to it. If you die and no one has access to the box, a court order must be obtained to open it.

A personal affairs record is a necessity for the married soldier because it serves as a vital source of information for his or her family.

A personal affairs record can be detailed, but make sure it includes at least the following:

- Insurance policy numbers and their amounts. Include automobile and homeowner's policies.
- Previous years' tax records.
- Copies of titles and bills of sale.
- Information on bank accounts.
- A list of all pay allotments.
- Information regarding any veterans' benefits to which you may be entitled.

If you are married, be sure someone in your family knows how to pay your household bills, when they are due, and where to find them.

Military Records

Keep a file of all records about your military service. Keep copies of orders, discharge certificate, awards, citations, letters of appreciation and commendation, medical and dental records, Leave and Earnings Statements, and other information about your military history, even old NCOERs. Information is frequently needed throughout your active service career and afterward, when you apply for certain benefits.

Emergency Data

Your DD Form 93, *Record of Emergency Data,* must be accurate and up-to-date at all times. This record tells your military personnel office (MILPO) where your next of kin can be located immediately. It gives the name of the person you want to receive your pay if you are missing in action as well as other information of benefit to your dependents.

Family Care Plan

The wrong time for you, either as dual military parents or a single parent, to begin planning who will take care of your children is when you find yourself on a short-notice deployment. AR 600-20, *Army Command Policy,* stipulates that every single-parent soldier, dual military parents, and single and dual military pregnant soldiers must develop a family care plan. The plan, DA Form 5305, as a minimum includes proof that a guardian has agreed to care for dependent children under the age of eighteen. Powers of attorney for medical care, guardianship, and the authorization to start or stop financial support should be in the packet, and the children should have military ID cards. Lastly, the regulation requires a letter of instruction to the guardian/escort. This letter should contain specific instructions needed for the guardian to ensure the care of the dependents.

Although not required for the packet, birth certificates, Social Security cards, shot records, other medical or insurance cards, medication dosages if necessary, and lists of family member addresses and phone numbers in case of emergency should be kept in a central location (an accordion-style organizer or file cabinet special drawer is suitable) and labeled to make it easy for the guardian to find documents fast. You might also want to contact financial institutions, children's doctors, schools, and day-care providers prior to deployment, so there will not be questions when your guardian comes to sign your child out of school to take him or her to the doctor.

Power of Attorney

A power of attorney is a legal document by which you give another person the power to act as your agent, either for some particular purpose or for the transaction of your business in general. In the wrong hands, a power of attorney can ruin you because the agent who holds such a power has, within the limits granted by it, full authority to deal with your property without consulting you. Grant it only to someone you can trust and then only when you must.

You may never need a power of attorney, or if you do need one, it may only be required to perform certain acts and no others—a limited or special power of attorney. Always consult a legal assistance officer or a lawyer before assigning a power of attorney, and cancel it as soon as it is no longer required.

Bank Accounts

If you are married, you and your spouse should decide who manages the accounts. Make them joint accounts so that if anything happens to you, your family will have ready access to funds.

Current regulations require soldiers to have guaranteed direct deposit to a financial institution. With a guaranteed direct deposit from the U.S. Army Finance Center, you do not have to bother with anything but picking up your Leave and Earnings Statement on payday.

FAMILY CARE PLAN

For use of this form, see AR 600-20; the proponent agency is DCSPER

PRIVACY ACT STATEMENT

AUTHORITY: 10 U.S.C. Section 3013, Secretary of the Army: Army Regulation 600-20, Army Command Policy and E.O. 9397 *(SSN)*

PRINCIPAL PURPOSE: To emphasize to soldiers the significance of their responsibilities to the military service and their family members while performing required military duties.

ROUTINE USES: None

DISCLOSURE: Mandatory; Failure to maintain a Family Care Plan could subject the soldier to separation, administrative action, or disciplinary action under the UCMJ.

PART I - SOLDIER'S FAMILY CARE

	INITIALS
A. I was counseled on ______________________ *(date)*, and fully understand the policy on family member care responsibilities. I understand that I must arrange for care of my family members, remain available for deployment and training, and report for duty as required without interference of responsibility for family members. I assume responsibility for all obligations for such things as child care, food, adequate housing, transportation, and emergency needs of my family members regardless of age.	
B. I have made and will maintain arrangements for the care of my family members during all the following: 1. Duty; 2. Exercises/field duty; 3. Permanent Change of Station; 4. Alerts; 5. Annual Training; 6. Temporary Duty; 7. Unit Training Assembly; 8. Active Duty Training; 9. Unaccompanied Tours; 10. Mobilization; 11. Deployment; 12. Other Military Duty; 13. Emergencies; 14. Leave/non-duty Time	
C. I understand the importance of ensuring the proper care for my family members, and ensuring my own readiness and deployability as well. I further understand that in light of the critical nature of both these requirements:	
1. Failure to make and maintain adequate family member care arrangements in accordance with the Army's policy is grounds for disciplinary action or separation.	
2. Nonavailability for worldwide assignment and/or unit deployment may lead to my separation from the Army.	
3. If arrangements for the care of my family members fail to work, I am not automatically excused from prescribed duties, unit deployment, or reassignment.	
4. If I fail to maintain a Family Care Plan or provide false information regarding my plan, I am subject to separation, administrative action, or disciplinary action under UCMJ.	
5. I must maintain an up-to-date Family Care Plan and revise my Plan when circumstances change. I understand that Family Care Plans may be tested at the discretion of the commander.	
6. I will receive no special consideration in duty assignments or duty stations based on my responsibilities for my family members unless enrolled in the Exceptional Family Member Program *(EFMP)* in accordance with AR 600-75.	
D. I have made all necessary arrangements *(legal, educational, financial, religious, special, etc.)* to ensure a smooth, rapid turnover of family member care responsibilities in case this plan is implemented.	
E. I have arranged for necessary travel required to transfer my family members to a designated person. If my principal designee is not in the local area, I have arranged with a nonmilitary person in the local area to assume temporary guardianship of my family members until they are transferred to my principal care designee, or that designee arrives to assume responsibility for their care.	
F. A copy of DA Form 5841-R *(Power of Attorney)* or **equivalent documents** and a copy of DA Form 5840-R *(Certificate of Acceptance as Guardian)* for each escort or guardian whether temporary or long-term is attached to this plan.	
G. The following additional required documents are completed, included in this plan, and will be put into effect as part of my Family Care Plan.	
1. DD Form 1172 *(Application for Uniformed Services Identification Card)* for each family member whether they have a currently valid ID card or not.	
2. DD Form 2558 *(Authorization to Start, Stop or Change an Allotment for Active Duty or Retired Personnel)* or other proof of financial support for expenses incurred by guardian and family members.	
3. Copies of Letters of Instruction *(which have been forwarded to designated escorts or guardians along with powers of attorney and other pertinent documents)*, outlining all special instructions concerning the care of my family members have also been included in my Family Care Plan.	
H. I have thoroughly briefed escorts and guardians on the full extent of their responsibilities and on procedures for gaining access to military/civilian facilities, services, entitlements and benefits on behalf of my family members.	
I. I am confident that my Family Care Plan is workable, and to the best of my knowledge, the guardian *(s)* and escort *(s)* I have designated will be both willing and able to carry out the responsibilities of caring for my family members.	

PART II - DESIGNATION OF GUARDIANS/ESCORTS

A. *I (We) have designated the following temporary guardian to care for my (our) family member (s) until responsibility is transferred to escort or principal (long-term) guardian.*

1. TYPED OR PRINTED NAME	2a. COMPLETE ADDRESS *(Including Street, Apartment Number, P.O. Box Number, Rural Route Number, City, State, and ZIP + 4 where applicable)*
3. TELEPHONE NUMBER *(Include Area Code)*	
	2b. E- MAIL ADDRESS

DA FORM 5305-R, APR 1999 DA FORM 5305-R, MAR 1992 IS OBSOLETE USAPA V1.00

B. *I (We) have designated the following individual(s) as principal long-term guardian(s) for my (our) family member (s). The designated guardian(s) reside in the continental United States or United States territories.*

1. TYPED OR PRINTED NAME	2a. COMPLETE ADDRESS *(Including Street, Apartment Number, P.O. Box Number, Rural Route Number, City, State, and ZIP + 4 where applicable)*
3. TELEPHONE NUMBER *(Include Area Code)*	2b. E-MAIL ADDRESS

C. *I (We) have designated the following individual(s) as escort for my(our) family member(s) if evacuation from OCONUS becomes necessary (applies only to persons assigned OCONUS):*

1. TYPED OR PRINTED NAME	2a. COMPLETE ADDRESS *(Including Street, Apartment Number, P.O. Box Number, Rural Route Number, City, State, and ZIP + 4 where applicable)*
3. TELEPHONE NUMBER *(Include Area Code)*	2b. E-MAIL ADDRESS

PART III - DUAL MILITARY COUPLES ONLY
MILITARY SPOUSE AND COMMANDER CERTIFICATION

A. **Spouse:** *We have made arrangements and will maintain arrangements for the care of our family member (s) in all circumstances required by our commitment to the military and our family.*

1. SIGNATURE OF SPOUSE	2. DATE *(YYYY/MM/DD)*
3. TYPED OR PRINTED NAME OF SPOUSE	4. SSN

5. **Recertification**	a. INIT.	DATE	b. INIT.	DATE	c. INIT.	DATE	d. INIT.	DATE	e. INIT.	DATE

B. **Commander:** *I have counseled the military spouse assigned to my unit, reviewed the Family Care Plan, and I am satisfied that the members have made adequate family care arrangements.*

1. SIGNATURE OF COMMANDER	2. DATE	3. UNIT ADDRESS
4. TYPED OR PRINTED NAME OF COMMANDER		

5. **Recertification**	a. INIT.	DATE	b. INIT.	DATE	c. INIT.	DATE	d. INIT.	DATE	e. INIT.	DATE

PART IV - SOLDIER AND COMMANDER CERTIFICATION

A. **Soldier:** *I (We) have made arrangements and will maintain arrangements for the care of my (our) family member(s) in all circumstances required by my (our) commitment to the military and my (our) family.*

1. SIGNATURE OF SOLDIER	2. DATE *(YYYY/MM/DD)*
3. TYPED OR PRINTED NAME OF SOLDIER	4. SSN

5. **Recertification**	a. INIT.	DATE	b. INIT.	DATE	c. INIT.	DATE	d. INIT.	DATE	e. INIT.	DATE

B. **Commander:** *I have reviewed the Family Care Plan, and I am satisfied that the members have made adequate family care arrangements that will allow for a full range of military duties and for worldwide availability as defined here.*

1. SIGNATURE OF COMMANDER	2. DATE	3. UNIT ADDRESS
4. TYPED OR PRINTED NAME OF COMMANDER		

5. **Recertification**	a. INIT.	DATE	b. INIT.	DATE	c. INIT.	DATE	d. INIT.	DATE	e. INIT.	DATE

REVERSE OF DA FORM 5305-R, APR 1999 USAPA V1.00

Your Will

The importance of having a will cannot be overemphasized. You may not consider that you "own" very much, but not having a will could cause many legal complications after your death. If you were to die without a will—*intestate*—your estate would be distributed according to the descent and distribution laws of your state of legal residence, or in the case of real property located in another state, the laws of that state.

If you are married, both you and your spouse should have wills, even if each will makes the same distribution of property and assets. It is particularly important to have a will if you have minor children so that their interests can be protected through a guardianship of your choice in the event both you and your spouse die.

Once you have made your will, review it periodically to keep it up-to-date. As circumstances change, you may want to update it to be sure that it still expresses your desires about the distribution of your property and assets.

Keep your will in a safe place. The safest place to keep it (and other important papers) is in a safe-deposit box at your bank. It is not a bad idea to send a copy of your will together with a statement as to the location of the original to the principal beneficiary or the person named in the will as the executor.

Commercial Life Insurance

It is beyond the scope of this book to discuss all the things to look for when you are shopping for life insurance. What kind of policy to get and how much insurance you may need depends strictly upon your individual or family situation. You are particularly insurable if you are still relatively young and you have school-age children who depend upon you. Shop around. There are numerous good individual and group insurance plans available; there are some pretty bad ones available as well (and plenty of unscrupulous insurance agents willing to take your money from you).

Servicemember's Group Life Insurance (SGLI)

Maximum coverage is $400,000, unless you decline coverage or request a reduced amount of coverage. DoD currently pays the premiums to servicemembers who are deployed in a designated combat zone for $150,000 of SGLI coverage. When you leave the service, your SGLI is convertible to Veterans Group Life Insurance (VGLI).

The Servicemembers Civil Relief Act (SCRA)

SCRA provides protection of rights, privileges, immunities, and benefits to servicemembers while serving on active duty. These benefits include: protection against paying taxes in both the home state and the state in which servicemembers are stationed, exemption from personal property taxes when stationed in a state which is not their domicile, the ability to have civil court cases delayed, and special treatment of certain financial obligations. Servicemembers may also qualify for lowering their interest rates to 6 percent for obligations incurred prior to entering active service. For more information go to *www.defenselink.mil/specials/relief_act/index.html* or see a legal assistance attorney. All mobilized Reserve Component (RC) soldiers can receive finance support and information from the local servicing finance office or defense military pay office (DMPO).

Re-employment Rights

RC soldiers who are mobilized are exempt from the Uniformed Services Employment and Reemployment Rights Act (USERRA) five-year limit for retaining re-employment rights. In regards to questions about employment or re-employment rights service members can check the Employer Support of the Guard and Reserve (ESGR) web site at: *www.ESGR.org*.

HOUSING

Renting

Military families often must rent local housing while waiting for government quarters to become available. If you find yourself in that situation, you might want to consider renting an apartment on a month-by-month basis. Should you sign a lease for a specified period of time and then have to break it because a set of quarters unexpectedly becomes available, you have to forfeit your deposit (usually an amount equal to a month's rent).

Renting an apartment gives single soldiers a degree of independence and privacy not available in the barracks, and for this reason, many soldiers want to move off post.

Whether a single soldier can move off post depends on the following:

- Your post commander's policy. It is also up to the commanding officer of your unit. Some commanders are liberal in granting this privilege; it depends upon your unit's mission. Commanders of headquarters units can be more liberal than those of tactical or combat support units.
- The amount and quality of troop housing available. Some small, specialized units have trouble finding adequate troop housing, especially at overcrowded installations in metropolitan areas. Where sufficient troop housing is available, however, commanders normally fill the billets up first before allowing lower-ranking single personnel to move off post.
- Nonabuse of the privilege. Your commander will revoke permission to live off post as soon as you start coming to work late, running up debts, or causing disturbances among the local population.

Be sure that you can afford to live off post. Your military pay combined with your housing and subsistence allowances may be enough, depending on the geographical area, but just enough and no more. If supporting yourself in an apartment leaves you flat broke at the end of the month, you are better off living in the barracks.

Some soldiers find it a good idea to team up with two or three friends and rent a place by splitting all the costs. This is an excellent idea if your companions can be trusted to pay their share, take care of the communal areas, and respect your privacy and personal property.

OWNERSHIP OF PROPERTY

Joint ownership of property can have certain advantages in establishing an automatic and known passage of ownership upon the death of one owner and can also have certain disadvantages. Inquire into federal and state laws regarding ownership of family property, and take actions that put your estate in the most favorable ownership positions.

In the event of your death, your immediate personal effects will be forwarded at government expense to the person entitled to their custody. This does not give the recipient legal title to them, but they should be retained for disposition under the law.

If you own real estate in your name and it is not paid for, show on your personal affairs record whether there is a mortgage or a deed of trust against it, along with the name of the person or organization to whom you are indebted. Also include information about property taxes and insurance.

Transfer of automobile ownership is sometimes complicated because of varying state laws. Remember that joint titling may make you or your spouse subject to personal property taxes; active-duty personnel are generally exempt from payment of personal property taxes, so adding your spouse's name to an automobile title can cost you a lot of money.

INCOME TAXES

Military pay in general is subject to income tax. You do not pay tax on subsistence, quarters, and uniform allowances. Dislocation allowance, special duty pays, and hardship pay, however, are taxable.

Any nonmilitary earnings, including the pay received while employed during off-duty hours and the income of any of your dependents, are taxable. Military pay is excluded from federal income tax for service in any area that the president of the United States designates by executive order to be a combat zone. This exclusion is unlimited for enlisted members. If you spend a single qualifying day in the combat zone, your pay for the entire month is excluded from taxable income. Bonuses and special pays are also excluded from taxable income if within the previously stated limitations and earned in the same month in which you served in a combat zone.

The Soldiers' and Sailors' Civil Relief Act assures that a state in which a soldier is stationed but which is not the servicemember's legal residence cannot tax service pay. Legal residence is established at enlistment or thereafter when a soldier executes DD Form 2058, *State of Legal Residence Certificate.*

The following states do not withhold income tax from the pay of military personnel: Alaska, Florida, Nevada, New Hampshire, South Dakota, Tennessee, Texas, Washington, and Wyoming. Soldiers claiming legal residence in foreign countries or U.S. territories are also exempt from paying state income taxes. Appendix K, "State Tax Withholding," to AR 37-104-3 contains specific information relative to each state for which withholding tax applies.

AGENCIES AND PEOPLE THAT CAN HELP

In addition to what follows, you can refer to the "Guide for Obtaining Information and Assistance" table on page 67 for more information.

Army Community Services (ACS)

The ACS is an official Department of the Army organization established to provide information, aid, guidance, and referral services to military personnel and their families. ACS activities are monitored by the Army Adjutant General. The ACS web page is at *www.myarmylifetoo.com/*

The ACS provides a wide variety of services, including the following:

- Referrals for handicapped dependents.
- Family counseling services.
- Financial planning services.
- Lending services to provide bedding, linens, and housewares to military families until they can get settled at a new post.
- Volunteer services providing transportation to dependents when required.
- Child abuse information and referral.
- An emergency food locker from which needy families may draw supplies.

Army Emergency Relief (AER)

The Army Emergency Relief operates as a part of the Army Community Services. AER provides badly needed financial assistance to soldiers and their dependents. A local AER officer can authorize interest-free cash loans. Large loans must be approved by Headquarters, AER. The AER web site is at *www.aerhq.org.*

AER loans may be approved for the following purposes:

- Defray living expenses because of nonreceipt of military pay.
- Provide money to help defray emergency travel expenses.
- Help pay rents, security deposits, and utilities.
- Help pay "essential [privately owned vehicle] POV expenses."
- Pay funeral expenses above and beyond those allowed by the government.

- Pay grants to the widows and orphans of deceased soldiers, in some cases.
- Provide cash to buy food when it is not available from the ACS food locker.
- Provide money to replace lost funds.

Soldiers must apply for AER loans through their unit commanders by filling out DA Form 1103, *Application for AER Financial Assistance*. The soldier must document his or her expenses or financial situation, and an allotment must be executed before the AER will disburse any money.

Each year, AER disburses millions of dollars to help soldiers and their families. The only source for these funds is cash donations by Army members solicited annually during Army-wide fund-raising drives.

The Army Family Action Plan (AFAP)

Today, more than half the active Army force is married. The Army now pays considerable attention to soldiers' families.

> A partnership exists between the Army and Army families. The Army's unique missions, concept of service[,] and lifestyle of its members all affect the nature of this partnership. Towards the goal of building a strong partnership, the Army remains committed to assuring adequate support to families in order to promote wellness, to develop a sense of community, and to strengthen the mutually reinforcing bonds between the Army and its families.

The Army Family Action Plan includes four major themes: relocation, medical, family support and role identity, and education and youth. The specific areas range from developing videos for overseas orientation programs, developing family member support groups at installations and units, and attempting to correct medical staff shortages, to providing English-as-a-second-language instruction for family members whose native language is other than English. As an NCO, regardless of whether you now have a family or plan to have one someday, your understanding and full support of the Army Family Action Plan is essential to its success.

Following are brief definitions of the critical elements of the plan's philosophy. Their applications are much more far-reaching than to just the Army Family Action Plan itself—they are essential ingredients to the cohesion that makes the Army work.

Partnership. Partnership has to exist between the Army as an institution and the individuals who are part of it: soldiers, civilians, and family members. Partnership is a cohesion of the Army and family members based on mutual understanding of the mission and commitment to one another. It is a reciprocal relationship, based on moral and ethical responsibilities and statutory and regulatory requirements. Partnership between its members makes the Army an institution, not just a job or a workplace.

Wellness. Wellness is the concern for developing those strengths, skills, aptitudes, and attitudes that contribute to the wholeness and health of body, mind, and spirit. Wellness is achieved by concentrating on what is working well, and by drawing on the characteristics of the Army's many healthy families and then transmitting those characteristics to the people who need assistance.

Sense of Community. This is the center of the partnership, with all members offered the challenge and opportunity to work together for the common good. It means that each member of the Army community has a special responsibility to make the institution a better place in which to live and work.

Partnership, wellness, sense of community—all are important to military community residents and officials. The following are a few of the many examples that illustrate the value of the AFAP:

- Quality child care is a top priority to the increasing number of spouses who work. AFAP initiatives bring about increased appropriated fund support for child care, fees for child care based on family income, better-trained and higher-paid caregivers and more of them, parent advisory boards, and an ongoing study of the demand for child care.
- Since relocation assistance and sponsorship are paramount, AFAP requests increased allowances for transportation of household goods, especially for junior enlisted soldiers. An automated relocation assistance system provides housing and other relocation information about areas in the United States and abroad.
- Because of the AFAP, reservists may shop in commissaries during a specified number of days during the year.

Since the first AFAP conference was held in 1983, many laws have been passed or amended to resolve more than a hundred quality-of-life issues affecting the Army family.

Legal Assistance

A legal assistance officer will advise you on such matters as a will, power of attorney, divorce and separation actions, estates, tax problems, and other civil matters. The legal assistance officer can also provide you with a very useful "legal checkup," which is designed to identify any potential legal problems that you may have.

This officer is not normally permitted to represent you in civil court or to give you advice in matters of a criminal nature. Neither may he or she advise you about court-martial investigations or charges (a military counsel appointed by the judge advocate will assist you in such cases). If your problem requires the services of a civilian lawyer, the legal assistance officer can refer you, through cooperating bar associations, to civilian legal advisors or legal aid bureaus.

The *Servicemember's Legal Guide,* 2nd edition, published by Stackpole Books, provides comprehensive information on what soldiers and their families need to know about the law.

Chaplains

Chaplains are available to help soldiers, family members, and civilians with any type of concern they may have, be it spiritual, work related, or otherwise. Chaplains can help in areas ranging from marriage and family counseling to stress management and suicide prevention. Soldiers seeking counseling don't necessarily have to be churchgoers to use the chaplains to help them through the rough times. Lastly, Army chaplain regulations state that any communications to a chaplain acting as a spiritual advisor must be kept in confidence and cannot be told to anyone else without permission.

Disability Soldier Support System (DS3)

The DS3 program provides each soldier seriously injured during combat operations in the global war on terrorism and his or her family with a personal DS3 advocate, called a soldier/family management specialist. When a soldier receives a disability rating of 30 percent or greater, and a special category designation, the soldier is designated DS3. Soldiers will continue to receive DS3 support for five years after they leave active duty.

MEDICAL INSURANCE—TRICARE

Army health-care beneficiaries—you and your family—should take a long-term view toward medical and dental health. Eat foods that contribute to a longer life. Exercise regularly for the same reason. Rest properly. Brush and floss after meals. Get periodic physical and dental examinations. Follow the advice of doctors, dentists, and other Army health- and medical-care providers. Stay healthy to limit the effects of illness or disease. Beware of unsafe acts and unsafe conditions to avoid injury. When a person is ill or injured, nothing matters more than recovery.

When an active-duty soldier becomes sick or gets hurt, the Army direct-care medical system provides care at no cost. In fact, AR 40-3, *Medical, Dental, and Veterinary Care,* prohibits active-duty soldiers, including active-duty reserve component soldiers, from seeking and obtaining medical and dental care from civilian sources without prior authorization from the local Army medical treatment facility commander. So, while soldiers are on active duty, they do not need medical and dental insurance. But Army family members do—and they have it provided by TRICARE, and the Dependent Dental Plan, which is offered through TRICARE.

Eligibility for TRICARE is determined by the Defense Enrollment Eligibility Reporting System (DEERS), a database of uniformed servicemembers (sponsors), family members, and others worldwide who are entitled under the law to TRICARE benefits. Active duty and retired servicemembers are automatically registered in DEERS, but it's the sponsor's responsibility to ensure that his or her eligible family members are registered correctly in DEERS. All sponsors should ensure that their family members' status (marriage, divorce, new child, etc.), residential address, telephone numbers, and e-mail address are current in DEERS so that TRICARE can send out information and have claims processed quickly and accurately.

TRICARE

TRICARE is a healthcare program for members of the uniformed services and their families, and survivors and retired members and their families. TRICARE brings together the health-care resources of each of the military services and supplements them with networks of civilian health-care professionals to provide better access and high-quality service while maintaining the capability to support military operations. There are three TRICARE regions in the United States, each with an assigned lead agent who is responsible for the military health services system in that region.

Under TRICARE, family members have two basic choices for seeking medical care: (1) the Enrolled Choice (TRICARE Prime) and (2) the Non-Enrolled Choice (TRICARE Extra/TRICARE Standard). Active-duty members must enroll in TRICARE Prime, and thus are not eligible for the Non-Enrolled Choice.

Choice 1. Enrolled Choice (TRICARE Prime) provides the most comprehensive health-care benefits to the patient at the lowest cost. TRICARE Prime guarantees priority access to care at a military treatment facility or, where available, an off-post, civilian, contracted doctor's office.

All active-duty military members must enroll in this choice and must use military facilities. Family members must also enroll to use this option. Those who select the Enrolled Choice will be assigned to a primary care manager (PCM). This is a health-care provider who you will see first for all of your medical needs. If necessary, your PCM will refer you to specialty medical care, when needed. There are no enrollment fees for active-duty families in TRICARE Prime.

Choice 2. The Non-Enrolled Choice (TRICARE Extra/TRICARE Standard) allows family members to seek medical care from any physician of their choice in the civilian community. The Non-Enrolled Choice is a more costly option than the Enrolled Choice. This choice incorporates two programs (TRICARE Extra and TRICARE Standard). Medical expenses are covered under these programs when family members are not enrolled in TRICARE Prime. A single deductible covers the use of either program.

Active enrollment and preauthorization are not required for your family to use the Non-Enrolled Choice, but a nonavailability statement must be obtained for civilian inpatient care. See your local health benefits advisor for more information.

TRICARE Standard is the basic TRICARE health care program, offering comprehensive health care coverage, for people not enrolled in TRICARE Prime. (Active duty service members are automatically enrolled in Prime, and many other beneficiaries choose to enroll.) Standard does not require enrollment.

Fee-for-service flexibility: Standard is a fee-for-service plan that gives beneficiaries the option to see any TRICARE-certified/authorized provider (doctor, nurse-practitioner, lab, clinic, etc.). Standard offers the greatest flexibility in choosing a provider, but it will also involve greater out-of-pocket expenses for you, the patient. You also may be required to file your own claims.

Costs: Standard requires that you satisfy a yearly deductible before TRICARE cost sharing begins, and you will be required to pay co-payments or cost shares for outpatient care, medications, and inpatient care. A nonavailability statement for civilian inpatient care may be required for areas surrounding military treatment facilities.

TRICARE Extra is an option that allows Standard beneficiaries to save money by making civilian doctors' appointments with doctors (nurse practitioners, labs, clinics, etc.) who are "participating" providers. Providers who participate in TRICARE agree to accept, as payment in full for services they render, the TRICARE maximum allowable charge (TMAC).

Nonparticipating providers may, by law, charge up to 15 percent above the TMAC for their services, and the TRICARE Standard beneficiary is responsible for the amount above the TMAC.

Participating providers will file claims forms for the TRICARE beneficiary. (Certified providers may or may not file claims on behalf of the Standard patient; the doctor may choose to do so, or not, on a case-by-case basis.)

Using the Non-Enrolled Choice allows family members the freedom to choose any civilian physician. Some physicians' services will be less costly than others. Your family members may continue to use military facilities on a space-available basis, but obtaining appointments will become very difficult.

TRICARE Pharmacy

Prescriptions may be filled (up to a ninety-day supply for most medications) at a military treatment facility (MTF) pharmacy free of charge, although not all medications are available at MTF pharmacies. The TRICARE Mail Order Pharmacy (TMOP) is available for prescriptions you take on a regular basis. You can receive up to a ninety-day supply (for most medications) of your prescription through the mail by using TMOP. Finally, prescription medications that your doctor requires you to start taking immediately can be obtained though a retail network pharmacy as part of the TRICARE Retail Pharmacy (TRRx) program.

What Will TRICARE Cost?

The charts below provide examples of cost shares for families using TRICARE. Health benefits advisors at the military treatment facilities or representatives at the TRICARE Service Centers can assist you and your family in obtaining the medical care and services you need.

ACTIVE DUTY FAMILY MEMBERS

	TRICARE Prime E-1 thru E-4	TRICARE Prime E-5 and above	TRICARE Extra/ Standard Families of E4 and below	TRICARE Extra/ Standard Families of E5 and above
Annual deductible (individual/family)	None	None	$50/$100	$150/$300
Civilian outpatient visit	$0	$0	Extra: 15% Standard: 20%	Extra: 15% Standard: 20%
Civilian inpatient admission	$0	$0	Greater of $25 or $13.90/day	Greater of $25 or $13.90/day
Civilian inpatient mental health	$0	$0	$20 per day	$20 per day

If you have questions about your military healthcare benefits under TRICARE, there are many places to get answers. A member handbook may be obtained by visiting or calling your local TRICARE Service Center; by calling the health benefits advisor at your nearest military hospital or clinic; or by visiting the web site at *www.tricare.osd.mil.* Each medical facility has a health benefits advisor, Managed Care Office, or TRICARE Service Center. This should be your first contact for information. Additionally, below are telephone numbers for each region, where you can call and get information about TRICARE and your healthcare benefits.

TRICARE West *www.triwest.com*
(888)-TRIWEST; (888) 874-9378

Alaska; Arizona; California; Colorado; Hawaii; Idaho; Iowa, except for the Rock Island Arsenal area; Kansas;

Minnesota; Missouri, except for the St. Louis area; Montana; Nebraska; Nevada; New Mexico; North Dakota; Oregon; South Dakota; the extreme western portion of Texas ; Utah; Washington; and Wyoming.

TRICARE North *www.healthnetfederalservices.com* (877) TRICARE; (877) 874-2273

Connecticut, Delaware, the District of Columbia, Illinois, Indiana, the Rock Island Arsenal area of Iowa, Kentucky, Maine, Maryland, Massachusetts, Michigan, the St. Louis area of Missouri, New Hampshire, New Jersey, New York, North Carolina, Ohio, Pennsylvania, Rhode Island, the Fort Campbell area of Tennessee, Vermont, Virginia, West Virginia, and Wisconsin.

TRICARE South *www.humana-military.com* (800) 444-5445

Alabama, Arkansas, Florida, Georgia, Louisiana, Mississippi, Oklahoma, South Carolina, most of Tennessee, and the eastern portion of Texas.

TRICARE OVERSEAS 1-888-777-8343

TRICARE Prime and *TRICARE Standard* for active duty and their families. Only TRICARE Standard for Military retirees, and their families who live overseas. Retirees cannot enroll in TRICARE Prime, but they can use TRICARE Standard.

TRICARE Reserve Select (TRS)

TRICARE Reserve Select is a new premium-based TRICARE health plan offered for purchase by certain members and former members of the Reserve Component (RC) and their families, if specific eligibility requirements are met. TRS coverage is available to eligible RC members who were called or ordered to active duty, under Title 10, in support of a contingency operation on or after September 11, 2001. RC Members and their Reserve Component unit will need to agree for the member to stay in the Select Reserve for one or more whole years to qualify. TRS coverage must be purchased. TRS members pay a monthly premium for health care coverage (for self-only or for self and family). Adjusted effective the first of each year, the premiums for calendar year 2005 are: $75.00 for TRS member-only coverage, $233.00 for TRS member and family coverage.

TRICARE for Life (TFL)

TFL is Medicare wraparound coverage available to:

- Medicare-entitled uniformed service retirees, including retired guard members and reservists.
- Medicare-entitled family members and widows/widowers (dependent parents and parents-in-law are excluded).
- Medicare-entitled Congressional Medal of Honor recipients and their family members.
- Certain Medicare-entitled unremarried former spouses.

TRICARE pays the balance on the Medicare claim—everything Medicare did not pay—for everything that is a TRICARE benefit.

TRICARE Supplements

TRICARE supplements are not part of the TRICARE program. The different commercial plans are designed to be secondary coverage to TRICARE. Dependent on the level of coverage, TRICARE supplements pay the cost share, deductible and eligible excess charges under the TRICARE Standard, and Extra options so that on a combined basis, eligible participants have 100 percent coverage in most cases. For more detailed information, check with any of the various associations representing the different members of the Armed Forces.

TRICARE Dental Program (TDP)

Active-duty soldiers receive all dental care, at no cost, from military dental treatment facilities and are therefore ineligible for the TRICARE Dental Program. The TDP is a voluntary dental plan open to families of all active-duty, selected reserve, and individual ready reserve soldiers ordered to active duty for more than thirty consecutive days.

Sponsors must have at least twelve months remaining on their service commitments at the time of enrollment. After completing the initial twelve-month enrollment period, they may continue in the TDP on a month-by-month basis.

Soldiers failing to pay premiums or disenrolling before completing the twelve-month lock-in are responsible for payment of all remaining premiums. Unless disenrolling for a valid reason, soldiers are prohibited from reentering the program for twelve months.

Soldiers may disenroll from the TDP before completion of the mandatory twelve-month enrollment for the following reasons: when a sponsor or family member loses Defense Enrollment Eligibility Reporting System (DEERS) eligibility, when TDP enrolled members relocate outside the CONUS service area, or when an active-duty member transfers with enrolled family members to a duty station where space-available dental care for the enrolled members is readily available at the local uniformed services dental treatment facility.

TRICARE Management Activity (TMA)

United Concordia Companies, Inc, administers and underwrites the TDP. For further information, call the TRICARE Dental Program, United Concordia Companies, Inc. (UCCI), at (800) 866-8499. For enrollment information, call (888) 622-2256. See also the UCCI web site: *www.ucci.com/was/ucciweb/-tdp/tdp.jsp,* or you can contact your nearest TRICARE Service Centers, a military dental treatment facility, or a uniformed services personnel office.

LONG-TERM CARE

TRICARE or Medicare do not cover long-term care. The Federal Long-Term Care Insurance Program is an important benefit for members of the Army family, including retiree members and qualified relatives. It is insurance that helps you pay for care to help you perform daily activities if you have an ongoing illness or disability. It also includes the kind of care you would need if you had a severe cognitive problem such as Alzheimer's disease. It is help with eating, bathing, dressing, transferring from a bed to a chair, toileting, continence, etc. This type of care isn't received in a hospital and isn't intended to cure you. It is not acute care. It is chronic care that you might need for the rest of your life. It can be received in your own home, at a nursing home, or at another long-term care facility.

If you are younger than forty and healthy and you retire, the Federal Long-Term Care Insurance Program may not be the best deal. You may obtain comparable coverage at a lower monthly premium from one of the large companies that handle long-term care. Check the premiums calculator offered by the Office of Personnel Management on the Internet at *www.ltcfeds.com/ltcWeb/-do/assessing_your_needs/ratecalc* for more information. To qualify, you must answer more questions about your health and habits than regular military personnel. Retirees can also call (800) 582-3337 Monday through Friday from 8 A.M. to 8 P.M. EST.

21

Separation, Discharge, and Retirement

SEPARATIONS

How and why a soldier leaves the Army depends on many factors, according to AR 635-200, *Active Duty Enlisted Administrative Separations*. Separation policies in AR 635-200 promote readiness of the Army by providing an orderly means to accomplish the following:

- Ensure that the Army is served by individuals capable of meeting required standards of duty performance and discipline.
- Maintain standards of performance and conduct through characterization of service in a system that emphasizes the importance of honorable service.
- Achieve authorized force levels and grade distribution.
- Provide for the orderly administrative separation of soldiers in a variety of circumstances.

AR 635-200 provides the authority for separation of soldiers upon expiration of term of service (ETS); the authority and general provisions governing the separation of soldiers before ETS to meet the needs of the Army and its soldiers; the procedures to implement laws and policies governing voluntary retirement of soldiers of the Army for length of service; and the criteria governing uncharacterized separations and the issuance of honorable, general, and under other than honorable conditions discharges.

The following selected entries are the authorized types of separations under the provisions of AR 635-200:

- *Chapter 4—Separation for Expiration of Service Obligation.* A soldier will be separated upon expiration of enlistment or fulfillment of service obligation. Noncommissioned officers under the Indefinite Reenlistment Program can request separation from active duty at any time. Approval will be granted, however, only to those soldiers who have fulfilled their

Active Duty Service Obligation. Soldiers requesting voluntary separation in lieu of Personnel Change in Status (PCS), must request separation within thirty days of being notified of the assignment. Soldiers will establish a separation date within six months from the date of application. Any separation date outside the six-month window must be fully justified.

- *Chapter 5—Separation for Convenience of the Government.* A chapter 5 separation covers the following: involuntary separation due to parenthood, lack of jurisdiction as ordered by a U.S. court or judge thereof, aliens not lawfully admitted to the United States, personnel who did not meet procurement medical fitness standards, failure to qualify medically for flight training, personality disorders, concealment of arrest record, and failure to meet Army body composition and weight-control standards.
- *Chapter 6—Separation Because of Dependency or Hardship.* Soldiers of the active Army and the reserve components serving on active duty or active duty for training may be discharged or released because of genuine dependency or hardship. Dependency exists when death or disability of a member of a soldier's (or spouse's) immediate family causes the family or one of its members to rely upon the soldier for principal care or support. Hardship exists when in circumstances not involving death or disability of a member of the soldier's (or spouse's) immediate family, separation from the service will materially affect the care or support of the family by alleviating undue and genuine hardship.
- *Chapter 7—Defective Enlistments, Reenlistments, and Extensions.* This chapter provides the authority, criteria, and procedures for the separation of soldiers because of minority, erroneous enlistment or extension of enlistment, defective enlistment agreement, and fraudulent entry.
- *Chapter 8—Separation of Enlisted Women for Pregnancy.* Chapter 8 provides authority for voluntary separation of enlisted women because of pregnancy. An enlisted woman who elects to remain on active duty when counseled may, if she is pregnant, subsequently request separation. Conversely, an enlisted woman who requested separation in writing may subsequently request withdrawal of the separation request.
- *Chapter 9—Alcohol or Other Drug Abuse Rehabilitation Failure.* A soldier who is enrolled in the Alcohol and Drug Abuse Prevention and Control Program (ADAPCP) for substance abuse may be separated because of inability or refusal to participate in, cooperate in, or successfully complete such a program.
- *Chapter 10—Discharge in Lieu of Trial by Court-Martial.* A soldier who has committed an offense or offenses punishable by a bad conduct

discharge or dishonorable discharge under the provisions of the Uniform Code of Military Justice and the Manual for Courts-Martial may submit a request for discharge for the good of the service. The request does not prevent or suspend disciplinary proceedings. (See AR 635-200, pages 43–45 for details.)

- *Chapter 11—Entry-Level Status Performance and Conduct.* This chapter provides guidance for the separation of personnel because of unsatisfactory performance or conduct (or both) while in entry-level status. It covers inability, lack of reasonable effort, or failure to adapt to the military environment.
- *Chapter 12—Retirement for Length of Service.* A soldier who has completed twenty years' active federal service and who has completed all required service obligations is eligible to retire. Upon retirement, the soldier is transferred to the U.S. Army Reserve Control Group (retired) and remains in that status until active service time plus control group time equals thirty years, and then is placed on the retired list. A Regular Army soldier who has completed at least thirty years of active federal service will, upon request, be placed on the retired list.
- *Chapter 13—Separation for Unsatisfactory Performance.* A soldier may be separated per this chapter when unqualified for further military service because of unsatisfactory performance, under the following circumstances: (1) the soldier will not develop sufficiently, or (2) the seriousness of the circumstance is such that retention would have an adverse impact on military discipline, good order, and morale, and (3) it is likely that the soldier will be a disruptive influence, and (4) it is likely that the circumstances will continue to recur, and (5) the ability of the soldier to perform duties, including potential for advancement or leadership, is unlikely, and (6) the soldier meets retention medical standards.
- *Chapter 14—Separation for Misconduct.* This chapter establishes procedures for separating personnel for misconduct because of minor disciplinary infractions, a pattern of misconduct, commission of a serious offense, conviction by civil authorities, desertion, and absence without leave. A discharge under other than honorable conditions is normally appropriate for a soldier discharged under this chapter.
- *Chapter 15—Discharge for Homosexual Conduct.* Homosexual conduct is grounds for separation from the Army. This includes preservice, prior service, or current service homosexual conduct. (See the section on homosexuality in chapter 5 for more information.)
- *Chapter 19—Qualitative Management Program (QMP).* This chapter contains policies and procedures for voluntary and involuntary separation, for the convenience of the government, of RA NCOs and USAR NCOs serving in AGR status, under the QMP. Soldiers separating under this chapter have their discharges characterized as honorable.

DISCHARGES

For whatever reason, sooner or later each soldier must quit the service. In this section, we will consider the various types of discharges, the operation of the U.S. Army transfer facilities, retirement, and veterans' rights.

Honorable Discharge

An honorable discharge is given when an individual is separated from the military service with honor. An honorable discharge cannot be denied to a person solely on the basis of convictions by courts-martial or actions under Article 15 of the Uniform Code of Military Justice. Denial must be based on patterns of misbehavior and not isolated instances. An honorable discharge may be awarded when disqualifying entries in an individual's service record are outweighed by subsequent honorable and faithful service over a greater period of time during the current period of service.

Unless otherwise ineligible, a member may receive an honorable discharge if he or she has, during the current enlistment or extensions thereof, received a personal decoration or is separated by reason of disability incurred in the line of duty.

General Discharge

A general discharge is issued to an individual whose character of service has been satisfactory but not sufficiently meritorious to warrant an honorable discharge. Such persons would have, for example, frequent punishments under Article 15 of the UCMJ or be classified as general troublemakers.

Other than Honorable Discharge

Discharges that fall within this category are given for reasons of misconduct, homosexuality, or security, or for the good of the service, and are covered by AR 635-200. No person shall receive a discharge under other than honorable conditions unless afforded the right to present his or her case before an administrative discharge board with the advice of legal counsel.

Uncharacterized Separations

There are two types of uncharacterized separations: those given when a soldier is in entry-level status and those given because of void enlistments or inductions.

Bad Conduct or Dishonorable Discharge

A soldier will be given a bad conduct discharge pursuant only to an approved sentence of a general or special court-martial. A soldier will be given a dishonorable discharge pursuant only to an approved sentence of a general court-martial. The appellate reviews must be completed and the affirmed sentence ordered duly executed. Dishonorable and bad conduct discharges result in expulsion from the Army.

TRANSITION ACTIVITIES

U.S. Army transfer facilities provide an informal, quiet atmosphere centrally located at a post where soldiers being separated may be processed within acceptable time limits. AR 635-10 prescribes that overseas returnees, except retirees, be separated on the first workday after their arrival at the separation transfer point, when possible. Personnel being released from active duty who are discharged before expiration of term of service (ETS) or the period for which ordered to active duty are separated by the third workday after approved separation. All others are separated on their scheduled separation dates, except for those individuals who elect to be separated on the last workday before a weekend or a holiday.

Medical Examination

There is no statutory requirement for soldiers to undergo a medical exam incidental to separation. It is Army policy, however, to accomplish a medical examination if a soldier is active Army and retiring after twenty or more years of active duty; if a soldier is being discharged or released and requests a medical examination; if review of the soldier's health record by a physician or physician's assistant warrants an exam; or if an examination is required by AR 40-501, *Standards of Medical Fitness*.

Each soldier undergoing separation processing will have his or her medical records screened by a physician, regardless of whether a separation physical has been requested. Advise your soldiers that a separation physical may be one of the most important medical examinations of their lives. Separation physicals end in a personal interview with a doctor. That interview is the proper time to bring up every single medical fact incident to military service. This interview substantiates service connection should a soldier, after discharge, request disability compensation from the Department of Veterans Affairs based on military service. Above all, each soldier being separated or retired from the service should make a copy of his or her medical and dental records and keep them after discharge.

Army Career and Alumni Program

The Army Career and Alumni Program (ACAP) is a transition and job assistance initiative located at military sites worldwide. Each ACAP site includes a transition assistance office (TAO) and a job assistance center (JAC), which are available for all active and reserve component soldiers, Army civilians, and military and civilian family members. The TAO provides eligible clients with transition advice and serves as a focal point for problems. The JAC provides clients with job search training, individual assistance and counseling, and a referral service. For more information go to *www.acap.army.mil/*.

Transition Assistance. The TAO synchronizes current preservice transition services on an individual basis to help personnel leaving the Army and provides the following:

- First step in the transition process.
- Individual transition plans.
- Awareness of available resources.
- Defense Outplacement Referral System.
- Federal and public sector job information.

Ideally, the TAO staff likes to see you 180 days before your separation or retirement date, but if that is not possible, you are eligible to be seen at the ACAP office until you are discharged from the Army.

Job Assistance. The JAC conducts individual, small-, and large-group workshops to accomplish the following:

- Target your second career.
- Prepare for interviews.
- Find hidden markets for your skills.
- Evaluate job offers.
- Build negotiating skills.
- Teach you to dress for success.
- Track job leads.
- Evaluate employment agencies, job fairs, and automated résumé services.
- Develop your résumé.
- Help with essential correspondence.

Like the TAO staff, the JAC staff encourages you to start the ACAP process 180 days prior to your discharge date.

Employment Network. The Army Employment Network (AEN) is an ACAP database that contains information from employers who are committed to considering Army personnel for employment. The AEN provides the company name, location of all branches of the company, total number of personnel hired annually, the types of positions for which a company hires, points of contact, and in some cases a listing of currently available positions.

The network is linked to regional and federal Office of Personnel Management computers that list federal jobs, and is also tied to the Department of Veterans Affairs, which with the ACAP conducts a combined three-day job training seminar, three-hour training session, and six-hour training workshop. Clients choose the seminar, session, or workshop, depending on their needs and available time. For more information about the ACAP, call toll-free in the continental United States (800) 445-2049. If you are stationed overseas, call DSN 221-0993. If you are an NCO, you should visit your local ACAP office and learn more about the program, then relate it to every soldier you supervise.

RETIREMENT

> My sword I give to him that shall succeed me in my pilgrimage, and my courage and skill to him that can get it.
>
> —John Bunyan

The important thing to remember is that when a soldier puts the uniform into the closet for the last time, he or she does not have to stay in there with it. Those who do often pass quickly. You should begin early in your career to think of retirement not as a thing that comes near the end of active life, but the point of departure between the end of one exciting and fulfilling career and the beginning of another.

Making the Decision

Only you can make the decision to retire. If you are married, you will want to discuss the decision thoroughly with your spouse and family, but in the final analysis, it is you who must submit that application for retirement.

Army Retirement Services, Office of the Deputy Chief of Staff for Personnel (ODCSPER), Headquarters, Department of the Army (HQDA), provides information on benefits and entitlements to active-duty personnel preparing for retirement. It also provides information to retirees through Army installation Retirement Services Offices (RSOs). The Retirement Services home page is located at *www.odcsper.army.mil/Directorates/retire/army_retirement_services_office/pocs.asp*.

Read the literature on retirement procedures and veterans' benefits so that when you arrive at the transfer point for discharge, you will already know what to expect. Do not wait for someone else to tell you what your rights and benefits are. If you are to be retired at a post that does not have a transfer activity, your processing will be done at the local military personnel office. To an extent, you will be on your own there unless the personnel officer has people as experienced as the commander of a transfer activity in processing retirements.

Submission and Withdrawal of Retirement Applications

Any soldier who has completed nineteen or more years' service may apply for retirement. The request must be made within twelve months of the requested retirement date, except that the retirement approval authority is authorized to set a minimum time for submission, which cannot be less than two months before the desired retirement date. Generally, to be eligible, all service obligations incurred as a result of schooling, promotion (unless a waiver is granted), and duty tours must be completed.

A retirement application cannot be withdrawn unless it is established that retaining the soldier concerned will be for the convenience or best interest of the government or will prevent an extreme hardship to either the soldier or his immediate family. The hardship must have been unforeseen at the time of the retirement application. Requests for withdrawal must be fully documented.

Terminal Leave

Deciding whether to take terminal leave may not be an easy decision. Whether to take it depends upon how much leave a soldier has accrued at the time of retirement, how much leave he or she may have previously cashed in for pay, and what plans the retiree may have for job-hunting activities, travel, or vacation.

Personnel taking terminal leave will be allowed to finish processing at the local transfer activity before departure on leave. On the day of retirement, a telephone call from the retiree, verifying his status and whereabouts, is all that is needed to finish outprocessing; the retiree's DD Form 214 will be sent via registered mail. Arrangements to pick up retired ID cards may be made at any military installation.

Allotments

Retirees are permitted to continue allotments that they had in effect while on active duty with few exceptions.

Requests to establish, discontinue, or change an authorized allotment after retirement may be submitted to the Retired Pay Operations Office by letter over your signature. No specific form is required. Forms are provided, however, with USAFAC Pam 20-194, *Retired Pay Information,* a copy of which should be forwarded to you by the Retired Pay Operations Office, U.S. Army Finance and Accounting Center, Indianapolis, Indiana.

Ceremonies

Each soldier who retires from the U.S. Army is authorized to participate in a retirement review in honor of the occasion. These reviews are generally held on the last day of the month, and all personnel retiring from the service on that day at any specific post or installation are honored at the same special formation. You will be given the option to accept or decline a ceremony during your pre-retirement processing.

Checks

If you do not already have your active-duty paychecks going to a financial institution, consider doing so when you retire. The direct deposit system guarantees the deposit of your retirement check in the bank or credit union of your choice.

Discharge Certificates

Your DD Form 214, *Certificate of Release or Discharge from Active Duty,* is the most important of all the documents you will accumulate during your retirement processing; it is one of the most important documents you will ever receive during your military career. At the time of your retirement you will receive copies 1 (original) and 4 (carbon) of DD Form 214. Be sure to make copies of these forms and protect the originals. Do not let the originals out of your possession.

Military Installation Privileges

Retired members, their dependents, and unmarried surviving spouses are authorized the use of various facilities on military installations when adequate facilities are available. This privilege includes commissary stores, post exchanges, Clothing Sales Stores, laundry and dry-cleaning plants, military theaters, Army recreation services facilities, officer and NCO messes, and medical facilities.

Army regulations regarding exchange and commissary privileges for retired personnel apply overseas only to the extent agreed upon by the foreign governments concerned.

Mobilization Planning

All eligible retired Regular Army personnel are subject to mobilization. If you change address, ensure that you notify Commander, HRC-ST LOUIS, ATTN: ARPC-PLM-O, 1 Reserve Way, St. Louis, MO 63132-5200 or through *www.hrc.army.mil.*

At the announcement of mobilization, retired personnel will be ordered to active duty in their retired grade. Initially, current medical fitness retention standards will apply until such time as the secretary of the Army directs the application of mobilization standards.

Retired Pay

If you are medically retired due to a disability incurred while on active duty, your retired pay is on your monthly active-duty pay multiplied by the percentage of disability.

The authority for nondisability retired pay, commonly known as length-of-service retired pay, is contained in Title 10, USC. Military retired pay is not based on financial need, and is not a pension, but is regarded as delayed compensation for completing twenty or more years of active military service. Nondisability retired pay falls under one of three different retirement systems:

- For those who entered active service before September 8, 1980, retirement pay base is computed using the highest grade satisfactorily held by the member.
- Those entering after September 7, 1980, fall under the High-3 system, where the retired pay is based on an amount equal to the total of the highest thirty-six months of active-duty basic pay, whether or not consecutive, divided by thirty-six. For the above two systems, each year of service is worth 2.5 percent toward the retirement multiplier. The longer

a soldier is on active duty, the higher the multiplier and the higher the retirement pay, up to the maximum of 75 percent.

- Personnel who entered the service after July 31, 1986, may either select the High-3 system or elect to receive a one-time lump-sum career status bonus of $30,000 and have their retired pay computed under the post-1986 retirement system REDUX. Under REDUX, a soldier retires at 40 percent of basic pay at twenty years service, with this multiplier applied against the average basic pay, similar to the High-3 described above. At age sixty-two, two adjustments are made to the REDUX retiree's compensation. The first adjusts the multiplier to what it would have been under High-3. For example, a twenty-year retiree's multiplier would increase from 40 to 50 percent, and a twenty-four-year retiree's multiplier to 60 percent. The second adjustment applies the full consumer price index (CPI) for every retirement year to this amount to compute a new base retirement salary, so that at age sixty-two, the REDUX and High-3 retirement salaries are equal. From this point on, REDUX cost-of-living allowances are again set at CPI minus 1 percent.

Army retirees receive the *Army Echoes* newsletter, retired pay statements, federal income tax statements (1099-R), and other correspondence originating from Defense Finance and Accounting Service-Cleveland Center (DFAS-CL). To receive these important documents, retirees must keep their address at DFAS-CL up-to-date by writing to: DFAS, U.S. Military Retirement Pay, PO Box 7130, London, KY 40742-7130; or FAX it to: 1-800-469-6559.

The DFAS web site, *www.dod.mil/dfas/* allows the retiree to make changes such as federal tax, direct deposit/electronic funds transfer (EFT), allotment (except annuitants), home address, savings bonds, and state tax changes, directly to his or her pay account in a secure electronic environment and to request the Form 1099 federal income tax statement.

Retired Personnel Records

Military personnel records for retired personnel (except general officers) are on file at the U.S. Army Reserve Human Resources Command in St. Louis, MO. Write to National Personnel Records Center, ATTN: Army Reference Branch (NCPMA), 9700 Page Avenue, St. Louis, MO 63132-5100. Be sure to give them your SSAN when you send your request. Your request will take some time, so be patient.

You should, however, make copies of all the important documents in your military personnel file at some point before you retire.

If you believe that an error or injustice has occurred and desire to request a review of your case by the Army Board for Correction of Military Records, you should apply in writing on DD Form 149, *Application for Correction of Military or Naval Record*. The application should be addressed to Army Board for Correction of Military Records, Department of the Army, Washington, DC 20310.

Survivor Benefit Program (SBP)

The SBP allows retired personnel to provide an annuity to certain designated survivors. Various amounts and types of coverage may be elected, with the maximum being 55 percent of the amount of a member's retired pay at the time of death. These persons may be the widows or widowers, dependent children, or other persons with an insurable interest in a retired soldier. A detailed description of the SBP plan may be found at *www.armyg1.army.mil/rso/sbp.asp.*

Wearing the Uniform, Military Titles and Signatures, Awards, and Decorations

Wearing of the uniform by retired personnel is a privilege granted in recognition of faithful service to the country. Retired personnel may wear the uniform when such wear is considered appropriate.

Retired personnel wear the same uniform prescribed for active-duty personnel. Retired personnel not on active duty may wear the uniform with decorations and awards. The shoulder sleeve insignia for U.S. Army retirees is authorized for wear on the left shoulder by retired personnel. The shoulder sleeve insignia of a former wartime unit may be worn on the right shoulder by retired personnel who served in the unit.

All retired personnel not on active duty are permitted to use their military titles socially and in connection with commercial enterprise. Such military titles must never be used in any manner that may bring discredit to the Army or in connection with commercial enterprises when such use, with or without the intent to mislead, gives rise to any appearance of sponsorship, sanction, endorsement, or approval by the Department of the Army or the Department of Defense.

Retired personnel who have not received the awards to which they are entitled or who desire replacement of items previously issued that were lost, destroyed, or are unfit for use without fault or neglect on the veteran's part may obtain them upon written application.

Requests should be addressed to the Commander, U.S. Army Reserve Components Personnel and Administration Center, 9700 Page Boulevard, St. Louis, MO 63132. The application should include a statement or explanation of the circumstances surrounding the loss or nonissue of the items concerned. Replacements are made at cost. No money should be mailed for replacements until you are instructed to do so.

VETERANS' RIGHTS AND BENEFITS

The benefits discussed in this section are available to all veterans regardless of status. All Department of Veterans Affairs (DVA or VA) benefits (with the

VETERANS' BENEFITS TIMETABLE

You Have *(after separation from service)*	Benefits	Where to Apply
Time varies	**GI Education:** The VA will pay you while you complete high school, go to college, or learn a trade, either on the job or in an apprenticeship program. Vocational and educational counseling is available.	Any VA office
10 years	**Veterans Educational Assistance Program:** The VA will provide financial assistance for the education and training of eligible participants under the voluntary contributory education program. Vocational and educational counseling is available upon request.	Any VA office
12 years, although extensions are possible under certain conditions	**Vocational Rehabilitation:** As part of a rehabilitation program, the VA will pay for tuition, books, tools, or other expenses and provide a monthly living allowance. Employment assistance is also available to help a rehabilitated veteran get a job. A seriously disabled veteran may be provided services and assistance to increase independence in daily living.	Any VA office
No time limit	**GI Loans:** The VA will guarantee your loan for the purchase of a home, manufactured home, or condominium; repair, alteration, or improvement of a home; or refinancing of an existing home loan.	Any VA office
No time limit	**Disability Compensation:** The VA pays compensation for disabilities incurred or aggravated during military service.	Any VA office
1 year from date of mailing of notice of initial determination	**Appeal to Board of Veterans Appeals:** Appellate review will be initiated by a notice of disagreement and completed by a substantive appeal after a statement of the case has been furnished.	VA office or hospital making the initial determination
No time limit	**Medical Care:** The VA provides hospital care covering the full range of medical services. Outpatient treatment is available to all service-connected conditions, or non-service-connected conditions in certain cases. Alcohol and drug dependence treatment is available.	Any VA office
Time varies	**Burial Benefits:** The VA provides certain burial benefits, including interment in a national cemetery and partial reimbursement for burial expense.	VA national cemetery having grave space, any VA office
No time limit	**Readjustment Counseling:** General or psychological counseling is provided to assist in readjusting to civilian life.	Any Vet Center, VA office, or hospital
Within 90 days of separation	**One-Time Dental Treatment:** The VA provides one-time dental care for certain service-connected dental conditions.	Any VA office or hospital
No time limit	**Dental Treatment:** Treatment for veterans with dental disabilities resulting from combat wounds or service injuries and certain POWs and other service-connected disabled veterans.	Any VA office or hospital
1 year from date of notice of VA disability rating	**GI Insurance:** Low-cost life insurance (up to $10,000) is available for veterans with service-connected disabilities. Veterans who are totally disabled may apply for a waiver of premiums on these policies.	Any VA office
120 days or 1 year beyond with evidence of insurability; or up to 1 year if totally disabled	**Veterans Group Life Insurance (VGLI):** SGLI may be converted to a 5-year nonrenewable term policy. At the end of the 5-year term, VGLI may be converted to an individual policy with a participating insurance company.	Office of Servicemember's Group Life Insurance, 213 Washington St., Newark, NJ 07102, or any VA office
No time limit	**Employment:** Assistance is available in finding employment in private industry, in federal service, and in local or state employment service.	Local or state employment service, U.S. Office of Personnel Management, Labor Department, any VA office
Limited time	**Unemployment Compensation:** The amount of benefit and payment period varies among states. Apply after separation.	State employment service
90 days	**Reemployment:** Apply to your former employer for employment.	Employer
30 days	**Selective Service:** Male veterans born in 1960 or later years must register.	At any U.S. post office; overseas at any U.S. embassy or consulate

exception of insurance and certain medical benefits) payable to veterans or their dependents require that the particular period of service upon which the entitlement is based be terminated under conditions other than dishonorable. Honorable and general discharges qualify the veteran as eligible for benefits. Dishonorable discharges and bad conduct discharges issued by general courts-martial are a bar to VA benefits. Other bad conduct discharges and discharges characterized as other than honorable may or may not qualify depending upon a special determination made by the VA, based on the facts of each case. To prove your eligibility for VA benefits, ensure that you keep a complete copy of your medical records and protect your DD Form 214, *Discharge Certificate.* More detailed information can be found on the VA web site at *www.va.gov/.*

Travel and Transportation Allowances

Soldiers are authorized travel allowances from their last duty station to their home. Shipment and storage of household goods incident to retirement is authorized on a one-time basis, subject to weight limitations and other controls. Specific information relative to shipment and storage of household goods is contained in DA Pam 55-2, *Personal Property Shipping Information.*

Retired soldiers are eligible for space-available travel, category 4, within the continental limits of the United States or DOD-owned or DOD-controlled aircraft. Dependents of retired personnel are not authorized space-available travel on military aircraft flying within the continental limits of the United States and therefore may not accompany retired members on such flights.

Department of Veterans Affairs (Disability) Compensation

If you believe that you have a condition that may entitle you to VA compensation, file your claim at the time of separation. If the VA, upon reviewing your medical records, finds that you do have grounds for seeking compensation, an appointment for a physical exam will be made for you at the Department of Veterans Affairs hospital closest to your retirement home. Your claim will be processed based upon the examination results.

You cannot receive both VA compensation for disability and an Army retirement check. Therefore, the amount of your VA disability is deducted from your regular retirement check (which is issued by the U.S. Army Finance Center). Your monthly income will remain the same, except that part will be paid by the Department of the Army and part by the VA.

Conversion of Servicemember's Group Life Insurance (SGLI) to Veterans Group Life Insurance (VGLI)

A servicemember has 120 days after separation to apply for Veterans Group Life Insurance (VGLI), with no exam requirements. Beyond the 120 days, a soldier has one year to apply, but there are then some exam requirements. During the 120 days after separation, the SGLI coverage continues without premiums.

You can keep your VGLI coverage for your lifetime, as long as you continue paying premiums. At any time, however, you may convert your VGLI coverage to an individual policy of life insurance with a commercial company that participates in the program at the company's standard premium rate regardless of your health. No disability or other supplemental benefits will be provided on converted policies. You may convert up to the amount of VGLI coverage you hold. The link at *www.insurance.va.gov/sgliSite/conversion/conversion.htm* provides information on how to convert to an individual policy with a list of participating companies.

Employment

Priority referral to job openings and training opportunities is given to eligible veterans, with preferential treatment for disabled veterans. Additionally, the job service assists veterans who are seeking employment by providing information about job marts, on the job training and apprenticeship training opportunities, and so on, in cooperation with VA regional offices and Veterans Outreach Centers.

Veterans may seek employment with the federal government and receive some breaks when applying for federal employment:

- A five-point preference is given to those who served during any war, in any campaign, in an expedition for which a campaign medal has been authorized, or for 180 consecutive days between January 31, 1955, and October 15, 1976.
- A ten-point preference is given to those who were awarded the Purple Heart, have a current service-connected disability, or are receiving compensation, disability retirement benefits, or pension from the VA.
- A veteran with a 30 percent or more disability may receive appointment without competitive examination with a right to be converted to career appointments and retention rights in reductions in force.

Education Benefits

See your Army Continuing Education System (ACES) counselor for details on the GI Bill, the Veterans Educational Assistance Program (VEAP), and other education benefit programs. For more information visit the GI Bill web site at *www.gibill.va.gov/*.

GI Loans

The purpose of VA GI loans is to buy a home; to buy a residential unit in certain condominium projects; to build a home; to repair, alter, or improve a home; to refinance an existing home loan; to buy a manufactured home (with or without a lot); to buy a lot for a manufactured home that you already own; to improve a home through installation of solar heating and/or cooling system or other weatherization improvements; to purchase and simultaneously improve a home with energy-conserving measures; to refinance an existing VA loan to reduce the interest rate; to refinance a manufactured home loan in order to acquire a lot; and to simultaneously purchase and improve a home. Eligibility requirements vary, based on period of service (except that all veterans, to be eligible, must have an other than dishonorable discharge certificate).

The loan terms are subject to negotiation between the veteran and the lender. The repayment period or maturity of GI home loans may be as long as thirty years and thirty-two days. Newly discharged veterans have certificates of eligibility mailed to their homes by the VA shortly after discharge. Other veterans may secure their certificates by sending VA Form 26-1880, *Request for a Certificate of Eligibility for VA Home Loan Benefits,* along with required supporting documents, to the VA regional office nearest them. Active-duty personnel may also take advantage of these loans.

One-Time Dental Treatment

In addition to dental conditions that qualify for treatment because of service connection, veterans are entitled to a one-time dental treatment without review of service records to establish service connection. This treatment must be applied for within ninety days of separation. Do not fail to take advantage of this very important benefit. Contact the local VA office or go to the VA web site *www.1010ez.med.va.gov/sec/vha/1010ez/* and apply on-line.

Unemployment Compensation

The purpose of unemployment compensation for veterans is to provide income for a limited period of time to help them meet basic needs while searching for employment. The amount and duration of payments vary because they are governed by state laws. Benefits are paid from federal funds. Veterans should apply immediately after discharge at the nearest state employment service, not at the VA. A copy of DD Form 214 is needed to establish type of separation from the service.

VA Medical Benefits

The Department of Veterans Affairs provides a Medical Benefits Package, a standard enhanced health benefits plan available to all enrolled veterans. Through it the VA offers the whole spectrum of medical benefits to qualified veterans: aids and services for the blind, alcohol treatment, domiciliary care, drug treatment, hospitalization care for dependents or survivors, nursing home care, outpatient dental treatment, outpatient medical treatment, and prosthetic appliances.

The VA maintains an annual enrollment system to manage the provision of quality hospital and outpatient medical care and treatment to all enrolled veterans. A priority system ensures that veterans with service-connected disabilities and those below the low-income threshold are able to be enrolled in the VA's healthcare system. Veterans who are receiving compensation or who would be eligible to receive compensation (except for retirement pay) who need treatment for an ailment connected with their service are admitted as beds are available. Under certain circumstances, veterans who were not discharged or retired for disability or who are not receiving compensation and who apply for treatment of a non-service-connected disability may be admitted to a VA hospital. Any veteran with a service-connected disability may receive VA outpatient medical treatment.

Vocational Rehabilitation

Generally, a veteran is eligible for vocational rehabilitation for twelve years following discharge or release from active service. A four-year extension is possible under certain circumstances, and further extensions may be granted for veterans who are seriously disabled when it is determined by the VA to be necessary because of disability and need for vocational rehabilitation.

Eligible disabled veterans may get training up to a total of four years or its equivalent in part-time or a combination of part-time and full-time training.

Eligibility for this training is determined by the VA.

VA Correspondence and Records

Keep a file of every paper the VA sends you. Your dealings with the VA will require patience and persistence; the required degree of each will depend to a large extent on how busy your local VA office is. Invariably, VA personnel are courteous, and they try to be helpful, but processing your claim may take some time.

Burial

Burial is available to any deceased veteran of wartime or peacetime service (other than for training) who was discharged under conditions other than dishonorable at all national cemeteries having available grave space, except Arlington Cemetery.

Eligible veterans' dependents may receive a headstone or grave marker without charge, shipped to a designated consignee. The cost of placing the marker in a private ceremony must be borne by the applicant. The VA may pay an amount not to exceed the average actual cost of a government headstone or marker as a partial reimbursement for the cost incurred by the person acquiring a nongovernment headstone or marker for placement in a cemetery other than a national cemetery.

SOURCES

AR 612-10, *Reassignment Processing and Army Sponsorship (and Orientation) Program.*

AR 614-30, *Overseas Service.*

AR 635-10, *Processing Personnel for Separation.*

AR 635-200, *Active Duty Enlisted Administrative Separations.*

Retirement Services Office Handbook for Retired Soldiers and Family Members; also see *www.armyg1.army.mil/rso/retiree_information/RetireeHandbookMar05.doc#Chapter15.*

VA FS 1S-1, *Federal Benefits for Veterans and Dependents.*

Army Retirement Services web site: *www.armyg1.army.mil/rso/-mission.asp.*

Index